Advanced Information and Knowledge Processing

Series Editors
Professor Lakhmi Jain
Lakhmi.jain@unisa.edu.au
Professor Xindong Wu
xwu@cs.uvm.edu

Also in this series

Dirk Husmeier, Richard Dybowski and Stephen Roberts (Eds)
Probabilistic Modeling in Bioinformatics and Medical Informatics
1-85233-778-8

Ajith Abraham, Lakhmi Jain and Robert Goldberg (Eds)
Evolutionary Multiobjective Optimization
1-85233-787-7

K.C. Tan, E.F.Khor and T.H. Lee
Multiobjective Evolutionary Algorithms and Applications
1-85233-836-9

Nikhil R. Pal and Lakhmi Jain (Eds)
Advanced Techniques in Knowledge Discovery and Data Mining
1-85233-867-9

Amit Konar and Lakhmi Jain
Cognitive Engineering
1-85233-975-6

Miroslav Kárný (Ed.)
Optimized Bayesian Dynamic Advising
1-85233-928-4

Yannis Manolopoulos, Alexandros Nanopoulos, Apostolos N. Papadopoulos
and Yannis Theodoridis
R-trees: Theory and Applications
1-85233-977-2

Sanghamitra Bandyopadhyay, Ujjwal Maulik, Lawrence B. Holder and Diane J. Cook (Eds)
Advanced Methods for Knowledge Discovery from Complex Data
1-85233-989-6

Marcus A. Maloof (Ed.)
Machine Learning and Data Mining for Computer Security
1-84628-029-X

Sifeng Liu and Yi Lin
Grey Information
1-85233-995-0

Vasile Palade, Cosmin Danut Bocaniala and Lakhmi Jain (Eds)
Computational Intelligence in Fault Diagnosis
1-84628-343-4

Mitra Basu and Tin Kam Ho (Eds)
Data Complexity in Pattern Recognition
1-84628-171-7

Samuel Pierre (Ed.)
E-learning Networked Environments and Architectures
1-84628-351-5

Arno Scharl and Klaus Tochtermann (Ed.)
The Geospatial Web
1-84628-826-5

Ngoc Thanh Nguyen

Advanced Methods
for Inconsistent
Knowledge
Management

 Springer

Ngoc Thanh Nguyen, DSc, PhD, Professor
Institute of Information Science and Engineering
Wroclaw University of Technology
Str. Janiszewskiego 11/17
50-370 Wroclaw
Poland

British Library Cataloguing in Publication Data
A catalogue record for this book is available from the British Library

Library of Congress Control Number: 2007929956

AI&KP ISSN 1610-3947
ISBN 978-1-84628-888-3   e-ISBN 978-1-84628-889-0

Printed on acid-free paper

9 8 7 6 5 4 3 2 1

Springer Science+Business Media
springer.com

Foreword

Nowadays in the knowledge society, each member deals with a number of tasks related to knowledge management. The most often realized tasks are: decision making, knowledge integration, selection, and retrieval. In all these tasks one has to solve inconsistency of knowledge. Inconsistency is a feature of knowledge which is characterized by the lack of possibility for inference processes. Therefore, solving inconsistency of knowledge is a basic and very essential subtask in many tasks of knowledge management. The whole management process may become impossible if the inconsistency is not resolved.

This book presents a set of methods for resolving inconsistency of knowledge. It originally treats the inconsistency on two levels, syntactic and semantic, and proposes methods for processing inconsistency on these levels. The methods proposed here are consensus based. They are worked out on the basis of mathematical models for representing inconsistency as well as tools for measuring and evaluating the degree of inconsistency, defined by the author.

The presented material shows that the solution of inconsistency is strongly related to knowledge integration processes. Therefore, along with inconsistency resolution tools, the author proposes algorithms for knowledge integration, such as ontology integration, or agent knowledge states integration. The author has put across a deep and valuable analysis of the proposed models by proving a number of interesting and useful theorems and remarks. Owing to these analysis results one can decide to use the worked out algorithms for concrete practical situations.

The author also presents two concrete applications of the proposed methods. The first refers to recommendation processes in intelligent learning systems. Using the method for rough classification, a model for representing learner profiles, learning scenarios, and the choice of a proper scenario for a new learner is proposed. The recommendation mechanisms are built by means of consensus methods and clustering algorithms. As a result, there is the possibility to adapt the learning path to learner needs and preferences. The second application is related to the conception of a multiagent metasearch engine for information retrieval from the Internet.

The conception consists of the structure agent knowledge and a set of procedures enabling knowledge exchange, recommendation processes, and decision-making processes of the agents.

Another aspect of this book is related to quality analysis of expert knowledge using consensus methods. The author has shown the relationships between the consistency degree of expert solutions for some problem and the distance between their consensus and the proper solution of the problem. He has proved, with some restrictions, that the consensus of the set of expert solutions is better than these solutions. The results are original and very interesting. I would like to congratulate Professor Nguyen for his wonderful contribution.

In my opinion, the methods for knowledge inconsistency resolution and integration included in this book are very valuable and many readers such as postgraduate and PhD students in computer science, as well as scientists who are working on knowledge management, ontology integration, and multiagent systems, will find it interesting.

Lakhmi C. Jain

Preface

Inconsistent knowledge management (IKM) is a subject which is the common point of knowledge management and conflict resolution. IKM deals with methods for reconciling inconsistent content of knowledge. Inconsistency in the logic sense has been known for a long time. Inconsistency of this kind refers to a set of logic formulae which have no common model. However, inconsistency of knowledge has a larger aspect which may be considered on two levels: syntactic and semantic. On the syntactic level inconsistency may be treated in the same way as the inconsistency of logic formulae mentioned above, but in a larger context. On the semantic level, on the other hand, inconsistency appears when these formulas are interpreted in some concrete structures and some real world. For solving a large number of conflicts, and especially, for resolving inconsistency of knowledge on the semantic level, consensus methods have been shown to be useful.

This book is about methods for processing inconsistent knowledge. The need for knowledge inconsistency resolution arises in many practical applications of computer systems. This kind of inconsistency results from the use of various sources of knowledge in realizing practical tasks. These sources often are autonomous and they use different mechanisms for processing knowledge about the same real world. This can lead to inconsistency. This book provides a wide snapshot of some intelligent technologies for knowledge inconsistency resolution.

This book completes the newest research results of the author in the period of the last five years. A part of these results has been published in prestigious international journals and conference proceedings. In this book, along with other new results, the results are completed, extended, and presented in a comprehensive and unified way.

The material of each chapter of this book is self-contained. I hope that the book can be useful for graduate and PhD students in computer science; participants of courses in knowledge management and multiagent systems; researchers and all readers working on knowledge management and/or ontology integration; and specialists from social choice.

I wish to express my great gratitude to Professor Lakhmi C. Jain, the editor of this series, for his encouragement, inspiration, and interest. Thanks are also due to my colleagues at the Institute of Information Science and Engineering of Wroclaw University of Technology, for their nurturing of this project. Special thanks go to Catherine Brett for her kind contacts and advice in preparing this book. Finally, I cordially thank my wife Bich Ngoc and my sons Ngoc Trung and Ngoc Khanh for their great patience and understanding during the preparation of this book.

This work was supported by the Polish Ministry of Science and Higher Education under the grant no N516 013 32/1733.

Ngoc Thanh Nguyen

Table of Contents

1. Inconsistency of Knowledge

This chapter is an introduction to the topics of inconsistency of knowledge and inconsistent knowledge management. It describes the subject of this book as well as its structure.

1.1. Introduction

What is inconsistency of knowledge? In knowledge-based systems the notion *consistency of knowledge* is most often understood as a situation in which a knowledge base does not contain contradictions. Thus inconsistency of knowledge appears if there are some contradictions. However, this definition is not satisfactory because the notion *inconsistency* is only replaced by the notion *contradiction*. Contradiction is easily defined in classical logic-based knowledge bases, where contradiction can be understood as a situation in which a set of logic formulae has no model; that is, on the basis of these formulae one can infer *false*. For example, for the set of formulae $\{\neg x \vee y, x, \neg y, x \vee \neg y\}$ with the inference engine of standard logic one can easily notice that no model exists because in any interpretation formulae x, $\neg y$ and $\neg x \vee y$ may not be satisfied simultaneously. In nonlogic knowledge bases the notion of contradiction is more difficult to define.

The notion of inconsistency of knowledge is more complex than the notion of contradiction. In general for setting an inconsistency of knowledge it is necessary to set the following three components:

- A subject to which the inconsistency refers: If we assume that a knowledge base contains knowledge about some real world then the subject of inconsistency may be a part of the real world.
- A set of elements of knowledge related to this subject: Such an element may be, for example, a formula or a relational tuple in the base.
- Definition of contradiction: In the case of logic-based bases the contradiction is simple to identify owing to the criterion of contradiction

of a set of formulae. In the case of nonlogic bases contradiction needs to be indicated referring to the subject of inconsistency.

In the case of logic-based knowledge bases the inconsistency of knowledge is reduced to the contradiction of a set of formulae. The definition of contradiction in this case is well known, very strong, and independent of that to which the subject refers. Thus the most important is the second component, which is a set of logic formulae.

In the case of nonlogic bases all three components are important; without one of them it is hard to set the inconsistency. As an example of inconsistency in a nonlogic base of knowledge let's consider the following relation representing a state of knowledge about the weather forecasts for some regions of a country.

Region_ID	Day	Temperature	Rain	Sunshine
r_1	d_1	15–30	Yes	Yes
r_1	d_2	18–32	Yes	No
r_1	d_1	20–32	No	No
r_2	d_1	23–30	Yes	No
r_2	d_2	22–29	No	No

We may notice that in this base there is an inconsistency. The inconsistency subject is pair (*Region_ID, Day*) and the set of elements being in inconsistency consists of the first and third tuples. They represent different forecasts for the same region on the same day. The contradiction is based on the fact that for the same region and the same day one of the parameters *Temperature*, *Rain*, and *Sunshine* assigns different values.

As in database systems, without elimination of inconsistency a knowledge base does not have the best utility. Referring to database systems the data inconsistency problems are solved by means of integrity constraint management systems that take care of satisfaction of these constraints. Owing to the well-defined and simple structure of data the constraints are easily formulated and the procedures for their realization are effective. In addition, integrity constraints look after the consistency on the lower level of data semantics and similar constraints may also be used in knowledge bases. Inconsistency of knowledge, however, most often refers to some integral objects or processes in the real world such as real objects, problems, events, scenarios, and the like. In general, consistency of knowledge means a condition that the pieces of knowledge included in a knowledge base and describing these integral objects are not contradictory. For this reason conditions for achieving knowledge consistency are more difficult to formulate and the algorithms for their realization are more complex and in many cases require using heuristic strategies.

It is also worth noticing that in referring to data inconsistency one uses the term "elimination" whereas in referring to knowledge inconsistency one uses the term "processing" which means that inconsistency of knowledge is not always an undesirable thing as data inconsistency is, but something natural in knowledge bases, which is useful for reflecting the real world. Methods for processing inconsistency of knowledge have the following purposes:

- Inference from inconsistency [3, 17, 22]: "Omitting" of inconsistent elements of a knowledge base and determining logic consequences of the remaining consistent elements.
- Determination of the representatives [13, 112]: A representative of a set of inconsistent elements of knowledge is an element that best represents them. For determining a representative all inconsistent elements are taken into account.
- Integration of inconsistent elements [48, 53, 54, 81, 82]: Creating new element(s) of knowledge that reflect all the elements in the base.

In general, we can distinguish the following aspects of knowledge inconsistency.

1. *Centralization Aspect*: This aspect refers to inconsistency of knowledge within one knowledge base. The reasons of inconsistency are the following:
   - Knowledge is acquired in a period of time and its "topicality" depends on the timestamps [44, 63, 153]. "New" knowledge is inconsistent with "old" knowledge because of the change of the real world to which the knowledge refers. Thus some pieces of knowledge may be inconsistent with some others if the temporal feature is taken into account.
   - The indeterminacy of the relationships between events taking place in the real world.
   - Inaccuracy of the devices responsible for knowledge acquisition and processing.
   - The indeterminacy of knowledge processing procedures.
   - Knowledge is extracted from data in a database or a data warehouse, by using, for example, data mining methods. Extracted knowledge is then dependent on the data and some of its elements may be inconsistent.

The main aim of inconsistency resolution in this case is to achieve consistency of knowledge because from the integrity point of view there is no profit in an inconsistent base of data or knowledge. For this kind of inconsistency one can actualize the knowledge base by removing from it the nonactual information, so that the remaining information should be consistent. However, knowledge extracted from data using these methods may cause the loss of useful rules. In this aspect inconsistency of knowledge is an undesirable thing which should be removed for correct functioning of knowledge bases.

2. *Distribution Aspect*: This aspect is related to inconsistency between different knowledge bases. This kind of inconsistency may take place in distributed environments. The circumstances of this kind of inconsistency are:

   - Several knowledge-based systems function in a distributed environment and reflect the same real world, or the same part of it. For the same subject (i.e., conflict issue) the sites may generate different versions (i.e., conflict content) of knowledge [105, 133]. For example, agents in a multiagent system may have different opinions on some matter or experts solving the same problem may give different solutions. Thus they are in conflict of knowledge.
   - The independency (autonomy) of the owners of knowledge bases. Very often the owner of a knowledge base is an agent or some autonomous software. Thus it processes the knowledge in an independent way.
   - The uncertainty and incompleteness of the knowledge, which may cause the inconsistency.
   - The indeterminacy of mechanisms processing the knowledge within a knowledge-based system.

The main aim of inconsistency resolution in this case is different from the aim for the centralization aspect. It seems that for this kind of inconsistency knowledge base revision methods are not useful because knowledge consistency is achieved by removing some elements of knowledge from the base. In this way the removed pieces of knowledge are treated differently from the remaining pieces. Such an assumption cannot be accepted in this case because it seems that all opinions of the agents or solutions given by the experts should be treated in the same way in the inconsistency resolution task. The aim of this task is to determine a version of inconsistent pieces of knowledge, which is needed for further processing. Consensus methods have been proved to be useful in this case. In this aspect inconsistency is a natural thing, which should not be removed but processed for extracting valuable knowledge.

The above-presented aspects seem to cover the sources of knowledge inconsistency.

1.2. Levels of Knowledge Inconsistency

From the state of the literature we may divide methods of knowledge inconsistency resolution into two levels: *syntactic* and *semantic*.

Syntactic level refers mainly to logic-based bases of knowledge. As mentioned above, owing to very strong conditions for contradiction, the subject of inconsistency is not needed. Here one has to deal with a set of logic formulae which is contradictory. We propose the adjective *syntactic* for this level because of the condition for contradiction meaning that the set of formulae is contradictory in each interpretation of the formulae.

On the syntactic level the approaches for inconsistency resolution can be divided into three groups. The first group consists of approaches based on knowledge base revision, the second group includes approaches relying on paraconsistent logics, and the methods belonging to the third group deal with measures of inconsistency. The methods belonging to the first group are most often used in deductive databases, making it possible to remove some formulae from the base to produce a new consistent database [36, 37, 47, 95, 140]. Such a process may be performed by confronting the formulae with the actual state of the real world to which the database refers. The disadvantage of this approach is that it is too complex to localize the inconsistency and to perform optimal selection, that is, with minimal loss of useful information.

The second group consists of paraconsistent logic-based methods. Paraconsistent logics give sensible inferences from inconsistent information. Hunter [58] and other authors have defined the following logics: weakly negative logic which uses the full classical language; four-valued logic which uses a subset of the classical language; quasi-logical logic which uses the full classical language and enables effectively rewriting data and queries to a conjunction normal form; and finally argumentative logic which reasons with consistent subsets of classical formulae. Hunter has stated that paraconsistent logics can localize inconsistency and their conclusions are sensible with respect to the data. In these logics the inconsistency does not need to be resolved. However, this kind of logic does not offer concrete strategies for acting on inconsistency and the means for reasoning in the presence of inconsistency in the existing logical systems are still scant.

The third group includes methods that enable "monitoring" the inconsistency by measuring its degree. For this aim Hunter [59] proposes a measure for inconsistency in a set of formulae; Knight [70] measures up the inconsistency in a set of sentences. Fuzzy logic is useful in inconsistency leaving for software development [86]. Other authors [11, 40] have used labelling mechanisms in resolving inconsistency of data in databases.

Apart from the above-mentioned groups there are a lot of other works devoted to solving knowledge inconsistency on the syntactic level. Among others, in the work [16] an argued consequence relation, taking into account the existence of consistent arguments in favour of a conclusion and the absence of consistent arguments in favour of its opposite, has been investigated. In another work [5] the authors propose a method for drawing conclusions from systems that are based on classical logic with the assumption that the knowledge included in the systems might be inconsistent. The author of the work [50] solves the inconsistency problem on the syntactic level for deductive bases using nonmonotonic negation.

On the semantic level logic formulae are considered as referring to a concrete real world which is their interpretation. Inconsistency arises if in this world a fact and its negation may be inferred. In the example concerning weather forecasts presented in Section 1.1 one may infer the fact "*Sunshine is in region r_1 in day d_1,*" as well as the fact "*There is no sunshine in region r_1 in day d_1.*" As mentioned above, for setting inconsistency on this level three parameters need to be determined: the inconsistency subject, the set of knowledge elements being in inconsistency, and the definition of contradiction.

Up to now there are three known approaches for leaving inconsistency on the semantic level. The first consists of such methods that, similar to the methods in the first group of methods for inconsistency resolution on the syntactic level, enable localization of the inconsistency and its removal. These methods mention the procedures for checking data consistency using integrity constraints in database systems [33, 128]. However, structures in knowledge bases are more complex and such methods may be ineffective. Also, it is not so simple to define integrity constraints for knowledge bases. The second approach is related to Boolean reasoning and the third concerns using consensus methods.

In Boolean reasoning [23, 132] an inconsistency resolution task is formulated as an optimisation problem, which is next transformed to such a form of Boolean formula that the first implicant is the solution of the problem. In the last approach for solving inconsistency the consensus of the knowledge elements which are in inconsistency is determined and is accepted as the representative of these elements. In other words, a new state of knowledge arises by replacing the elements being in inconsistency by their consensus. Consensus choice algorithms in turn are dependent to a large degree on the structure used for describing the real world.

The task of determining the inconsistency degree is also important on the semantic level. Nguyen and Malowiecki [118] have defined consistency functions which enable calculating the consistency level for so-called conflict profiles.

Each of these levels of inconsistency may be considered referring to the above-mentioned aspects. This is illustrated in Figure 1.1.

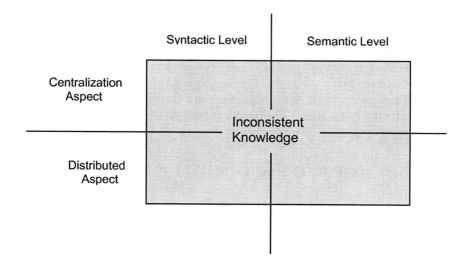

Figure 1.1. Levels and aspects of knowledge inconsistency.

1.3. Knowledge Inconsistency and Integration

In order to merge several information systems or to enable the semantic communication between them it is necessary to integrate their knowledge. Generally, a problem of knowledge integration may be formulated as follows. For a given set of knowledge pieces referring to an object (or objects) of the real world, one should eliminate the inconsistency, if any, appearing in this set. According to Reimer [139] knowledge integration can be considered in two aspects: integration of different knowledge bases and integration of different representations of the same knowledge but on different levels of representation. Corresponding to the first aspect the inconsistency mentioned in the definition of knowledge integration agrees with the notion of inconsistency presented in the previous subsections. Corresponding to the second aspect inconsistency is understood as some mismatch not of knowledge, but of its different structures.

It seems that the first kind of knowledge integration is more important, and is also a harder task for realization. One can see a close relationship between the knowledge integration process in this aspect and the idea for knowledge inconsistency resolution presented in this chapter. It seems that inconsistency resolution is a natural subtask which is necessary to be realized in the integration task. Knowledge integration is also needed for group decision-making processes and here of course knowledge inconsistency should be resolved. In the work [52] a conflict resolution model for group decision making is proposed based on the conflict index which integrates multiple possibility distributions into a new one to represent compromised knowledge.

Inconsistency of knowledge has also been considered in the aspect of uncertainty which has been investigated on different levels [4, 93].

1.4. The Subject of this Book

The main subject of this book is related to the distribution aspect of knowledge inconsistency resolution. As described in Section 1.2 the problems of knowledge inconsistency resolution in the centralization aspect, especially on the syntactic level, have been solved in many works of other authors. The author of this book for a couple of years has been dealing with these problems referring to the distribution aspect. Using consensus methods for these problems is an original approach and a number of works on this topic done by the author have been published. The materials presented in this book are coherent in the sense that they refer to the topic of knowledge inconsistency resolution in the distribution aspect. Some results included in them have been published, however, in this book they are extended, improved, and presented in a more comprehensive and unified way. In addition, this book also contains many materials not published previously. The details of the characteristics of the materials are presented in the conclusions of particular chapters.

The main contributions of this book consist in brief of the following elements.

- General model for conflict and knowledge inconsistency. This model contains such elements as conflict representation and consistency measures for conflict profiles.

- General model of consensus, which contains postulates for consensus choice functions, their classes, an approach to set susceptibility to consensus, and methods for its achievement.

- Representation method for inconsistent knowledge: several structures have been proposed, such as relational, disjunctive, conjunctive, and fuzzy-based. In each of these structures the possibility for representing positive knowledge and negative knowledge has been investigated.

- Consistency measures for conflict profiles which enable calculating the degree of conflict and choosing corresponding methods for conflict resolution.

- Method for knowledge inconsistency resolution on the syntactic level referring to distribution aspect with disjunctive, conjunctive, and fuzzy-based structures of inconsistency.

- Method for knowledge inconsistency resolution on the semantic level with disjunctive and conjunctive structures of inconsistency.

- Method for inconsistency resolution for ontologies based on consensus tools. A new classification of ontology conflicts has also been proposed.

- Consensus-based method for reconciling inconsistency of knowledge of experts. A model for inconsistency of expert knowledge has been built. It has been proved that a high degree of inconsistency is often profitable and with some restrictions the consensus of experts' opinions is better than each of these solutions.

- Method for determination of a learning scenario in intelligent tutoring systems using consensus tools and rough classification algorithms.

- Project of a multiagent system as a metasearch engine for information retrieval in the Internet. In this project the knowledge inconsistency resolution method is used for reconciling inconsistent knowledge and answers given by different agents for the same query, as well as in recommendation procedures.

1.5. The Structure of this Book

The content of this book can be divided into three parts. In the first part (Chapters 2 and 3) we present the theoretical foundation for conflict analysis and consensus choice tools. In the second part (Chapters 4–9) the inconsistency of knowledge is investigated on two levels: syntactic and semantic. For each level we propose the structures for representing inconsistency and algorithms for its solution. The detailed analysis of these algorithms is also presented. The methods based on consistency measures for inconsistency processing are worked out. A set of postulates for consistency measures which determine the classes of inconsistency functions is defined and analyzed. Next these functions are used for investigation of susceptibility to consensus for knowledge conflict profiles.

In this part we also deal with the analysis of expert knowledge inconsistency and conflicts of ontologies. It turns out that inconsistency of expert opinions on some matters may be very useful. Ontology mismatch (or inconsistency) may take place on three levels: instance level, concept level, and relation level. On each level we define the inconsistency and work out a method for inconsistency processing.

In the third part (Chapters 10 and 11) we present two applications of the proposed methods for inconsistency resolution. The first application is related to the problem of recommendation in intelligent tutoring systems. For a given learner the opening learning scenario is determined by a consensus-based procedure on the basis of the knowledge about similar scenarios passed by other learners. Owing to this the learning process is changed dynamically to better suit actual learner characteristics. The second application refers to the aspect of inconsistency of agent knowledge. It includes a detailed conception of a metasearch engine with using multiagent technologies. The aim of the project is to create a consensus-based multiagent system to aid users in information retrieval from the Internet. A more detailed description of the chapters is presented as follows.

Chapter 2 presents a general model for conflict and knowledge inconsistency. A definition of inconsistency referring to the distribution aspect is included. This model contains such elements as conflict representation and consistency measures for conflict profiles. For measuring consistency a set of postulates is proposed and five consistency functions are defined and analyzed. Some methods for improving the consistency are also worked out.

Chapter 3 is devoted to a couple of new problems of consensus theory. A set of classes for consensus choice functions is defined and analyzed. The problems of evaluating the quality of consensus and susceptibility to consensus are solved. Several methods for achieving susceptibility to consensus are worked out and some methods for reducing the number of consensuses are also given.

Chapter 4 is concerned with a general model for knowledge integration referring to its inconsistency in distribution aspect. This chapter presents the aspect of knowledge inconsistency in the integration process. We propose a multivalue and multiattribute model for knowledge integration and show the placement of the inconsistency aspect in the integration process. The postulates for knowledge integration and algorithms for this process are worked out.

The purpose of Chapter 5 is to present the process of knowledge inconsistency resolution and knowledge integration on the syntactic level. The contributions of this chapter are based on the solutions of these problems in the distribution aspect. Here as the structure of inconsistency we use such logic structures as conjunctive and disjunctive. Fuzzy conjunctive structure is also considered.

Chapter 6 deals with the solutions of knowledge inconsistency resolution and knowledge integration on the semantic level. Here conjunctive and disjunctive structures interpreted in a real world are investigated. For each structure the notion of semantic is defined and analyzed. The distance functions for these structures are defined and the problem of dependencies between attributes is also investigated.

Chapter 7 presents a fuzzy-based approach to a consensus problem. In Chapter 3 (Section 3.6) weights for achieving consensus susceptibility are used. The weights serve to express the credibility of experts or agents who generate given opinions. This chapter presents an approach in which weights are used for expressing the credibility of opinions. We call a set of such opinions a *fuzzy conflict profile*. Postulates for consensus functions and algorithms for consensus determination are given.

Chapter 8 has a special character and is devoted to the analysis of expert knowledge. We show different types of conflict profiles consisting of expert solutions of some problem and investigate the relationship between the consensus of a profile to the proper solution of this problem. Although the proper solution is not known, we show that in certain situations the consensus is more similar to it than the solutions proposed by the experts. In this way in some degree we prove the hypothesis that the wisdom of the crowd is greater than the wisdom of single autonomous units.

The idea of Chapter 9 is concerned with inconsistency resolution for ontologies. Ontology is a very popular structure for knowledge and the problem of its inconsistency in different systems appears fairly frequently. If integration of some systems has to be performed, their ontologies must also be integrated. In this process it is often necessary to resolve conflicts (or inconsistency) between ontologies. In this chapter we present a classification of ontology conflicts and consensus-based algorithms for their resolution.

Chapter 10 deals with application of the methods for inconsistency resolution presented in previous chapters. Its subject is related to recommendation processes in intelligent tutoring systems. Using methods for rough classification, a model for representation of learning scenarios and the choice of proper scenario for a new learner is built. The recommendation mechanisms presented in this chapter are based on consensus methods and clustering algorithms. Owing to them there is a possibility to adapt the learning path to learner profiles.

Chapter 11 includes a detailed conception of a metasearch engine using multiagent technologies. We present a consensus-based approach for integrating answers generated by different agents for a given query. Moreover, this multiagent system uses the features of agent technology for making the system a recommender system. The aim of the project is to create a consensus-based multiagent system to aid users in information retrieval from the Internet.

Finally, some conclusions and directions for the future research are included in Chapter 12.

2. Model of Knowledge Conflict

The aim of this chapter is to introduce the subject of conflict analysis, its representation, and tools useful in its resolution. These tools consist of consistency functions which measure the degree of the coherence of elements being in a conflict. Conflict is something we often have to deal with in our everyday life and in many kinds of computer systems. Because of its very rich and varied nature, in this book we investigate only one class of conflicts related to knowledge management.

2.1. Introduction

Conflict can be considered in many cases as inconsistency. Conflict, however, seems to have more a specific meaning than inconsistency. Inconsistency most often refers to states of resources (such as knowledge base, database, etc.) of one or more integral systems, whereas with a conflict we have in mind some inconsistency between a few autonomous unities. Thus conflict refers to a set of unities and a concrete matter. It then is suitable for the kind of inconsistency on distributed aspect analyzed in Chapter 1. Thus conflict is very often considered in distributed environments, in which several autonomous systems function and have to co-operate in order to realize some common tasks.

Let's consider a distributed system which is understood as a collection of independent computers connected to each other by a network and equipped with distributed software and data [27]. In such a kind of system independence is one of the basic features of the sites, meaning that within the confines of available resources each of them does independent data processing, and takes care of consistency of data. Most often each system site is placed in a region of the real world and its task relies on storing and processing information about this region. Regions occupied by the sites often overlap. This redundancy is needed for the following reasons.

- Uncertain and incomplete information (data) of the sites referring to regions they occupy.

- Entrusting one region to several sites may cause a complement of sites' information and owing to this it can enlarge the credibility of information-processing results.

However, the autonomy feature of sites and their indeterminism in information processing may cause disagreement (conflict) between sites referring to a common subject. Independent sites may generate different versions of information about the same real world. This in turn may cause trouble in information processing of the whole system.

As shown in Figure 2.1, for the same event in the real world four agents may generate different scenarios. Thus there arises a conflict profile:

Conflict profile = {Scenario 1, Scenario 1, Scenario 2, Scenario 3},

where Scenario 1 appears two times and each of Scenarios 2 and 3 appears only once.

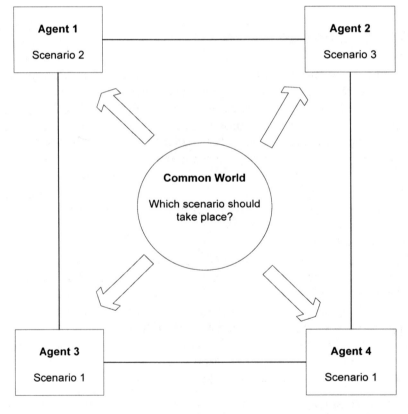

Figure 2.1. An example of conflict in an agent-based distributed environment.

Another, more practical example refers to a multiagent system serving intrusion detection in a network system [61, 72]. It is assumed that the network system consists of a set of sites. Two types of agents are designed: monitoring agents (MA) and managing agents (MaA). Monitoring agents observe the sites, process the captured information and draw conclusions that are necessary to evaluate the current state of system security. Managing agents are responsible for managing the work of monitoring agents (Figure 2.2). Each monitoring agent monitors its area consisting of several sites. If an attack appears, the agent must deduce the kind, source, and the path of propagation of this attack. It is assumed that the areas of the monitoring agents might mutually overlap. Owing to such an assumption the credibility of monitoring agents' results could be high, the sources of attacks might be more quickly established, and the risks of security breach of the main sites might be reduced. Each managing agent manages a set of monitoring agents.

The deduction results of monitoring agents referring to the same site may be inconsistent, meaning that for the same attack and the same site different agents may diagnose different sources of attack, propagation paths, and so on. In other words, they may be in conflict.

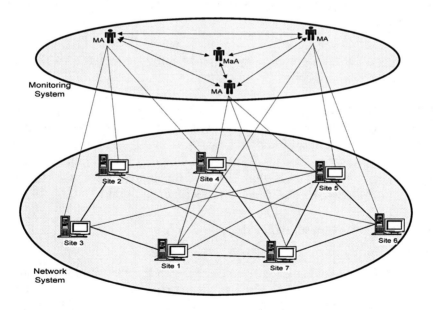

Figure 2.2. A multiagent system for intrusion detection.

The above examples show that conflict situations take place when for the same subject several sites cooperating in a distributed environment may generate different versions of data (e.g., different scenarios of a future event or different solutions of the same problem). In this chapter we deal with the definition of conflict and tools for its analysis. We restrict our consideration to conflict of knowledge and propose a formal model for its representation. We also define and analyze consistency measures of conflict profiles. Consistency is a very important parameter of conflict profiles, and its value could say some essential things about the conflict.

2.2. What is Conflict?

In the most general way one can say that a conflict takes place when at least two bodies have different opinions on the same subject. In a general context we can distinguish the following components of a conflict [104]:

- *Conflict body*: a set of participants of the conflict.
- *Conflict subject*: a set of matters which are occupied by the participants.
- *Conflict content*: a set of opinions of the participants on the conflict subject. These opinions represent the knowledge states of the participants on this subject.

Conflict has been a popular subject in such sciences as psychology and sociology. In computer science conflict analysis has been more and more needed because of using autonomous programs and processing data knowledge originating from these sources. The first formal model for conflict has been proposed by Pawlak [133]. Referring to the above-mentioned parameters the Pawlak conflict can be specified as follows.

- *Conflict body*: a set of agents.
- *Conflict subject*: a set of issues.
- *Conflict content*: a set of tuples representing the opinions of these agents on these issues. Each agent referring to each issue has three possibilities for presenting his opinion: (+), yes; (−), no; and (0), neutral.

For example [133], if there are five agents (#1, #2, #3, #4, #5) and five issues (*a*, *b*, *c*, *d*, *e*) then the opinion of an agent on these issues may be represented by a row in the following information table.

Agent	a	b	c	d	e
#1	–	–	+	+	+
#2	+	0	+	–	–
#3	+	–	+	–	0
#4	0	–	–	0	–
#5	+	–	–	–	–

Pawlak has created a set of tools that enable conflict analysis. This set consists of such elements as relations of coalition, neutrality, and conflict. Pawlak has used neither distance functions for measuring the similarity of agents' opinions nor the method for determination of conflict solution. In addition, Pawlak's model is very simple and does not allow the agents to express more complex opinions. As stated above, referring to a matter an agent has only three possibilities for expressing her opinion: *approval*, *objection*, and *neutrality*. An enhancement of Pawlak's model has been proposed by Skowron and Deya [144]. In this work the authors define local states of agents which may be interpreted as the sources of their opinions expressed referring to the matters in contention. This model considers conflicts on several levels, among others on the level of reasons of conflicts. In this approach it is still assumed that attribute values are atomic.

In this chapter we define conflicts in distributed environments with the above-mentioned parameters. We build a formalism which has the following purposes:

- Conflict can be defined on a general level.

- It is possible to calculate the inconsistency degree of conflict, and within conflict values of the attributes representing participants' opinions should more precisely describe these opinions. We realize this aim with the assumption that values of attributes representing conflict contents are not atomic as in Pawlak's approach, but sets of elementary values where an elementary value is not necessarily an atomic one. Thus we accept the assumption that attributes are multivalued, similar to Lipskis's [79] and Pawlak's [132] concepts of multivalued information systems.

- We introduce three kinds of conflict of participants' knowledge: positive, negative, and ignorance. Positive knowledge serves to express such types of opinion as "In my opinion it should be," negative knowledge, "In my opinion it should not be," and uncertain knowledge, "I have no basis to state if it should be." For example, an expert is asked to forecast the increase of GDP of a country. She can give her three kinds of opinions: an interval to which the increase should most likely belong, an interval (intervals) to which the increase should not belong, and an interval (intervals) to which she does not know if the increase may belong or not. An example of the expert's opinion is presented as follows.

Should be	Should not be	Uncertain
$[3, 5]$	$(-\infty, 2], (10, +\infty)$	$(5, 10]$

- Owing to this assumption a conflict participant functioning in some real world and having limited possibilities does not have to know "everything". In Pawlak's approach positive knowledge is represented by value "+", and negative knowledge by value "−". Some difference occurs between the semantics of Pawlak's "neutrality" and the semantics of "uncertainty" presented in this work. Namely, most often neutrality appears in voting processes and does not mean uncertainty, whereas uncertainty means that an agent or expert is not competent to express its opinions on some matter.

- We define the inconsistency level for conflict.

- Weights of conflict participants are taken into account in determining the inconsistency level.

- Criteria for susceptibility to consensus are defined for conflict.

In the next section we present a general model for conflict.

2.3. Conflict Representation

2.3.1. Basic Notions

In this section we present some notions needed for use in the next sections. In the context of the components of conflict defined in Section 2.2 (conflict body, subject, and content), we assume in this model that the conflict subject is given and for this subject the set of all potential opinions which may be included in the conflict content may be determined. We investigate the properties of behaviour of different cases of conflict content.

By U we denote a finite set of objects representing the potential opinions for the conflict subject. Symbol 2^U denotes the powerset of U, that is, the set of all subsets of U.

By $\Pi_k(U)$ we denote the set of all k-element subsets (with repetitions) of set U for $k \in \aleph$ ($\aleph$ is the set of natural numbers), and let

$$\Pi(U) = \bigcup_{k \in \aleph} \Pi_k(U).$$

Thus $\Pi(U)$ is the set of all nonempty subsets with repetitions of set U.

Each element of set $\Pi(U)$ is called a *conflict profile*. A conflict profile is then a subset with repetitions of set U and should represent a conflict content.[1]

In this work we do not use the formalism often used in consensus theory [13] in which the domain of consensus is defined as $U^* = \bigcup_{k>0} U^k$, where U^k is the k-fold Cartesian product of U. In this way we can specify how many times an object occurs in a profile and we can ensure that the order of objects belonging to a profile is not important. We also use in this book the algebra of sets with repetitions (multisets) defined by Lipski and Marek [80]. Some of its elements are presented by the following examples.

An expression

$$X = \{x, x, y, y, y, z\}$$

is called a set with repetitions with cardinality equal to 6. In this set element x appears two times, y three times, and z one time. Set X can also be written as

$$X = \{2 * x, 3 * y, 1 * z\}.$$

The sum of sets with repetitions is denoted by the symbol $\cup$ and is defined in the following way. If element x appears in set X n times and in Y n' times, then in their sum $X \cup Y$ this element should appear $n + n'$ times. For example, if $X = \{2 * x, 3 * y, 1 * z\}$ and $Y = \{4 * x, 2 * y\}$, then

$$X \cup Y = \{6 * x, 5 * y, 1 * z\}.$$

The difference of sets with repetitions is denoted by the symbol "–" and is defined in the following way. If element x appears in set X n times and in Y n' times, then the number of occurrences of x in their difference $X - Y$ should be equal to $n - n'$ if $n \geq n'$, and 0 otherwise. For example:

$$\{6 * x, 5 * y, 1 * z\} - \{2 * x, 3 * y, 1 * z\} = \{4 * x, 2 * y\}.$$

---

[1] In this work sets with repetitions refer only to conflict profiles, and any symbol representing a conflict profile also represents a set with repetitions.

A set X with repetitions is a subset of a set Y with repetitions $(X \subseteq Y)$ if each element from X does not have a greater number of occurrences than it has in set Y. For example,

$$\{2 * x, 3 * y, 1 * z\} \subseteq \{2 * x, 4 * y, 1 * z\}.$$

Set U can have two kinds of structure: the *macrostructure* and the *microstructure*. By a macrostructure of U we understand some relationship between its elements, for example, a binary relation on U, or some relationship between its elements and elements of another set, for example, some function from $U \times U$ to another set. In this work as the macrostructure of the set U we assume a distance function:

$$d: U \times U \rightarrow [0, 1],$$

which is

1. *Nonnegative*:

$$\forall x, y \in U: d(x,y) \geq 0,$$

2. *Reflexive*:

$$\forall x, y \in U: d(x,y) = 0 \text{ iff } x = y, \text{ and}$$

3. *Symmetrical*:

$$\forall x, y \in U: d(x,y) = d(y,x),$$

where $[0, 1]$ is the closed interval of real numbers between 0 and 1.

Thus function d is a half-metric because the above conditions include only a part of the metric conditions. Here there is the lack of a transitive condition because it is too strong for many practical situations [20].

By a microstructure of U we understand the structure of the elements of U. For example, if U is the set of all partitions of some set X then the microstructure of U is a partition of X, and as the macrostructure of U we can define a distance function between partitions of X.

Let us notice that a space (U, d) defined in the above way does not need to be a metric space. Therefore, we call it a *distance space* [103].

We distinguish the following classes of conflict profiles.

Definition 2.1.
A conflict profile $X \in \Pi(U)$ is called:
(a) Homogeneous, if all its elements are identical;, that is, $X = \{n * x\}$ for some $x \in U$ and n being a natural number
(b) Heterogeneous, if it is not homogeneous

(c) Distinguishable, if all its elements are different from each other

*(d) Multiple, referring to a profile Y (or X is a multiple of Y, written as X = n * Y) if*

$$Y = \{x_1, x_2, \ldots, x_k\}$$

and

$$X = \{n * x_1, \ n * x_2, \ldots, n * x_k\}$$

for k and n being natural numbers and n > 1

(e) Regular, if it is distinguishable or a multiple of some distinguishable profile

As defined above, a conflict profile $X \in \Pi(U)$ contains opinions of conflict participants on the given matter of contention. It should be the main subject for conflict analysis in order to solve it. In fact, if the profile is homogeneous then there is no conflict inasmuch as all the opinions are identical. However, for completeness of the theory, we assume that it is a special case of conflict.

2.3.2. Definition of Knowledge Conflict

We assume that there is given a finite set A of agents which work in a distributed environment. The term "agent" is used here in a very general sense: as an agent we may understand an expert or an intelligent and autonomous computer program. We assume that these agents have their own knowledge bases in which knowledge states can be distinguished. In general, by a state of agent knowledge we understand these elements of an agent knowledge base which reflect the state of the real world occupied by the agent referring to a given timestamp. Such a state may be treated as a view or an opinion of the agent on some matter. We realize that the structures of agent knowledge bases may be differentiated from each other. However, in this chapter we do not deal with them; this is the subject of the next chapters where we define concrete structures (logical or relational) of agent knowledge. We assume that there is a common platform for presenting the knowledge states of all agents.

We assume that the agents from set A work on a finite set of common subjects (matters) of their interest. This set is denoted by S.

Now by U we denote the set of all possible states of agent knowledge presented in the platform. Owing to this assumption two different states belonging to U should have different "content".

An agent $a \in A$ referring to subject (matter) $s \in S$ can generate the following kinds of knowledge:

- *Positive knowledge*: a state $u \in U$ is called the positive knowledge of agent a referring to subject s if in the opinion of the agent state u is the most proper description (alternative, scenario, etc.) related to subject s.
- *Negative knowledge*: a state $u \in U$ is called the negative knowledge of agent a referring to subject s if in the opinion of the agent state u cannot be the proper description (alternative, scenario, etc.) related to subject s.
- *Uncertain knowledge*: a state $u \in U$ is called the uncertain knowledge of agent a referring to subject s if it does not know if state u can be the proper description (alternative, scenario, etc.) related to subject s.

Thus positive knowledge represents the kind of agent opinions that something should take place, whereas by means of negative knowledge an agent can express its contrary opinion. Notice that for the same agent the state representing positive knowledge must be different from the state representing its negative knowledge.

In this way for a subject $s \in S$ we can define the following profiles:

- *Positive profile*: $X^+(s)$ – as the set of knowledge states from U representing positive knowledge of the agents referring to subject
- *Negative profile*: $X^-(s)$ – as the set of knowledge states from U representing negative knowledge of the agents referring to subject s
- *Uncertain profile*: $X^\pm(s)$ – as the set of knowledge states from U representing uncertain knowledge of the agents referring to subject s

Positive, negative, and uncertain profiles referring to subject s should satisfy the following conditions:

- They are pairwise disjoint.
- They are sets with repetitions because of the fact that some agents may generate the same knowledge state.

Now we can present the definition of knowledge conflict.

Definition 2.2.
A knowledge conflict referring to subject s appears if at least one of profiles $X^+(s)$ and $X^-(s)$ is heterogeneous.

From Definition 2.1 it follows that a conflict takes place if at least two agents generate different (positive or negative) knowledge states referring to the same subject. Notice that in this definition there is no reference to the uncertain profile $X^\pm(s)$. The reason is that the role of uncertain knowledge is not as important as the role of the two remaining kinds of knowledge. If referring to a subject the agents have identical positive and negative knowledge then although their states of uncertainty are different, then there is no conflict.

Sets $X^+(s)$ and $X^-(s)$ are also called *positive conflict profile* and *negative conflict profile*, respectively.

Below we present an example.

Example 2.1. Consider a group of experts who have to analyze the economic situation of a country and forecast its increase of GDP in a given year. An expert may generate an interval to which in his opinion the increase of GDP is most likely to belong. He may also give some other intervals to which in his opinion the increase of GDP should not belong. As a knowledge state we define a subset of the set of real numbers. In the following table the opinions of five experts are presented.

Expert	X^+	X^-	$X^\pm$
E_1	[3, 5]	$(-\infty, 3), (5, +\infty)$	$\varnothing$
E_2	[2, 6]	$(-\infty, 2), (6, 8)$	$[8, +\infty)$
E_3	4	$[1, 3], (7, +\infty)$	$(-\infty, 1), (3,4),$ $(4,7]$
E_4	[3, 5]	$(-\infty, 3), (5, +\infty)$	$\varnothing$
E_5	[3, 5]	$(-\infty, 3), (10, +\infty)$	$(5,10]$

In this way we have a conflict because the profiles X^+ and X^- are not homogeneous. Notice that the opinions of some experts (E_2, E_3, E_5) do not exhaust the set of all real numbers. This means they can have some ignorance. For example, expert E_5 does not know if the increase of GDP may belong to interval (5, 10] or not. ◆

2.3.3. Credibility Degree of Conflict Participants

In a conflict the roles of its participations (i.e., the agents) do not have to be the same. The need for differentiating agent roles follows from the fact that one agent may be more credible than another. Credibility of an agent or an expert in many cases should be a multidimensional value. For simplicity here we assume it to be a one-dimensional value. This value should play the following roles.

- It represents the competence of the agent.
- It represents the credibility of the agent.

We define this value by means of the following function,

$$w: A \times S \rightarrow [0,1],$$

where for a given agent a and a subject s value $w(a, s)$ is called the weight of agent a referring to subject s.

For simplicity, if the subject of conflict is known and if the elements of a conflict profile are well identified, then we may denote the weight of an element in a profile by $w(x)$ where x is an element of the profile. For example,

$$X = \{x_1, x_2, x_3, x_4\},$$

where $x_1 = $ "*Yes*", $x_2 = $ "*Yes*", $x_3 = $ "*No*", and $x_4 = $ "*Yes*". The weights can be written as

$$w(x_1) = 0.4; \quad w(x_2) = 0.1; \quad w(x_3) = 0.9; \quad w(x_4) = 1.$$

2.4. Consistency Measure for Conflict Profiles

2.4.1. Notion of Conflict Profile Consistency

Referring to conflict profiles one can say that the conflict represented by one profile is larger than that by another. Let's consider an example.

Example 2.2. Let agents participating in a conflict generate answers "*Yes*," "*No*," or "*Neutral*;" then it seems that profile

$$X = \{Yes, No, Neutral\}$$

represents a more serious conflict than profile

$$X' = \{Yes, Yes, No\},$$

which in turn seems to be worse than profile

$$X'' = \{Yes, Yes, Neutral\}.$$

Assume that our aim is to make a decision on the basis of participants' opinions. The basis of our observation relies on the fact that profile X contains all three potential opinions, each of which appears exactly one time. In this case we often say "*Nothing is known;*" that is, it is not possible to make any sensible decision. The second profile contains two opinions "*Yes*" and one opinion "*No.*" Here using the rule of majority we could suggest accepting "*Yes*" as the decision. However, not taking into account the opinion "*No*" in this case may cause doubt inasmuch as the relationship between the number of "*Yesses*" to the number of "*Nos*" is only 2 to 1. The third profile is in the smallest degree embarrassing because two of participants say "*Yes*" and the third is neutral.   ♦

For this reason an idea for measuring the degree of conflict has arisen. Referring to opinions belonging to conflict profiles one can observe that elements of a certain profile are more similar to each other (i.e., they are more convergent or more consistent) than elements of some other profile. In Example 2.2 opinions included in profile X' seem to be more consistent than opinions included in profile X, and opinions from profile X'' seem to be more consistent than opinions from profile X'. This shows that for a given profile it is needed to determine a value which would represent the degree (or level) of its consistency (or inconsistency). This value should be very useful in evaluating whether a conflict is "solvable." We propose to define this parameter for conflict profiles by means of consistency functions. For this aim we define a set of several postulates representing the intuitive conditions for consistency degree which should be satisfied by these functions. We also define several consistency functions and show which postulates they fulfil.

By symbol c we denote the consistency function for a conflict profile. This function has the signature:

$$c: \Pi(U) \rightarrow [0,1].$$

The idea of this function relies on measuring the consistency degree of profile elements. The consistency degree of a profile mentions the notion of indiscernibility defined by Pawlak for an information system [132, 145]. However, they are different conceptions. The difference is based on the fact that the consistency degree represents the coherence level of the profile elements and to measure it one should first define the distances between these elements. Indiscernibility, in turn, reflects the possibility for differentiating two tuples, and the distance function is not used.

By $C(U)$ we denote the set of all consistency functions for $\Pi(U)$.

The notion of inconsistency measure has been referred to in paraconsistent logics [18, 59, 69, 70]. The general idea of these works is based on measuring the inconsistency value for a set of formulae which are not consistent. In our approach the inconsistency is expressed by means of the distance function, and the consistency value is determined on its basis.

2.4.2. Postulates for Consistency Functions

The requirements for consistency functions are expressed in the following postulates. We assume that the universe U consists at least of two elements. Let $c \in C(U)$. The postulates are presented as follows.

P1a. Postulate for maximal consistency:
If X is a homogeneous profile then

$$c(X) = 1.$$

P1b. Extended postulate for maximal consistency:
For $Y, Z \in \Pi(U)$ where $Y = \{x\}$ and

$$X^{(n)} = (n * Y) \cup Z$$

being such a profile that element x occurs at least n times, and the numbers of occurrences of other elements from Z are constant, then the following equation should be true,

$$\lim_{n \to +\infty} c(X^{(n)}) = 1.$$

P2a. Postulate for minimal consistency:
If $X = \{a, b\}$ and $d(a,b) = \max_{x,y \in U} d(x, y)$ then

$$c(X) = 0.$$

P2b. Extended postulate for minimal consistency:
For $Y, Z \in \Pi(U)$, $Y = \{a, b\}$ and

$$X^{(n)} = (n * Y) \cup Z$$

being a profile such that elements a and b occur at least n times, and the numbers of occurrences of other elements from Z are constant, and

$$d(a,b) = \max_{x,y \in U} d(x,y),$$

then the following equation should take place,

$$\lim_{n \to +\infty} c(X^{(n)}) = 0.$$

P2c. Alternative postulate for minimal consistency:

If X = U then c(X) = 0.

P3. Postulate for nonzero consistency:
If there exist elements a, b ∈ X such that

$$d(a,b) < \max_{x,y \in U} d(x,y)$$

and X ≠ n * U for all n = 1, 2, . . . , then

$$c(X) > 0.$$

P4. Postulate for heterogeneous profiles:
If X is a he terogeneous profile then

$$c(X) < 1.$$

P5. Postulate for multiple profiles:
If profile X is a multiple of profile Y then

$$c(X) = c(Y).$$

P6. Postulate for greater consistency:
Let

$$d(x,X) = \Sigma_{y \in X} d(x,y)$$

denote the sum of distances between an element x of universe U and the elements of profile X. Let

$$D(X) = \{d(x,X): x \in U\}$$

be the set of all such sums. For any profiles X, Y ∈ Π(U) the following dependency should be true,

$$\left(\frac{\min (D(X))}{card(X)} \leq \frac{\min (D(Y))}{card(Y)} \right) \Rightarrow (c(X) \geq c(Y)).$$

P7a. Postulate for consistency improvement:
Let a and a' be such elements of universe U that

$$d(a,X) = \min \{d(x,X): x \in X\}$$

and

$$d(a',X) = \min \{d(x,X): x \in U\};$$

then

$$c(X-\{a\}) \leq c(X) \leq c(X \cup \{a'\}).$$

P7b. Second postulate for consistency improvement:
Let b and b' be such elements of universe U that

$$d(b,X) = \max \{d(x,X): x \in X\}$$

and

$$d(b',X) = \max \{d(x,X): x \in U\};$$

then

$$c(X \cup \{b'\}) \leq c(X) \leq c(X - \{b\}).$$

P8. Postulate for simplification:
For Y, Z $\in \Pi(U)$ and

$$X^{(n)} = (n * Y) \cup Z$$

then the following equation should be true,

$$\lim_{n \to +\infty} c(X^{(n)}) = c(Y).$$

The above-mentioned postulates illustrate intuitive conditions for consistency functions. However, some commentaries should be given.

- *Postulate for maximal consistency* (P1a): This postulate seems to be very natural because it requires that if in a profile only one element occurs then the consistency should be maximal. As stated earlier, a homogeneous profile in fact does not represent any conflict, thus for this situation the consistency should be maximal. In the example of the experts generating opinions about the GDP level for a country, if their opinions are the same then the consistency of their knowledge on this matter should be maximal.

- *Extended postulate for maximal consistency* (P1b): If in a given conflict profile some element is dominant (by its large number of occurrences) in such degree that the numbers of occurrences of other elements are insignificant, then the consistency should be near to the maximal value. This is consistent with the rule of majority.
- *Postulate for minimal consistency* (P2a): If a profile X consists of two opinions and their distance is maximal, that is,

$$X = \{a, b\} \text{ and } d(a,b) = \max_{x,y \in U} d(x,y),$$

then it represents the "worst conflict," so the consistency should be minimal.

- *Extended postulate for minimal consistency* (P2b): This postulate characterizes also a "very bad" conflict in which two maximally differing opinions dominate because their numbers of occurrences aim to infinity. For this situation the consistency should aim to 0. This postulate is also consistent with the rule of majority.
- *Alternative postulate for minimal consistency* (P2c): This postulate presents another aspect of "the worst conflicts," meaning that the profile is distinguishable and moreover, it consists of all possible opinions which may be generated. Referring to such kind of profiles we can say that everything is possible, and that is it is very hard to infer something from the situation. Therefore, the consistency degree should be minimal.
- *Postulate for nonzero consistency* (P3): This postulate defines a set of profiles with consistency degree larger than 0. In some sense it is complementary to postulates P2b and P2c which give consistency value 0 for those profiles nonreflected by postulate P3. In addition, if a profile contains at least two such elements that their distance is smaller than the maximal distance in the universe, and it is neither the universe nor its multiple, then this means that there is some coherence in it. For such profiles the consistency should be greater than 0.
- *Postulate for heterogeneous profiles* (P4): The consistency of "true" conflict may not be maximal. The maximal value of consistency is then reserved for profiles representing nonconflict situations. Thus if a profile is heterogeneous then its consistency may not be maximal, because the opinions represented by its elements are not identical.

- *Postulate for multiple profiles* (P5): If profile X is a multiple of profile Y then it means that the proportions of the numbers of occurrences of any two elements are identical in profiles X and Y. In other words, the quantity relationships between element x and element y $(x, y \in U)$ are the same in profiles X and Y. Thus these profiles should have the same consistency degree.
- *Postulate for greater consistency* (P6): The fact that

$$\frac{\min(D(X))}{card(X)} \leq \frac{\min(D(Y))}{card(Y)}$$

means that the elements of profile X are more concentrated than the elements of profile Y. In other words, profile X is denser than profile Y. Thus there should be $c(X) \geq c(Y)$.
- *Postulate for consistency improvement* (P7a): This postulate shows when it is possible to improve the consistency. According to this postulate removing the best element of a profile (i.e., the sum of distances between it and other elements is minimal) should worsen the inconsistency, whereas adding the best element of the universe referring to the profile (i.e., the sum of distances between it and elements of the profile is minimal) should improve the consistency.
- *Postulate for consistency improvement* (P7b): This postulate is dual to postulate P7a. It states that removing the worst element of a profile (i.e., the sum of distances between it and other elements is maximal) should improve the inconsistency, whereas adding the worst element of the universe referring to the profile (i.e., the sum of distances between it and elements of the profile is maximal) should worsen the consistency.

Postulates P7a and P7b are very useful in consistency improvement. According to them the consistency value should be larger if we add to a profile this element of universe U which generates the minimal sum of distances to the profile elements, or if we remove from the profile this element which generates the maximal sum of distances. For example, let

$$U = \{x, y, z, s, t, u, w\}$$

be such a universe that the distances between element w and other elements are much greater than the distances among elements x, y, z, t and u (see Figure 2.3). Let

$$X = \{x, y, z, s, t, w\},$$

$$d(u,X) = \min\{d(x,X): x \in U\}$$

and

$$d(w,X) = \max\{d(x,X): x \in X\}.$$

According to postulates P7a and P7b we can improve the consistency by moving element w or adding element u; that is

$$c(X) \le c(X - \{w\}) \quad \text{and} \quad c(X) \le c(X \cup \{u\}).$$

So we have

$$c(X) \le c(X - \{w\}) \le c(X - \{w\} \cup \{u\}) = c(\{x, y, z, s, t, u\})$$

and

$$c(X) \le c(X \cup \{u\}) \le c(X \cup \{u\} - \{w\}) = c(\{x, y, z, s, t, u\}).$$

- *Postulate for simplification* (P8): This postulate in a certain sense is a general form of postulates P1b and P2b regarding postulate P5. It requires accepting the consistency value of a profile as the consistency value of this part of the profile which dominates. In this case the dominating subprofile is $n * Y$, and because according to postulate P5 we have $c(n * Y) = c(Y)$, then the consistency is equal to the consistency of Y.

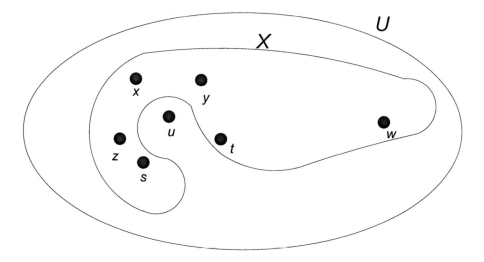

Figure 2.3. An example of profile X.

2.4.3. Analysis of Postulates

Let

$$P = \{P1a, P1b, P2a, P2b, P2c, P3, P4, P5, P6, P7a, P7b, P8\}$$

be the set of all postulates. A postulate $p \in P$ may be treated as an atomic logical formula for which the interpretation should be the set of pairs

$$<U, C(U)>$$

where U is a universe and $C(U)$ is the set of all consistency functions for conflict profiles from $\Pi(U)$.

We say that a postulate $p \in P$

- is *satisfied* if there exist a universe U and a function in $C(U)$ which satisfies postulate p
- is *u-true* if there exists a universe U for which p is satisfied by all functions from $C(U)$
- is *true* if it is *u*-true referring to all universes
- is *false* if it is not satisfied

We can build complex formulae on the basis of the atomic formulae using logic quantifiers and such logical connectives as $\vee$, $\wedge$, $\neg$, $\Rightarrow$. For these formulae we accept the same semantics as defined for atomic formulae and the semantic rules of classical logic.

We prove the following.

Theorem 2.1.

(a) *All postulates are independent, meaning that for each pair $p, p' \in P$ and $p \neq p'$ formula*

$$p \Rightarrow p'$$

is not true.

(b) *The set of all postulates is not contradictory, meaning that there exist a universe and a function which satisfies all the postulates; that is, formula*

$$P1a \wedge P1b \wedge P2a \wedge P2b \wedge P2c \wedge P3 \wedge P4 \wedge P5 \wedge P6 \wedge P7a \wedge P7b \wedge P8$$

is satisfied.

Proof.

(a) It is easy to check the lack of truth of all formulae $p \Rightarrow p'$ where p, $p' \in P$ and $p \neq p'$. The reason is that each postulate occupies a region in the set C of all consistency functions, and although these regions may overlap they are not included one in another. For example, consider postulates P1a and P1b. Postulate P1a deals with only heterogeneous profiles and postulate P1b deals with nonheterogeneous profiles; if a consistency function satisfies one of these postulates it does not have to satisfy the second.

(b) Here we should define a function which satisfies all postulates. Let

$$U = \{x, y\},$$

and consistency function c be defined as follows,

$$c(X) = \begin{cases} 1 & \text{if } X \text{ is heterogeneous} \\ 0 & \text{if } X = n * U \text{ for } n = 1,2,... \\ \dfrac{k}{k+l} & \text{if } X = \{k * x, l * y\} \text{ and } k > l \\ \dfrac{l}{k+l} & \text{if } X = \{k * x, l * y\} \text{ and } k < l \end{cases}$$

It is not hard to check that function c satisfies all postulates.   ♦

Below we present some other properties of the classes of consistency functions.

Theorem 2.2.
Let $X \in \Pi(U)$, card$(X) > 1$ and let $c \in C(U)$ be a consistency function satisfying postulate P6. Let x be such an element of universe U that

$$d(x, X) = \min\{d(t, X): t \in U\}$$

and y be such an element of profile X that

$$d(x, y) = \max_{z \in X} d(x, y).$$

The following dependence is true

$$c(X) \leq c(X - \{y\}).$$

Proof.
Let $Y = X - \{y\}$ and card$(X) = n > 1$, then card$(Y) = n - 1$. Let x' be such an element of universe U that

$$d(x',Y) = \min \{d(t,Y): t \in U\}.$$

We have then $d(x',Y) \le d(x,Y)$. Also, from

$$d(x,y) = \max_{z \in X} d(x,z)$$

it follows that

$$(n-1) \cdot d(x, y) \ge d(x,Y).$$

Thus

$$\frac{\min \{d(t,X):t \in U\}}{card(X)} = \frac{d(x,X)}{n} = \frac{d(x,Y)+d(x,y)}{n}$$

$$\ge \frac{d(x,Y)}{n-1} \ge \frac{d(x',Y)}{n-1} = \frac{\min \{d(t,Y):t \in U\}}{card(Y)}.$$

Because function c satisfies postulate P6, then there should be

$$c(X) \le c(Y). \qquad \blacklozenge$$

Owing to this property one can improve the consistency value for a profile by removing from it this element which is farthest from the element of U with the minimal sum of distances to the profile's elements.

This property also shows that if a consistency function satisfies postulate P6 then it should also partially satisfy postulate P7a.

Theorem 2.3.
Let $X \in \Pi(U)$ and let $c \in C(U)$ be a consistency function satisfying postulate P6. Let x be such an element of universe U that

$$d(x,X) = \min\{d(t,X): t \in U\};$$

then the following dependence is true

$$c(X) \le c(X \cup \{x\}).$$

Proof.
Let $Y = X \cup \{x\}$. Because

$$d(x,X) = \min\{d(t,X): t \in U\},$$

it implies that

$$d(x,Y) = \min\{d(t,Y): t \in U\}.$$

In addition we have $d(x, X) = d(x, Y)$. Taking into account the fact that

$$card\ (Y) = card(X) + 1$$

it follows

$$\frac{\min\{d(t,X):t \in U\}}{card(X)} \geq \frac{\min\{d(t,Y):t \in U\}}{card(Y)}.$$

Because function c satisfies postulate P6 then we have

$$c(X) \leq c(X \cup \{x\}).\qquad\qquad\blacklozenge$$

This property allows improving the consistency value by adding to the profile an element which generates the minimal sum of distances to the profile's elements. It also shows that if a consistency function satisfies postulate P6 then it should also partially satisfy postulate P7b.

Theorem 2.4.
Postulates P1a *and* P2a *in general are inconsistent with postulate* P7a; *that is, formula*

$$(P1a \wedge P2a) \Rightarrow \neg P7a$$

is u-true.

Proof.
We show that there exists a universe U for which any function c from $C(U)$ if satisfying postulates P1a and P2a cannot satisfy postulate P7a. Let then $U = \{a,b\}$ and $a \neq b$, then

$$d(a,b) = \max_{x,y \in U} d(x,y) > 0.$$

Let $X = U$; according to postulate P2a we have $c(X) = 0$. Because function c satisfies postulate P1a we have

$$c(X - \{a\}) = c(\{b\}) = 1.$$

In addition, we have

$$d(a,X) = \min\{d(t,X): t \in X\}$$

and

$$c(X - \{a\}) = 1 > c(X) = 0,$$

so function c cannot satisfy postulate P7a. $\blacklozenge$

Theorem 2.5.

Postulates P1a *and* P4 *in general are inconsistent with postulate* P7a; *that is, formula*

$$(P1a \land P4) \Rightarrow \neg P7a$$

is u-true.

Proof.

We show that there exists a universe U for which any function c from $C(U)$ if satisfying postulates P1a and P4 cannot satisfy postulate P7a. Let then $U = \{a,b\}$ and $a \neq b$; then

$$d(a,b) = \max_{x,y \in U} d(x,y) > 0.$$

Let $X = U$; according to postulate P4 we have $c(X) < 1$. Because c satisfies postulate P1a we have

$$c(X - \{a\}) = c(\{b\}) = 1.$$

Also, we have

$$d(a,X) = \min\{d(t,X): t \in X\}$$

and

$$c(X - \{a\}) > c(X),$$

so function c cannot satisfy postulate P7a.   ◆

Theorem 2.6.

Postulates P1a *and* P4 *in general are inconsistent with postulate* P7a; *that is, formula*

$$(P2a \land P3) \Rightarrow \neg P7b$$

is u-true.

Proof.

We show that there exists a universe U for which any function c from $C(U)$ if satisfying postulates P2a and P3 cannot satisfy postulate P7b. Let then $U = \{a,b\}$ and $a \neq b$; then

$$d(a,b) = \max_{x,y \in U} d(x,y) > 0.$$

Let $X = U$; we have

$$d(a,X) = \max\{d(t, X): t \in X\}$$

and

$$d(b,X) = \max\{d(t, X): t \in U\}.$$

According to postulate P2a we have $c(X) = 0$. In addition,

$$c(X \cup \{b\}) = c(\{a, b, b\}) > 0$$

according to postulate P3, so function c cannot satisfy postulate P7b.   ◆

Theorems 2.4 through 2.6 show some inconsistency between postulates P7a and P7b and other postulates. As stated above, postulates P7a and P7b play an important role in consistency improvement, and it has turned out that it is not always possible.

Postulate P8 in some sense is more general than postulates P1b and P2b. The following theorem proves this fact.

Theorem 2.7.
The following formulae

$$(P8 \wedge P1a) \Rightarrow P1b$$

and

$$(P8 \wedge P2a) \Rightarrow P2b$$

are true.

Proof.
For the first formula assume that for any universe U and any function $c \in C(U)$ let c satisfy postulates P8 and P1a. Let $Y, Z \in \Pi(U)$ where $Y = \{x\}$ and

$$X^{(n)} = (n * Y) \cup Z.$$

According to postulate P8 we have

$$\lim_{n \to +\infty} c(X^{(n)}) = c(Y),$$

and according to postulate P1a we have:

$$c(Y) = c(\{x\}) = 1.$$

Thus function c satisfies postulate P1b.
A similar proof may be done for the second formula.   ◆

2.4.4. Consistency Functions

In this section we present the definitions of five consistency functions and analyze their satisfaction referring to the defined postulates. These functions are defined as follows.

Let $X = \{x_1, \ldots, x_M\}$ be a conflict profile. We introduce the following parameters.

- The matrix of distances between the elements of profile X:

$$D^X = \left[d_{ij}^X\right] = \begin{bmatrix} d(x_1,x_1) & \cdots & d(x_1,x_M) \\ \vdots & \ddots & \vdots \\ d(x_M,x_1) & \cdots & d(x_M,x_M) \end{bmatrix}.$$

- The vector of average distances between an element to the rest (for $M > 1$) :

$$W^X = (w_1^X, w_2^X, \ldots, w_M^X),$$

where

$$w_i^X = \frac{1}{M-1}\sum_{j=1}^{M} d_{ji}^X$$

for $i = 1, 2, \ldots, M$. Notice that although in the above sum there are M components, the average is calculated only for $M - 1$. This is because for each i value $d_{ii}^X = 0$.

- Diameters of set X:

$$Diam(X) = \max_{x,y \in X} d(x, y),$$

and the maximal element of vector W^X:

$$Diam(W^X) = \max_{1 \le i \le M} w_i^X,$$

representing this element of profile X which generates the maximal sum of distances to other elements. Because the values of distance function d are normalized we assume that the diameter of universe U is equal to 1; that is,

$$Diam(U) = 1.$$

- The average distance in profile X:

$$d_{mean}(X) = \begin{cases} \dfrac{1}{M(M-1)} \sum_{i=1}^{M} \sum_{j=1}^{M} d_{ij}^{X} = \dfrac{1}{M} \sum_{i=1}^{M} w_i^{X} & \text{for } M > 1 \\ 0 & \text{for } M = 1 \end{cases}$$

Value $d_{mean}(X)$ represents the average of all distances between different elements of the profile. Notice that the word "different" refers only to the indexes of the elements. In fact some of them may be identical because of repetitions.

- The total average distance in profile X:

$$d_{t\_mean}(X) = \frac{\sum\limits_{x,y \in X} d(x,y)}{M(M+1)} \ .$$

This value serves to represent the average distance of all distances between elements of profile X. The sum of these distances is expressed by the numerator of the quotient. However, one can ask a question: why is k^2 not in the denominator, but $k(k+1)$ is? The answer is: in the numerator each distance $d(x,y)$, where $x \neq y$, occurs exactly twice, whereas each distance $d(x,y)$, where $x = y$, occurs exactly only once. Because $d(x, y) = 0$ for $x = y$, then adding such distance does not change the value of the numerator. However, in determining the average each distance should be taken into account twice. Thus the denominator should be $k(k+1)$, but not k^2. For example, see Figure 2.4 where we have profile $X = \{a, b\}$ and $M = 2$. In sum $\sum\limits_{x,y \in X} d(x,y)$ distance $d(a, b)$ appears twice because $d(a,b) = d(b,a)$, therefore for calculating the total average of distances each of the distances $d(a,a)$ and $d(b,b)$ should be taken into account twice. Thus the number of distances should be $2 \cdot 3 = 6$.

In fact, the value $d_{t\_mean}(X)$ of the total distance average and value $d_{mean}(X)$ of the distance average are dependent on each other referring to value M:

$$d_{t\_mean}(X) = \frac{M-1}{M+1} \, d_{mean}(X).$$

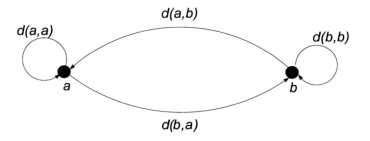

Figure 2.4. Profile $X = \{a, b\}$.

- The sum of distances between an element x of universe U and the elements of set X:

$$d(x, X) = \Sigma_{y \in X} d(x, y).$$

- The set of all sums of distances:

$$D(X) = \{d(x, X): x \in U\}.$$

- The minimal average distance from an element to the elements of profile X:

$$d_{min}(X) = \frac{1}{M} \min (D(X)).$$

These parameters are now applied for defining the following consistency functions,

$$c_1(X) = 1 - Diam(X),$$

$$c_2(X) = 1 - Diam(W^X),$$

$$c_3(X) = 1 - d_{mean}(X),$$

$$c_4(X) = 1 - d_{t\_mean}(X),$$

$$c_5(X) = 1 - d_{min}(X).$$

Some comments for the defined functions:

- $c_1(X)$: This function reflects the maximal distance between two elements of profile X. The intuitive sense of this function is based on the fact that if this maximal distance is equal to 0 (i.e., profile X is homogeneous) then the consistency is maximal (equal to 1). However, the density and coherence of profiles are not taken into account.

- $c_2(X)$: This function refers to the maximal average distance between an element of profile X and other elements of this profile. If the value of this maximal average distance is small, that is, the elements of profile X are near each other, then the consistency should be high. The density and coherence of profiles are in some degree taken into account by this function.
- $c_3(X)$: This function takes into account the average distance between elements of X. This parameter seems to be very representative for consistency. The larger this value is, the smaller is the consistency and vice versa. This function reflects to a large degree the density of profiles.
- $c_4(X)$: This function takes into account the total average distance between elements of X. As noted above, this function is dependent on function $c_3(X)$ and vice versa. However, there is an essential difference between these functions. Consider a distinguishable profile X in which all elements are maximally distanced from each other; that is,

$$\forall (x, y \in X, x \neq y): d(x, y) = 1.$$

For $card(X) = 2$ we have:

$$d_{t\_mean}(X) = 1/3 \quad \text{and} \quad d_{mean}(X) = 1.$$

For $card(X) = M > 2$ we can prove that $d_{mean}(X)$ is constant and $d_{mean}(X) = 1$, whereas

$$d_{t\_mean}(X) = \frac{M-1}{M+1}.$$

It seems that in this case function c_4 better reflects the consistency than function c_3. This is because the larger M is, the smaller is the inconsistency. However, for each value of M the value of function c_3 is constant and equals 0, whereas

$$c_4(X) = 1 - \frac{M-1}{M+1} = \frac{2}{M+1}.$$

Values of c_4 then better reflect this situation than those of c_3.

- $c_5(X)$: The minimal average distance between an element of universe U and elements of X. The elements of universe U which generate the minimal average distance to elements of profile X may be treated as representatives for this profile. The average distance between a representative to the profile elements also reflects the coherence of the profile. In clustering theory, this criterion is used for determining the centre of a group, called a *centroid*.

Table 2.1 presented below shows the results of the defined functions. The columns represent postulates and the rows represent the defined functions. Satisfying a postulate by a consistency function means that the function satisfies the postulate for all universes. The symbol + means that the presented function satisfies the postulate, the symbol – means that the presented function does not satisfy the postulate, and the symbol ± means partially satisfying the given postulate. From these results it implies that function c_5 partially satisfies postulates P7a and P7b. As follows from Theorems 2.2 and 2.3, if a function satisfies postulate P6 then it should partially satisfy postulates P7a and P7b. As we can see, function c_5 satisfies postulate P6.

From Table 2.1 it follows that function c_4 satisfies most postulates (9 over 12), and the next is function c_3 (8 postulates). However, neither function c_3 nor function c_4 satisfies postulate P5, which seems to be very natural. Function c_5 also is good in referring to the number of satisfied postulates. Function c_1 is very simple to calculate and it satisfies 6 postulates, although it does not satisfy any of postulates P6, P7a, P7b, or P8. Referring to functions c_2, c_3, and c_4 we know that they satisfy postulates P7a, P7b, that is, the postulates for consistency improvement. Below we present some other property of these functions referring to another kind of consistency improvement.

Table 2.1. Results of analysis of consistency functions regarding postulates

	P1a	P1b	P2a	P2b	P2c	P3	P4	P5	P6	P7a	P7b	P8
c_1	+	–	+	+	+	–	+	+	–	–	–	–
c_2	+	–	+	–	–	–	+	+	–	+	+	–
c_3	+	+	+	–	–	+	+	–	–	+	+	+
c_4	+	+	–	+	–	+	+	–	+	+	+	+
c_5	+	+	–	–	–	+	+	+	+	±	±	+

Theorem 2.8.

Let $X \in \Pi(U)$, $X = \{x_1, x_2, \ldots, x_M\}$, and let

$$X' = \{x_i \in X: w_i^X = Diam(W^X) \text{ and } 1 \leq i \leq M\}.$$

Then profile $X\backslash X'$ should not have a smaller consistency than X; that is,

$$c(X\backslash X') \geq c(X),$$

where $c \in \{c_2, c_3, c_4\}$.

Proof.

(a) For function c_2 the proof follows immediately from the notice that

$$Diam(W^X) \leq Diam(W^{X\backslash X'}).$$

(b) For function c_3 we have

$$\overline{d}(X) = \frac{1}{M}\sum_{i=1}^{M} w_i^X.$$

Because for each $x_i \in X'$ there is

$$w_i^X = Diam(W^X),$$

therefore there should be

$$\overline{d}(X) \geq \overline{d}(X \backslash X');$$

that is,

$$c_3(X\backslash X') \geq c_3(X).$$

(c) For function c_4 the proof is similar as for function c_3 ♦

This property shows another way for improving consistency referring to functions c_2, c_3, and c_4, which is based on removing from a profile those elements generating the maximal average distance.

2.4.5. Reflecting Weights in Consistency Measure

In Section 2.3.3 we have defined weights for conflict participants which have to reflect their competency and credibility. It is natural that these weights should be taken into account in the consistency value. First of all, these weights should be reflected in the distances between the opinions of the conflict participants. Formally, for reflecting the weights we introduce the set of participants; generally, we call them agents.

Let then X be a conflict profile which consists of opinions of agents from set A with such assumption that each agent has exactly one opinion in the profile. Of course, some agents may have the same opinion, therefore, X is a set of repetitions. For simplicity, we distinguish the elements of profile X, and for each $x \in X$ by w_x we denote the weight of the agent which is the author of opinion x. Notice that the way of weight representation is different from that presented in Section 2.3.3.

For two opinions $x, y \in X$ we define the weighted distance $d'(x,y)$ between them on the basis of distance function d taking weights of x and y into account, as follows,

$$d'(x, y) = w(x) \cdot w(y) \cdot d(x, y).$$

Using defined function d' in consistency functions $c_1, c_2, c_3, c_4,$ and c_5 we give new consistency functions as $c'_1, c'_2, c'_3, c'_4,$ and c'_5, respectively. Postulates P1–P8 can also be redefined using weighted distance function d'. We can notice that the satisfaction of postulates using distance function d can also be transformed to the satisfaction of postulates using weighted distance function d'.

In previous sections we have considered consistency improvement by removing those elements which spoilt the consistency, or adding new elements which enlarge this value. Here we also consider the problem of consistency improvement, but by modification of weights of the conflict participations. In some sense it is a banal problem because one can always modify the weights so that only one element has weight larger than zero. Owing to this there will arise a homogeneous profile which should have maximal value of consistency.

2.4.6. Practical Aspect of Consistency Measures

The aim of conflict solution most often consists in determining a version of data (or an alternative, or a scenario) which best represents the versions belonging to the conflict content (i.e., conflict profile). As stated above, the consistency value of a conflict profile delivers some image about the profile: it is dense (high value of consistency) or rare (low value of consistency). In corresponding to conflict a rare profile may provide that the conflict content is not "good" enough for the conflict to be solved. On the other hand, if the consistency value is high, one can say that the opinions of conflict participants are coherent enough, and such conflict may be solved. Let's consider an example, five witnesses of a crime describe the hair color of the criminal as follows.

Hair_color = {*blond, black, redhead, green, bald*}.

As can be seen, the opinions of the witnesses are very different, and having to deal with such information it is very hard to infer what is probably the color of the criminal's hair. However, if the conflict profile is presented as follows,

Hair_color = {*blond, blond, redhead, fair-haired, blond*},

then one can state that the probable hair color of the criminal is *blond*, and it is even more probable that he is *fair-haired*.

Another aspect of consistency refers to expert knowledge analysis. It very often happens that the same task is entrusted to several experts for solving. This is because experts as specialists of different domains can have different approaches to the problem. Owing to this the solutions given by experts should reflect different sides of the problem. In this situation if the consistency of expert opinions is high then of course the credibility of the final solution (determined on the basis of the solutions given by the experts) is also high. However, if the consistency is low, it is not a reason for concern.

As we show in Chapter 8, in expert knowledge analysis, the consistency of solutions given by experts for a problem does not have such essential significance. It is proved that if we can assume that the experts solve the problem with the same degree of credibility then a conflict profile with low consistency value can be better than a conflict profile with high consistency in the sense that the consensus determined on the basis of the first profile may be nearer to the proper solution than the consensus determined on the basis of the second profile. Consistency value then has sense for such conflict profiles which are sets of opinions of participants, referring to whom we cannot assume any degrees of credibility, as with the set of criminal witnesses presented above.

As a matter of fact there are many practical aspects of consistency measures. We can use the consistency degrees in multiagent systems and in all kinds of information systems where knowledge is processed by autonomous programs: in distributed database systems where data consistency is one of the key factors, and also in reasoning systems and many others.

2.5. Conclusions

The material on the subject of inconsistency measures for conflict profiles presented in this chapter is partially based on the material included in [83–85, 118–120]. However, in this chapter many postulates have been modified and postulate P8 has been introduced. Modification of postulates also causes new results of their analysis to arise. In addition, new consistency function c_5 has been defined and analyzed.

3. Consensus as a Tool for Conflict Solving

In this chapter we present a case study of consensus theory and a general model of consensus. This model uses the model for conflict presented in Chapter 2. We define the general notion of consensus and postulates for consensus choice functions. Next, classes of consensus functions are defined and analyzed referring to postulates. A number of other notions such as consensus susceptibility, quality of consensus, or reduction of consensus number are also presented and analyzed.

3.1. Introduction

In Chapter 2 we presented a model for conflict representation and other notions for evaluating conflict situations. In this chapter we propose a tool for conflict resolution. We focus on a specific kind of conflict: inconsistency[1] of knowledge. As pointed out in Chapter 1, inconsistency of knowledge may have two aspects: the *centralization aspect* and *distribution aspect.* We mention that the first aspect refers to inconsistency of knowledge which arises in the same knowledge base as the result of, among others, a dynamic real world. The second aspect concerns the inconsistency of different knowledge sources referring to the same real world. The knowledge conflicts of the second aspect are the subject of this chapter; for solving them we propose to use consensus methods.

The main subject of a consensus method is a conflict profile representing a conflict (or inconsistency) situation. A conflict profile is a set of different versions of knowledge about the same element of a real world. The task of a consensus method is to determine a version of knowledge which best reflects the given versions. The question is how to perform this task if the given versions may be different from each other or even contradictory to each other. For example, if the profile consists of two versions, *Yes* and *No* as the answers of two experts for the same question, then it is very hard

---

[1] Terms *inconsistency* and *conflict* in this context are equivalent.

to determine a final answer which best reflects the given answers. In this chapter we present an approach which gives the solution to this problem.

Consensus theory has arisen in social science and has a root in the choice theory [2]. However, there is an essential difference between these theories. Although the subject of a method in choice theory is a set X (of alternatives, objects) being a subset of a universe U, the choice is based on the selection of a subset of X, whereas the consensus of X must not be an element of X. Furthermore, a consensus of set X must not have the same structure as the elements of X, what is assumed in choice theory. At the beginning of consensus research the authors most often dealt with simple structures of the elements of universe U, such as linear or partial orders. Later, more complex structures such as n-trees, partitions, hierarchies, and the like have been also investigated. Most often homogeneous structures of the universe elements are assumed.

The organization of this chapter is the following. In Section 3.2 an overview of applications of consensus methods for solving conflicts in distributed environments is presented. Section 3.3 includes the definition of consensus choice functions, postulates for them, and the analysis of these postulates. In Section 3.4 the notion of consensus quality is presented. The notion of consensus susceptibility, its criteria, and their analysis are given in Section 3.5. Some approaches for achieving susceptibility to consensus for such profiles are presented in Section 3.6. Section 3.7 includes some methods for reducing the number of consensuses generated by a consensus function. Finally, some conclusions are given in Section 3.8.

3.2. Consensus Theory – A Case Study

3.2.1. An Overview

Consensus methods (similarly as data mining or knowledge discovery methods) deal with problems of data analysis in order to extract valuable information. However, consensus methods differ from data mining methods with regard to their aims as well as regard to the characteristics of datasets. The task of data mining is to discover patterns in existing data, which means that a data mining method is used when one is interested in searching some regular relationships between data. It takes into account only those records of data which firstly, appear more often, and secondly, include the same relationship between some values.

The dataset, being the domain for applying a data mining method, most often contains data from different sources that are of a temporal character.

It may, for example, include the data referring to the activities of an enter-
prise in a period of time. On the other hand, the characteristic of a dataset
being the domain for applying a consensus method is that it represents a
conflict situation in which several participants generate different opinions
on some common matter, or it contains inconsistency of data which is
caused by, for example, incomplete or uncertain data processing. In this
case a consensus method enables determining such a record of data which,
first, should best represent a set of data records, and, second, should be a
good compromise acceptable for the participants that are in conflict.

According to Barthelemy et al. [13, 14] problems considered by consensus theory can be classified into the two classes:

- Problems in which a certain and hidden structure is searched
- Problems in which inconsistent data related to the same subject are
  unified

The problems included in the first class seem to be very similar to the
problems of data mining. However, this class consists of problems of searching a structure of a complex or internally organized object. This object
can be a set of elements and the searched structure to be determined can be
a distance function between these elements. Data that are used to uncover
this structure usually come from experiments or observations. They should
reflect this structure, however, not necessarily in a precise and correct way.

The second class consists of problems that appear when the same subject (problem solving, choice task, etc.) is occupied by different autonomous units (such as experts or agents). Then the solutions of the problem
or the variants of the choice given by the experts (or agents) may differ
from each other. In such a case a particular method is desired that makes it
possible to deduce from the set of given alternatives only one alternative to
be used in further processing. This class contains two well-known consensus problems: the *Alternatives Ranking Problem* and *Committee Election
Problem*. The first of these problems can be described as follows [6, 46].
Let A be a nonempty and finite set of alternatives. A *profile P* on A is
defined as a finite set of linear orders on A. A *situation* is understood as an
ordered pair (A, P). For each situation (A, P) and each pair of alternatives
$x, y \in A$, a number $p(x,y)$ is defined that is equal to the number of orders
included in P in which the alternative x precedes the alternative y. Hence,
if an order p contains n alternatives then $p(x, y) + p(y, x) = n$ for $x \neq y$.
Moreover a binary relation W_p on A is defined as $(x, y) \in W_p$ if and only if
$p(x, y) > p(y, x)$. The problem is based on defining a consensus choice function which should determine an alternative on the basis of a situation (A, P).

The committee election problem can be described as follows. From a nonempty set $S = \{s_1, s_2, \ldots, s_m\}$ of m candidates, a committee (i.e., a nonempty subset of S) should be selected as the outcome of an election in which votes (as one-element subsets of S) are cast by $n > 0$ voters $v_1, v_2, \ldots, v_n$. These votes create a profile $P = (p_1, p_2, \ldots, p_n) \in S^n$, where p_i is the vote of v_i, for $i = 1, \ldots, n$. The problem is based on defining a consensus choice function which should determine a committee on the basis of a set of votes.

In the literature there are three approaches for defining consensus choice functions: *axiomatic, constructive,* and *optimization.*

In the axiomatic approach for the alternatives ranking problem a set of axioms has been fixed for the class of so-called *Condorcet social choice functions* (a consensus choice function C is a Condorcet function if and only if it satisfies the following Condorcet principle: for all situations (A, P) there should be $C(A, p) = \{x\}$, whenever $x \in A$ and $(x, y) \in W_p$ for all $y \in A\backslash\{x\}$). One of the Condorcet functions, called the *Kemeny median,* is the most popular one which determines the best alternative by determining an order nearest to those in P. A consensus function which for a given profile P assigns a nonempty subset of S called a committee of P, should be determined. Seven rational requirements have been defined for consensus choice [6]: *unrestricted domain* (*UD*), *Pareto* (*P*), *independent of irrelevant alternatives* (*IIA*), *no dictator* (*ND*), *neutrality* (*N*), *symmetry* (*S*), and *Condorcet consistency* (*Cc*). These axioms are presented briefly as follows.

- *Unrestricted domain* (*UD*): The consensus function should determine an alternative for each situation (A, P); that is, for any possible preference distribution of votes it should always be possible to calculate a consensus.
- *Pareto* (*P*): If an element $a \in A$ is preferable to element $b \in A$ in each order belonging to profile P, then a should also be more preferable than b in the consensus. In general, the Pareto condition requires that if all voters vote for the same alternative, then this alternative should be chosen as a consensus.
- *Independence of irrelevant alternatives* (*IIA*): The preference ordering of each pair of elements in the consensus is dependent only on their preference ordering in the orders belonging to the profile. This axiom is a condition for the integrity of the profile.
- *No dictator* (*ND*): The consensus for situation (A, P) should not be changed despite changing the indexes of profile elements; that is, all voters should be treated in the same way.

- *Neutrality* (*N*): The consensus for situation (*A*, *P*) should not be changed despite changing the indexes of elements of set *A*; that is, all votes should be treated in the same way.
- *Symmetry* (*S*): A consensus function should be symmetrical if conditions (*N*) and (*ND*) are satisfied; that is, it should justly treat the voters and the votes.
- *Condorcet consistency* (*Cc*): A consensus function *C* should satisfy condition *Cc*, if for any profiles P_1 and P_2 the following dependency is true,

$$C(P_1) \cap C(P_2) \neq \varnothing \ \Rightarrow \ C(P_1 \cup P_2) = C(P_1) \cap C(P_2);$$

  that is, if two groups of voters voting separately have common preferences then they should have the same preferences voting together.

It turns out that no consensus choice functions exist that satisfy all of the above-mentioned axioms simultaneously. Namely, Arrow [6] proved that if each order belonging to a profile consists of more than two elements, then all consensus choice functions fulfilling the conditions *UD*, *P*, and *IIA* do not satisfy the condition *ND*. Later, Young and Levenglick [158, 159] showed that the unique choice function satisfying the conditions *N*, *C*, *Cc*, *UD*, and *P* is the Kemeny median which requires the consensus to be as near as possible to the profile elements. In [13, 88, 89, 90] the authors have used axioms for determining consensus functions for such structures of objects as semilattices or weak hierarchies. In the majority of cases the most popular function is simply a median.

In the constructive approach consensus problems are solved on the levels of the *microstructure* and *macrostructure* of a universe *U* of objects representing all potential alternatives. The microstructure of *U* is understood as a structure of its elements. Such a structure may be, for example, a linear order of a set of alternatives (in the alternatives ranking problem), or a subset of the set of candidates (in the committee election problem). A macrostructure of *U* is understood as a relation between elements of *U*. Such a structure may be, for example, a preference relation or a distance (or similarity) function between objects from *U*. In a consensus problem objects of a profile should have the same structure, but their consensus may be of a different structure. The following microstructures have been investigated in detail: linear orders [6, 46, 157], semilattices [13], *n*-tree [35, 155], ordered partitions and coverings [30], incomplete ordered partitions [55], nonordered partitions [14], weak hierarchies [90], and time interval [102, 109, 114]. A large number of works were dedicated to develop heuristics based on the Kemeny median for determining consensus of collections of rankings, which is a NP-complete problem.

Within the optimization the approach defining consensus choice functions is often based on some optimality rules. These rules can be classified as follows.

- *Global optimality rule*: This requires that the chosen objects should be optimal in a global sense. The most popular requirement is that the choice should be "Pareto optimal," meaning that it is not possible to change the decision in a way that will make some objects better off without making some others worse off. This feature is called "unanimity" and for the alternatives ranking problem it means that if the object x is preferable to object y by all sites, then y should not be selected.
- *Condorcet's optimality rule*: The chosen alternative should be better than any other in direct comparison. It is a very strong criterion of choice, and of course such alternatives do not always exist.
- *Maximal similarity rules*: The chosen objects should be as similar as possible to the elements of the profile X.

Consensus theory has many applications in computer systems: in mobile systems [8], distributed systems [15], multiagent systems [39, 63, 65, 117], interactive systems [146], interface systems [122, 147], and communication systems [156].

3.2.2. Consensus versus Conflicts

Although the application of consensus methods to solving conflicts is something very natural, we now make an analysis of what consensus can bring to the resolution of conflicts. We have assumed that a conflict profile consists of opinions or alternatives given by some autonomous units such as experts or agents on some matter. In general, the elements of a conflict profile represent solutions of the same problem which are generated by these autonomous units. As mentioned in Chapter 1, the reason that these solutions may be different from each other follows from these circumstances.

- The independence of knowledge processing mechanisms of the units: This feature is the consequence of the autonomy of the units. Different knowledge processing procedures may give different results even when used for the same knowledge base. An example may refer to using different data mining methods which used for the same database may extract different rules.

- Differences in knowledge bases of the units: This is very possible because frequently autonomous units have their own knowledge bases, independent of other units. Knowledge in these bases comes from the observations of the units referring to the real world which is often dynamic, as well as from the results of their inferring processes.

- Indeterminism in knowledge processing, as well as the lack of completeness and certainty of information, may cause the arising of different results of inference, and in fact, generating different solutions to the same problem.

The aim of conflict resolution is to determine the proper solution of the problem on the basis on those generated by the autonomous units. The following two cases may take place [118, 123].

1. *The proper solution is independent of the opinions of the conflict participants.*

As an example of this kind of conflict we can consider different diagnoses for the GDP of the same country in a given year generated by different financial experts. The problem then relies on determining the proper GDP for the country which is unambiguous and really known only when the year finishes. Moreover, this value is independent of the given forecasts. A conflict in which the proper solution is independent of the opinions of the conflict participants is called *independent conflict.* The independence feature of conflicts of this kind means that the proper solution of the problem exists but is not known to the conflict participants. The reasons for this phenomenon may follow from many aspects, among others, from ignorance of conflict participation or the random characteristics of the solution which may make the solution very hard to be calculated in a deterministic way.

The example of GDP diagnosis is an example of the first case, whereas the forecast of the numbers cast in a lottery is an example of the second case. Thus the conflict participants for some reason have to "guess" this unknown solution. Their solutions are then assumed to reflect the proper solution but it is not known to what degree, as well as if in a valid and complete way. In other words, the solutions given by the conflict participants reflect the "hidden" and independent solution but it is not known to what degree. Thus one assumes that each of them is treated as partially valid and partially invalid (which of its parts is valid and which is invalid is not known). This degree may not be equal to 100% because if so, only one solution is needed and our approach is contradictory to itself.

If we assume that the proper solution should be determined on the basis of the given solutions, then it should be the consensus of the given solutions satisfying the following condition. It should best represent the given solutions. If it is possible to define some distance (or similarity) measure in the universe of all potential solutions then this requirement means that the consensus should be maximally near (or similar) to the given solutions. As we show later, this condition is included in a postulate for consensus choice functions.

2. *The solution is dependent on the opinions of the conflict participants.*

Conflicts of this kind are called *dependent conflicts*. In this case it is the opinions of conflict participants that decide about the solution. The committee election problem described above is an example of this kind of conflict. The result of the election is determined only on the basis of the voters' votes. In general, this case is of social or political character and the diversity between the participant opinions most often follows from differences of choice criteria or their hierarchy.

For dependent conflicts the consensus is also determined on the basis of the given solutions. However, it should not only best represent the given solutions, but also should be a good compromise which could be acceptable by the conflict participants. Thus the consensus should not only best represent the opinions but also should reflect each of them to the same degree (with the assumption that each of them is treated in the same way). The condition "acceptable compromise" means that any of the opinions should neither be "harmed" nor "favored". As we show in this chapter, these two conditions are in general inconsistent with each other because if one of them is satisfied then the second cannot be satisfied.

Let's consider an example.

Example 3.1. Let a set of four candidates (denoted by symbols A, B, C, D) be given and five voters have to choose a committee (as a subset of the candidates' set). Assume that the votes are the following,

$$\{A, B, C\},$$

$$\{A, B, C\},$$

$$\{A, B, C\},$$

$$\{A, B, C\},$$

$$\{D\}.$$

Let the distance between two sets of candidates be equal to the cardinality of their symmetrical difference. If the consensus choice is made only by the first condition then committee $\{A, B, C\}$ should be determined because the sum of the distances between it and the votes is minimal. However, we can note that it prefers the first four votes and totally ignores the fifth (the distances from the consensus to the votes are: 0, 0, 0, 0, and 4, respectively). Now, if we consider committee $\{A, B, C, D\}$ as the consensus then the distances would be 1, 1, 1, 1, and 3, respectively. In this case although the sum of distances between the consensus and the given votes is not minimal, the consensus neither is too far from the votes nor "harms" any of them.   ♦

We show later in this chapter that the choice based on the criterion of minimization of the sum of squared distances between consensus and the given solutions gives a more uniform consensus than the consensus chosen by minimization of the sum of distances. Therefore, the criterion of the minimal sum of squared distances is also very important, although it is less known in practical applications.

3.3. Consensus Functions

In this section we present a general model for consensus. This model differs from the models proposed by other authors by the fact that we do not assume the microstructure of the universe U. Owing to this, a number of interesting and generic properties of classes of consensus functions can be formulated.

3.3.1. Definition of Consensus Function

Let (U, d) be a distance space as defined in Chapter 2. We mention that U is a finite universe of objects and d is a distance function between these objects. Symbol $\Pi(U)$ denotes the set of all nonempty subsets with repetitions of universe U.

Below we present an axiomatic approach to the consensus choice problem.

Definition 3.1.
By a consensus choice function in space (U, d) we mean a function

$$C: \Pi(U) \to 2^U.$$

For a conflict profile $X \in \Pi(U)$ the set $C(X)$ is called the *representation* of X, and an element of $C(X)$ is called a *consensus* of profile X. Notice that $C(X)$ is a normal set (i.e., without repetitions).

Let $Con(U)$ denote the set of all consensus choice functions in space (U, d). For $X \in \Pi(U)$ and $x \in U$ let

$$d(x, X) = \sum_{y \in X} d(x, y)$$

and

$$d^n(x, X) = \sum_{y \in X} (d(x, y))^n$$

for $n \in \aleph$ and $n > 1$.

These symbols are needed to define the postulates for consensus functions presented in the next section.

3.3.2. Postulates for Consensus Function

The following definition presents ten postulates for consensus choice functions; eight of them were originally introduced in [103].

Definition 3.2.

A consensus choice function $C \in Con(U)$ satisfies the postulate of:

1. *Reliability (Re) iff*

$$C(X) \neq \varnothing.$$

2. *Unanimity (Un), iff*

$$C(\{n * x\}) = \{x\}$$

for each $n \in \aleph$ and $x \in U$.

3. *Simplification (Si) iff*

$$(Profile\ X\ is\ a\ multiple\ of\ profile\ Y) \Rightarrow C(X) = C(Y).$$

4. *Quasi-unanimity (Qu) iff*

$$(x \notin C(X)) \Rightarrow (\exists n \in \aleph : x \in C(X \cup (n * x)))$$

for each $x \in U$.

5. *Consistency (Co) iff*

$$(x \in C(X)) \Rightarrow (x \in C(X \cup \{x\}))$$

for each $x \in U$.

6. *Condorcet consistency (Cc), iff*

$$\left(C(X_1) \cap C(X_2) \neq \varnothing\right) \Rightarrow \left(C(X_1 \stackrel{\cup}{} X_2) = C(X_1) \cap C(X_2)\right)$$

for each $X_1, X_2 \in \Pi(U)$.

7. *General consistency (Gc) iff*

$$C(X_1) \cap C(X_2) \subseteq C(X_1 \stackrel{\cup}{} X_2) \subseteq C(X_1) \cup C(X_2)$$

for any $X_1, X_2 \in \Pi(U)$.

8. *Proportion (Pr) iff*

$$\left(X_1 \subseteq X_2 \wedge x \in C(X_1) \wedge y \in C(X_2)\right) \Rightarrow \left(d(x,X_1) \leq d(y,X_2)\right)$$

for any $X_1, X_2 \in \Pi(U)$.

9. *1-Optimality (O_1) iff*

$$\left(x \in C(X)\right) \Rightarrow \left(d(x,X) = \min_{y \in U} d(y,X)\right)$$

for any $X \in \Pi(U)$.

10. *2-Optimality (O_2) iff*

$$\left(x \in C(X)\right) \Rightarrow \left(d^2(x,X) = \min_{y \in U} d^2(y,X)\right)$$

for any $X \in \Pi(U)$.

The above postulates express some very intuitive conditions for consensus functions. Below we give some comments on them.

- According to postulate *Reliability* for each (nonempty) profile at least one consensus should exist. This requirement in some sense mentions such rules as "*It is possible to solve any conflict.*" Reliability is a known condition for a consensus choice function [90]. For the alternatives ranking problem this condition is called *unrestricted domain (UD)* [6].
- Postulate *Unanimity* requires that if a profile is homogeneous then the only consensus is the element belonging to this profile. It is a very intuitive requirement for many consensus choice tasks.
- According to postulate *Simplification* a consensus of a profile should also be a consensus of any of its multiples.
- According to postulate *Quasi-unanimity*, if an element x is not a consensus of a profile X, then it should be a consensus of a new profile X' containing X and n elements x for some n. In other words, each element from U should be chosen as the consensus of a profile X if it occurs in X

enough times. This postulate is to a certain degree consistent with the postulate *Unanimity* because if x occurs in a large enough number of times in a profile then this profile could be understood as a homogeneous one.

- Postulate *Consistency* is very intuitive; it states that if some element x is a consensus for a profile X, and if this element is added to X it should still be a consensus for the new profile. In the committee choice problem this postulate means that if somebody has been chosen for the committee and if there will be one vote added in which this person is chosen, then he should again be chosen in the collective choice. Consistency is a very important requirement for consensus functions because it enables the users to understand a consensus rule behavior if the results of separate choices are combined. Consistency was first defined by Condorcet ". . . if two disjoint subsets of voters V and V' would choose the same alternative using (social choice function) f, then their union should also choose this alternative using f" [157]. This form of consistency is presented in postulate *Condorcet consistency* (*Cc*). Our form is different from the Condorcet form, and as we show later, it is not the consequence of Condorcet consistency. In [13] a broad set-theoretic model for consensus methods was presented, in which the fundamental role of consistency could be appreciated.

- Postulate *General consistency* is in some sense more general than postulate *Condorcet consistency*. It sets some relationships between sets $C(X_1)$, $C(X_2)$, and $C(X_1 \cup X_2)$. The intuition is that a common consensus of two profiles should also be a consensus of their sum, and a consensus of the sum of two profiles should be a consensus of at least one of them.

- Postulate *Proportion* is a natural condition because the bigger the profile, the greater the difference is between its consensus and its elements.

- Postulate 1-*Optimality* requires the consensus to be as near as possible to elements of the profile. A consensus generated by a function satisfying this postulate plays a very important role because it can be understood as the best representative of the profile. This requirement is very popular not only in consensus theory but also in optimization theory. In choice theory Kemeny [6] first formulated this criterion for determining a linear order representing a set of linear orders. It then was called the *Kemeny median.*

- Postulate 2-*Optimality*, up to now not as popular as 1-*Optimality*, requires the sum of the squared distances between a consensus and the profile elements to be minimal. Notice that the role of a consensus is not only based on the best representation of a profile, but it should also be "fair;" that is, the distances from the consensus to the profile elements should be uniform. As proved below, postulate 2-*Optimality* specifies a class of consensus choice functions which, to a certain degree, satisfy this condition. In Chapter 8 we show some very interesting properties of this postulate referring to objects in Euclidean space.

The first three postulates (*Re, Co, Qu*) are independent of the structure of *U* (i.e., the distance function *d*), and the last three postulates (*Pr, O_1, O_2*) are formulated on the basis of this function. Postulates *Re, Co, Qu* are in a way very "natural" conditions, which should often be satisfied in the task of consensus choice.

3.3.3. Analysis of Postulates

Let *P* be the set of all postulates; that is,

$$P = \{Re, Un, Si, Qu, Co, Cc, Gc, Pr, O_1, O_2\}.$$

A postulate $p \in P$ may be treated as an atomic logical formula for which the interpretation should be the set of pairs

$$<U, Con(U)>,$$

where *U* is a universe and *Con(U)* is the set of all consensus functions for conflict profiles from $\Pi(U)$.

Similarly as for consistency functions we say that a postulate $p \in P$

- is *satisfied* if there exist a universe *U* and a function in *Con(U)* which satisfies postulate *p*
- is *c-satisfied* if for any universe *U* there exists a function in *Con(U)* which satisfies postulate *p*
- is *u-true* if there exists a universe *U* for which *p* is satisfied by all functions from *Con(U)*
- is *true* if it is *u*-true referring to all universes
- is *false* if it is not satisfied

We can build complex formulae on the basis of atomic formulae using logic quantifiers and such logical connectives as $\vee$, $\wedge$, $\neg$, $\Rightarrow$. For these formulae we accept the same semantics as defined for atomic formulae and the semantic rules of classical logic.

Below several essential properties of classes of consensus choice functions are presented. These properties refer to the relationships between postulates.

Theorem 3.1.
The following formulae are not true.

   (a) $p \Rightarrow p'$ for $p, p' \in P$ and $p \neq p'$.

   (b) $O_1 \wedge O_2$.

   (c) $Re \wedge Un \wedge Co \wedge Si \wedge Qu \wedge Cc \wedge Gc \wedge Pr \wedge O_1 \wedge O_2$.

Proof.

   (a) To prove the lack of truth of formula $p \Rightarrow p'$ it is needed to show a concrete universe in which there exists a consensus function satisfying postulate p but nonsatisfying postulate p'. For example, we show that formulae

$$O_1 \Rightarrow Re$$

and

$$Re \Rightarrow O_1$$

are not true. For the first dependency, let U be any universe, and let C_o be the empty function; that is,

$$C_o(X) = \varnothing \quad \text{for all} \quad X \in \Pi(U).$$

This function satisfies postulate O_1 but does not satisfy postulate Re. For the second formula, let $U = \{a, b\}$, $d(a,b) = 1$, and let consensus function C be defined as

$$C(X) = \{a, b\} \quad \text{for all } X \in \Pi(U).$$

This function satisfies postulate Re but does not satisfy postulate O_1 because if it satisfied postulate O_1 then there would be

$$C(\{a\}) = \{a\}.$$

   (b) Let $U = \{1, 2, \ldots, 6\}$ and let $d(x,y) = |x - y|$ for $x,y \in U$. Thus for profile $X = \{1, 5, 6\}$ the only consensus satisfying postulate O_1 is element 5, whereas the only consensus satisfying postulate O_2 is element 4. Thus formula $O_1 \wedge O_2$ may not be true.

   (c) This dependency is a result of dependency (b).   ♦

   From the above dependencies it follows that, firstly, the postulates are in pairs independent of each other, and secondly, in general there does not exist any consensus choice function which simultaneously satisfies the postulates O_1 and O_2. As a consequence, there does not exist any consensus choice function simultaneously satisfying all the postulates. The result presented here is similar to Arrow's result referred to consensus choice for linear orders [6].

Theorem 3.2.

The following formulae are c-satisfied.

(a) $Re \wedge Co \wedge Si \wedge Qu \wedge Cc \wedge Pr \wedge O_1$.

(b) $Re \wedge Co \wedge Si \wedge Qu \wedge Cc \wedge O_2$.

Proof.

Let U be any universe. Define the following consensus function

$$C_1(X) = \{x \in U: d(x, X) = \min_{y \in U} d(y, X)\}.$$

Notice that this function satisfies postulates Re, Si, Co, Qu, Cc, Pr, and O_1. On the other hand, function

$$C_2(X) = \{x \in U: d^2(x, X) = \min_{y \in U} d^2(y, X)\}$$

should satisfy postulates of reliability, simplification, consistency, Condorcet consistency, quasi-unanimous, and 2-optimal. Thus the formulae are c-satisfied. ◆

Notice that function C_2 does not satisfy postulate Pr.

It is easy to notice that if C is a function satisfying postulate O_1 then for each profile $X \in \Pi(U)$ there should be:

$$C(X) \subseteq C_1(X)$$

and if C is a function satisfying postulate O_2 then

$$C(X) \subseteq C_2(X).$$

Theorem 3.3.

The following formulae are true.

(a) $(O_1 \wedge Re) \Rightarrow Co \wedge Si$.

(b) $(O_1 \wedge Re) \Leftrightarrow (Pr \wedge Qu \wedge Re)$.

Proof.

(a) Let U be any universe and let consensus function C satisfy postulates O_1 and Re. Thus for any profile $X \in \Pi(U)$ there should be $C(X) \neq \varnothing$. Let $x \in C(X)$; then we have

$$d(x,X) = \min_{y \in U} d(y,X).$$

We should show that

$$x \in C(X \cup \{x\}).$$

Because

$$C(X \cup \{x\}) \neq \varnothing,$$

there must exist $x' \in U$ such that $x' \in c(X \cup \{x\})$, and

$$d(x',X') = \min_{y \in U} d(y,X')$$

where $X' = X \cup \{x\}$. Let us notice that there should be $x = x'$ because if $x \neq x'$ then

$$d(x,X') = d(x,X) \leq d(x',X) < d(x',X').$$

So function C satisfies postulate Co.

Satisfying postulate Si follows from the fact that if an element x generates the minimal sum of distances to the elements of profile X then the sum of distances from x to elements of a multiple of profile X is also minimal.

(b) Now let function C satisfy postulates Pr, Qu, and Re; we should also prove that C satisfies postulates O_1. Let $X \in \Pi(U)$; according to postulate Re we have $C(X) \neq \varnothing$. Let $x \in C(X)$, $y \in U$, and $y \neq x$. If $y \in C(X)$ then on the basis of postulate Pr we should have $d(x,X) = d(y,X)$, because $X \subseteq X$. If $y \notin C(X)$ then on the basis of the postulate Qu there should exist a number n such that $y \in c(X')$, where $X' = X \cup \{n*y\}$. Because $X \subseteq X'$, from satisfying postulate Pr it follows that

$$d(x,X) \leq d(y,X') = d(y,X).$$

Thus for all $y \in U$, there should be

$$d(x,X) \leq d(y,X),$$

meaning that C satisfies postulates O_1 and Re.

Let us now assume that C satisfies postulates O_1 and Re, and we should show that it also satisfies postulates Qu and Pr. For postulate Qu assume that $x \notin C(X)$ for some $x \in U$. Then we can find $y \in U$, $y \neq x$ such that

$$d(y,x) = \min_{z \in U} d(z,x).$$

Let n be a natural number where

$$n \ge \frac{d(x,X) - d(y',X)}{d(y,x)}$$

for all $y' \in C(X)$.

Let now $X' = X \cup \{n * x\}$, $z \in U$, and $z \ne x$; we have the following:

$$d(z,X') = d(z,X) + (n + 1)d(z,x)$$
$$> d(y',X) + nd(y,x)$$
$$\ge d(y',X) + d(x,X) - d(y',X)$$
$$= d(x,X) = d(x,X').$$

It implies that $x \in C(X')$, more strongly $C(X') = \{x\}$, so C satisfies Qu.

To prove that C satisfies Pr let us assume that $X_1, X_2 \in \Pi(U)$, $X_1 \subseteq X_2$, and $x \in C(X_1)$, $y \in C(X_2)$. We should show that $d(x,X_1) \le d(y,X_2)$. Notice that $d(x,X_1) \le d(y,X_1)$ because $x \in c(X_1)$, and $d(y,X_1) \le d(y,X_2)$ because $X_1 \subseteq X_2$, thus $d(x,X_1) \le d(y,X_2)$. ♦

From Theorem 3.3 it is easy to prove the following:

Theorem 3.4.
The following formulae are true.

(a) $(O_1 \wedge Re) \Leftrightarrow (Pr \wedge Qu \wedge Re \wedge Co \wedge Si)$

(b) $(Pr \wedge Qu \wedge Re) \Rightarrow Un$.

Theorem 3.4 states that if a consensus function satisfies postulates of *Reliability, Proportion, Quasi-unanimity, Consistent,* and *Simplification* then it should also satisfy the postulate of 1-*Optimality* and vice versa. Thus satisfying postulate O_1 is a very important property of consensus functions and it explains why this function is quite often used in practical settings. Property *Unanimity* of these functions confirms their intuitive nature [13].

Theorem 3.5.
The following formula is true.

$$(O_2 \wedge Re) \Rightarrow (Co \wedge Qu \wedge Un \wedge Si).$$

Proof.
Let U be any universe and let a consensus function $C \in \textbf{Con}(U)$ satisfy postulates O_2 and Re; we should show that C also satisfies postulates Co, Qu, Un, and Si. For satisfying Co let us notice that for each profile X we have $C(X) \ne \varnothing$. Let $x \in C(X)$; then of course

$$d^2(x,X) = \min_{y \in U} d^2(y,X).$$

We should show that $x \in C(X \cup \{x\})$. Because $C(X \cup \{x\}) \neq \varnothing$, then there must exist $x' \in U$ such that $x' \in C(X \cup \{x\})$, and there should be true

$$d^2(x',X') = \min_{y \in U} d^2(y,X'),$$

where $X' = X \cup \{x\}$. Notice that if $x \neq x'$ then

$$d^2(x,X') = d^2(x,X) \leq d^2(x',X) < d^2(x',X'),$$

thus there must be held $x = x'$, so $x \in C(X')$.

To prove that C satisfies Qu let us assume that $x \notin C(X)$ for some $x \in U$. Then we can find $y \in U$ and $y \neq x$ such that

$$d(y,x) = \min_{z \in U} d(z,x).$$

Let n be a natural number, where

$$n \geq \frac{d^2(x,X) - d^2(y',X)}{d^2(y,x)}$$

for all $y' \in C(X)$.

Let now $X' = X \cup \{n * x\}$, $y' \in C(X)$, $z \in U$ and $z \neq x$ (if U is a 1-element set then of course the statement is true). We have the following:

$$d^2(z,X') = d^2(z,X) + nd^2(z,x)$$
$$\geq d^2(y',X) + nd^2(y,x)$$
$$\geq d^2(y',X) + d^2(x,X) - d^2(y',X)$$
$$= d^2(x,X) = d^2(x,X').$$

It implies that $x \in C(X')$, so C satisfies Qu.

Satisfying postulate Un is obvious. Satisfying postulate Si follows from the fact that if an element x generates a minimal sum of squared distances to the elements of profile X then the sum of squared distances from x to elements of a multiple of profile X should also be minimal.   ♦

The above-proved theorems show very important properties of consensus choice functions specifying postulates O_1 and O_2. Satisfying one of these postulates implies satisfying many other postulates; owing to this the practical sense of postulates O_1 and O_2 is very essential.

Below we have an obvious property of functions C_1 and C_2 defined above.

Theorem 3.6.

Let U be any universe and let $X, Y \in \Pi(U)$; then

(a) If $C_1(X) \cap C_1(Y) \neq \varnothing$ then $C_1(X) = C_1(Y)$.

(b) If $C_2(X) \cap C_2(Y) \neq \varnothing$ then $C_2(X) = C_2(Y)$.

A consensus function C which satisfies postulate O_1 or postulate O_2 we call an O_1-function or O_2-function, respectively. A consensus determined by an O_1-function or O_2-function is called an O_1-consensus or O_2-consensus, respectively. As we stated above, C_1 is an O_1-function and C_2 is an O_2-function.

Below we present other properties which show the behavior of functions C_1 and C_2 for large profiles.

Theorem 3.7.

Let U be any universe and $Y, Z \in \Pi(U)$, and let

$$X^{(n)} = (n * Y) \cup Z;$$

then the following equations should be true.

(a) $\lim\limits_{n \to +\infty} C_1(X^{(n)}) = C_1(Y)$.

(b) $\lim\limits_{n \to +\infty} C_2(X^{(n)}) = C_2(Y)$.

Proof.

(a) We prove that there exists a natural number n_o such that for all $n > n_o$ there should be

$$C_1(X^{(n)}) = C_1(Y).$$

Toward this aim, we should show that if x is an O_1-consensus for Y (i.e., $x \in C_1(Y)$) then $x \in C_1(X^{(n)})$. This should be enough for proving the above inequality owing to Theorem 3.6. In addition, notice that if $C_1(Y) = U$ then the above equality is true because function C_1 is reliable.

Let now $x \in C_1(Y)$. Assume that $C_1(Y) \neq U$; let $y \in U \backslash C_1(Y)$; we have $d(y, Y) > d(x, Y)$. Let then n_y be such natural number that

$$n_y > \frac{d(y, Z) - d(x, Z)}{d(y, Y) - d(x, Y)}.$$

We have then

$$n_y(d(y,Y) - d(x,Y)) > d(y,Z) - d(x,Z),$$

and

$$n_y d(y,Y) + d(y,Z) > n_y d(x,Y) + d(x,Z);$$

that is,

$$d(y, X^{(n_y)}) > d(x, X^{(n_y)}).$$

Let now

$$n_o = \max \{n_y : y \in U \backslash C_1(Y)\};$$

then for each $n > n_o$ there should be

$$d(y, X^{(n)}) > d(x, X^{(n)})$$

for each $y \in U \backslash C_1(Y)$; that is, $x \in C_1(X^{(n)})$. So

$$\lim_{n \to +\infty} C_1(X^{(n)}) = C_1(Y).$$

(b) The proof for this equality is similar if we define the number n_y satisfying the condition:

$$n_y > \frac{d^2(y,Z) - d^2(x,Z)}{d^2(y,Y) - d^2(x,Y)}. \qquad \blacklozenge$$

Below we present other important properties of consensus functions satisfying postulate O_2.

For $X \in \Pi(U)$ we define the following relations.

- $\alpha_X^n \subseteq U \times U$, where

$$x \alpha_X^n y \Leftrightarrow d^n(x,X) \le d^n(y,X)$$

for $n \in \aleph$ and $d^n(x,X) = \sum_{y \in X} (d(x,y))^n$.

- $\overline{\alpha}_X \subseteq U \times U$, where

$$x \overline{\alpha}_X y \Leftrightarrow \overline{d}(x,X) < \overline{d}(y,X),$$

    for

$$\overline{d}(x,X) = \sum_{y \in X} \left[d(y,z) - \frac{1}{card(X)} d(x,X) \right]^2.$$

The interpretation of relation $\overline{\alpha}_X$ is that element x is in relation $\overline{\alpha}_X$ with element y iff the distances from x to elements of X are more uniform than the distances from y to elements of X.

Relation α_X^n is reflective, transitive, and coherent, whereas relation $\overline{\alpha}_X$ is transitive and coherent. It is obvious that if C is an O_i-function and $x \in C(X)$ then we should have $x\,\alpha_X^i\,y$ for all $y \in U$ and $i = 1, 2$. Also it is obvious that

$$C_i(X) = \{x \in U: x\,\alpha_X^i\,y \text{ for all } y \in U\}$$

for $i = 1, 2$.

Theorem 3.8.
Let $X \in \Pi(U)$, $x \in C_2(X)$, $z \in C_1(X)$, and $y \in U$; then the following dependencies are true.

(a) $x\,\alpha_X^1\,y \vee x\,\overline{\alpha}_X\,y$.

(b) $\left(C_1(X) \cap C_2(X) = \varnothing\right) \Rightarrow x\,\overline{\alpha}_X\,z$.

Proof.
(a) Let $K = card(X)$, $x \in c(X)$, and $y \in U$; then we have

$$\overline{d}(x,X) = \sum_{z \in X}[d(x,z) - \tfrac{1}{K}d(x,X)]^2$$

$$= \sum_{z \in X}[(d(x,z))^2 - \tfrac{1}{K}d(x,z)d(x,X) + \tfrac{1}{K^2}(d(x,X))^2]$$

$$= \sum_{z \in X}(d(x,z))^2 - \tfrac{2}{K}\sum_{z \in X}d(x,z)d(x,X) + \tfrac{1}{K^2}\sum_{z \in X}(d(x,X))^2$$

$$= d^2(x,X) - \tfrac{2}{K}(d(x,X))^2 + \tfrac{1}{K}(d(x,X))^2$$

$$= d^2(x,X) - \tfrac{1}{K}(d(x,X))^2.$$

In a similar way we should obtain

$$\overline{d}(y,X) = d^2(y,X) - \tfrac{1}{K}(d(y,X))^2.$$

Let us assume that relation $x\,\alpha_X^1\,y$ does not occur; that is,

$$d(x,X) > d(y,X).$$

It then implies

$$\frac{1}{K}(d(x,X))^2 > \frac{1}{K}(d(y,X))^2.$$

In addition we have

$$d^2(x,X) \le d^2(y,X)$$

because $x \in C_2(X)$; thus there should be

$$\bar{d}(x,X) < \bar{d}(y,X),$$

or

$$x\,\bar{\alpha}_X\,y.$$

In a similar way we can show that if $x\,\bar{\alpha}_X\,y$ is not true, then there must be $x\,\alpha_X^1\,y$.

(b) Because $C_1(X) \cap C_2(X) = \varnothing$, from (a) it follows that for $x \in C_2(X)$ and $y \in C_1(X)$ we have $x\,\alpha_X^2\,y$ and not $x\,\alpha_X^1\,y$; then $x\,\bar{\alpha}_X\,y$ should follow.

$\blacklozenge$

Theorem 3.8 shows that if x is an O_2-consensus for profile X then in comparison to any element y of universe U consensus x is either nearer to the profile elements, or the uniformity measure $\bar{d}$ for x is smaller than for y. It means that there may exist an element z which has a smaller sum of distances to X than x, but the value of $\bar{d}$ for z will be greater. In comparison to an O_1-consensus, an O_2-consensus always has a lesser or equal value of $\bar{d}$, which means that the distances from this consensus to the profile elements are more uniformly distributed.

It is known that postulate O_1 defines a very popular criterion not only for consensus choice (well known among others as Kemeny's median) [68], but also for many optimization tasks. This is natural because the chosen element is the best representative for the profile. However, according to the above results, postulate O_2 also seems to be a very good one, especially in consensus choice, where not only the best representation is required, but also the uniformity of the distances between consensus and the profile elements is important. Consider the example below.

Example 3.2. From a set of candidates (denoted by symbols A, B, C, D, E) five voters have to choose a committee (as a subset of the candidates' set), similarly to that in Example 3.1. Assume that the conflict profile is the following.

$$X = \{\{A, B, C\}, \{A, B, C\}, \{A, B, C\}, \{A, B, E\}, \{D, E\}\}.$$

Let the distance between two sets of candidates be equal to the cardinality of their symmetrical difference. If the consensus choice is made only by postulate O_1 then committee

$$\{A, B, C\}$$

should be determined because the sum of distances between it and the votes is minimal. However, one can note that it prefers the first three votes while totally ignoring the fifth (the distances from this committee to the votes are: 0, 0, 0, 2, and 5, respectively). If now as the consensus we take committee

$$\{A, B, C, E\}$$

then the distances would be 1, 1, 1, 1, and 4, respectively. In this case the consensus is neither too far from the votes nor does it "harm" any of them. This is because the distances generated by the second committee are more uniform than those by the first. The sum of squared distances for the first committee is 29 whereas for the second committee it is 20.   ♦

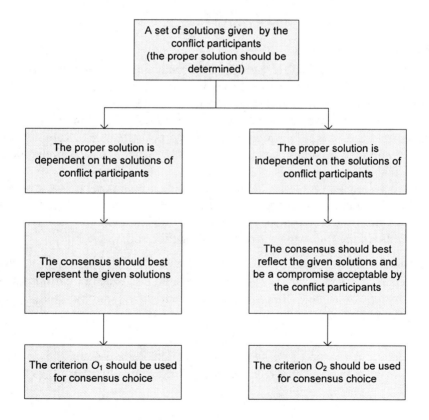

Figure 3.1. Scheme for applications of consensus functions.

As we can see, postulate Gc very rarely appears in the properties of the postulates. The reason is that Gc is a very strong postulate which consists in fact of two conditions. The first condition is in some sense a weaker condition than that in the Condorcet consistency postulate. However, the second condition is too strong to be satisfied simultaneously with other postulates. This condition in general may not be satisfied simultaneously with any of the postulates O_1 and O_2.

After the analysis of consensus functions and referring to the considerations given in Section 3.2.2 we propose the scheme for the applications of consensus functions presented in Figure 3.1.

3.3.4. Other Consensus Choice Functions

In [104] several consensus functions have been investigated. Here we present some of them. We define the following functions

$$C_n(X) = \{x \in U: d^n(x,X) = \min_{y \in U} d^n(y,X)\}$$

for $X \in \Pi(U)$, $n \in \aleph$.

For $n = 1, 2$ the justification for consensus choice functions was presented earlier. The sense of functions with $n > 2$ is that in some cases the procedure for determining distance function values may be very complex, and as a consequence, the consensus choice made by function C_1 or C_2 will be a very time-consuming problem. Sometimes it is easier to calculate the power of a distance value than to calculate the distance. For example, in an Euclidean space it is easier to calculate the second power of a value of distance between two points, and as the consequence (this is shown in Chapter 8), determining a consensus on the basis of function C_2 is less complex than determining a consensus on the basis of function C_1.

We prove the following properties of functions C_n.

Theorem 3.9.
For each universe U and each $n \in \aleph$, function C_n satisfies postulates of Reliability, Consistency, Quasi-unanimity, Unanimity, Condorcet consistency, and Simplification.

Proof.
For functions C_1 and C_2 this was proved in Theorems 3.4 and 3.5. In general, for a given number $n \in \aleph$ let's define a distance function d' such that

$$d'(x,y) = (d(x,y))^n.$$

Notice that the distance function d' satisfies all three conditions (i.e., non-negative, reflexive, and symmetric), thus (U, d') is a distance space. Notice also that the function corresponding to function C_n which is defined for space (U, d) can be then treated as C_1 in space (U, d'). Therefore function C_n in space (U, d) should have all properties of function C_1 in space (U, d'). ◆

Theorem 3.10.
For each $X \in \Pi(U)$ there exists $X^* \subseteq U$ such that the following dependency is true.

$$\lim_{n \to +\infty} C_n(X) = X^*.$$

Proof.
Let $X \in \Pi(U)$. We prove that there exists $X^* \subseteq U$ and $n_0 \in \aleph$ such that for all $n \geq n_0$ there should be

$$C_n(X) = X^*.$$

Let $card(X) = K$; we define the following sets with repetitions

$$P_x = \{d(x,z): z \in X\}$$

for $x \in U$, and

$$P = \{P_x: x \in U\}.$$

We define a lexicographical relation η on P as follows. Let $P_x, P_y \in P$; we denote by $<x_1, x_2, \ldots, x_K>$ and $<y_1, y_2, \ldots, y_K>$ the nonincreasing sequences which arise after sorting elements of P_x and P_y, respectively. Let now

$$q = \begin{cases} 1 & \text{if } x_1 \neq y_1 \\ K & \text{if } x_j = y_j \text{ for all } j = 1,\ldots,K \\ k & \text{if } x_k \neq y_k \text{ and } x_j = y_j \text{ for } j = 1,\ldots,k-1; k < K \end{cases} \quad ;$$

then

$$<P_x, P_y> \in \eta \Leftrightarrow x_q \leq y_q.$$

Notice that η is a linear order on P. Let $<P_x, P_y> \in \eta$ for some $x,y \in U$; then $x_q \leq y_q$ and we have the following:

$$d^n(y,X) - d^n(x,X)$$

$$= \sum_{z \in X} (d(y,z))^n - \sum_{z \in X} (d(x,z))^n$$

$$= \sum_{z \in X} y_i^n - \sum_{z \in X} x_i^n \geq y_q^n - (K - q + 1) x_q^n.$$

From the definition of the number q it follows that there exists a natural number n_{xy} such that for all natural numbers n if $n \geq n_{xy}$ then

$$d^n(x,X) \leq d^n(y,X).$$

Let now

$$P_{min} = \{x \in U: (\forall y \in U) (<P_x, P_y> \in \eta)\}.$$

Of course if $x,y \in P_{min}$ then $P_x = P_y$. For $x \in P_{min}$, $y \in U$ there must be held

$$d^n(x,X) \leq d^n(y,X)$$

for each $n \geq n_{xy}$. Let $x \in P_{min}$ and

$$n_0 = \max \{n_{xy}: y \in U\};$$

then for each $n \geq n_0$ we should have

$$d^n(x,X) \leq d^n(y,X)$$

for all $y \in U$; it means that

$$C_n(X) = P_{min}.$$

Let's now set $X^* = P_{min}$ and the theorem should be proved.   ◆

From this theorem it follows that for each profile X beginning from some n_0 the consensus function C_n should give the same value.

Now we deal with the dependency of consensus functions in two distance spaces with dependent distance functions. Two distance functions d_1 and d_2 in spaces (U, d_1) and (U, d_2) are dependent on each other if for any $x, x', y, y' \in U$,

$$d_1(x,x') \geq d_1(y,y') \Leftrightarrow d_2(x,x') \geq d_2(y,y').$$

Let then distance functions d_1 and d_2 be dependent on each other. We define consensus choice functions C_n^1 and C_n^2, where

$$C_n^i(X) = \{x \in U: d_i^n(x,X) = \min_{y \in U} d_i^n(y,X)\}$$

for $i = 1, 2$. We have the following.

Theorem 3.11.
Let distance functions d_1 and d_2 be dependent on each other and $X \in \Pi(U)$; then the following dependency is true.

$$\lim_{n \to +\infty} C_n^{\;1}(X) = \lim_{n \to +\infty} C_n^{\;2}(X).$$

Proof.
We show that there exists $X^* \subseteq U$ and $n_0 \in N$ such that for all $n \geq n_0$ there should be

$$C_n^{\;1}(X) = C_n^{\;2}(X) = X^*.$$

Letting $K = card(X)$ we define the following sets with repetitions

$$P_x^{\;i} = \{d_i(x,z): z \in X\}$$

for $x \in U$ and

$$P^i = \{P_x^{\;i}: x \in U\}.$$

In set P^i we define a linear order η^i in the same way as in the proof of Theorem 3.10. Let

$$P^i_{min} = \{x \in U: (\forall y \in U)(<P_x^{\;i}, P_y^{\;i}> \in \eta^i)\}.$$

Notice that $<P_x^{\;1}, P_y^{\;1}> \in \eta^1$ if and only if $<P_x^{\;2}, P_y^{\;2}> \in \eta^2$, because the functions d_1 and d_2 are dependent upon each other, thus $P^1_{min} = P^2_{min}$. Also from the proof of Theorem 3.10 it follows that there exist numbers $n_0^{\;i}$ such that if $n \geq n_0^{\;i}$, then $C_n^{\;i}(X) = P^i_{min}$ for $i = 1,2$. Letting now $n_0 = \max\{n_0^{\;i}: i = 1, 2\}$, $n \geq n_0$ and $X^* = P^1_{min} = P^2_{min}$, we should have

$$C_n^{\;i}(X) = C_n^{\;i}(X) = X^*.$$

The theorem is then proved.   ◆

From Theorem 3.11 it follows that if we use two dependent distance functions then for the same profile beginning from some n_0 the consensus functions $C_n^{\;1}$ and $C_n^{\;2}$ should determine the same values.

3.4. Quality of Consensus

For conflict profiles and their consensuses we introduce a measure which allows evaluating these consensuses referring to the profiles.

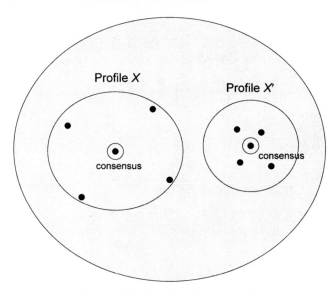

Figure 3.2. Quality of consensus.

Definition 3.3.
Let $X \in \Pi(U)$, $C \in \textbf{Con}(U)$, and $x \in C(X)$. By the quality of consensus x in profile X we call the following value

$$\hat{d}(x,X) = 1 - \frac{d(x,X)}{card(X)}.$$

Thus the quality of a consensus in a profile reflects the average distance from the consensus to the elements of this profile. The aim of introducing this measure is not to compare the quality of consensuses within a profile but to compare the quality of consensuses within different profiles. Within a profile it is obvious that for getting a consensus with the maximal quality it is enough to determine an O_1-consensus. Let's see the example in Figure 3.2. We can notice that the consensus of profile X has lower quality than the consensus of profile X'.

If x is an O_1-consensus then instead of $\hat{d}(x, X)$ we write $\hat{d}(X)$ because as all O_1-consensuses have the same (maximal) quality.

The problem we want to solve here is, having a given profile, how to improve the quality of its consensus. For solving this problem we consider the modification of the profile toward this aim. By the profile modification we mean adding or removing elements to or from this profile.

We have the following properties.

Theorem 3.12.
Let x be an O_1-consensus for profile X; let $X^{(k)}$ be such a profile that

$$X^{(k)} = X \cup \{k * x\}$$

for any $k \in \aleph$; then there should be

$$\hat{d}(X) \le \hat{d}(X^{(n)}) \le \hat{d}(X^{(n+1)})$$

for all $n \in \aleph$. The equality takes place iff X is a homogeneous profile.

Proof.
Notice that after adding x to profile X this element is still an O_1-consensus for X. Moreover we have

$$d(x,X) = d(x,X^{(1)}).$$

Also, $card(X^{(1)}) = card(X) + 1$, thus there should be

$$1 - \frac{d(x,X)}{card(X)} \le 1 - \frac{d(x,X^{(1)})}{card(X^{(1)})};$$

that is,

$$\hat{d}(X) \le \hat{d}(X^{(1)}).$$

By induction we can prove that $\hat{d}(X^{(n)}) \le \hat{d}(X^{(n+1)})$. The equality takes place if and only if X is a homogeneous profile because only in this case $d(x,X) = d(x,X^{(n)}) = 0$. ◆

The above theorem shows that if we increase a heterogeneous profile by adding to it an O_1-consensus then we can improve the consensus quality. From the proof we can easily prove that

$$\lim_{n \to +\infty} \hat{d}(X^{(n)}) = 1.$$

The following theorem shows that if we add to a profile such an element of it that minimizes the sum of distances to its elements, and this element is not too far from an O_1-consensus of this profile, then the consensus quality should be improved.

Theorem 3.13.
Let x be such an element of profile X that

$$d(x,X) = \min\{d(y,X): y \in X\}$$

and let there exist an O_1-consensus y of X such that

$$d(y,x) \leq \frac{1}{card(X)} d(y,X);$$

then the following inequality should be true

$$\hat{d}(X) \leq \hat{d}(X \cup \{x\}).$$

Proof.
Let $X' = X \cup \{x\}$, and let z be an O_1-consensus of X'. We have

$$d(z,X') \leq d(y,X').$$

On the other hand

$$d(y,X') = d(y,X) + d(y,x)$$

$$\leq d(y,X) + \frac{1}{card(X)} d(y,X)$$

$$= \frac{card(X)+1}{card(X)} d(y,X).$$

It implies that

$$\frac{1}{card(X)+1} d(z,X') \leq \frac{1}{card(X)} d(y,X),$$

which means

$$\hat{d}(X) \leq \hat{d}(X'). \qquad \blacklozenge$$

In general, we can expect that the larger the consistency value of a profile the higher the quality of its consensus. A case of this situation is illustrated in Figure 3.2. However, this is true only for consistency function c_5 (see Section 2.4.4, Chapter 2), and not always true for the remaining consistency functions.

3.5. Susceptibility to Consensus

In this section we present the definition, criteria, and their analysis for profile susceptibility to consensus. Because of reliability of consensus functions, in a distance space for each profile one may always determine its consensus (e.g., using one of criteria O_1 and O_2). However, one should give the answer for the following question. Is the consensus sensible and may it be accepted as the solution of the conflict? In other words, is the profile susceptible to consensus [64]?

To illustrate this problem let's consider an example.

Example 3.3. Let a space (U, d) be defined as follows. $U = \{a, b\}$ where a and b are objects of some type, and distance function d is given as

$$d(x,y) = \begin{cases} 0 & \text{for } x = y \\ 1 & \text{for } x \neq y \end{cases}$$

for $x, y \in U$.

Let X be a profile, as a set with repetitions, where

$$X = \{a, b\};$$

that is, each of objects a and b occurs exactly once in the profile. Assume that X represents the result of some voting in which two voters take part; each of them casts one vote (for a or b). There is one vote for a and one vote for b. It is easy to note that for profile X the O_1- or O_2-consensus should be equal to a or b. But it intuitively seems that neither of them is a good consensus, because there is lack of compromise in this conflict situation. Let us now consider another profile

$$X' = \{2 * a, b\}$$

in which there are three votes: two of them are for a and one is for b. For this profile the only consensus should be a and it seems to be a good consensus; that means this profile is susceptible to consensus. ◆

The above example shows that although consensus may always be chosen for a conflict profile, it does not have to be a good one. Below we try to characterize the situations in which conflict profiles are susceptible to consensus.

3.5.1. Criteria for Consensus Susceptibility

For a given distance space (U, d), $X \in \Pi(U)$ and $card(X) = K$, first we define the following parameters [106],

$$d^i_{t\_mean}(X) = \frac{\sum\limits_{x,y \in X} (d(x,y))^i}{k(k+1)} \quad \text{for } i = 1,2.$$

$$d_x^i(X) = \frac{\sum_{y \in X}(d(x,y))^i}{k} \qquad \text{for } i = 1,2.$$

$$d_{\min}^i(X) = \min_{x \in U} d_x^i(X) \qquad \text{for } i = 1,2.$$

$$d_{\max}^i(X) = \max_{x \in U} d_x^i(X) \qquad \text{for } i = 1,2.$$

For $i = 1$ the index i may be omitted; thus symbols d_{t_mean} and $d_{\min}$ are consistent with those defined earlier in Section 2.4.

The interpretations of these parameters are the following:

- $d_{t\_mean}^i(X)$: For $i = 1$ we have interpreted this value as the total average distance of all distances in profile X. The justification for this pattern is given in Section 2.4 (Chapter 2). For $i = 2$ this value is treated as the total average of all squared distances in profile X.
- $d_x^i(X)$: This value represents the average distance of all distances between object x and the elements of profile X.
- $d_{\min}^i(X)$: The minimal value of $d_x^i(X)$ for $x \in U$.

Definition 3.4
Let $X \in \Pi(U)$ be a profile. We say that profile X is susceptible to consensus in relation to postulate O_i for $i = 1, 2$ (or O_i-susceptible to consensus) if and only if the following inequality takes place,

$$d_{t\_mean}^i(X) \geq d_{\min}^i(X) .$$

The idea of the above definition lies in such intuition that because value $d_{t\_mean}^i(X)$ represents the average distance in profile X, and $d_{\min}^i(X)$ represents the average distance from the consensus to the elements of the profile, then X is susceptible to consensus (i.e., it is possible to determine a "good" consensus for X) if the second value is not greater than the first. Satisfying the above inequality means that the elements of profile X are "dense" enough for determining a good consensus. In other words, opinions represented by these elements are consistent enough for determining a good compromise.

For the profile X from Example 3.3 the above-defined values are calculated as follows.

$$d_{t\_mean}(X) = \frac{2 \cdot (0+1+0)}{2 \cdot 3} = \frac{1}{3}$$

and

$$d_{min}(X) = \frac{1}{2}.$$

Of course $\frac{1}{3} < \frac{1}{2}$, thus profile X is not O_1-susceptible to consensus. The same result may be deduced for $i = 2$. For profile X' we have the following.

$$d_{t\_mean}(X') = \frac{2 \cdot 2}{3 \cdot 4} = \frac{1}{3},$$

and

$$d_{min}(X') = \frac{1}{3}.$$

Thus $d_{t\_mean}(X') = d_{min}(X')$, meaning that profile X' is O_1-susceptible to consensus. Similarly we can state that profile X' is not O_2-susceptible to consensus, but profile X' is O_2-susceptible to consensus. Definition 3.4 is then consistent with the intuition.

Definition 3.5.
Let $X \in \Pi(U)$ be a profile. We say that X is i-regular for $i = 1, 2$ if and only if for each pair of objects $x, y \in U$ the following equality takes place.

$$d_x^i(X) = d_y^i(X).$$

Notice that profile X defined in Example 3.3 is *i*-regular for $i = 1, 2$, whereas profile X' is not *i*-regular (or *i*-irregular) for $i = 1, 2$.
Below we present some results of the analysis.

Theorem 3.14.
Each i-regular profile X, where $card(X) > 1$, is not O_i-susceptible to consensus for $i = 1, 2$.

Proof.
For $i = 1$: Let X be a 1-regular profile in space (U, d) and let $card(X) = k$; then we have

$$d_x(X) = \frac{\sum\limits_{y \in X} d(x,y)}{k}.$$

This value should be the same for all $x \in U$; thus the sum $\sum_{y \in X} d(x,y)$ is also the same for all $x \in U$. Let it be equal to $s_X > 0$. We have then

$$d_{\min}(X) = \frac{s_X}{k}.$$

On the other hand, the value $d_{t\_mean}(X)$ is equal to

$$d_{t\_mean}(X) = \frac{\sum\limits_{x,y \in X} d(x,y)}{k(k+1)} = \frac{ks_X}{k(k+1)} = \frac{s_X}{k+1}.$$

It follows that

$$d_{\min}(X) > d_{t\_mean}(X);$$

this means that profile X is not O_1-susceptible to consensus.

The proof for $i = 2$ is similar.   ◆

Theorem 3.14 implies that it is not worth determining the consensus for a regular profile because it is not susceptible to consensus.

Theorem 3.15.
Let $X, X' \in \Pi(U)$ be such profiles that X is i-regular and $X' = X \cup \{x\}$ for some $x \in X$; then profile X' is O_i-susceptible to consensus for $i = 1, 2$.

Proof.
For $i = 1$: Because profile X is 1-regular, thus similarly as in the proof of Theorem 3.14 we can assume that $d_{\min}(X) = s_X/k$ where $card(X) = k$. It is easy to notice that for profile X' the value $d_{\min}(X')$ can be achieved for element x and is equal to $s_X/(k + 1)$. Value $d_{t\_mean}(X)$ can be calculated as follows:

$$d_{t\_mean}(X) = \frac{\sum\limits_{y,z \in X'} d(y,z)}{(k+1)(k+2)}$$

$$= \frac{\sum_{y,z \in X} d(y,z) + 2\sum_{y \in X} d(x,y)}{(k+1)(k+2)} = \frac{ks_X + 2s_X}{(k+1)(k+2)} = \frac{s_X}{k+1}.$$

Thus we should have

$$d_{\min}(X) = d_{t\_mean}(X),$$

This means that profile X is O_1-susceptible to consensus.

The proof for $i = 2$ is similar.   ◆

Theorem 3.15 shows the way for achieving the susceptibility to consensus for an i-regular profile; it is enough to add to it any of its elements. The practical sense of this theorem is the following. If in an impasse conflict situation any of the opinions does not dominate the other then it is enough to invite an additional participant for the possibility of determining a sensible consensus.

From the practical point of view, a special and interesting case is that universe U consists of real numbers, and the distance $d(x,y)$ is equal to $|x-y|$ for $x, y \in U$. We show now the conditions which should be satisfied for a profile consisting of real numbers to be susceptible to consensus. Assuming that we have to deal with such kind of distance spaces, then the following property is true [106].

Theorem 3.16.
In space (U, d) if a profile $X \in \Pi(U)$ consists of an odd number of elements then it is always O_i-susceptible to consensus for $i = 1, 2$.

Proof.

(a) For $i = 1$: Because $card(X)$ is an odd number then $card(X) = 2k - 1$ for k being a natural number. If $k = 1$ then of course the equality

$$d_{t\_mean}(X) = d_{\min}(X) = 0$$

takes place; that is, the theorem is true in this case. Assume that $k > 1$. Let us denote by $(a_1, a_2, \ldots, a_{2k-1})$ an increasing sequence which arises after sorting elements of profile X. Let us consider the following distances,

$$d(a_{k-i}, a_{k+i}) = |a_{k-i} - a_{k+i}| \quad \text{for } 1 \le i < k.$$

Each distance $d(a_{k-i}, a_{k+i})$ where $1 \le i < k$ generates a set D_i consisting of the following elements (which indeed are sets of distances):

- 2-element sets which consist of pairs of distances

$$\{d(a_{k-i},a_j), d(a_j,a_{k+i})\}$$

or

$$\{d(a_{k+i},a_j), d(a_j,a_{k-i})\}$$

for $k-i \le j \le k+i$.
Notice that

$$d(a_{k-i},a_{k+i}) = d(a_{k-i},a_j) + d(a_j,a_{k+i})$$
$$= d(a_{k+j},a_j) + d(a_j,a_{k-i}).$$

- 1-element sets which consist of distances $d(a_j,a_{k+i})$ or $d(a_{k+i},a_j)$ for $1 \le j < k-i$ and $d(a_{k-i},a_j)$ or $d(a_j,a_{k-i})$ for $k+i < j \le 2k-1$.
  Notice that

$$d(a_{k-i},a_{k+i}) \le d(a_j,a_{k+i}) = d(a_{k+i},a_j)$$

for $1 \le j < k-i$, and

$$d(a_{k-i},a_{k+i}) \le d(a_{k-i},a_j) = d(a_j,a_{k-i})$$

for $k+i < j \le 2k$.

Notice also that for a given i the number of sets in set D_i is equal to

$$2(2i + 2(k-i-1)) = 2(2k-2).$$

The elements of these sets are nonrepeated and their sum is not smaller than $d(a_{k-i}, a_{k+i})$. Also as follows from index definition, each distance occurs in all sets D_i (for $i = 1, 2, \ldots$) at most once.

Now we calculate the values which decide about the susceptibility to consensus for profile X. One can prove that value $d_{min}(X)$ can be achieved for $x = a_k$, thus

$$d_{min}(X) = \frac{1}{2k-1} \sum_{1 \le i \le k-1} d(a_{k-i},a_{k+i}),$$

and

$$d_{t\_mean}(X) = \frac{1}{2k(2k-1)} \sum_{1 \le s,t \le 2k-1} d(a_s,a_t).$$

Notice that because $(2k-2)/k \ge 1$ for $k > 1$, we have the following:

$$\frac{1}{2k(2k-1)} \sum_{1 \le s,t \le 2k-1} d(a_s, a_t)$$

$$\ge \frac{1}{2k(2k-1)} \sum_{1 \le i \le k-1} \left(\sum_{d \in D_i} \left(\sum_{z \in d} z \right) \right)$$

$$\ge \frac{1}{2k(2k-1)} 2(2k-2) \sum_{1 \le i \le k-1} d(a_{k-i}, a_{k+i})$$

$$= \frac{2k-2}{k} d_{\min}(X) \ge d_{\min}(X).$$

Profile X is then O_1-susceptible to consensus.

(b) For $i = 2$: notice that

$$(d(a_i, a_j))^2 \ge (d(a_i, a_k))^2 + (d(a_k, a_j))^2$$

for $1 \le i \le k$ and $k \le j \le 2k-1$. It implies that

$$\sum_{\substack{1 \le i \le k \\ k \le j \le 2k-1}} (d(a_i, a_j))^2 \ge k \sum_{1 \le i \le k-1} \left((d(a_k, a_{k+i}))^2 + (d(a_k, a_{k-i}))^2 \right).$$

The value $d_{\min}^2(X)$ should be achieved for $x = 1/n \sum_{i=1}^{n} a_i$, thus

$$d_{\min}^2(X) = \frac{1}{2k-1} \sum_{1 \le i \le 2k-1} (d(a_i, x))^2$$

$$\le \frac{1}{2k-1} \sum_{1 \le i \le k-1} \left((d(a_k, a_{k+i}))^2 + (d(a_k, a_{k-i}))^2 \right)$$

$$\le \frac{1}{k(2k-1)} \sum_{\substack{1 \le i \le k \\ k \le j \le 2k-1}} (d(a_i, a_j))^2 = d_{t\_mean}^2(X).$$

It follows that profile X is also O_2-susceptible to consensus.   ◆

Theorem 3.16 shows that if for a competition the number of jury members is odd and if their opinions are in the form of real numbers then it is always possible to determine a sensible consensus. This result explains why the numbers of jury members in many contests are odd numbers.

In the case when $card(X)$ is an even number then profile X is not always O_1-susceptible or O_2-susceptible to consensus. The interesting case is when $card(X) = 2$; let $X = \{a, b\}$ where $a \neq b$. We have

$$d(a, b) = |a - b| > 0.$$

Notice that

$$d_{min}(X) = \frac{|a - b|}{2} > \frac{|a - b|}{3} = d_{t\_mean}(X).$$

So profile X cannot be O_1-susceptible to consensus. Similarly we can prove that it is also not O_2-susceptible to consensus. This is consistent with the consideration in Example 3.3.

Below we present the notion of susceptibility to consensus of a profile in the context of other profile.

Definition 3.6.
Profile $X \in \Pi(U)$ is susceptible to consensus in the context of profile

$$Y \in \Pi(U) \text{ if } X \subset Y \text{ and } d^i_{max}(X) \leq d_{min}(X).$$

The above definition serves in such situations as when profile X is not susceptible to consensus but its context (profile Y) is more nonsusceptible to consensus. In other words, the conflict encompassed by profile X is not meaningful in the relation to the conflict represented by profile Y. In this case the consensus determined for profile X could be acceptable.

3.5.2. Consensus Susceptibility versus Consistency

Now we analyze the relationships between consistency values of conflict profiles and their susceptibility to consensus.

In Chapter 2 we defined five consistency functions:

$$c_1(X) = 1 - Diam(X),$$

$$c_2(X) = 1 - Diam(W^X),$$

$$c_3(X) = 1 - d_{mean}(X),$$

$$c_4(X) = 1 - d_{t\_mean}(X),$$

$$c_5(X) = 1 - d_{min}(X).$$

Here we present some dependencies between profile consistency and consensus susceptibility. These dependencies show that in general the two notions are coherent. The following properties are true.

Theorem 3.17.
For each $j = 1, \ldots, 5$ if $c_j(X) = 1$ then profile X is O_i-susceptible to consensus for $i = 1, 2$.

Proof.
For each $j = 1, \ldots, 5$ it is easy to show that $c_j(X) = 1$ if and only if profile X is homogeneous. In this case we have

$$d^i_{min}(X) = d^i_{t\_mean}(X) = 0$$

for $i = 1, 2$; that is, profile X is O_i-susceptible to consensus for $i = 1, 2$. ◆

This property shows the coherence between consistency measures and consensus susceptibility. In the case when a profile has maximal consistency then it is also susceptible to consensus. However, if a profile has minimal consistency then it should not necessarily be susceptible to consensus. The following properties show that the intuition is true only for functions c_3, c_4, and c_5 and false for functions c_1 and c_2.

Theorem 3.18.
(a) For each $j = 3, 4$ if $c_j(U)$ is minimal then profile X is not O_i-susceptible to consensus for $i = 1, 2$.

(b) If $c_5(X) = 0$ then profile X is not O_i-susceptible to consensus for $i = 1, 2$.

Proof.
(a) We assume that $card(X) > 1$, because if $card(X) = 1$ then X is a homogeneous profile and of course it is O_i-susceptible to consensus for $i = 1, 2$. For function c_3 notice that if $c_3(U)$ is minimal, that is, $c_3(U) = 0$, then $d_{mean}(U) = 1$; that is,

$$\frac{\sum\limits_{x,y \in U} d(x,y)}{card(U)(card(U)-1)} = 1.$$

From this equality it follows that $d(x,y) = 1$ for all $x,y \in U$ and $x \neq y$. Thus in a profile $X \in \Pi(U)$ we should have

$$d_{min}^i(X) = 1$$

and

$$d_{t\_mean}^i(X) = \frac{card(X)-1}{card(X)} < d_{min}^i(X),$$

for $i = 1, 2$. Thus profile X cannot be O_i-susceptible to consensus for $i = 1$, 2. For function c_4 the proof is identical with the notion that $c_4(U)$ is minimal if and only if $d_{t\_mean}(U)$ is maximal; that is,

$$d_{t\_mean}(U) = \frac{card(U)-1}{card(U)}.$$

(b) For function c_5 notice that if $c_5(X) = 0$ then

$$d_{min}^i(X) = 1;$$

this means that $d(x,y) = 1$ for all $x,y \in X$ and $d(x,y) = 1$ for all $x \in U$ and $y \in U$ where $x \neq y$. Thus

$$d_{t\_mean}^i(X) = \frac{card(X)-1}{card(X)} < d_{min}^i(X);$$

then profile X cannot be O_i-susceptible to consensus for $i = 1, 2$.   ◆

For functions c_1 and c_2 it is not possible to formulate a relationship between the minimal value of $c_1(U)$ or $c_2(X)$ and the susceptibility to consensus because these functions take into account only the behavior of some elements of the profile. The behavior of other elements is not reflected by them. Nevertheless functions c_1 and c_2 have many practical applications.

Another aspect of the relationship between consistency measures and consensus susceptibility is based on the investigation of the behavior of consistency in situations when a profile is susceptible to consensus. It turns out that the behaviors of defined consistency functions are not similar.

From Theorem 3.18 it follows that if profile X is O_i-susceptible to consensus for $i = 1, 2$ then $c_5(X) > 0$, $c_3(U) > 0$, and $c_4(U) > 0$. However, referring to functions c_1 and c_2 similar results may not be deduced.

Referring to functions c_4 and c_5 we have the following.

Theorem 3.19.
If profile X is O_1-susceptible to consensus then there should be:

$$c_4(X) \geq \frac{2}{card(X)+1} \quad and \quad c_5(X) \geq \frac{2}{card(X)+1}.$$

Proof.
Notice that because profile X is O_1-susceptible to consensus, then

$$d_{t\_mean}(X) \geq d_{min}(X).$$

In addition, we know that

$$d_{t\_mean}(X) = \frac{card(X)-1}{card(X)+1} \quad d_{mean}(X) \leq \frac{card(X)-1}{card(X)+1}.$$

So there should be

$$c_5(X) = 1 - d_{t\_mean}(X) \geq 1 - \frac{card(X)-1}{card(X)+1} = \frac{2}{card(X)+1}.$$

Because $c_4(X) \geq c_5(X)$ then there should also be

$$c_4(X) \geq \frac{2}{card(X)+1}.$$

The same result may be similarly proved for a profile O_2-susceptible to consensus. ♦

This theorem shows some threshold for the minimal values of consistency of a profile susceptible to consensus. Theorems 3.17 to 3.19 state some coherence between two notions: conflict profile consistency and susceptibility to consensus. We can see that these two notions are not contradictory to each other, but they are also independent. We mention that the criterion for susceptibility to consensus allows us to evaluate if a determined consensus will be sensible, whereas consistency value tells us about the coherence degree of the elements of a conflict profile. From the above results it follows that if the consistency is very low then the profile may not be susceptible to consensus, and if a profile is susceptible to consensus then its consistency value is larger than some positive value.

3.6. Methods for Achieving Consensus Susceptibility

In this section we present some methods for achieving susceptibility to consensus for such profiles which are not susceptible to consensus. We deal with the following two methods toward this aim:

- Profile modification by adding or removing elements
- Profile modification by weight determination for its elements

In the first method we show several situations when adding or removing elements to or from the profile may cause achieving the susceptibility to consensus. In the second method we work out an algorithm for profile element weight modification for this purpose.

3.6.1. Profile Modification

In this section we present some results which allow achieving the susceptibility to consensus for a profile by its modification. The theorem presented below shows that if a profile is not susceptible to consensus then it should become susceptible if we add to it a large enough number of occurrences of any element of the universe.

Theorem 3.20.
Let $X \in \Pi(U)$ be such a profile that X is not O_1-susceptible to consensus. Let $x \in U$; then there exists a natural number $n_o \in \aleph$ such that profile

$$X' = X \cup \{n_o * x\}$$

is O_1-susceptible to consensus.

Proof.
We know that an O_1-function also satisfies the postulate of *Quasi-unanimous* (defined in Section 3.2.2), according to which if an element x is not a consensus of profile X then there exists a natural number n such that x is a consensus of profile $Y = X \cup \{n * x\}$. Letting $card(X) = k$, for profile Y we have

$$d_{\min}(Y) = \frac{1}{k+n}\left(\sum_{y \in X} d(x,y)\right) = \frac{d(x,X)}{k+n}$$

and

$$d_{t\_mean}(Y) = \frac{1}{(k+n)(k+n+1)}\left(\sum_{y,z \in X} d(y,z) + 2(n-1)\sum_{y \in X} d(x,y)\right)$$

$$= \frac{1}{(k+n)(k+n+1)}\left(\sum_{y,z \in X} d(y,z)\right)$$

$$+ \frac{1}{(k+n)(k+n+1)}\left(2(n-1)\sum_{y \in X} d(x,y)\right)$$

$$= \frac{k(k+1)}{(k+n)(k+n+1)} d_{t\_mean}(X) + \frac{2(n-1)}{(k+n)(k+n+1)} d(x,X).$$

Thus inequality

$$d_{min}(Y) \leq d_{t\_mean}(Y)$$

is equivalent to inequality

$$d(x, X) \leq \frac{k(k+1)}{(k+n+1)} d_{t\_mean}(X) + \frac{2(n-1)}{(k+n+1)} d(x,X).$$

Notice that for $n \rightarrow +\infty$ the first component on the right side of the above inequality should aim at 0 and the second component aims at $2d(x, X)$. It then implies that with a large enough value of n the above inequality should be true. That is, the profile Y with such a value of n should be O_1-susceptible to consensus. ♦

The same result can be proved for O_2-susceptibility.

In general, the higher the value of consistency of a profile is, the larger the possibility for it to be susceptible to consensus. Although it is not true in all cases,[2] we can accept it for trying to achieve the consensus susceptibility. As we know, postulates P7a and P7b show that inconsistency may be enlarged if we add to the profile its O_1-consensus, or remove this element from it which generates the maximal sum of distances to the remaining elements.

3.6.2. Using Weights

In this section we present another approach for achieving susceptibility to consensus, which is based on determining weights for the elements of a conflict profile. In this approach an element is assigned with a weight value representing the degree (or level) of this element in determining consensus. Weights assigned to conflict participants can be interpreted as the degrees of their credibility, and in consequence, the credibility of their opinions. Weights also can represent the degrees (or participation) of the profile elements in the consensus determination process. This approach may be useful in such practical applications in which conflict participants

---

[2] This is because of the lack of restrictions for the distance function d; with the assumption that d is a half-metric it seems to be impossible for this statement to be true.

may not achieve the compromise (consensus) because of too large differences of their opinions on some subject (i.e., the consistency value is too low). In such cases one of the possible solutions may be based on assigning the participants with their priorities which can be represented by the weights. Owing to modification of these priorities one may determine a profile which is susceptible to consensus, and then the participants can achieve the compromise. Such an approach can find applications, for example, in creating intelligent user interfaces [124, 126].

The weight function has been defined in Section 2.3.3 (Chapter 2). We mention the assumption that the profile elements represent the opinions of the conflict participants; each of these opinions belongs to one participant and each participant can give only one opinion. A weight function for each participant assigns a real number belonging to interval [0,1]. Thus we have the following weight function,

$$w: X \to [0,1].$$

Function w can be treated as a fuzzy function

Having the weight function we define the following postulate O_i^w for consensus choice in which the weight function is taken into account,

$$(x \in c(X)) \Rightarrow \left(\sum_{y \in X} w(y)(d(x,y))^i = \min_{z \in U} \sum_{y \in X} w(y)(d(z,y))^i \right)$$

for $i = 1, 2$.

Two consensus functions satisfying postulate O_i^w (for $i = 1,2$) can be defined as follows.

$$C_i^w(X) = \left\{ x \in U: \sum_{y \in X} w(y)(d(x,y))^i = \min_{z \in U} \sum_{y \in X} w(y)(d(z,y))^i \right\}$$

for $i = 1, 2$.

One can notice that function C_i^w corresponds to function C_i defined in Section 3.3.3.

The expressions serving to evaluate the susceptibility to consensus of profiles now have the following forms (for simplicity we do not change the symbols for these expressions).

$$d_{t\_mean}^i(X) = \frac{\sum_{x,y \in X} w(y)(d(x,y))^i}{k(k+1)},$$

$$d_x^i(X) = \frac{\sum\limits_{y \in X} w(y)(d(x,y))^i}{k}$$

and

$$d_{\min}^i(X) = \min_{x \in U} d_x^i(X)$$

for $i = 1, 2$.

Now let's consider the following problem [110].

Assume that a profile $X \in \Pi(U)$ is not O_i-susceptible to consensus. How can function w be constructed such that profile X is O_i^w-susceptible to consensus for $i = 1, 2$?

A very simple answer to the above question may be the following. Set $w(x) = 0$ for each $x \in X$, then the susceptibility is achieved because the equality $d_{t\_mean}^i(X) = d_{\min}^i(X) = 0$ holds. Unfortunately, this answer is not satisfactory because in this case any element of U may be a consensus for X. We are interested in the minimal modification of function w (at the beginning, we assume $w(x) = 1$ for any $x \in X$) so that profile X becomes susceptible to profile X, that is, to achieve the inequality

$$d_{t\_mean}^i(X) \geq d_{\min}^i(X).$$

First let's consider an example.

Example 3.4. Let a space (U, d) be defined as $U = \{a, b, c\}$ where $a, b,$ and c are objects of some type, and distance function d is defined as

$$d(x,y) = \begin{cases} 0 & \text{for } x = y \\ 1 & \text{for } x \neq y \end{cases} \quad \text{for all } x,y \in U.$$

Let X be a profile where

$$X = \{25 * a, 25 * b, 25 * c\}.$$

Assume that X represents the result of some voting in which 75 voters take part; each of them casts one vote (for a or b or c). For each object there are exactly 25 votes. It is easy to note that profile X is neither O_1-susceptible nor O_2-susceptible to consensus. Now we assume that the votes for elements a and b will have weight equal to 0.5, and the votes for element c will have weight equal to 1; that is,

$$w(a) = 0.5, \quad w(b) = 0.5, \quad \text{and} \quad w(c) = 1.$$

Thus

$$d^i_{t\_mean}(X) = \frac{2 \cdot (0.5 \cdot 25 \cdot 25 + 0.5 \cdot 25 \cdot 25 + 0.25 \cdot 25 \cdot 25)}{75.76}$$

$$= \frac{2.5 \cdot 25 \cdot 25}{75 \cdot 38} = \frac{62.5}{3 \cdot 38},$$

and

$$d^i_{min}(X) = \frac{50 \cdot 0.5}{75} = \frac{1}{3}$$

for c being a consensus. Of course we have $62.5/3.38 > 1/3$, so profile X becomes O_1^w-susceptible to consensus with new weight function w. ◆

The following theorem presents the possibility of weight modification for achieving consensus susceptibility.

Theorem 3.21.

If profile X is not O_i-susceptible to consensus for the weights equal to 1, then there always exists a weight function w such that $w(x) > 0$ for any element $x \in X$ for which profile X is O_i^w-susceptible to consensus ($i = 1, 2$).

Proof.
We present the proof for $i = 1$. The proof for $i = 2$ is similar. For simplicity for $i = 1$ we do not use the index i in the expressions.

Because profile X is not O_1-susceptible to consensus, the following inequality should take place,

$$d_{t\_mean}(X) = \frac{\sum\limits_{x,y \in X} d(x,y)w(y)}{k(k+1)} < d^i_{min}(X) = \frac{\sum\limits_{y \in X} d(x',y)w(y)}{k}$$

for $card(X) = k$, $x' \in C_1(X)$ and $w(x) = 1$ for each $x \in X$. Thus for each $z \in U$ we have

$$\frac{\sum\limits_{x,y \in X} d(x,y)w(y)}{(k+1)} < \sum\limits_{y \in X} d(z,y)w(y)$$

or

$$\frac{\sum\limits_{x,y \in X} d(x,y)w(y)}{(k+1)} - \sum\limits_{y \in X} d(z,y)w(y) < 0.$$

After transforming the above inequality, we have the following.

$$\sum\limits_{y \in X} w(y) \left(\frac{\sum\limits_{x \in X} d(x,y)}{k+1} - d(z,y) \right) < 0.$$

Denoting

$$\alpha(y) = \frac{\sum\limits_{x \in X} \delta(x,y)}{(k+1)},$$

we obtain

$$\sum\limits_{y \in X} w(y)(\alpha(y) - d(z,y)) < 0.$$

For any given element $z \in U$, set X can be divided into two disjoint sets X' and X'' such that for each $y \in X'$ inequality $\alpha(y) - d(z,y) \le 0$ is true and for each $y \in X''$ inequality $\alpha(y) - d(z,y) > 0$ is true. Notice that because profile X is not O_1-susceptible to consensus, there exists $z \in U$ such that set X'' is not empty. Then the last inequality can be written as

$$\sum\limits_{y \in X''} w(y)(\alpha(y) - d(z,y)) < \sum\limits_{y \in X'} w(y)(\alpha(y) - d(z,y)),$$

where $w(y) = 1$ for each $y \in X$. We show that it is possible to modify function w so that all its values are greater than 0 and the following inequality will be true.

$$\sum\limits_{y \in X''} w(y)(\alpha(y) - d(z,y)) \ge \sum\limits_{y \in X'} w(y)(\alpha(y) - d(z,y)).$$

Because set X'' is not empty, the sum on the left side of the above inequality is greater than 0. Thus it is possible to maintain $w(y) = 1$ for each $y \in X''$, and for elements $y \in X'$ to decrease values $w(y)$ so that $w(y) > 0$ and the above inequality is true. In this way the theorem has been proved. ◆

We now present an algorithm which for a profile being non-O_1-susceptible to consensus minimally modifies the values of weight function

w (at the beginning they are equal to 1) so that X becomes susceptible to consensus referring to criterion O_1^w.

The idea of this algorithm is based on the following steps. At first, we count the consensus according to function C_1; next we determine sets X' and X'' on the basis of the proof of Theorem 3.21. Having these sets we can minimally modify the values of function w so that the inequality

$$d_{t\_mean}(X) \geq d_{min}(X)$$

takes place. The algorithm is presented as follows.

Algorithm 3.1.

Input: Profile X being non-O_1-susceptible to consensus and $card(X) = k$, $w(x) = 1$ for each $x \in X$.

Result: New values of function w, for which profile X is O_1^w-susceptible to consensus.

Procedure:

    BEGIN

       1. Determine $z \in U$ such that $d(z,X) = d_{min}(X)$;

       2. Divide set X into disjoined sets X' and X'' so that for each $y' \in X'$ and $y'' \in X''$ the inequalities $\alpha(y') - d(z,y') \leq 0$ and $\alpha(y'') - d(z,y'') > 0$, follow, respectively, where

$$\alpha(y) = \frac{\sum\limits_{x \in X} d(x,y)}{(k+1)}$$

      for $y \in X$;

       3. For each $y \in X'$ set maximal value of $w(y)$ such that $w(y) > 0$ and the following inequality holds true

$$\sum\limits_{y \in X''} w(y)(\alpha(y) - d(z,y)) \geq \sum\limits_{y \in X'} w(y)(\alpha(y) - d(z,y));$$

       4. For each $y \in X''$ set $w(y) = 1$;

    END.

The idea for an algorithm aiming to minimally modify the values of function w so that X becomes O_2^w-susceptible is similar, and the algorithm is presented as follows.

Algorithm 3.2.

Input: Profile X being non-O_2-susceptible to consensus and $card(X) = k$, $w(x) = 1$ for each $x \in X$.

Result: New values of function w, for which profile X is O_2^w-susceptible to consensus.

Procedure:

BEGIN

1. Determine $z \in U$ such that $d^2(z,X) = d^2_{min}(X)$;.

2. Divide set X into disjoined sets X' and X'' so that for each $y' \in X'$ and $y'' \in X''$ the inequalities $\alpha(y') - (d(z,y'))^2 \leq 0$ and $\alpha(y'') - (d(z,y''))^2 > 0$ follow, respectively, where

$$\alpha(y) = \frac{\sum\limits_{x \in X} (d(x,y))^2}{(k+1)};$$

3. For each $y \in X'$ set maximal value of $w(y)$ such that $w(y) > 0$ and the following inequality becomes true.

$$\sum_{y \in X''} w(y)(\alpha(y) - (d(z,y))^2) \geq \sum_{y \in X'} w(y)(\alpha(y) - (d(z,y))^2);$$

4. For each $y \in X''$ set $w(y) = 1$.

END.

We can see that the computational complexity of Algorithms 3.1 and 3.2 is not large and is linear to the number of elements of profile X except step 1. For step 1 some special procedure should be used, and its complexity is dependent on the microstructure of universe U. In some cases this problem is NP-complete and it is necessary to work out a heuristic algorithm.

3.7. Reduction of Number of Consensuses

Very often for a conflict profile X a consensus function determines more than one consensus; that is, $card(C(X)) > 1$ for some function $C \in Con(U)$. This phenomenon in many cases may make the knowledge management process difficult because it is necessary to determine only one consensus. In this section we deal with the methods for reducing the number of consensuses generated by a consensus function [115]. First consider an example.

Example 3.5. From a set of candidates (denoted by symbols $A, B, C, \ldots$) four voters have to choose a committee (as an 1- or 2-element subset of the candidates' set). With this aim each of the voters votes on such committee which in her opinion is the best one. Assume that the votes are the following:

$$\{A, B\}, \{A,C\}, \{B,C\}, \text{ and } \{A\}.$$

Let the distance between two sets of candidates be equal to the cardinality of their symmetrical difference. Using function C_1 (the most practically applied function) to determine the consensus for conflict profile

$$X = \{\{A, B\}, \{A,C\}, \{B,C\}, \{A\}\}$$

from the universe U being the collection of all 1- or 2-element subsets of $\{A, B,C\}$, we obtain the following consensuses,

$$C_1(X) = \{\{A, B\}, \{A,C\}, \{A\}\}.$$

One can see that the number of the consensuses is equal to three and thus the choice result is not unambiguous. It is then needed to reduce the representative number in some way. Notice also that if we use C_2 to determine consensus, then there should be only two consensuses

$$C_2(X) = \{\{A, B\}, \{A,C\}\}. \qquad \blacklozenge$$

3.7.1. Additional Criterion

We define the following functions. For $X \in \Pi(U)$,

$$\overline{C}_1(X) = \{x \in C_1(X): \overline{d}(x,X) = \min_{y \in C_1(X)} \overline{d}(y,X)\},$$

$$\overline{C}_2(X) = \{x \in C_2(X): \overline{d}(x,X) = \min_{y \in C_2(X)} \overline{d}(y,X)\},$$

$$C_{12}(X) = \{x \in C_2(X): d(x,X) = \min_{y \in C_2(X)} d(y,X)\},$$

$$C_{n1}(X) = \{x \in C_1(X): d^2(x,X) = \min_{y \in C_1(X)} d^2(y,X)\},$$

for $n \in \aleph$.

We have the following theorem.

Theorem 3.22.
For each conflict profile $X \in \Pi(U)$ the following dependencies are true.

(a) $C_{21}(X) = \overline{C_1}(X)$.

(b) $C_{12}(X) = \overline{C_2}(X)$.

Proof.
(a) In the proof of Theorem 3.8 we showed that

$$\overline{d}(x,X) = d^2(x,X) - \tfrac{1}{K}(d(x,X))^2$$

for each $x \in U$ and $card(X) = K$. Assume that $x \in \overline{C_1}(X)$; then for each $y \in C_1(X)$ inequality $\overline{d}(x,X) \le \overline{d}(y,X)$ should be true; that is,

$$d^2(x,X) - \tfrac{1}{K}(d(x,X))^2 \le d^2(y,X) - \tfrac{1}{K}(d(y,X))^2.$$

In addition, because $x, y \in C_1(X)$ then $d(x,X) = d(y,X)$ and from the above inequality it follows that

$$d^2(x,X) \le d^2(y,X);$$

this means $x \in C_{21}(X)$. Similarly we can prove that if $x \in C_{21}(X)$ then $x \in \overline{C_1}(X)$. Thus

$$C_{21}(X) = \overline{C_1}(X).$$

(b) The proof for this equality is similar to that in (a)   ♦

Theorem 3.22 shows a very important result in using the second choice functions to the consensus choice. Concretely, if for a profile X in the first step we use function C_1, and in the second step we choose from $C_1(X)$ those consensuses best referring to postulate O_2, then it turns out that these consensuses are also the best referring to the uniformity of the distances between them and the profile elements, and vice versa. Similar results may be obtained if in the first step we use function C_2 and in the second step we choose from $C_2(X)$ those consensuses which best refer to postulate O_1. These consensuses also best refer to the uniformity of the distances between them and the profile elements, and vice versa.

Owing to the two-step consensus choice most often we can decrease the number of consensuses and choose those which satisfy not one but several postulates simultaneously.

Example 3.6. For the profile defined in Example 3.5 if in the first step we use function C_1 and in the second step we use function C_2 then the result will contain not three but two consensuses, which are:

$$C_{21}(X) = \{\{A,B\}, \{A,C\}\}. \qquad \blacklozenge$$

Similarly as in the proof of Theorem 3.11 we can prove that if all elements x of $C_1(X)$ generate different sets

$$\{d(x,y): y \in X\}$$

then there exists a natural number n_o such that $C_{n1}(X)$ contains exactly one element for each $n > n_o$.

3.7.2. Profile Modification

In this method we propose the choice in two steps: in the first step the consensus is chosen on the basis of some criterion. If the number of consensuses is large then we modify the profile to decrease this number. Modification of a profile may be based on:

- Adding a new element to the profile
- Removing some element form the profile

In the first case we create a new profile by adding all consensuses to the previous profile, and next using the same or other criterion to make the second choice. This method is very effective because in the second choice the number of consensuses always equals one. We have the following.

Theorem 3.23.
For each profile $X \in \Pi(U)$ and function C_i where $i =1, 2, \ldots$, the following dependency is true.

$$C_i(X \cup \{x\}) = \{x\},$$

for $x \in C_i(X)$.

Proof.
First we prove that each if $x \in Y$ then $x \in C_i(X \cup Y)$. Let $X' = X \cup \{x\}$; for any $y \in U$ and $y \neq x$ we have

$$d^i(x,X') = \sum_{z \in X'} (d(x,z))^i = d^i(x,X)$$

$$< \sum_{z \in X}\left(d(y,z)\right)^i + (d(y,x))^i = d^i(y,X').$$

Thus x is the only consensus for profile X'.   ◆

The following example illustrates this method.

Example 3.7. From Example 3.5 we have

$$C_1(X) = \{\{A,B\}, \{A,C\}, \{A\}\}.$$

After adding one of these consensuses (say $\{A,B\}$) to the profile X we have new profile

$$X' = \{\{A,B\}, \{A,B\}, \{A,C\}, \{B,C\}, \{A\}\},$$

for which

$$C_1(X') = \{A,B\};$$

that is, $C_1(X')$ contains exactly one consensus.   ◆

In the second case we propose to reduce the consensus number by removing from the profile those elements which "spoil" its consistency. The way to eliminate such elements is defined in postulate P7b for consistency functions (Chapter 2, Section 2.4). According to this postulate from the profile X we should eliminate such an element a for which

$$d(a,X) = \max\{d(x,X): x \in X\}.$$

Thus the element a should most "spoil" its consistency, and if we remove this element from X then the consistency of the new profile should increase, and owing to this the consensus set may be small.

The reduction method we propose in this case is based on several steps of consensus choice. At the first step, we make the choice on the basis of function C_1. If the number of consensuses is large then in the second step we remove from the profile the element which most "spoils" the consistency of X and make the second choice for this profile still using function C_1, and so on. The process should be stopped when the number of consensuses is equal to one. The following example should illustrate this method.

Example 3.8. With the same assumptions from Example 3.5, let us consider the following profile,

$$X = \{\{A,B\}, \{C\}, \{B,C\}, \{A,C\}, \{A\}, \{D\}\}.$$

Using consensus function C_1 we obtain three representatives:

$$C_1(X) = \{\{A\}, \{A,C\}, \{C\}\}.$$

For reducing this number we notice that the last vote, that is, $\{D\}$, most spoils the profile consistency because the value $d(\{D\},X)$ is maximal. After removing this element, we have the following profile,

$$X' = \{\{A,B\}, \{C\}, \{B,C\}, \{A,C\}, \{A\}\},$$

for which the choice on the basis of function C_1 gives only one consensus

$$C_1(X') = \{\{A,C\}\}. \qquad \blacklozenge$$

However, this method does not always guarantee success. If in universe U the distance between any two elements is identical and we deal with a distinguishable profile then the consensus function should give

$$C_1(X) = X.$$

Also value $d(x,X)$ is identical for all $x \in X$, so removing any element from X does not improve the situation. The number of consensuses will be equal to one if in the profile only one element remains.

3.8. Conclusions

In this chapter we have worked out a general model for consensus choice tasks. The model is called general bcause we have not assumed the microstructure of universe U. In this model the following elements have been defined and analyzed: a set of ten postulates for consensus choice functions; several classes of consensus functions; criteria for susceptibility to consensus for conflict profiles; criterion for quality of consensus and method for improving the quality; relationships between criteria for susceptibility to consensus and consistency values of conflict profiles; methods for achieving susceptibility to consensus for conflict profiles; and methods for reducing the number of consensuses. We have defined two notions for evaluating a consensus and a profile: consensus quality and susceptibility to consensus. As has been shown, along with the notion of profile consistency, these three notions are independent of each other. Some of these notions have been presented in our earlier publications. However, in this chapter a deeper analysis has been done, and a number of new and original results have been presented.

The tools proposed here should give a general image for solving consensus tasks and should enable someone to make a decision as to which consensus choice function should be applied to a concrete practical situation.

In the next chapters we deal with concrete microstructures of universe U.

4. Model for Knowledge Integration

This chapter presents the aspect of knowledge inconsistency in the integration process. It is natural that in the knowledge integration process resolving inconsistency is needed because the knowledge may originate from different sources. We propose a model for knowledge integration and show the placement of the inconsistency aspect in the integration process.

4.1. Introduction

One of the fundamental challenges for artificial intelligence is developing methods to enable cooperation between autonomous and intelligent systems. One of the necessary conditions for successful cooperation is the consistency of knowledge of these systems. Knowledge integration is the task of creating a new piece of knowledge on the basis of other different pieces of knowledge. This task is very often required because of the autonomy of the systems and nondeterministic mechanisms for knowledge processing which may cause the appearance of such situations that knowledge about the same real world may be reflected differently in different systems. This task is difficult because it is hard to indicate the inconsistency of knowledge as well as to reconcile the inconsistency. However, without solving this problem cooperation between the systems is not possible.

In multiagent environments the knowledge integration task has an essential meaning because cooperation is one of the main elements in agent functioning. The realization of this task is needed for the following reasons:

- A new agent has to be created on the basis of some other agents and has to take over the functions of these agents.
- Several agents want to cooperate for realizing a common task.

In both cases one should pay particular attention to knowledge integration because it is well known that having inconsistent knowledge, the agents may disturb each other instead of co-operating. Figure 4.1 presents a general scheme for the knowledge integration process.

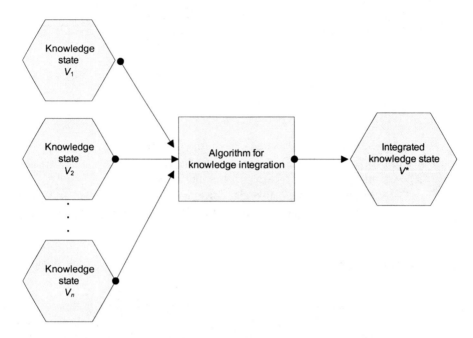

Figure 4.1. The general scheme for knowledge integration.

Reimer [139] has considered knowledge integration processes in two aspects: integration of different knowledge bases and integration of different knowledge representations but on different levels of representation. Apart from the above-mentioned aspects of knowledge integration other authors consider this task necessary in identifying how new and prior knowledge interact while incorporating new information into a knowledge base [93].

The subject of this chapter is to present a consensus-based model for knowledge integration. It is obvious that the inconsistency which may take place during an integration process should be considered as referring to the distribution aspect. Therefore, the consensus tool is useful here for solving inconsistency of knowledge. In this model we define a relational structure for representing the knowledge being integrated. Next the conditions for integration results are specified, and integration algorithms are worked out. Our original contributions consist of new algorithms for knowledge integration as well as a proposal for structures of different kinds of agent knowledge.

This chapter is organized as follows. Section 4.2 presents a general model of knowledge integration. We define a formal problem of integration, a set of postulates for this process, and some results of their analysis. In Section 4.3 a concrete integration task is formulated and solved which refers to knowledge integration in a multiagent environment. Section 4.4 includes postulates for the integration process and their analysis. In Section 4.5 algorithms for integration are presented. Finally some conclusions are included in Section 4.6.

4.2. A General Model for Knowledge Integration

4.2.1. Basis Notions

For representing agent knowledge conflict an approach based on using relational structures has been presented in [104, 105]. In this chapter we use some notions defined in those works. On their basis two kinds of knowledge (positive and negative) can be represented.

Formally, we assume that a real world is described by means of the following elements:

- A finite set A of attributes.
- Each attribute $a \in A$ has a *domain* as a set V_a of elementary values. A value of attribute a may be a subset of V_a as well as some element of V_a. Set 2^{V_a} is called the *super domain* of attribute a. Letting

$$V = \bigcup_{a \in A} V_a,$$

the real world can then be denoted by the pair (A, V).

For $B \subseteq A$ let's denote

$$V_B = \bigcup_{b \in B} V_b$$

and

$$\overline{2}^{V_B} = \bigcup_{b \in B} 2^{V_a}.$$

By an elementary value we mean a value which is not divisible in the system. Thus it is a relative notion; for example, one can assume the following values to be elementary: time units, set of numbers, partitions of a set, and so on.

We define the following notions. Let $T \subseteq A$.

- A *complex tuple* (or *tuple* for short) of type T is a function

$$r: T \to \overline{2}^{V_T}$$

such that $r(a) \subseteq V_a$ for all $a \in T$. Instead of $r(a)$ we write r_a and a tuple of type T is written as r_T.

The set of all tuples of type T is denoted by $TUPLE(T)$.

For example, let

$$T = \{a, b\},$$
$$V_a = \{0, 1, 2\},$$
$$V_b = \{+, -\}.$$

Some tuples of type $\{a, b\}$ are the following,

a	b
$\{1\}$	$\varnothing$
$\{0, 2\}$	$\{+, -\}$

A tuple r of type T may be written as a set:

$$r = \{(a, r_a): a \in T\}.$$

- An *elementary tuple* of type T is a function

$$r: T \rightarrow V_T$$

such that $r(a) \in V_a$ for all $a \in T$. If $V_a = \varnothing$ then $r(a) = \varepsilon$, where symbol ε represents a special value used for the case when the domain is empty. The set of all elementary tuples of type T is denoted by $E\text{-}TUPLE(T)$.

For example, for $A = \{a, b, c\}$, $V_a = \{0, 1, 2\}$, $V_b = \{+, -\}$ and $V_c = \varnothing$, some elementary tuples of type $\{a, b, c\}$ are the following.

a	b	c
1	+	ε
2	−	ε

An elementary tuple r of type T may also be written as a set:

$$r = \{(a, r_a): a \in T\}.$$

- By symbol ϕ we denote the set of all empty tuples, that is, all of whose values are empty. By symbol ϕ_E we denote the set of all empty elementary tuples, that is, all of whose values are equal to ε.
- By symbol θ we denote the set of all partly empty tuples, that is, where at least one value is empty. Expression $r \in \theta$ means that in tuple r at

least one attribute value is empty and expression $r \notin \theta$ means that in tuple r all attribute values are not empty. Of course we have $\phi \subset \theta$. By symbol θ_E we denote the set of all partly empty elementary tuples.

- The sum of two tuples r and r' of type T is a tuple r'' of type T such that $r''_a = r_a \cup r'_a$ for each $a \in T$. This operation is written as

$$r'' = r \cup r'.$$

More generally, a sum of two tuples r and r' of types T and T', respectively, is a tuple r'' of type $T'' = T \cup T'$ such that

$$r'' = \begin{cases} r_t \cup r_{t'} & \text{for } t \in T \cap T' \\ r_t & \text{for } t \in T \setminus T' \\ r_{t'} & \text{for } t \in T' \setminus T \end{cases}.$$

- The product of two tuples r and r' of type T is also a tuple r'' of type T such that $r''_a = r_a \cap r'_a$ for each $t \in T$. This operation is written as

$$r'' = r \cap r'.$$

More generally, a product of two tuples r and r' of types T and T', respectively, is a tuple r'' of type $T'' = T \cap T'$ such that $r''_t = r_t \cap r'_t$ for each $t \in T \cap T'$. This is written as:

$$r'' = r \cap r'.$$

- Let $r \in TUPLE(T)$ and $r' \in TUPLE(T)$ where $T \subseteq T'$; we say that tuple r is included in tuple r', if and only if $r_a \subseteq r'_a$ for each $a \in T$. This relation is written as

$$r \prec r'.$$

The idea for multivalue structures was initiated by Lipski [79] and Pawlak [132] for representing uncertainty of knowledge. The usefulness of this kind of structure in logics has been proved in [7].

4.2.2. Distance Functions between Attribute Values

In this section we deal with the way to measure the distance between attribute values in complex tuples. A distance is measured between two values of the same attribute.

Let $a \in A$ be an attribute; as the distance function for values of attribute a we understand a function:

$$d_a : 2^{V_a} \times 2^{V_a} \to [0, 1].$$

The original conception of this function has been presented in [105]. In this work two distance functions have been defined. Here we introduce their definitions with some modification and improvement.

We assume that V_a is a finite set, and let $card(V_a) = N$.

4.2.2.1. Functions Minimizing Transformation Costs

The general idea of this function relies on determining the distance between two sets as the minimal cost needed for transformation of one set into the other. A set X is transformed into a set Y by means of such operations as *Adding*, *Removing*, and *Transformation* which are used referring to the elements of set X, so that in the result set Y is obtained. We define the following cost functions:

- Function E_{AR}

$$E_{AR}: V_a \to [0, 1]$$

specifies the cost for adding (or removing) an elementary value to (or from) a set.

- Function E_T

$$E_T: V_a \times V_a \to [0, 1]$$

specifies the cost for transformation of one elementary value into another.

For functions E_{AR} and E_T we accept the following assumptions:

1. Function E_T is a metric; that is, for any $x, y, z \in V_a$ the following conditions are held:

$$E_T(x,y) \geq k0 \text{ and } E_T(x,y) = 0 \text{ iff } x = y.$$

$$E_T(x,y) = E_T(y,x).$$

$$E_T(x,y) + E_T(y,z) \geq E_T(x,z).$$

2. For any $x, y \in V_a$ there should be

$$\left| E_{AR}(x) - E_{AR}(y) \right| \leq E_T(x,y) \leq E_{AR}(x) + E_{AR}(y).$$

Condition (1) is natural because function E_T may be treated as a distance function between the elements from set V_a. For condition (2) notice that its first inequality is equivalent to the following inequalities,

$$E_{AR}(y) \le E_T(x,y) + E_{AR}(x),$$

and

$$E_{AR}(x) \le E_T(x,y) + E_{AR}(y).$$

The intuition of the first inequality is based on seeing that the minimal cost for transforming set $\{x\}$ into set $\{x, y\}$ where $x, y \in V_a$ can be achieved by adding element y to set $\{x\}$. The cost needed for this operation is equal to $E_{AR}(y)$ and should not be greater than the cost for transforming element x into element y and next adding element x. For the second inequality one can justify similarly. The second inequality of condition (2) requires that the cost of transformation of one elementary value into another should not be greater than the sum of removing the cost of the first element and adding the cost of the second. The intuition is that if one wants to transform set $\{x\}$ into set $\{y\}$ then generally the cost is not minimal if one removes x from set $\{x\}$ and next adds y to it.

Notice that we do not propose a concrete form of functions E_{AR} and E_T. This is possible if the structure of elementary values belonging to set V_a is known. Below we give an example.

Example 4.1. Let V_a be the set of all partitions of set

$$X = \{1, 2, 3\}.$$

We assume that the cost of adding (or removing) a partition is 1, and the cost of transforming a partition into another is defined according to the conception of Day in [34] and is equal to the minimal normalized number of elements which need to be moved from one class to another class. For example, the cost for transforming partition $\{\{1,2\}, \{3\}\}$ into partition $\{\{1,3\}, \{2\}\}$ is equal to $\tfrac{2}{3}$. Thus if we have two sets of partitions:

$$X = \big\{\{1,2\}, \{3\}\big\}, \{\{1,3\}, \{2\}\},$$

and

$$Y = \big\{\{1,2,3\}\big\},$$

then the minimal cost for transforming set X into set Y is equal to the costs for transformation of the partitions in set X into the partition in set Y, for which the sum is equal to $\tfrac{1}{3} + \tfrac{1}{3} = \tfrac{2}{3}$. ◆

Definition 4.1.
By distance function minimizing the transformation cost we understand the function:

$$\delta_a: 2^{V_a} \times 2^{V_a} \to [0,1]$$

which for a pair of sets X, $Y \subseteq V_a$ assigns a number

$$\delta_a(X,Y) = \frac{T(X,Y)}{\sum_{x \in V_a} E_{AR}(x)},$$

where $T(X,Y)$ represents the minimal cost needed for transforming set X into set Y.

Note that δ_a in fact is not a concrete distance function, but represents a class of distance functions. To this class belong many distance functions defined in other works, for example, the distance function between equivalence relations [34], between ordered partitions and coverings [31, 32], between semilattices [88], and between n-trees [35].

The following remark is directly implied from Definition 4.1.

Remark 4.1. *The following properties are true for any X, $Y \subseteq V_a$.*

(a) $\delta_a(X,Y) = \delta_a(X \backslash Y,\ Y \backslash X)$.

(b) $\delta_a(X,Y) = \delta_a(V_a \backslash X,\ V_a \backslash Y)$.

(c) $\delta_a(X,Y) \leq 1$, *the equality occurs iff* $(X = \varnothing \wedge Y = V_a)$ *or*
       $(Y = \varnothing \wedge X = V_a)$.

(d)   *Function δ_a is a metric.*

The above remark shows that elements belonging simultaneously to two sets X and Y do not have any shares in the distance between them (*a*), the distance between two sets is equal to the distance between their complements (*b*), the definition of distance function is correct referring to the normalization (*c*), and this function is really suitable for distance measures (*d*).

4.2.2.2. Functions Reflecting Element Shares in the Distance

This kind of function is based on determining the value of shares of each element of set V_a in the distance between two subsets of this set. Of course, the share of an element depends on the sets between which the distance is measured.

Let $a \in A$; we define the three-argument share function:

$$S_a: 2^{V_a} \times 2^{V_a} \times V_a \to [0, 1]$$

such that value $S_a(X,Y,z)$ represents the share of element z in the distance between two sets X and Y.

We accept the following assumptions for function S_a.

For any $X, Y, Z \subseteq V_a$:

$$\forall z \in X \div Y: S_a(X,Y,z) = 1/N,$$

$$\forall z \in X \cap Y: S_a(X,Y,z) = 0,$$

$$\forall z \in V_a \setminus (X \cup Y): S_a(X,Y,z) \leq 1/N,$$

$$\forall z \in V_a: (X = Y) \Rightarrow (S_a(X,Y,z) = 0),$$

$$\forall z \in V_a: S(X,Y,z) = S_a(Y,X,z),$$

$$\forall z \in V_a: S_a(X,Y,z) + S_a(Y,Z,z) \geq S_a(X,Z,z).$$

The first three conditions require that the share of a value z belonging to only one of sets X and Y is equal to $1/N$; if z belong to both sets then the share is 0 and for z being outside sets X and Y the share should not be larger than for an element being in $X \div Y$. The next three conditions require function S_a to be reflexive, symmetric, and transitive referring to its first two arguments. It is worthwhile to note that the above conditions are coherent; that means a function S_a fulfilling all of them always exists. The remark below shows some property of function S_a. Its proof should be implied directly by the conditions for function S_a.

Remark 4.2.
For any $X, X', Y, Y' \subseteq V_a$ the following dependency is true:

If $X \cup Y = X' \cup Y' = V_a$ and $X \cap Y \subseteq X' \cap Y'$ then
$$S_a(X,Y,z) \geq S_a(X',Y',z) \text{ for each } z \in V_a.$$

The distance between two sets should now be defined as the sum of contributions of elementary values referring to these sets, by means of the following function,

$$\rho_a: 2^{V_a} \times 2^{V_a} \to [0,1].$$

Definition 4.2.
For any sets $X, Y \subseteq V_a$ their distance $\rho_a(X,Y)$ is equal to

$$\rho_a(X,Y) = \frac{N}{2N-1} \sum_{z \in V_a} S_a(X,Y,z).$$

From Definition 4.2 and the properties of function S it is easy to prove the following properties which also justify the form of this function.

Remark 4.3.
For any $X, X', Y, Y' \subseteq V_a$:

(a)   If $(X \cup Y = X' \cup Y' = V_a)$ and $(X \cap Y \subseteq X' \cap Y')$ then
$$\rho_a(X,Y) \geq \rho_a(X',Y').$$

(b) $\rho_a(X,Y) \geq \dfrac{card(X \div Y)}{N(2N-1)}.$

(c)   Function ρ_a is a metric.

A distance function of this kind should be useful for such a structure of set V_a, where relations between its elements occur. Such relations may be, for example, linear or partial orders. For the first kind of the structures nine Condorcet choice functions were presented and analyzed [46].

Example 4.2.
Let V_a be the collection of some elementary values. Distance function

$$\gamma(X_1,X_2) = \frac{1}{card(V_a)} card(X_1 \div X_2)$$

for $X_1, X_2 \subseteq V_a$ is an example of function ρ_a.   ◆

Notice that the above definitions determine large classes of functions δ_a and ρ_a. Below we present two groups of these functions, each of them is characterized by one of the following properties.

Definition 4.3.
(a)   Function $\partial \in \{\delta_a, \rho_a\}$ is proportional (P) iff the following depend-ency is true for any $X, X', Y, Y' \subseteq V_a$,

$$(X \div Y \subseteq X' \div Y') \Rightarrow (\partial(X,Y) \leq \partial(X',Y')),$$

(b)   Function $\partial \in \{\delta_a, \rho_a\}$ is quasi-proportional (QP) iff for any $X, X', Y, Y' \subseteq V_a$:

$$(X \cup Y = X' \cup Y' \wedge X \div Y \subseteq X' \div Y') \Rightarrow (\partial(X,Y) \leq \partial(X',Y')).$$

The idea of proportional functions is based on the condition that the larger the symmetric difference between two sets is, the greater their dis-tance. This condition is intuitive because the elements belonging to the symmetric difference should have the largest share. It also means that other elements may have a share greater than zero, but the shares of elements belonging to the symmetric difference are decisive for the dis-tance. The idea of functions from the second group is based on the same condition as in the first group with a requirement that the sum of sets X and Y is constant.

We denote proportional functions ρ_a and δ_a by symbols ρ_a^P and δ_a^P, and quasi-proportional functions ρ_a and δ_a by symbols ρ_a^{QP} and δ_a^{QP}, respectively. We have the following property.

Theorem 4.1.
The following dependencies are true for all $X, X', Y, Y' \subseteq V_a$.

(a) Conditions P and QP are equivalent for functions δ_a.

(b) Function δ_a is proportional iff $E_T(x,y) = E_{AR}(x) + E_{AR}(y)$ for all $x, y \in V_a$.

(c) $\rho_a^P(X,Y) = \dfrac{card(X \div Y)}{N(2N-1)}.$

(d) Function ρ_a^P is also quasi-proportional.

(e) $(X \div Y = X' \div Y') \Rightarrow (\partial(X,Y) = \partial(X',Y'))$ *for* $\partial \in \{\rho_a^P, \delta_a^P, \delta_a^{QP}\}.$

(f) $(X \cup Y = X' \cup Y' \wedge X \div Y = X' \div Y') \Rightarrow (\rho_a^{QP}(X,Y) = \rho_a^{QP}(X',Y')).$

Proof.

(*a*) We show that function δ_a^P is also quasi-proportional and function δ_a^{QP} is also proportional. The first statement is obvious. For the second statement assume that $X \div Y \supseteq X' \div Y'$. Denote $C = X \backslash Y, D = Y \backslash X, C = X' \backslash Y'$ and $D' = Y' \backslash X'$. Note that

$$X \div Y = C \div D = C \cup D \quad \text{and} \quad X' \div Y' = C' \div D' = C' \cup D',$$

thus we have

$$\delta_a(X,Y) = \delta_a(C,D) \quad \text{and} \quad \delta_a(X',Y') = \delta_a(C',D').$$

Denote

$$E = (C \cup D) \backslash (C'' \cup D'), C'' = C' \cup E \quad \text{and} \quad D'' = D' \cup E,$$

dependencies

$$C'' \cup D'' = C \cup D \quad \text{and} \quad C \div D \supseteq C'' \div D''$$

should be true. Because function δ_a is quasi-proportional, so

$$\delta_a(C,D) \geq \delta(C'',D'').$$

Also, we have

$$\delta_a(C',D') = \delta_a(C'',D'');$$

then

$$\delta_a(C,D) \geq \delta_a(C',D');$$

that is,

$$\delta_a(X,Y) \geq \delta_a(X',Y').$$

It then implies that quasi-proportional function δ_a is also proportional.

(b) $\Rightarrow$) Let function δ_a be proportional and let

$$X = \{x\}, \quad Y = \{y\}, \qquad X' = \{x, y\}, \qquad Y' = \varnothing;$$

then we have

$$\delta_a(X,Y) = \delta_a(X',Y') \quad \text{because } X \div Y = X' \div Y'.$$

Apart from this we have

$$\delta_a(X,Y) = E_T(x,y) \quad \text{and} \quad \delta_a(X',Y') = E_{AR}(x) + E_{AR}(y),$$

so

$$E_T(x,y) = E_{AR}(x) + E_{AR}(y).$$

$\Leftarrow$) Let for any $x, y \in V_a$ dependence

$$E_T(x,y) = E_{AR}(x) + E_{AR}(y)$$

follow, and let

$$X \div Y \supseteq X' \div Y',$$

then

$$\delta_a(X,Y) = \sum_{x \in X \div Y} E_{AR}(x) \geq \sum_{x \in X' \div Y'} E_{AR}(x) = \delta_a(X',Y').$$

(c) Let

$$w_a = \frac{1}{N(2N-1)}.$$

Notice that because function ρ is a metric we have the following,

$$\rho_a^P(X,Y) \leq \rho_a^P(X \cup Y,X) + \rho_a^P(X \cup Y,Y).$$

From $X \cup Y \supseteq X$ and $X \cup Y \supseteq Y$ is implied

$$\rho_a^P(X \cup Y,X) = w_a \cdot card((X \cup Y) \div Y) = w_a \cdot card(X \setminus Y),$$

and

$$\rho_a^P(X \cup Y,Y) = w_a \cdot card(Y \setminus X),$$

thus

$$\rho_a^P(X,Y) \leq w_a \cdot card(X \setminus Y) + w_a \cdot card(Y \setminus X) = w_a \cdot card(X \div Y).$$

Also one can easily prove that

$$w_a \cdot card(X \div Y) \leq \rho_a^P(X,Y),$$

so

$$\rho_a^P(X,Y) = w_a \cdot card(X \div Y) = \frac{card(X \div Y)}{N(2N-1)}.$$

(*d*) The proof is implied directly from conditions (*P*) and (*QP*).

(*e*) and (*f*) The proof is obvious.   ♦

Theorem 4.1 shows important properties of proportional and quasi-proportional functions and relationships between them.

4.3. Knowledge Integration Problem

We assume that some real world is commonly shared by several agents that function in a distributed environment. Their states of knowledge may refer to the same elements of the real world as well as to its various elements. A knowledge state of an agent is represented by a tuple of some type. Assume that the agents want to integrate their knowledge. We define the problem of knowledge integration as follows.

Given a conflict profile

$$X = \{r_i \in TUPLE(T_i): T_i \subseteq A \text{ for } i = 1, 2, \ldots, n\}$$

one should determine a tuple r^* of type $T^* \subseteq A$ which best represents the given tuples.

Tuple r^* is called an integration of profile *X*.

Notice that the integration problem is different from a consensus problem in that there is no assumption that the tuples representing the agent knowledge states are of the same type, as in the consensus problem [104].

The following example should illustrate this problem.

Example 4.3. Consider a meteorological distributed system in which the sites are meteorological stations in different places of a region. Each station uses an agent whose task consists in monitoring the weather phenomena occurring in his subregions and determining the weather forecast for the next day. Assume that the forecasts refer to the occurrences of such phenomena as air pressure, rainfall, snow, sunshine, temperature, and wind. The elements of the real world are the following:

- A = {*Pressure, Wind_Direction, Wind_Speed, Temperature, Rain, Sunshine, Snow*}.
- $V_{Pressure}$ = set of integers representing air pressure measured in unit hPa.
- $V_{Wind\_Direction}$ = {W, E, S, N, W–S, W–N, E–N, E–S}.
- V_{Wind_Speed} = set of integers representing speeds of wind measured in unit m/s.
- $V_{Temperature}$ = set of integers representing Celsius degrees.
- V_{Rain} = {Yes, No}.
- $V_{Sunshine}$ = {Yes, No}.
- V_{Snow} = {Yes, No}.

The knowledge states of six agents are presented as follows.

Agent	1	2	3	4	5	6
Pressure	990–995		990–997	992–999	993–997	992–998
Wind_ Direction	{W, W–N}	{E, E–N}	{S, W–S}	{S, W–S}	{W–N}	∅
Wind_ Speed	10–12	5–10	20–30	40–50	0–10	
Tempera- ture	15–25	20–24	12–21	12–21	22–24	17–20
Rain	No	Yes	No	No	Yes	Yes
Sunshine	No	No	No	No	Yes	No
Snow	Yes	No				Yes

◆

We accept the following interpretations:

- If referring to an attribute a an agent gives value $v \subseteq V_a$ as a set of elementary values, then this fact is interpreted that in the opinion of the agent the proper value should be included in set v. In the above example, one of agents has assigned to attribute *Temperature* value 12–20 meaning that the proper temperature for the next day, in her opinion, should not be lower than 12 and should not be higher than

20 Celsius degrees. In this sense it follows that in the opinion of the agent the proper value should not be included in set $V_a\backslash v$. Thus set $V_a\backslash v$ may be treated as the negative knowledge of the agent.

- The empty windows referring to some attribute in the above table mean that the agents have not dealt with this parameter and they have no opinions on this matter. If an attribute has no value in a tuple then we define it as *indefinite* in this tuple. Otherwise the attribute has a *definite* value.

- Empty value (denoted by symbol $\emptyset$) of an attribute means that in the opinion of the agent this attribute has no value. In the above example, one of the agents assigns to attribute *Wind_Direction* the empty value meaning that in his opinion there will not be any wind in the region.

4.4. Postulates for Knowledge Integration

In order to integrate different states of knowledge coming from different sources, some rational premises (postulates) must be proposed. These postulates are used in order to verify the fulfillment of minimal requirements to initialize the process of knowledge integration and then to find an agreement of inconsistent or incomplete data related to the same objects in the case of conflicts.

P_1. *Closure of knowledge – 1*
The type of the integration should be included in the sum of types of the profile elements; that is,

$$T^* \subseteq \bigcup_{i=1}^{n} T_i .$$

P_2. *Closure of knowledge – 2*
The integration should be included in the sum of profile elements; that is,

$$r^* \prec \bigcup_{i=1}^{n} r_i .$$

P_3. *Consistency of knowledge*
The common part of profile elements should be included in the integration; that is,

$$\bigcap_{i=1}^{n} r_i \prec r^*.$$

P_4. *Superiority of knowledge – 1*

For each attribute $a \in T^*$ value r^*_a depends only on definite values from

$$\{r_{ia}: i = 1, 2, \ldots, n\}.$$

P_5. *Superiority of knowledge – 2*

If sets of attributes T_i ($i = 1, 2, \ldots, n$) are disjoint with each other then

$$r^* = \left[\bigcup_{i=1}^{n} r_i\right]_{T^*},$$

where $\left[\bigcup_{i=1}^{n} r_i\right]_{T^*}$ is the sum $\bigcup_{i=1}^{n} r_i$ restricted to attributes from set T^*.

P_6. *Maximal similarity*

Let d_a be a function measuring the distance between values of attribute $a \in A$ then the difference between integration r^* and the profile elements should be minimal in the sense that for each $a \in T^*$ the sum

$$\sum_{r \in Z_a} d(r^*_a, r),$$

where

$$Z_a = \{r_{ia}: r_{ia} \text{ is definite}, i = 1, 2, \ldots, n\}$$

should be minimal.

Below we give some comments on these postulates.

- Postulate P_1 requires the integration to have such a type T^* that does not exceed the types of the given tuples. This requirement is natural because if an attribute is not a subject of interest of any source than it should not be reflected in the integration. Thus in some sense this postulate expresses the closure of knowledge.
- According to postulate P_2 the integration should not "surprise" in the sense that the values appearing in the integration should be included in the profile elements. This is a strong requirement for knowledge closure.
- Postulate P_3 is similar to the Pareto criterion for consensus choice; that is, if all agents or experts have some common opinion then this opin-

ion should occur in the integration. In other words, the integration should be consistent with knowledge from the sources.

- According to postulate P_4 the basis for determining the value for attribute a in the integration should consist only of definite values from set $\{r_{ia}: i = 1, 2, \ldots, n\}$. This means that if an agent's knowledge state does not refer to the subject represented by attribute a then she does not have any influence on the integration referring to this subject. Thus if only one agent has been involved in the subject, then only her opinion decides about the integration on this matter. This is then the condition for superiority of knowledge.

- Postulate P_5 also expresses a condition for superiority of knowledge. This means if the subjects covered by agents have nothing in common, then the integration should consist of all their opinions. This postulate is very useful when the scopes of agents' interest are disjoint; then their knowledge should be fully honored in the integration result.

- Postulate P_6 is a standard condition for consensus choice and should be useful for integration determining. This criterion is very natural and popular in consensus determining. Its justification is based on the requirement that the integration should best represent the given opinions of the agents, thus it should minimally differ from these opinions. This criterion mentions the criterion O_1 defined in Chapter 3.

The fact that integration r^* satisfies a postulate P_i is represented by expression

$$r^* \vdash P_i.$$

Now we present some properties of these postulates.

Theorem 4.2.
Postulates $P_1, P_2, \ldots, P_6$ are not consistent in the sense that not for each profile an integration satisfying all postulates exists.

Proof.
For the proof we should show a profile for which no integration satisfying all postulates exists. For this purpose we define a simple profile X where all tuples have the same 1-attribute type, for which the domain is set $\Re \times \Re$ where $\Re$ is the set of real numbers. Let then the tuples belonging to profile X be as follows.

$$X = \{(a, \{(0,1)\}), (a, \{(1,0)\}), (a, \{(0,0)\}), (a, \{(1,1)\})\}.$$

As the distance function between these sets of points on the plane accept the Euclidean distance function. If we use postulate P_6 for integration determination then it is easy to show that r^* may not be one of the profile elements, but should be $r^* = (a, \{(0.5, 0.5)\})$. Thus postulate P_2 is not satisfied.   ◆

Theorem 4.2 implies that the defined postulates in general are not coherent. This is an advantage rather than a disadvantage because this property means that the postulates are not dependent on themselves. However, as shown in Theorem 4.3 below, by using some distance functions these postulates may be consistent.

Theorem 4.3.
If distance functions of type ρ or proportional distance functions of type δ are used then satisfying postulates P_1 and P_6 should imply satisfying postulates P_2, P_3, P_4, and P_5; that is,

$$((r^* \,|{-}\, P_1) \wedge (r^* \,|{-}\, P_6)) \Rightarrow$$
$$((r^* \,|{-}\, P_2) \wedge (r^* \,|{-}\, P_3) \wedge (r^* \,|{-}\, P_4) \wedge (r^* \,|{-}\, P_5)).$$

Proof.
A brief proof of the theorem is presented as follows. Let X be a profile

$$X = \{r_i \in TUPLE(T_i): T_i \subseteq A \text{ for } i = 1, 2, \ldots, n\}$$

and r^* be its integration satisfying postulates P_1 and P_6 using distance functions of type ρ or proportional distance functions of type δ. We show that r^* should also satisfy the remaining postulates.

(a) For postulate P_2 assume that it is not satisfied. This means that there exists an attribute $a \in T^*$ and an element $x \in V_a$ such that $x \in r^*_a$ but $x \notin \bigcup_{i=1}^{n} r_i$. Let $r^{*\prime}_a = r^*_a \backslash \{x\}$; using distance functions of type ρ or proportional distance functions of type δ we have:

$$d_a(r^*_a, r_a) > d_a(r^{*\prime}_a, r_a)$$

for each $a \in T^*$. Thus r^* could not satisfy postulate P_6.

(b) For postulate P_3 similarly we assume that it is not satisfied. There exist an attribute $a \in T^*$ and an element $x \in V_a$ such that $x \in \bigcap_{i=1}^{n} r_i$ but $x \notin r^*_a$. Let then $r^{*\prime}_a = r^*_a \cup \{x\}$; using distance functions of type ρ or proportional distance functions of type δ we have:

$$d_a(r^*_a, r_a) > d_a(r^{*\prime}_a, r_a)$$

for each $a \in T^*$. Thus r^* could not satisfy postulate P_6.

(c) Satisfaction of postulate P_4 follows directly from the satisfaction of postulate P_6.

(d) For postulate P_5 notice that if sets of attributes T_i ($i = 1,2, \ldots, n$) are disjoint from each other then for each $a \in T^*$ set

$$Z_a = \{r_{ia} : i \in \{1,2, \ldots, n\} \text{ and } r_{ia} \text{ is definite}\}$$

has exactly one element. Because postulate P_6 is satisfied, this element should be equal to the value of integration referring to attribute a, that is, r^*_a. Notice that because sets T_i are disjoint with each other, sum $\bigcup_{i=1}^{n} r_i$ is simply a tuple of type $\bigcup_{i=1}^{n} T_i$. Thus after making its restriction to attributes belonging to set T^* we should have the integration. That is, postulate P_5 is also satisfied. ◆

Theorem 4.3 is an important property of postulates P_6 and P_1. As stated above, postulate P_6 is very popular and has been proved to be useful in practical applications for inconsistency situations. It turned out in this case that with using some kinds of distance functions if an integration satisfies this postulate and postulate P_1 then the remaining postulates characteristic of the knowledge integration process are also satisfied. Thus with using a proper distance function it is possible to determine an integration r^* which satisfies all postulates simultaneously.

Notice, however, that if the distance function is not of type ρ or proportional distance functions of type δ then Theorem 4.3 is not true. An example is included in the proof of Theorem 4.2 where the distance function between points on the Euclidean plane is of type δ, but it is not propositional. Therefore, postulate P_2 is not satisfied. Below we show that in general satisfying postulates P_1 and P_6 should imply satisfying postulates P_3, P_4, and P_5.

Theorem 4.4.
If distance functions of type ρ or δ are used then satisfying postulates P_1 and P_6 should imply satisfying postulates P_3, P_4, and P_5; that is,

$$\big((r^* \,|\!- P_1) \wedge (r^* \,|\!- P_6)\big) \Rightarrow \big((r^* \,|\!- P_3) \wedge (r^* \,|\!- P_4) \wedge (r^* \,|\!- P_5)\big).$$

Proof.
For the proof of this theorem we can use paragraphs (b) through (d) of the proof of Theorem 4.3, noting that in these paragraphs the assumption of proposition has not been used . ◆

As shown in Chapter 3, criterion O_2 also has very important properties and could be useful for integration determining. However, in many cases of distance functions criterion O_2 causes higher complexity of the algorithm for determining the integration. But in some cases using criterion O_1 causes higher complexity than O_2. Therefore we propose to consider using criterion O_1 or O_2 when applying postulate P_6 to achieve the effectiveness of the integration procedure.

4.5. Algorithms for Integration

As shown in Theorems 4.3 and 4.4, by using distance functions of type ρ or proportional distance functions of type δ for a given profile it is possible to determine an integration which satisfies all postulates simultaneously and in the general case we would have all postulates satisfied except postulate P_2. Therefore, it is very important to determine such an integration which satisfies postulates P_1 and P_6.

Below we present an algorithm for integration. The idea of this algorithm is based on determining subprofiles for attributes and next for each subprofile determining its integration.

Algorithm 4.1.

Input: Profile

$$X = \{r_i \in TUPLE(T_i): T_i \subseteq A \text{ for } i = 1, 2, \ldots, n\}$$

and distance functions σ_a for attributes $a \in A$.

Output: Tuple r^* of type $T^* \subseteq A$ which is the integration of tuples from X.

Procedure:

BEGIN

1. Set $A = \bigcup\limits_{i=1}^{n} T_i$;

2. For each $a \in A$ determine a set with repetitions

$$X_a = \{r_{ia}: r_i \subseteq X \text{ for } i = 1, 2, \ldots, n\};$$

3. For each $a \in A$ using distance function σ_a determine a value v_a such that

$$\sum_{i=1}^{n} \sigma_a(v_a, r_{ia}) = \min_{v'_a \subseteq V_a} \sigma_a(v'_a, r_{ia}) ;$$

4. Create tuple r^* consisting of values v_a for all $a \in A$;
END.

The most important step in the above algorithm is step 3 which for each subprofile determines its integration satisfying postulate P_6. The integration problem of this type has been formulated and analyzed in [104]. In that work a set of postulates for integration has been defined, and algorithms for its determining have been worked out. Therefore, these algorithms could be used for this case and we would like to encourage the reader to refer to the above-mentioned work.

As stated above, in general all postulates cannot be satisfied. Therefore, it is only possible to achieve a partial satisfaction of these postulates. Concretely, as follows from the proof of Theorem 4.4, the partial satisfaction refers to postulate P_6. For this purpose we can modify Algorithm 4.1 by changing step 3 as follows.

For each $a \in A$ using distance function σ_a determine a value v_a such that

$$\sum_{i=1}^{n} \sigma_a(v_a, r_{ia}) = \min_{v'_a \subseteq W_a} \sigma_a(v'_a, r_{ia}),$$

where

$$W_a = \bigcup_{i=1}^{n} r_{ia}.$$

Owing to this step postulate P_2 should be satisfied but postulate P_6 is satisfied only partially. The advantage of this modification is that the complexity of the algorithm decreases owing to the restriction of the space of searching (not whole set 2^{V_a} but only its subset 2^{W_a}).

Example 4.4. Consider the profile given in Example 4.3 where the subprofiles for attributes are the following:

$X_{Pressure} = \{990–995, 990–997, 992–999, 993–997, 992–998\}.$

$X_{Wind\_Direction} = \{\{W, W–N\}, \{E, E–N\}, \{S, W–S\},$
$$\{S, W-S\}, \{W-N\}, \varnothing\}.$$

$X_{Wind\_Speed} = \{10–12, 5–10, 20–30, 40–50, 0–10\}.$

$X_{Temperature} = \{15–25, 20–24, 12–21, 12–21, 22–24, 17–20\}.$

$X_{Rain} = \{No, Yes, No, No, Yes, Yes\}.$

$$X_{Sunshine} = \{No, No, No, No, Yes, No\}.$$

$$X_{Snow} = \{Yes, No, Yes\}.$$

For determining an integration for a subprofile we can use different algorithms for different structures of attribute values. For number intervals several algorithms have been worked out in [100, 102]; for sets of elementary values an algorithm is proposed in [19]. For elementary values, a simple algorithm is proposed in [31].

Thus the integration satisfying postulates P_1 and P_6 for the subprofiles, which create the integration r^*, is the following.

Pressure	Wind_ Direction	Wind_ Speed	Tem-perature	Rain	Sun-shine	Snow
991–997	W	15–22	16–22	{Yes, No}	No	Yes

♦

From the integration algorithm it follows evidently that if all elements of the profile are identical then the result of the integration should be the same.

4.6. Conclusions

In this chapter a general model for knowledge integration is presented. We assume that knowledge states to be integrated are represented by a multi-attribute and multivalue structure. A knowledge state is represented by a tuple of some type. The same structure is used for the result of the integration process. Although in this chapter we use the same structure for representing inconsistency as in work [105], some novel elements have been introduced here. Firstly, the algebra of multiattribute and multivalue tuples allows calculating the sum and the intersection of tuples of different types. Secondly, a profile may consist of tuples of different types, and the postulates reflect this fact. And finally, the proposed algorithms serve to perform the knowledge integration processes, not only for consensus calculation. As mentioned, the algorithms worked in [105] are very useful for integration determining and may be used here in the integration process. In the next chapter we deal with processing inconsistency on the syntactic level.

5. Processing Inconsistency on the Syntactic Level

The purpose of this chapter is to present the problems of knowledge inconsistency resolution and knowledge integration on the syntactic level. Its main contribution consists in the solutions of these problems in the distribution aspect. Here as the structure of inconsistency we use such logic structures as conjunctive and disjunctive. Fuzzy conjunctive structure is also investigated.

5.1. Introduction

Inconsistency of knowledge may appear in many situations, especially in distributed environments in which autonomous programs operate. Inconsistency may lead to conflicts, for which resolution is necessary for the correct functioning of an intelligent system. Inconsistency of knowledge in general means a situation in which some autonomous programs (such as agents) generate different versions (or states) of knowledge on the same subject referring to a real world. In this chapter we propose two logical structures for representing inconsistent knowledge: conjunction and disjunction. For each of them we define the distance function and formulate the consensus problem, the solution of which would resolve the inconsistency. Next, we work out algorithms for consensus determination. Consensus methodology has been proved to be useful in solving conflicts and should be also effective for knowledge inconsistency resolution [98, 99, 101].

We assume that there is given a finite set of agents which work in a distributed environment. The term *agent* is used here in a very general sense: as an agent we may understand an expert or an intelligent and autonomous computer program. An example of such an environment is a multiagent system [44]. We assume that these agents have their own knowledge bases. In general, by a state of agent knowledge we understand a state of the agent knowledge base. Such a state may be treated as a view or opinion of the agent on some subject or matter.

In this chapter we assume that a knowledge state of an agent is represented by a standard logic expression in which an agent expresses his knowledge in the form of a conjunction or a disjunction of literals. A literal is built by a symbol belonging to a given set of symbols (positive literal) or by a symbol with a negation symbol (negative literal) [108].

We assume that a real world can be divided into sets of facts, events, and the like, referring to which agents can give their opinions relying on assigning a given fact or event a logical value (*true* or *false*). We assume also that the set of all facts and events of a real world is finite and it is possible to use a finite set of symbols for their representation.

5.2. Conjunctive Structure of Knowledge

5.2.1. Basic Notions

On the syntactic level we assume that for representing knowledge an agent or expert uses a finite set L of symbols representing the positive logical value (i.e., value *true* in classical logic) referring to concrete events and objects in a real world. A literal is defined as follows.

- Positive literal: A symbol from L, for example, a, b, and so on
- Negative literal: A symbol from L preceded by negation symbol "$\neg$", for example, $\neg a$, $\neg b$, and so on

Each literal may then represent the logic value of an event or an object in the real world: if it is a positive literal then the value is *true* and if it is a negative one, the value is *false*. On this level we do not consider the further interpretation of literal symbols (this is the subject of Chapter 6; here we only assume that different symbols refer to different elements of the real world.

A conjunction of literals (positive or negative) is a logic formula in which literals are connected by symbol of conjunction "$\wedge$". More formally, by a conjunction we understand the following expression:

$$t_1 \wedge t_2 \wedge \cdots \wedge t_k,$$

where $t_i \in L$ or $t_i = \neg t_i'$ where $t_i' \in L$, for $i = 1, 2, \ldots, k$.

A state of agent knowledge is represented by a conjunction. If on some matter an agent gives its opinion as a conjunction

$$t_1 \wedge t_2 \wedge \cdots \wedge t_k$$

then it is interpreted that in the opinion of this agent the facts or events represented by positive literals from $t_1, t_2, \ldots, t_k$ should take place, and those represented by negative literals should not take place. We also accept the interpretation that those facts or events which are not included in the opinion belong to the agent's ignorance. Owing to this interpretation agents or experts must not be assumed to "know everything."

We assume that in a conjunction a symbol may not occur more than once. The reasons are:

- Conjunction

$$t_1 \wedge t_2 \wedge t_3 \wedge \cdots \wedge t_k,$$

where $t_1 = t_2 = t$ for $t \in L$ (symbol t occurs twice), is in the context of classical logic equivalent to conjunction

$$t_1 \wedge t_3 \wedge \cdots \wedge t_k,$$

where symbol t occurs only one time.

- Conjunction

$$t_1 \wedge t_2 \wedge \cdots \wedge t_k,$$

where $t_1 = t$ and $t_2 = \neg t$ for $t \in L$, is equivalent to *false*. Such kind of conjunctions should not appear because we assume that an agent has its own "sensible" opinion on a given subject.

Notice that the order of literals in a conjunction is not important.

By *Conj(L)* we denote the set of all conjunctions with symbols from set *L*. Notice that because of the limitation of set *L* and referring to the above restrictions, set *Conj(L)* is also finite.

Example 5.1. Let's consider a real world consisting of weather forecasts for some region of a country. Let there be a set of agents:

$$Agent = \{a_1, a_2, a_3\},$$

and a set of symbols:

$$L = \{t_1, t_2, t_3, t_4\},$$

which represent the following facts.

- t_1: The temperature in the region will be higher than 0.
- t_2: The region will be sunny.
- t_3: It will snow in the region.
- t_4: The wind will be strong.

For this common subject the agents generate the following set of knowledge states:

Agent	Knowledge State
a_1	$t_1 \wedge \neg\, t_2 \wedge t_4$
a_2	$\neg t_1 \wedge t_3 \wedge t_4$
a_3	$t_2 \wedge \neg t_3 \wedge \neg t_4$

Thus in the opinion of agent a_1 in the considered region the temperature will be higher than 0, but there will be no sunshine and the wind will be strong.   ◆

Notice that in a conjunction x one may distinguish two sets of symbols: the first consists of those symbols in the conjunction which belong to positive literals, and the second consists of the remaining symbols. A conjunction x can be then represented by a pair (x^+, x^-) where x^+ is the set of symbols of positive literals appearing in x and x^- is the set of symbols of negative literals occurring in x. For example, the representation of conjunction

$$x = a \wedge \neg\, b \wedge c$$

for $a, b, c \in L$ is pair (x^+, x^-) where $x^+ = \{a, c\}$ and $x^- = \{b\}$.

Sets x^+ and x^- are called the positive and negative components of the conjunction, respectively.

Definition 5.1.
A conjunction (x^+, x^-) where $x^+, x^- \subseteq L$ is nonconflicting if

$$x^+ \cap x^- = \emptyset.$$

That means a nonconflicting conjunction is not equivalent to *false*. We consider only this kind of conjunctions because they are sensible for agents to express their opinions; a conflicting conjunction (i.e., not nonconflicting) is equivalent to *false* and is not useful for this purpose.[1]

Definition 5.2.
Let $x = (x^+, x^-) \in Conj(L)$ and $x' = (x'^+, x'^-) \in Conj(L)$ be nonconflicting conjunctions. We say that
(a) Conjunction x is inconsistent with conjunction x' if:

$$x^+ \cap x'^- \neq \emptyset \quad \text{or} \quad x'^+ \cap x^- \neq \emptyset.$$

---

[1] In this case one has to deal with the inconsistency in the centralization aspect.

(b) Two nonconflicting conjunctions are sharply inconsistent if they are inconsistent and

$$x^+ \cap x'^+ = \emptyset \quad and \quad x^- \cap x'^- = \emptyset.$$

From condition (*a*) in Definition 5.2 it follows that if conjunction x is inconsistent with conjunction x' then:

$$(x^+ \cup x'^+) \cap (x^- \cup x'^-) \neq \emptyset.$$

Two sharply inconsistent conjunctions do not have any common symbols in their positive and negative components. It is obvious that the consequence of two inconsistent conjunctions is *false*.

More generally, we have the following.

Definition 5.3.
A set of nonconflicting conjunctions

$$X = \{x_i = (x_i^+, x_i^-) \in Conj(L): i = 1, 2, \ldots, n\}$$

is inconsistent if

$$\bigcup_{x \in X} x^+ \cap \bigcup_{x \in X} x^- \neq \emptyset,$$

otherwise it is consistent.

Thus if set X is consistent then conjunction

$$\left(\bigcup_{x \in X} x^+, \bigcup_{x \in X} x^- \right)$$

is a logical consequence of conjunctions from X.

5.2.2. Distance Function between Conjunctions

In this section we define the distance function $d_\wedge$ between conjunctions. This function should help in evaluating the difference between conjunctions. Owing to this function it will be possible to get to know about the inconsistency level of a conflict profile, and in consequence, to determine the consensus for the conflict.

First we need to give the definition of the distance between finite sets.

Definition 5.4.
By the distance between two finite sets X_1, X_2 we understand the following number

$$\eta(X_1, X_2) = \begin{cases} \dfrac{card(X_1 \div X_2)}{card(X_1 \cup X_2)} & for \ \ X_1 \cup X_2 \neq \varnothing \\ 0 & for \ \ X_1 \cup X_2 = \varnothing \end{cases}.$$

Between finite sets there are also other distance functions defined, such as

$$\eta'(X_1, X_2) = card(X_1 \div X_2).$$

This function is a very popular one. However, the advantages of the function η defined in Definition 5.4 are the following.

- Its values are normalized into interval [0, 1]; this is very useful when the number of all elements is not known.
- It distinguishes the component sets in a very clear way: if sets X_1 and X_2 are disjoint and at least one of them is nonempty, then their distance is maximal (i.e., equals 1).

Next we define the distance of two conjunctions x_1 and x_2 as follows.

Definition 5.5.
By the distance between two conjunctions x_1, $x_2 \in Conj(L)$ we understand the following number,

$$d_\wedge(x_1, x_2) = \frac{w_1 \cdot \eta(x_1^+, x_2^+) + w_2 \cdot \eta(x_1^-, x_2^-)}{w_1 + w_2},$$

where

- $\eta(x_1^+, x_2^+)$: *the distance between sets of nonnegated symbols in conjunctions x_1 and x_2.*
- $\eta(x_1^-, x_2^-)$: *the distance between sets of negated symbols in conjunctions x_1 and x_2.*
- w_1 *and* w_2 *are the weights of distances* $\eta(x_1^+, x_2^+)$ *and* $\eta(x_1^-, x_2^-)$ *in distance $d_\wedge(x_1, x_2)$, respectively, which satisfy the conditions:*

$$w_1 + w_2 = 1 \quad and \quad 0 < w_1, w_2 < 1.$$

In a conjunction positive literals can be considered as the positive knowledge of agents, and negative literals are considered as their negative knowledge. Using values w_1 and w_2 we can distinguish the weights of the distances between positive and negative parts of agent knowledge states.

It is obvious that values of function $d_\wedge$ are normalized; that is, they belong to interval [0, 1].

The distance function $d_\wedge$ defined above is of course a metric. Notice also that the distance of two sharply inconsistent conjunctions is always maximal and equal to 1.

5.2.3. Integration Problem and Postulates for Consensus

The integration problem is formulated as follows.

For a given conflict profile of conjunctions

$$X = \{x_i = (x_i^+, x_i^-) \in Conj(L): i = 1, 2, \ldots, n\}.$$

It is necessary to determine a conjunction $x^* \in Conj(L)$ called a consensus of set X.

Notice that a profile X consists of positive profile

$$X^+ = \{x_i^+: i = 1, 2, \ldots, n\}$$

and negative profile

$$X^- = \{x_i^-: i = 1, 2, \ldots, n\}.$$

We now define the following consensus function for profiles of conjunctions.

Definition 5.6.
By a consensus function for profiles of conjunctions we understand a function

$$C: \Pi(Conj(L)) \to 2^{Conj(L)}.$$

which satisfies one or more of the following postulates.
P1. *For each conjunction $(x^{*+}, x^{*-}) \in C(X)$ there should be:*

(a) $\bigcap_{x \in X} x^+ \subseteq x^{*+}$

and

(b) $\bigcap_{x \in X} x^- \subseteq x^{*-}$.

P2. *For each conjunction $(x^{*+}, x^{*-}) \in C(X)$ there should be:*

(a) $x^{*+} \subseteq \bigcup_{x \in X} x^+$

and

(b) $x^{*^-} \subseteq \bigcup_{x \in X} x^-$.

P3. *If profile X is consistent then conjunction*

$$\left(\bigcup_{x \in X} x^+, \bigcup_{x \in X} x^- \right)$$

should be a consensus of X.

P4. *For each conjunction* $(x^{*^+}, x^{*^-}) \in C(X)$ *there should be*:

$$x^{*^+} \cap x^{*^-} = \varnothing$$

P5. *A consensus* $x^* \in C(X)$ *should minimize the sum of distances*:

$$\sum_{x \in X} d_\wedge(x^*, x) = \min_{x' \in Conj(L)} \sum_{x \in X} d_\wedge(x', x).$$

P6. *For each symbol* $z \in L$ *and a consensus* $x^* \in C(X)$ *the form of appearance (i.e., as a positive or negative literal) of z in* x^* *depends only on its forms of appearance in conjunctions belonging to X.*

In a consensus $(x^{*^+}, x^{*^-}) \in C(X)$ set x^{*^+} is called the *positive component*, and set x^{*^-} the *negative component*.

Some commentary should be made for the defined postulates.

- Postulate $P1$a means that the common part of positive profiles should be included in the positive component of the consensus. The sense of this postulate follows from the Pareto criterion: if all voters vote for the same candidate then she should be finally chosen. On the other hand, postulate $P1$b requires the same for negative profiles. These conditions seem to be very intuitive, because if in the opinions of all agents (or experts) some event should take place (or should not take place), then the consensus should take this fact into account.
- Postulates $P2$a and $P2$b are in some sense dual to postulates $P1$a and $P1$b. Concretely, consensus should not exceed the profiles. This means that the positive and negative components of the consensus should be included in the sums of positive profiles and negative profiles, respectively. These postulates come from the rule of the closed world. Objects which do not belong to the world do not exist.
- Postulate $P3$ is specific for the logic character of the profile. For example, in classical logic one of the consequences of formulae $a \wedge b \wedge \neg c$ and $d \wedge e$ should be $a \wedge b \wedge \neg c \wedge d \wedge e$. Generally, if profile X is consistent then the conjunction

$$\left(\bigcup_{x \in X} x^+ , \bigcup_{x \in X} x^- \right)$$

is a logic consequence of conjunctions belonging to profile X. This is because the conjunction is in fact the following formula,

$$t_1 \wedge t_2 \wedge \cdots ,$$

where $t_i \in \bigcup_{x \in X} x^+ \cup \bigcup_{x \in X} x^-$ for $i = 1, 2, \ldots$. This formula is a consequence of the conjunctions belonging to X. In addition, this formula is also the "largest" consequence of the conjunctions belonging to X. To explain this statement let's use an example. Let $x_1 = a \wedge b \wedge \neg c$ and $x_2 = a \wedge d$; then the consequences of these formulae are, for example, $a \wedge b$, $b \wedge \neg c \wedge d$, and so on. But the "largest" consequence is $a \wedge b \wedge c \wedge d$. This is because there is no consequence which contains more symbols than this formula. Postulate $P3$ requires this formula to be a consensus of given conjunctions. This requirement is justified inasmuch as this formula reflects all given conjunctions. Moreover, it is equivalent with the set of all formulae belonging to the profile.

Another aspect of this postulate refers to the superiority of knowledge. It means that if only one agent (or expert) states that some fact should take place, then this should be reflected in the consensus.

Let's consider an example for the conflict profile given below.

Agent	Knowledge state
a_1	$t_1 \wedge \neg\, t_2 \wedge t_4$
a_2	$\neg t_2 \wedge t_3 \wedge t_4$
a_3	$t_3 \wedge t_1 \wedge \neg t_5$

According to postulate $P3$ the consensus should be in the form of the conjunction

$$t_1 \wedge \neg\, t_2 \wedge t_3 \wedge t_4 \wedge \neg\, t_5.$$

- Postulate $P4$ requires the consensus to be nonconflicting. For a practical sense of consensus this requirement is justified because if it were a conflicting conjunction it would be equivalent to *false* and thereby there would be no profit in it.
- Postulate $P5$ is a popular criterion for consensus and is consistent with the criterion O_1 defined in Chapter 3. This criterion is natural for satisfying the condition for "the best representation."
- Postulate $P6$ is very essential from the point of view of knowledge precedence. This follows from the assumption that knowledge of an agent

need not be complete, and events or scenarios which are not included in his opinion, belong to his ignorance. For this reason, referring to an event as the basis for determining its status in the consensus, only those opinions in which the event is referred to should be taken into account. As an example consider the conflict profile given below.

Agent	Knowledge state
a_1	$t_1 \wedge \neg\, t_2 \wedge t_3$
a_2	$\neg t_2 \wedge t_3 \wedge t_1$
a_3	$t_3 \wedge t_1 \wedge \neg t_5$
a_4	$t_3 \wedge t_1 \wedge \neg t_2$

For the status of symbol t_5 in the consensus we take into account only the opinion of agent a_3 because only this agent includes this symbol in her opinion. For the status of symbol t_2 we take into account the opinions of agents a_1, a_2, and a_4.

By C_{co} we denote the set of all consensus functions for profiles of conjunctions. Notice also that although the postulates defined above are for consensus functions, they may also be considered to be satisfied by a particular consensus for a profile.

5.2.4. Analysis of Postulates

In this section we present several properties of postulates and the relationships between consensus functions satisfying them.

Notice that we can consider satisfying the defined postulates referring to a consensus function in general, as well as to its behavior for one argument in particular.

The fact that a consensus function C satisfies a postulate P for a given profile X of the function is written as

$$C(X) \mathrel{|\!\!-} P.$$

The fact that a consensus function C satisfies a postulate P (i.e., the postulate is satisfied for all arguments of the function) is written as

$$C \mathrel{|\!\!-} P.$$

Last, if a postulate P is satisfied for all functions from C_{co} then we write

$$C_{co} \mathrel{|\!\!-} P.$$

The first theorem presented below shows that postulates $P1$ and $P2$ are the consequences of postulate $P5$.

Theorem 5.1.

A consensus function which satisfies postulate P5 should also satisfy postulates P1 and P2; that is;

$$(C \vdash P5) \Rightarrow (C \vdash P1 \wedge C \vdash P2)$$

for each $C \in C_{co}$.

Proof.

Let X be a profile, $X \in \Pi(Conj(L))$, and let $C \in C_{co}$ be a consensus function satisfying postulate $P5$. Let $(x^{*^+}, x^{*^-}) \in C(X)$ be a consensus of profile X. For proving that postulate $P1$ is satisfied by C we should show that

$$\bigcap_{x \in X} x^+ \subseteq x^{*^+}$$

and

$$\bigcap_{x \in X} x^- \subseteq x^{*^-}.$$

For the first dependence let's assume that

$$\bigcap_{x \in X} x^+ \not\subseteq x^{*^+} ;$$

this means that there exists a symbol t such that $t \in \bigcap_{x \in X} x^+$ but $t \notin x^{*^+}$. In this case create set $x^{*\prime^+} = x^{*^+} \cup \{t\}$. Then we have

$$\sum_{x \in X} \eta(x^{*\prime^+}, x^+) < \sum_{x \in X} \eta(x^{*^+}, x^+)$$

because

$$\eta(x^{*\prime^+}, x^+) < \eta(x^{*^+}, x^+) \quad \text{for each } x \in X.$$

In consequence,

$$\sum_{x \in X} d(x'^*, x) < \sum_{x \in X} d(x^*, x),$$

where

$$x'^* = (x'^{*^+}, x^{*^-}).$$

This result is contradictory to the assumption that conjunction (x^{*^+}, x^{*^-}) is a consensus for X, which satisfies postulate $P5$.

The proof for dependence

$$\bigcap_{x \in X} x^- \subseteq x^{*-}$$

can be performed in similar way.
For postulate $P2a$ assume that

$$x^{*+} \not\subset \bigcup_{x \in X} x^+ .$$

Then there should exist a symbol t such that $t \in x^{*+}$ but $t \notin \bigcup_{x \in X} x^+$. In this case let

$$x^{*\prime+} = x^{*+} \setminus \{t\}.$$

We should have

$$\sum_{x \in X} \eta(x^{*\prime+}, x^+) < \sum_{x \in X} \eta(x^{*+}, x^+)$$

because

$$\eta(x^{*\prime+}, x^+) < \eta(x^{*+}, x^+)$$

for each $x \in X$. As its consequence

$$\sum_{x \in X} d(x'^*, x) < \sum_{x \in X} d(x^*, x),$$

where

$$x'^* = (x'^{*+}, x^{*-}).$$

The proof for $P2b$ is similar.   ◆

The above theorem presents a very important property of postulate $P5$ because postulates $P1$ and $P2$ are very intuitive. Also, they represent very essential features of the voting process.

Theorem 5.2.
Let X be a consistent profile and $C \in C_{co}$ be a consensus function. If function C satisfies postulate $P2$ or postulate $P5$ for profile X, then it should also satisfy postulate $P4$ for X; that is,

$$(C(X) \mid\!- P2) \vee (C(X) \mid\!- P5) \Rightarrow (C(X) \mid\!- P4) .$$

Proof.
First, we prove that if $C(X)$ satisfies postulate $P2$ then it should also satisfy postulate $P4$; that is,

$$(C(X) \mathbin{|\!-} P2) \Rightarrow (C(X) \mathbin{|\!-} P4).$$

Let $(x^{*+}, x^{*-}) \in C(X)$. According to postulate $P2$ we have

$$x^{*+} \subseteq \bigcup_{x \in X} x^{+} \quad \text{and} \quad x^{*-} \subseteq \bigcup_{x \in X} x^{-}.$$

Because X is a consistent profile, then

$$\bigcup_{x \in X} x^{+} \cap \bigcup_{x \in X} x^{-} = \varnothing.$$

Thus

$$x^{*+} \cap x^{*-} = \varnothing.$$

$C(X)$ then satisfies postulate $P4$. Now we prove

$$(C(X) \mathbin{|\!-} P5) \Rightarrow (C(X) \mathbin{|\!-} P4).$$

For this it is sufficient to notice that according to Theorem 5.1:

$$(C(X) \mathbin{|\!-} P5) \Rightarrow (C(X) \mathbin{|\!-} P2).$$

Then using the statement above we have the proof.   ◆

Postulates $P1$ through $P5$ are not contradictory on the argument level; that is, there exists a function $C \in C_{co}$ and a profile X for which all of the postulates are satisfied. However, these postulates are contradictory on the function level; that is, a consensus function which satisfies all postulates for all arguments does not exist. We have the following.

Theorem 5.3.

(a) $(\exists C \in C_{co})(\exists X \in \Pi(Conj(L))): \big(C(X) \mathbin{|\!-} P1 \wedge \cdots \wedge C(X) \mathbin{|\!-} P5\big).$

(b) $\neg\big[(\exists C \in C_{co}):(C \mathbin{|\!-} P1 \wedge \cdots \wedge C \mathbin{|\!-} P5)\big].$

Proof.

(a) For proving this statement we define a concrete function and show a concrete profile for which all postulates are satisfied. Let function C be defined as follows.

$$C(X) = \Big\{x^{*} \in Conj(L): \sum_{x \in X} d_{\wedge}(x^{*}, x) = \min_{x' \in Conj(L)} \sum_{x \in X} d_{\wedge}(x^{*}, x')\Big\}.$$

As we can see, this function satisfies postulate $P5$. Now let's define the profile X:

$$X = \{n * x\}$$

for some $x \in Conj(L)$, x is nonconflicting, and $n \in \aleph$. That is, profile X is consistent and homogeneous (see Definition 2.1, Chapter 2). It is obvious that

$$C(X) = \{x\}.$$

Thus postulates $P1$, $P2$, and $P3$ are satisfied. For postulate $P4$, notice that because x is nonconflicting, its positive and negative components are disjoint. In this way we have shown that all postulates are satisfied for $C(X)$.

(b) We show that for each function C satisfying postulate $P5$ there exists a profile X such that $C(X)$ does not satisfy postulate $P3$.

Let $C \in C_{co}$, and let profile X be defined as follows,

$$X = \{99 * (\{t\}, \varnothing), (\{t'\}, \varnothing)\}$$

for some $t, t' \in L$, and $t \neq t'$. Thus X contains 99 occurrences of the same conjunction $(\{t\}, \varnothing)$ and one conjunction $(\{t'\}, \varnothing)$. Let $x^* \in C(X)$; notice that because C satisfies postulate $P5$ then x should have the form:

$$x^* = (\{t\}, \varnothing).$$

Anyway, x may not contain symbol t' because for x the sum of distances should be:

$$\sum_{x \in X} d_{\wedge}(x^*, x) = w_1,$$

where w_1 has been defined in Definition 5.5. In the meantime for

$$x' = (\{t, t'\}, \varnothing)$$

the sum should be:

$$\sum_{x \in X} d_{\wedge}(x', x) = \frac{1}{2} \cdot 100 \cdot w_1$$

$$= 50 \cdot w_1 > \sum_{x \in X} d_{\wedge}(x^*, x).$$

Thus postulate $P3$ may not be satisfied.   ◆

From Theorems 5.1 and 5.2 we can deduce that satisfying postulate $P5$ implies satisfying postulates $P1$, $P2$, and $P4$ simultaneously. From Theorem 5.3 it is known that a consensus function satisfying all postulates does not exist. However, in Theorem 5.5 we show some restriction which causes satisfying postulate $P3$ in the case of satisfying postulate $P5$. Before this theorem we present a property allowing us to determine independently positive and negative components of consensus satisfying postulate $P5$.

Let X be a profile

$$X = \{(x_i^+, x_i^-): i = 1, 2, \ldots, n\}.$$

On its basis we create the profiles:

$$X' = \{(x_i^+, \varnothing): i = 1, 2, \ldots, n\},$$

$$X'' = \{(\varnothing, x_i^-): i = 1, 2, \ldots, n\}.$$

Then we have the following.

Theorem 5.4.

The positive and negative components of a consensus satisfying postulate P5 can be determined in an independent way; that is, conjunction (x^{*+}, x^{*-}) is a consensus of profile X if and only if conjunction $(x^{*+}, \varnothing)$ is a consensus of profile X' and conjunction $(\varnothing, x^{*-})$ is a consensus of profile X''.

Proof.

The proof follows directly from the definition of distance function $d_\wedge$ between conjunctions (see Definition 5.5). For determining a consensus (x^{*+}, x^{*-}) satisfying postulate $P5$ each component may be determined independently. Also, notice that a consensus satisfying postulate $P5$ for profile X' should have the negative component as an empty set, and for profile X'' should have the positive component as an empty set.   ◆

Another important property of a consensus satisfying postulate $P5$ is that if all positive and negative components of a profile are nonempty then the components of the consensus may not be empty.

Theorem 5.5.

For any profile X if for each $x \in X$ we have $x^+ \neq \varnothing$ then $x^{*+} \neq \varnothing$, and also if for each $x \in X$ we have $x^- \neq \varnothing$ then $x^{*-} \neq \varnothing$.

Proof.

Let's assume that for a profile X each of its positive components is nonempty. Let

$$X = \{(x_i^+, x_i^-): i = 1, 2, \ldots, n\}$$

and let

$$X^+ = \{x_i^+: i = 1, 2, \ldots, n\}.$$

Notice that

$$\sum_{i=1}^{n} \eta(\varnothing, x_i^+) = n$$

because $\eta(\varnothing, x_i^+) = 1$ (the maximal value for distance η) for each $i = 1$, $2, \ldots, n$. Notice also that for any $t \in x_i^+$ for some i there should be

$$\eta(\{t\}, x_i^+) = \frac{card(x_i^+) - 1}{card(x_i^+)} < 1.$$

So

$$\sum_{i=1}^{n} \eta(\{t\}, x_i^+) < \sum_{i=1}^{n} \eta(\varnothing, x_i^+).$$

That means the positive component of the consensus cannot be empty. The proof for the negative consensus component is identical.   ◆

Now we present the relationship between postulates $P3$ and $P5$. As we have shown earlier, these postulates are in general contradictory. However, there is some class of profiles which satisfy both of them.

Before presenting Theorem 5.6 we define notion of *strong distinguishable profile* which is consistent and all positive and negative components are nonempty and disjoint with each other. That is, a consistent profile X

$$X = \{(x_i^+, x_i^-): i = 1, 2, \ldots, n\}$$

is strong distinguishable if all sets x_1^+, x_1^-, x_2^+, x_2^-, $\ldots$, x_n^+, x_n^- are non-empty and disjoint with each other. It follows that in a strong distinguishable profile any symbol from L may occur at best once.[2]

Theorem 5.6.
Let $C \in C_{co}$ be a consensus function and let X be a strong distinguishable profile. If function C satisfies postulate P5 for profile X, then it should also satisfy postulate P3 for this profile; that is,

$$(C(X) \,|\!- P5) \Rightarrow (C(X) \,|\!- P3).$$

Proof.
Let X be a strong distinguishable profile; that is, any symbol from L occurs at best one time in X. We can then write:

$$X = \{(x_i^+, x_i^-): i = 1, 2, \ldots, n\}$$

where all sets x_1^+, x_1^-, x_2^+, x_2^-, $\ldots$, x_n^+, x_n^- are disjoint with each other.

Let $C \in C_{co}$ be a consensus function satisfying postulate $P5$ and let

---

[2] This definition is consistent with the definition of a distinguishable profile given in Definition 2.1 (Chapter 2).

$$x = (x_i^+, x_i^-),$$

where

$$x_i^+ = \bigcup_{x \in X} x^+$$

and

$$x_i^- = \bigcup_{x \in X} x^-.$$

Define positive and negative profiles of X as

$$X^+ = \{x_i^+ : i = 1, 2, \ldots, n\}$$

and

$$X^- = \{x_i^- : i = 1, 2, \ldots, n\}.$$

Using the results of Theorem 5.5 we show that set x_i^+ is the positive component of a consensus belonging to $C(X)$, and x_i^- is the negative component of this consensus. Concretely we show that x_i^+ and x_i^- minimize the sums

$$\sum_{i=1}^{n} \eta(x^+, x_i^+) \quad \text{and} \quad \sum_{i=1}^{n} \eta(x^-, x_i^-),$$

respectively. We deal with the first case; the proof for the second case is similar.

Let $\alpha_i = \eta(x^+, x_i^+)$ for $i = 1, 2, \ldots, n$. Notice that

$$\alpha_i = \frac{card(x_i^+)}{card(x^+)}.$$

Thus

$$\sum_{i=1}^{n} \eta(x^+, x_i^+) = n - 1$$

because

$$\sum_{i=1}^{n} \alpha_i = n$$

owing to the assumption that X is a strong distinguishable profile.

Since X is a strong distinguishable profile, all sets x_i^+ for $i = 1, 2, \ldots,$ n are disjoint with each other. Thus we can replace a set x_i^+ by a symbol

$t_i \in L$ so that all symbols t_i for $i = 1, 2, \ldots, n$ are different from each other. For this new profile

$$T = \{t_i: i = 1, 2, \ldots, n\}$$

we can easily prove that set T is a consensus satisfying postulate $P5$, and of course also postulate $P3$ because set T is the representative of x^+. ♦

We should refer to postulate $P6$ which does not specify in a concrete way what should (or should not) belong to the consensus, but requires determining the basis for consensus choice. This condition is not reflected by postulate $P5$. Below let's consider an example.

Example 5.2. Let profile X be defined as

$$X = \{99 * t_1, \neg t_2\},$$

where $t_1, t_2 \in L$. Thus profile X consists of 99 identical conjunctions t_1 and one conjunction $\neg t_2$. According to postulate $P5$ the consensus should be t_1 because it minimizes the sum of distances from the consensus to the elements of the profile. Symbol t_2 does not appear in the consensus because it occurs in the profile only one time. However, postulate $P6$ as the basis of the status for symbol t_2 takes only this one opinion in which it appears. Thus because only one agent gave an opinion about the event represented by t_2 the status of this symbol should be the same as in this opinion. ♦

The way to determine the basis for setting the status for a symbol in the consensus follows from postulate $P6$. Let $X \in \Pi(Conj(L))$ be a profile; the consensus basis $X(t)$ for a symbol $t \in L$ is defined as

$$X(t) = \{n_1 * t, n_2 * (\neg t)\},$$

where n_1 is the number of conjunctions belonging to X in which literal t appears, and n_2 is the number of conjunctions belonging to X in which literal $\neg t$ appears. Thus those conjunctions in which neither t nor $\neg t$ appears are not taken into account.

For example, for profile

$$X = \{99 * t_1, \neg t_2\}$$

we have

$$X(t_1) = \{99 * t_1\}$$

and

$$X(t_2) = \{\neg t_2\}.$$

As stated above, postulates *P5* and *P6* are inconsistent with each other. However, after determining the consensus bases for particular symbols according to postulate *P6*, postulate *P5* may be useful for determining the final status for this symbol in the consensus. It may be easily shown that for the example given above the status for symbol t_1 should be literal t_1 whereas the status for symbol t_2 should be literal $\neg t_2$.

5.2.5. Heuristic Algorithm for Determining Consensus

Theorems 5.1, 5.2, 5.3, and 5.5 show that the criterion defined in postulate *P5* is very important, because in general a consensus satisfying this postulate also satisfies other postulates. Therefore, working out an algorithm for determining consensus satisfying this postulate should be done.

According to Theorem 5.4 we found out that determining the positive and negative components of a consensus for a given profile of conjunctions may be performed independently. Thus the task for calculation of conjunction $(x^{*+}, x^{*-}) \in C(X)$ where

$$X = \{x_i = (x_i^{+}, x_i^{-}) \in Conj(L): i = 1, 2, \ldots, n\}$$

can be divided into two similar subtasks. One of these subtasks refers to determining positive component x^{*+} such that

$$\sum_{x \in X} \eta(x^{*+}, x^{+}) = \min_{x' \subseteq L} \sum_{x \in X} \eta(x', x^{+})$$

and the other refers to determining positive component x^{*-} such that

$$\sum_{x \in X} \eta(x^{*-}, x^{-}) = \min_{x' \subseteq L} \sum_{x \in X} \eta(x', x^{-}).$$

In general we propose an algorithm for the following optimization problem.

Given a finite universe U and a profile $Y \in \Pi(U)$ one should determine a subset $y^* \subseteq U$ for which

$$\sum_{y \in Y} \eta(y^*, y) = \min_{y' \subseteq U} \sum_{y \in Y} \eta(y', y).$$

It is possible to prove that this problem is a NP-complete problem. Therefore, other approaches such as genetic or heuristic algorithms should be worked out. In this chapter we propose an effective heuristic algorithm for this problem. Notice that the same problem, but with distance function

$$\eta'(y_1, y_2) = card(y_1 \div y_2)$$

is not NP-complete, and there has been worked out an effective optimal algorithm [31].

The idea of our algorithm is simple and can be presented as follows.

First, we calculate the number of appearances of each element (from those occurring in the profile) in the sets belonging to the profile. Using postulate $P1$ we create the first element of consensus y^* as the set of all common elements of the sets belonging to the profile. Next, we improve the consensus by considering the addition to it of those elements which have the maximal frequency and help to decrease the sum of distances. The next improvement consists in checking if adding an element of the profile decreases the sum of distances. If so, the consensus is extended by this element. The algorithm will stop when all elements of the profile have been checked.

Below we present the heuristic algorithm.

Algorithm 5.1.

Input: Profile $Y \in \Pi(U)$.

Output: Set $y^* \subseteq U$ which minimizes the sum of distances to elements of profile Y.

Procedure:

BEGIN

    1. Set $Z := \bigcup_{y \in Y} y$; $y^* := \varnothing$; and $n := card(Y)$;

    2. For each element $z \in Z$ calculate $f(z)$ as the number of its appearances in sets belonging to profile Y;

    3. For each $z \in Z$ if $f(z) = n$ then set $y^* := y^* \cup \{z\}$ and set $Z := Z \setminus \{z\}$;

    4. Calculate $S^* = \sum_{y \in Y} \eta(y^*, y)$;

    5. Find $z \in Z$ such that $f(z)$ is maximal;

    6. Set $y' := y^* \cup \{z\}$, $Z := Z \setminus \{y\}$;

    7. Calculate $S(y') = \sum_{y \in Y} \eta(y', y)$, if $S(y') \le S^*$ then set

$$S^* := S(y') \text{ and } y^* := y';$$

    8. If $Z \ne \varnothing$ then GOTO 5;

    9. For each $y \in Y$ do

        Begin

           Set $y'' := y^* \cup y$;

           If $S(y'') \le S^*$ then set $y^* := y''$ and $S^* := S(y'')$

        End;

END.

The algorithm given above is not complex; its computational complexity can be easily proved to be $O(m^2 n)$ where $m = card(Z)$ and $n = card(Y)$.

Now we can use Algorithm 5.1 to determine the consensus of a profile of conjunctions. The idea of this algorithm is based on using Algorithm 5.1 to determine the consensuses for profiles consisting of positive and negative components, respectively. Next, these consensuses are checked for removing the common part of them.

The algorithm is presented as follows.

Algorithm 5.2.

Input: Profile $X \in \Pi(Conj(L))$, where $X = \{(x_i^+, x_i^-): i = 1,2, \ldots, n\}$.

Output: Consensus (x^{*+}, x^{*-}) satisfying postulates $P4$ and $P5$.

Procedure:

BEGIN

    1. Set $Y^+ := \{x_i^+ : i = 1, 2, \ldots, n\}$;

    2. Set $Y^- := \{x_i^- : i = 1, 2, \ldots, n\}$;

    3. For profile Y^+ using Algorithm 5.1 determine its consensus x^{*+};

    4. For profile Y^- using Algorithm 5.1 determine its consensus x^{*-};

    5. If $x_i^{*+} \cap x_i^{*-} = \varnothing$ then GOTO END;

    6. Calculate $S(x^*) = \sum_{x \in X} d_\wedge(x^*, x)$ where $x^* = (x_i^{*+}, x_i^{*-})$

    7. Set $T := x_i^{*+} \cap x_i^{*-}$;

    8. For each $z \in T$ do

        Begin

            8.1. Set $x' = (x^{*+}\setminus\{z\}, x^{*-})$ and $x'' = (x^{*+}, x^{*-}\setminus\{z\})$;

            8.2. Calculate $S(x') = \sum_{x \in X} d_\wedge(x', x)$ and

$$S(x'') = \sum_{x \in X} d_\wedge(x'', x);$$

            8.3. If $S(x') \leq S(x'')$ then set $x^{*+} := x^{*+}\setminus\{z\}$ else

                   if $S(x'') < S(x')$ then set $x^{*-} := x^{*-}\setminus\{z\}$;

        End;

END.

It is easy to show that the computational complexity of Algorithm 5.2 is $O(m^2 n)$ where $m = \max\{card(\bigcup_{x \in X} x^+), card(\bigcup_{x \in X} x^-)\}$ and $n = card(X)$.

Let's note that for a strong distinguishable profile a consensus satisfying postulate $P5$ also satisfies postulate $P3$. However, a consensus determined by a heuristic algorithm may not fulfill this rule. Fortunately, Algorithm 5.2 possesses this property and we can prove the following.

Theorem 5.7.

Algorithm 5.2 has the following properties:

  (a) For any profile X the consensus determined by Algorithm 5.2 satisfies postulates P1, P2, and P4.

  (b) For a strong distinguishable profile X the consensus determined by Algorithm 5.2 satisfies postulate P3.

  (c) For any profile X if for each $x \in X$ we have $x^+ \neq \varnothing$ then $x^{*+} \neq \varnothing$, and also if for each $x \in X$ we have $x^- \neq \varnothing$ then $x^{*-} \neq \varnothing$.

Proof.

(a) Satisfying postulate $P1$ results from step 3 of Algorithm 5.1 because in set y^* it includes all such element z that $f(z) = card(Y)$; that is, z appears in all elements of the profile, and these elements are still in the final form of the consensus. For postulate $P2$ notice that using step 1 of Algorithm 5.1 in Algorithm 5.2 causes set Z to be defined as the sum of all positive (or negative) components. Next, the other elements of consensus y^* are chosen only from Z. Thus the consensus must be a subset of Z. Postulate $P4$ should be satisfied owing to step 8 of Algorithm 5.2, which causes removing the common elements of sets x_i^{*+} and x_i^{*-} from one of them.

(b) Let X be a strong distinguishable profile. We investigate only the determination of the consensus of its positive components; for the negative components the consideration is identical. If X contains only one conjunction then the theorem is obviously true. Now assume that the cardinality of X is greater than 1. For all elements $z \in Z$ the numbers $f(z)$ calculated in step 2 of Algorithm 5.1 should equal 1 because profile X is strong distinguishable. The set y^* calculated in step 3 should be empty, and the sum S^* calculated in step 4 should be equal to n. The loop consisting of steps 5–8 the first time should add to set y^* a new element z (where z is any element of Z) because this should decrease the sum of distances from n to $(n - 1) + (k - 1)/k$, where k is the cardinality of the element w of profile Y, to which z belongs. Notice that the loop will add to set y^* all elements from w because other elements of w should decrease the sum of distances.

At last, when whole w is added to set y^*, the sum of distances should equal $(n - 1)$; it is also the minimal sum of the distances (see the proof of Theorem 5.5). This minimal sum should not be changed if a whole element of profile Y is added to y^*. Therefore, owing to step 9 of Algorithm 5.1 y^* should contain all elements of Y; that is, postulate $P3$ is satisfied.

(c) See the proof of Theorem 5.5 and notice that owing to step 6 of Algorithm 5.1 set y^* will not be empty.   ◆

We now present an algorithm which reflects both postulate $P5$ as well as postulate $P6$.

Algorithm 5.3.

Input: Profile $X \in \Pi(Conj(L))$, where $X = \{(x_i^+, x_i^-): i = 1, 2, \ldots, n\}$.

Output: Consensus (x^{*+}, x^{*-}) satisfying postulates P5 and P6.

Procedure:

BEGIN

    1. Set $Z:= \{t \in L$: there exists a conjunction $x \in X$ in which symbol t appears$\}$;

    2. Set $(x^{*+}, x^{*-}):= (\emptyset, \emptyset)$;

    3. For each $t \in Z$ set

$$X(t) = \{n_t * t, n_t' * (\neg t)\} \, ,$$

    where n_t is the number of conjunctions belonging to X in which literal t appears, and n_t' is the number of conjunctions belonging to X in which literal $\neg t$ appears.

    4. For each $t \in Z$ do

      Begin

        4.1. If $n_t \cdot w_1 < n_t' \cdot w_2$ then set $x^{*-}:= x^{*-} \cup \{t\}$;

        4.2. If $n_t \cdot w_1 \geq n_t' \cdot w_2$ then set $x^{*+}:= x^{*+} \cup \{t\}$;

      End;

END.

In the above algorithm postulate P6 is used in step 3, and postulate P5 is used in step 4. Notice that because the consensus basis $X(t)$ consists only of two kinds of literals, then the sum of distances will be smallest if we include in the consensus the literal which appears no fewer times than the other, taking into account the weights w_1 and w_2 defined for distance function $d_\wedge$. It also follows that although consensus determined by this algorithm only partially satisfies postulate P5, it satisfies postulates P1 and P2.

The computational complexity of Algorithm 5.3 is $O(mn)$ where $m = card(Z)$ and $n = card(X)$.

5.3. Disjunctive Structure of Knowledge

We now deal with the dual structure for knowledge on the syntactic level, that is, the disjunctive structure. This structure is very popular in knowledge representation by experts and agents, especially for such kinds of knowledge as uncertain or incomplete. Owing to its simplicity and representation power it is also the structure most often used in logic programming languages such as Prolog and Datalog, and in deductive databases. In addition, we can see that the negation of a conjunction gives a disjunction, for example, $\neg(a \wedge b \wedge c) \equiv (\neg a) \vee (\neg b) \vee (\neg c)$, where symbol "$\equiv$" represents the semantic equivalence. Disjunctive structure can then be very useful in representing negative knowledge for those experts who use conjunctions to represent their positive knowledge.

First, we present some basic notions.

5.3.1. Basic Notions

Using disjunctive structure an agent opinion has the form:

$$l_1 \vee l_2 \vee \ldots \vee l_k \, ,$$

where l_i is a literal (positive or negative) for $i = 1, 2, \ldots, k$ and $k \in \aleph$. The symbols for building literals belong to set L (see Section 5.2.1).

Notice that owing to this structure an agent may express its opinion in types other than conjunction structure; viz. an agent can now give its opinion in the form of a disjunction referring to a number of scenario attributes.

Notice that formula

$$l_1 \vee l_2 \vee \ldots \vee l_k$$

can be treated as a clause. We can then write

$$(l_1 \vee l_2 \vee \ldots \vee l_k) \equiv (h_1 \vee h_2 \vee \ldots \vee h_{k'}) \vee (\neg b_1 \vee \neg b_2 \vee \ldots \vee \neg b_{k''}),$$

where $h_1, h_2, \ldots, h_m$ are positive literals and $\neg b_1, \neg b_2, \ldots, \neg b_n$ are negative literals among $l_1, l_2, \ldots, l_k$. Furthermore we have

$$(l_1 \vee l_2 \vee \ldots \vee l_k) \equiv (h_1 \vee h_2 \vee \ldots \vee h_{k'}) \vee \neg(b_1 \wedge b_2 \wedge \ldots \wedge b_{k''})$$

$$\equiv (b_1 \wedge b_2 \wedge \ldots \wedge b_{k''}) \rightarrow (h_1 \vee h_2 \vee \ldots \vee h_{k'}).$$

Symbol "$\rightarrow$" represents the logic implication.

Formula

$$(b_1 \wedge b_2 \wedge \ldots \wedge b_{k''})$$

is called the *body* of the clause, and formula

$$(h_1 \vee h_2 \vee \ldots \vee h_{k'})$$

is called the *head* of the clause. It is a well-known form of clause. The above-mentioned transformation shows that the disjunction structure should be very useful in practice for agents to express their opinions, because an expert has now the possibility to represent her opinion as a rule,

If precondition *then* **postcondition.**

As a equivalent form for clause

$$(b_1 \wedge b_2 \wedge \cdots \wedge b_{k''}) \rightarrow (h_1 \vee h_2 \vee \cdots \vee h_{k'})$$

we use the following,

$$b_1, b_2, \ldots, b_{k''} \rightarrow h_1, h_2, \ldots, h_{k'}.$$

Or more generally:

$$b \rightarrow h,$$

where b is the body and h is the head of the clause, for $b, h \subseteq L$.

Clauses have been classified into the following groups: the group of Horn clauses (definite clauses) and the group of nondefinite clauses. A Horn clause has at most one symbol in its head, and a nondefinite clause has two or more symbols in the head. The inference mechanisms of clauses are dependent on the so-called closed world assumptions [129]. However, in this work we do not deal with the inference process of clauses in the logical sense, but in the qualitative sense.

By *Clause(L)* we denote the set of all clauses with symbols from set L.

Similarly as for conjunctions a clause

$$x = b \rightarrow h$$

can be then represented by a pair

$$(x^+, x^-),$$

where x^+ is the set of symbols belonging to the head of x and x^- is the set of symbols belonging to the body of x; that is, $x^+ = h$ and $x^- = b$. For example, the representation of clause

$$x = (t_1, t_2 \rightarrow t_3)$$

for $t_1, t_2, t_3 \in L$ is pair (x^+, x^-), where $x^+ = \{t_3\}$ and $x^- = \{t_1, t_2\}$.

If body $b = \varnothing$ then the clause will have form

$$\rightarrow h,$$

if head $h = \varnothing$ then the clause will have form

$$b \rightarrow,$$

and if $b = h = \varnothing$ then the clause is

$$\rightarrow .$$

This clause is called *empty* and represents the value *false*.

Sets x^+ and x^- are called the positive and negative components of the clause, respectively. An empty clause is then represented by pair $(\varnothing, \varnothing)$. A clause in which both components are nonempty is called a *complete* clause.

Definition 5.7.

A clause (x^+, x^-), where $x^+, x^- \subseteq L$, is nonconflicting if the following condition is satisfied,

$$x^+ \cap x^- = \varnothing.$$

That means that a nonconflicting clause is not equivalent with *true*. An opinion of an expert or an agent in the form of conflicting clauses (equivalent with *true*) has no value in practice. Therefore, we consider only nonconflicting clauses because they are sensible for agents to express their opinions.

Definition 5.8.

Let $x = (x^+, x^-) \in Clause(L)$ and $x' = (x'^+, x'^-) \in Clause(L)$ and let $t \in x^+ \cap x'^-$. We say that clause (x''^+, x''^-) where

$$x''^+ = (x^+ \cup x'^+) \setminus \{t\} \quad and \quad x''^- = (x^- \cup x'^-) \setminus \{t\}$$

is the consequence of clauses x and x'.

For example, for the given clauses

$$x = (a, b \to c, d)$$

and

$$x' = (e, f \to a)$$

their consequence is the following clause,

$$x'' = (b, e, f \to c, d).$$

The above definition presents in fact the well-known rule for generating the consequence of two clauses [129]. Furthermore, we have the following.

Definition 5.9.

A profile of clauses $X \in \Pi(Clause(L))$ is called inconsistent if one of their consequences is empty clause $(\varnothing, \varnothing)$ (i.e., clause $\to$). A profile which is not inconsistent, is called consistent.

For example, profile

$$X = \{a, b \to c, c \to, \to a, \to b\}$$

is inconsistent because the consequence is an empty clause, but profile

$$X' = \{a, b \to c, c \to, \to a\}$$

is a consistent one for which clause $(b \to)$ is a consequence, but the empty clause is not a consequence.

5.3.2. Distance Function between Clauses

In this section we define the distance function $d_\vee$ between clauses. This function should help in evaluating the difference between clauses. Owing to this function it will be possible to learn about the inconsistency level of a conflict profile, and in consequence, to determine the consensus for the conflict.

For defining the distance function between clauses we need the distance function η between sets which has been defined in Section 5.2.2.

The definition of the distance of two clauses x_1 and x_2 is presented as follows.

Definition 5.10.
By the distance between two clauses $x_1, x_2 \in Clause(L)$ we understand the following value,

$$d_\vee(x_1, x_2) = \frac{w_1 \cdot \eta(x_1^+, x_2^+) + w_2 \cdot \eta(x_1^-, x_2^-)}{w_1 + w_2} ,$$

where

- $\eta(x_1^+, x_2^+)$: *The distance between sets of positive components in clauses x_1 and x_2.*
- $\eta(x_1^-, x_2^-)$: *The distance between sets of negative components in clauses x_1 and x_2.*
- w_1 *and* w_2 *are the weights of distances* $\eta(x_1^+, x_2^+)$ *and* $\eta(x_1^-, x_2^-)$ *in distance* $d_\vee(x_1, x_2)$, *respectively, which satisfy the following conditions,*

$$w_1 + w_2 = 1 \quad and \quad 0 < w_1, w_2 < 1.$$

In a clause (similarly as in a conjunction) positive literals can be considered as the positive knowledge of agents, whereas negative literals are considered as their negative knowledge. Using values w_1 and w_2 we can distinguish the weights of distances between positive and negative parts of agent knowledge states.

In the aspect of precondition and postcondition of a clause, the distance between two clauses is in fact the sum of distances between their pre- and postconditions. In some situations the preconditions are more important and in other situations the postconditions are more important. For reflecting this aspect the values of parameters w_1 and w_2 may be modified. If pre- and postconditions have the same importance, then we may set $w_1 = w_2 = \frac{1}{2}$.

The above-defined distance function $d_\vee$ is of course a metric. Its values are also normalized to interval $[0, 1]$.

Notice that the distance between two inconsistent clauses (i.e., their consequence is the empty clause) is maximal (i.e., equals 1). It is then the justification for this function.

The above-defined distance function $d_\vee$ is of course a metric.

5.3.3. Integration Problem and Postulates for Consensus

We now formulate the integration problem as follows.

For a given set of clauses

$$X = \{x_i = (x_i^+, x_i^-): i = 1, 2, \ldots, n\}$$

it is necessary to determine a clause $x^* = (x^{*+}, x^{*-})$ *called a consensus of set X.*

Example 5.3. Let's consider a real world consisting of weather forecasts in some region of a country, similar to the one in Example 5.1. Let there be a set of agents:

$$Agent = \{a_1, a_2, a_3, a_4\},$$

and a set of symbols:

$$L = \{t_1, t_2, t_3, t_4, t_5\},$$

which represent the facts:

- t_1: The temperature in the region will be higher than 0.
- t_2: The region will be sunny.
- t_3: It will snow in the region.
- t_4: The wind will be strong.
- t_5: It will rain.

Assume that for some common region the agents generate the following set of knowledge states.

Agent	Knowledge state
a_1	$t_1 \to t_5$
a_2	$\to t_2, t_5$
a_3	$t_2, t_3, t_4 \to$
a_4	$t_2, t_3 \to t_4$

Thus in the opinion of agent a_1 in the considered region if the temperature is higher than 0, then it will be raining. ♦

More generally, we need to define the following consensus function.

Definition 5.11.

By a consensus function for profiles of clauses we understand a function:

$$C: \Pi(Clause(L)) \to 2^{Clause(L)}.$$

which satisfies one or more of the following postulates.

P1. *For each clause* $(x^{*+}, x^{*-}) \in C(X)$ *there should be*:

(a) $\bigcap_{x \in X} x^+ \subseteq x^{*+}$

and

(b) $\bigcap_{x \in X} x^- \subseteq x^{*-}$.

P2. *For each clause* $(x^{*+}, x^{*-}) \in C(X)$ *there should be*:

(a) $x^{*+} \subseteq \bigcup_{x \in X} x^+$

and

(b) $x^{*-} \subseteq \bigcup_{x \in X} x^-$.

P3. *If profile X is consistent then any clause*

$$(x^+, x^-)$$

which is a consequence of all clauses from X, should be its consensus.

P4. *If profile X consists of nonempty and nonconflicting clauses then for each clause* $(x^{*+}, x^{*-}) \in C(X)$ *there should be*:

(a) $x^{*+} \cap x^{*-} = \varnothing$

and

(b) $x^{*+} \cup x^{*-} \neq \varnothing$.

P5. *A consensus $x^* \in C(X)$ should minimize the sum of distances*:

$$\sum_{x \in X} d_\vee(x^*, x) = \min_{x' \in Clause(L)} \sum_{x \in X} d_\vee(x', x).$$

P6. *For each symbol $z \in L$ and a consensus $x^* \in C(X)$ the form of appearance (i.e., as a positive or negative literal) of z in x^* depends only on its forms of appearance in clauses belonging to X.*

In a consensus $(x^{*+}, x^{*-}) \in C(X)$ set x^{*+} is called the *positive component*, and set x^{*-} the *negative component*.

We give some commentary to the defined postulates.

- Postulates $P1$ and $P2$ contain the same requirements as their counterparts defined for profiles of conjunctions. They are in some sense Pareto-based criteria.
- Postulate $P3$ is specific for the logical character of the profile. For example, if there are three clauses in the profile:

$$a \rightarrow b, \quad b \rightarrow c, \quad \text{and} \quad c \rightarrow d$$

then their consequence should be the following clause,

$$a \rightarrow d$$

and this clause should be the consensus of the profile. Consensus has been known to be useful in reconciling inconsistent elements of the conflict profile. However, if a profile does not contain inconsistency, then the natural requirement is that its consequence should be a consensus.
- Postulate $P4$ requires the consensus to be a nonconflicting and nonempty clause for those profiles which consist of nonconflicting and nonempty clauses. For a practical sense of consensus this requirement is well justified because if it were a conflicting clause it would be equivalent to *true* and if it were an empty one it would be equivalent to *false*. In both cases determination of consensus is not justified because there would be no profit in it.
- Postulate $P5$ is known to be a popular criterion for consensus choice, as it is consistent with the postulate with the same name defined in Section 5.2.3. This criterion is natural for satisfying the condition for "the best representation." It is also consistent with the criterion O_1 defined in Chapter 3.
- Postulate $P6$ has here the same aspects as the same postulate for conjunctions.

By C_{cl} we denote the set of all consensus functions for profiles of clauses.

The postulates defined above may be considered to be satisfied by:

- A particular consensus for a given profile
- A profile
- A consensus function

Now we present some properties of consensus functions referring to the postulates. A large part of these properties is similar to those of the postulates for consensus determination of profiles of conjunctions.

Theorem 5.8.

A consensus function $C \in C_{cl}$ which satisfies postulate P5 should also satisfy postulates P1 and P2; that is,

$$(C \mid\!- P5) \Rightarrow (C \mid\!- P1 \wedge C \mid\!- P2).$$

Proof.

The proof for this theorem is similar to the proof of Theorem 5.1 because the basis of consensus determination is distance function η between sets.

♦

We note that similarly as for conjunctions (Theorem 5.4), determining consensus satisfying postulate $P5$ for a given profile can be performed independently for its positive and negative profiles.

The theorem presented below shows the properties for clauses similar to the one given in Theorem 5.2. However, postulate $P4$ for clauses is different from that defined for conjunctions.

Theorem 5.9.

Let profile X consist of complete clauses and $C \in C_{cl}$ be a consensus function. If function C satisfies postulate P5 for profile X, then it should also satisfy postulate P4b for X; that is,

$$(C(X) \mid\!- P5) \Rightarrow (C(X) \mid\!- P4b).$$

Proof.

Let profile X consist of complete and nonconflicting clauses and let consensus function C satisfy postulate $P5$. We show that

$$x^{*+} \neq \varnothing \quad \text{and} \quad x^{*-} \neq \varnothing.$$

For the first dependence notice that because of the completeness of profile X each element of the positive profile

$$X^+ = \{x_i^+ : i = 1, 2, \ldots, n\}$$

is nonempty. Thus set x^{*+} which minimizes the sum

$$\sum_{i=1}^{n} \eta(x^{*+}, x_i^+)$$

should not be empty. The reason is that if it were empty, the sum would be equal to n, whereas for any $j \in \{1, 2, \ldots, n\}$ we would have:

$$\sum_{i=1}^{n} \eta(x_j^+, x_i^+) < n$$

because

$$\eta(x_j^+, x_j^+) = 0.$$

The proof for the second dependence is identical. Thus we should have:

$$x^{*+} \cup x^{*-} \neq \varnothing$$

and as the consequence

$$C(X) \vdash P4b. \qquad\qquad \blacklozenge$$

Notice that without the assumption of profile completeness the following dependency is not true.

$$(C(X) \vdash P5) \Rightarrow (C(X) \vdash P4b).$$

Here is an example.

Example 5.4. Let profile X consist of six nonempty and nonconflicting clauses:

$$X = \{ \rightarrow t_1, \rightarrow t_2, \rightarrow t_3, t_1 \rightarrow, t_2 \rightarrow, t_3 \rightarrow \}.$$

Let C be a function satisfying postulate $P5$. Then the only element of $C(X)$ is the empty clause; that is,

$$C(X) = \{ \rightarrow \}.$$

Thus function C does not satisfy postulate $P4b$. $\qquad\qquad \blacklozenge$

In general, satisfying postulate $P5$ does not imply satisfaction of postulate $P4a$ either. Let's consider an example.

Example 5.5. Let the profile consist of two clauses:

$$X = \{ t_1 \rightarrow t_2, t_2 \rightarrow t_1 \}.$$

Letting C be a function satisfying postulate $P5$, we have

$$C(X) = \{ t_1 \rightarrow t_2, t_2 \rightarrow t_1, t_1 \rightarrow t_1, t_2 \rightarrow t_2 \}.$$

Because of the presence of clause $t_1 \rightarrow t_1$ function C does not satisfy postulate *P4a*.   ♦

However, postulates *P1*, *P2*, *P3*, *P4*, and *P5* are not contradictory on the argument level; that is, there exist a function $C \in C_{cl}$ and a profile X for which all of the postulates are satisfied. However, these postulates are contradictory on the function level; that is, a consensus function which satisfies all postulates for all arguments does not exist. We have the following.

Theorem 5.10.
The following dependencies are true.

> *(a)* $(\exists C \in C_{cl})(\exists X \in \Pi(Clause(L))): \big(C(X) \vdash P1 \wedge \cdots \wedge C(X) \vdash P5\big).$

> *(b)* $\neg\big[(\exists C \in C_{cl}):(C \vdash P1 \wedge \cdots \wedge C \vdash P5)\big].$

Proof.
(a) For proving this statement we define a concrete function and show a concrete profile, for which all postulates are satisfied. Let function C be defined as follows.

$$C(X) = \Big\{x^* \in Clause(L): \sum\nolimits_{x \in X} d_\vee(x^*,x) = \min_{x' \in Clause(L)} \sum\nolimits_{x \in X} d_\vee(x^*,x')\Big\}.$$

As we can see, this function satisfies postulate *P5*. Now let's define the profile X as follows,

$$X = \{k * x\}$$

for some $x \in Clause(L)$, x is nonconflicting, nonempty, and $k \in \aleph$. That is, profile X is homogeneous. It is obvious that

$$C(X) = \{x\}.$$

Thus postulates *P1*, *P2*, *P3* are satisfied. For postulate *P4a*, notice that because x is nonconflicting, then its positive and negative components are disjoint. Postulate *P4b* should also be satisfied because x is a nonempty clause. In this way we have shown that all postulates are satisfied for $C(X)$.

(b) We show now that for each function C satisfying postulate *P5* there exists a profile X such that $C(X)$ does not satisfy postulate *P3*.
Let $C \in C_{cl}$, and let profile X be defined as

$$X = \{99 * (t_1 \rightarrow t_2), t_2 \rightarrow t_3\}$$

for some $t_1, t_2, t_3 \in L$. Thus X contains 99 appearances of the same clause $t_1 \rightarrow t_2$ and one clause $t_2 \rightarrow t_3$. Let $x^* \in C(X)$; notice that because C satisfies postulate *P5* then x should have the form:

$$x^* = t_1 \to t_2 .$$

However, the consequence of the whole profile X should be clause

$$x = t_1 \to t_3,$$

which may not be a consensus from $C(X)$ because

$$\sum_{x \in X} d_\vee (x^*, x) = w_1 + w_2 ,$$

where w_1 and w_2 have been defined in Definition 5.10.

In the meantime for x this sum should be:

$$\sum_{x \in X} d_\vee (x, x) = \cdot 99 \cdot w_2 + w_1 > \sum_{x \in X} d_\vee (x^*, x).$$

Thus postulate $P3$ cannot be satisfied.   ◆

Theorem 5.10 shows that the defined postulates are consistent on the profile level, but they are contradictory on the level of the consensus function. More concretely, postulates $P3$ and $P5$ are most often inconsistent with each other. Postulate $P5$ reflects the numbers of occurrences of symbols in the profile, whereas postulate $P3$ does not refer to these numbers. It follows, as stated above, that postulate $P5$ is not good for profiles which have nonempty consequences; that is, they are not logically inconsistent. This postulate is good only for conflict situations described by inconsistent sets of clauses.

Now we deal with working out algorithms for consensus determination.

5.3.4. Heuristic Algorithm for Consensus Determination

As is known, satisfying postulate $P5$ implies also satisfying postulates $P1$, $P2$, but satisfying postulate $P4b$ takes place only with the assumption of completeness of profiles. Postulate $P4a$ is in some sense independent of postulate $P5$. Postulate $P3$ is not suitable for conflict situations. Thus we need to work out an algorithm for determining consensus, which satisfies postulates $P4a$, $P4b$, and $P5$. For this purpose we use Algorithm 5.1 which is useful for determining consensus of positive and negative profiles.

The idea of the algorithm is presented as follows. First, Algorithm 5.1 is used for determining consensuses for positive and negative profiles which satisfy postulate $P5$. If both these consensuses are empty then they are replaced by nonempty consensuses of positive and negative profiles after removing empty components from them. Next, it is checked if the positive and negative components of consensus are disjoint. If not, the same procedure is used (steps 5–8 of Algorithm 5.2) for eliminating their common elements.

The algorithm is presented below.

Algorithm 5.4.

Input: Profile $X \in \Pi(Clause(L))$, where
$$X = \{(x_i^+, x_i^-): x_i^+ \cup x_i^- \neq \varnothing \text{ for } i = 1, 2, \ldots, n\}.$$

Output: Consensus (x^{*+}, x^{*-}) satisfying postulates *P4a*, *P4b*, and *P5*.

Procedure:

BEGIN

1. Set $Y^+ := \{x_i^+: i = 1, 2, \ldots, n\}$;
2. Set $Y^- := \{x_i^-: i = 1, 2, \ldots, n\}$;
3. For profile Y^+ using Algorithm 5.1 determine its consensus x^{*+};
4. For profile Y^- using Algorithm 5.1 determine its consensus x^{*-};
5. If $x^{*+} \cup x^{*-} \neq \varnothing$ then GOTO 13;
6. Create $Y'^+ := \{x_i^+ \in Y^+: x_i^+ \neq \varnothing\}$;
7. Create $Y'^- := \{x_i^- \in Y^-: x_i^- \neq \varnothing\}$;
8. For profile Y'^+ using Algorithm 5.1 determine its consensus $x^{*'+}$;
9. For profile Y'^- using Algorithm 5.1 determine its consensus $x^{*'-}$;
10. Set $y_1 := (x^{*'+}, x^{*'-})$; $y_2 := (x^{*'+}, \varnothing)$; $y_3 := (\varnothing, x^{*'-})$;
11. Find j ($j = 1, 2, 3$) so that $\sum_{x \in X} d_\vee(y_j, x)$ is minimal;
12. Set $(x^{*+}, x^{*-}) := y_j$;
13. If $x_i^{*+} \cap x_i^{*-} = \varnothing$ then GOTO END;
14. Calculate $S(x^*) = \sum_{x \in X} d_\vee(x^*, x)$, where $x^* = (x_i^{*+}, x_i^{*-})$;
15. Set $T := x_i^{*+} \cap x_i^{*-}$;
16. For each $z \in T$ do
    Begin
    16.1. Set $x' = (x^{*+} \setminus \{z\}, x^{*-})$ and $x'' = (x^{*+}, x^{*-} \setminus \{z\})$;
    16.2. Calculate $S(x') = \sum_{x \in X} d_\vee(x', x)$ and
    $$S(x'') = \sum_{x \in X} d_\vee(x'', x);$$
    16.3. If $S(x') \leq S(x'')$ then set $x^{*+} := x^{*+} \setminus \{z\}$ else
    if $S(x'') < S(x')$ then set $x^{*-} := x^{*-} \setminus \{z\}$;
    End;

END.

It is not hard to show that the computationl complexity of Algorithm 5.4 is $O(m^2 n)$ where $m = \max\{card(\bigcup_{x \in X} x^+), card(\bigcup_{x \in X} x^-)\}$ and $n = card(X)$

Algorithm 5.4 possesses the following properties.

Theorem 5.11.

The following statements are true.

  (a) For any profile $X \in \Pi(Clause(L))$ the consensus determined by Algorithm 5.4 satisfies postulates P1, P2, and P4.

  (b) For any profile $X \in \Pi(Clause(L))$ with complete clauses (i.e., $x^+ \neq \varnothing$ and $x^- \neq \varnothing$ for each $x \in X$) generated by steps 3 and 4 of Algorithm 5.4 consensus (x^{*+}, x^{*-}) is complete; that is, $x^{*+} \neq \varnothing$ and $x^{*-} \neq \varnothing$.

Proof.

  (a) Satisfying postulate P1 results from step 3 of Algorithm 5.1 because it adds to set y^* all such elements z that $f(z) = card(Y)$; that is, z appears in all elements of the profile, and these elements are still in the final form of the consensus. For postulate P2 notice that using step 1 of Algorithm 5.1 in Algorithm 5.4 causes set Z to be defined as the sum of all positive (or negative) components. Next, the elements of consensus y^* are chosen only from Z. Thus the consensus must be a subset of Z. Postulate P4a should be satisfied owing to steps 14–16 of Algorithm 5.4 which cause removal of the common elements of sets x_i^{*+} and x_i^{*-} from one of them. Satisfaction of postulate P4b follows from steps 8–10 of Algorithm 5.4 which make the choice of consensus between only nonempty positive and negative components and next combine the nonempty consensus. Notice that the consensuses for profiles Y'^+ and Y'^- are nonempty (see the proof of Theorem 5.9).

  (b) The proof also follows directly from the proof of Theorem 5.9. Note that in this case steps 6–12 are not needed, and generated consensus satisfies at once postulate P4b. ◆

  For postulate P6 we can formulate an algorithm similar to Algorithm 5.3 for conjunctions which also takes into account postulate P5.

5.4. Fuzzy Structure of Knowledge

In this section we deal with fuzzy structure for inconsistency representation on the syntactic level. In Section 5.2 an agent or expert referring to an event or scenario may only assign his opinion by means of one of two values (*true* or *false*). For example, if in his opinion the event represented by symbol a should not take place then he can generate literal $\neg a$. We now consider the possibility for an agent (expert) to describe his opinion in more precise way using fuzzy-based approach.

5.4.1. Basic Notions

We assume that referring to a real event or scenario represented by symbol t an expert can give a degree in which in her opinion the event (or scenario) should take place. For example, if symbol t represents scenario "*The temperature will be higher than* 0," then the pair $(t, 0.7)$ should represent an opinion that with certainty 0.7 the temperature will be higher than 0.

In fuzzy structures we use only one form of literal; this is a fuzzy literal

$$(t, v) \, ,$$

where $t \in L$ and $v \in [0, 1]$.

Thus a positive literal t used in Sections 5.2 and 5.3 is a special case of this kind and may be interpreted as equivalent to fuzzy literal

$$(t, 1)$$

and a negative literal $\neg t$ may be interpreted as equivalent to fuzzy literal

$$(t, 0).$$

Notice that the above assumption is not novel; it is simply the basic assumption for fuzzy logic. We consider two kinds of fuzzy formulas:

- As a *fuzzy conjunction* we define the following expression,

$$(t_1, v_1) \wedge (t_2, v_2) \wedge \cdots \wedge (t_k, v_k) \, ,$$

  where $t_1, t_2 \in L$ and $v_1, v_2, \ldots , v_k \in [0, 1]$.
- As a *fuzzy clause* we define the expression:

$$(t_1, v_1) \vee (t_2, v_2) \vee \cdots \vee (t_k, v_k) \, ,$$

  where $t_1, t_2 \in L$ and $v_1, v_2, \ldots , v_k \in [0, 1]$.

Fuzzy conjunctions and fuzzy clauses may be very useful for agent knowledge representation. Similarly as earlier we also assume that if a symbol does not appear in an opinion of an agent then the fact or event represented by this symbol belongs to the agent's ignorance.

5.4.2. Distance Function

For defining distance functions for fuzzy conjunctions and fuzzy clauses we consider the following situations:

1. Two fuzzy formulas contain the same set of symbols. In this case the following distance function is reasonable.

Definition 5.12.

   (a) Let there be given two fuzzy conjunctions:

$$x = (t_1, v_1) \wedge (t_2, v_2) \wedge \cdots \wedge (t_k, v_k),$$

   and

$$x' = (t_1, v_1') \wedge (t_2, v_2') \wedge \cdots \wedge (t_k, v_k').$$

As the distance between conjunctions x and x' we understand the value:

$$d_{\wedge}^{f}(x,x') = \sum_{i=1}^{k}\left|v_i - v_i'\right|.$$

   (b) Let there be given two fuzzy clauses:

$$x = (t_1, v_1) \vee (t_2, v_2) \vee \cdots \vee (t_k, v_k),$$

   and

$$x' = (t_1, v_1') \vee (t_2, v_2') \vee \cdots \vee (t_k, v_k').$$

As the distance between clauses x and x' we understand the value:

$$d_{\vee}^{f}(x,x') = \sum_{i=1}^{k}\left|v_i - v_i'\right|.$$

The functions defined above are sensible because they reflect the distance for each symbol. Apart from these functions one may also use well-known distance functions for vectors such as the cosine function [141] for document space, or the Euclidean function for mathematical vector space.

2. Two fuzzy formulas contain different sets of symbols. In this case none none of the above-mentioned distance functions is reasonable. Let's consider an example.

Let there be given two fuzzy conjunctions:

$$x = (t_1, 0.3) \wedge (t_2, 0.5)$$

and

$$x' = (t_1, 0.8).$$

We can say that referring to the fact or event represented by symbol t_1 these two conjunctions differ from each other in a degree equal to 0.5. However, this difference is not known in the case of the fact or event represented by symbol t_2. The reason is that along with our assumption about the incompleteness of agent knowledge in the case of conjunction x' the agent has investigated only the fact or event represented by symbol t_1 and is ignorant as to the part of the real world represented by symbol t_2. Thus we have no basis to determine the degree of the difference between these conjunctions.

Despite the lack of possibility to calculate the distance function for fuzzy formulae in this case as we show below, using postulate $P6$ defined in Sections 5.2.3 and 5.3.3 and distance functions $d_\wedge^f$ and $d_\vee^f$ defined above we can solve the consensus problem.

5.4.3. Integration Problem and Algorithm for Consensus Choice

The integration problem for fuzzy conjunctions may be formulated as follows.

For a given set of fuzzy conjunctions

$$X = \{x_i = (t_1^{(i)}, v_1^{(i)}) \wedge (t_2^{(i)}, v_2^{(i)}) \wedge \cdots \wedge (t_{k_i}^{(i)}, v_{k_i}^{(i)}): i = 1, 2, \ldots, n\}$$

it is necessary to determine a fuzzy conjunction

$$x^* = (t_1, v_1) \wedge (t_2, v_2) \wedge \cdots \wedge (t_k, v_k),$$

called a consensus of set X.

The integration problem for fuzzy clauses is similar.

We cannot assume that the sets of symbols included in particular conjunctions are identical. Therefore, the direct use of postulate $P5$ (Section 5.2.3) for consensus choice is impossible. However, we may combine postulates $P5$ and $P6$ as shown in Algorithm 5.3 for this aim.

Below we present a similar algorithm to Algorithm 5.3. Its idea relies on determining the consensus basis for each symbol (postulate $P6$), and next using postulate $P5$ and distance function $d_\wedge^f$ to determine the fuzzy value for this symbol.

This algorithm is presented as follows.

Algorithm 5.5.

Input: Profile

$$X = \{x_i = (t_1^{(i)}, v_1^{(i)}) \wedge (t_2^{(i)}, v_2^{(i)}) \wedge \cdots \wedge (t_{k_i}^{(i)}, v_{k_i}^{(i)}): i = 1, 2, \ldots, n\}.$$

Output: Consensus $x^* = (t_1, v_1) \wedge (t_2, v_2) \wedge \cdots \wedge (t_k, v_k)$.

Procedure:

BEGIN

    1. Set $Z:=\{t \in L:$ there exists a conjunction $x \in X$, in which symbol t appears$\}$;

    2. Set $k:= card(Z)$;

    3. For each $t \in Z$ determine

$$X(t) = \{(t, v): \text{there exists a conjunction in } X \text{ containing literal } (t, v)\};$$

    4. Set $i:= 1$;

    5. For each $t \in Z$ do

      Begin

        5.1. Set $t_i:= t$;

        5.2. Create $Y = \{v: (t, v) \in X(t)\}$;

        5.2. Sort the elements of Y in an increasing order;

        5.3. Set $v_i:= y_{\left\lfloor \frac{l+1}{2} \right\rfloor}$ where $l = card(Y)$ and $\left\lfloor \frac{l+1}{2} \right\rfloor$ is the greatest integer not greater than $\dfrac{l+1}{2}$;

        5.4. Set $i:= i + 1$;

      End.

END.

The algorithm for fuzzy clauses may be formulated in the same way.

We should now show that in Algorithm 5.5 postulate *P5* is reflected. In fact it is used in step 5 of the algorithm. Notice that set $X(t)$ can be treated as a profile in which all literals refer to the same symbol t. We can then write:

$$X(t) = \{(t, y_1), (t, y_2), \ldots, (t, y_l)\}.$$

Value v should be such that it minimizes the sum

$$\sum_{i=1}^{l} d_{\wedge}^{f}\left((t,v),(t,y_i)\right) = \min_{v' \in [0,1]} \sum_{i=1}^{l} d_{\wedge}^{f}\left((t,v'),(t,y_i)\right).$$

In fact the above dependence is equivalent to:

$$\sum_{i=1}^{l} |v - y_i| = \min_{v' \in [0,1]} \sum_{i=1}^{l} |v' - y_i|.$$

It is not hard to prove that the value v determined in step 5 should satisfy this condition. In fact value v may belong to the interval

$$y_j \leq x \leq y_{j'},$$

where

$$j = \left\lfloor \frac{l+1}{2} \right\rfloor \quad \text{and} \quad j' = \left\lfloor \frac{l+2}{2} \right\rfloor.$$

Notice that in the case when the inconsistency refers to numbers very often the final value is determined as the average of these numbers. That is,

$$v = \frac{1}{l} \sum_{i=1}^{l} y_i.$$

This manner of calculating v is consistent with criterion O_2 defined in Chapter 3, requiring minimization of the sum of squared distances between the consensus and the elements of the profile.

5.5. Conclusions

As has been shown, using symbols for representing inconsistency of knowledge may be powerful in many cases. In this chapter we have used symbols for describing inconsistency in three structures: conjunction, clause, and fuzzy conjunction and clause. For each of them we have defined the consensus problem as well as the consensus function, for which a set of postulates has been proposed for expressing the conditions for consensus. The results of postulates are very interesting and help us to get to know about their relationships. These relationships have then been used in formulating the algorithms for consensus choice.

6. Processing Inconsistency on the Semantic Level

In this chapter some solutions of knowledge inconsistency resolution and knowledge integration on the semantic level are presented. The conjunctive and disjunctive structures of inconsistency interpreted in a real world are investigated. For each structure the notion of semantics is defined and analyzed. The distance functions for these structures are defined and the problem of dependencies between attributes is also investigated.

6.1. Introduction

In the previous chapter we have assumed that an event or a fact of a real world is represented by a symbol, and an agent or expert in her opinion assigns to this symbol one of the logic values (*true*, *false*), or one of the fuzzy values. Symbols in an agent opinion may be in one of two relationships: conjunction or disjunction. The advantages of this approach are based on the simplicity of representation, and in consequence, the effectiveness of inconsistency processing. However, there are some disadvantages of this model, presented as follows:

- The representation power is restricted. Among others, the dependencies between real world facts or events may not be exposed by symbols themselves. It is necessary to use a metalanguage for this purpose.
- Because of diversification and the large number of real world facts and events, the set of symbols may be very large, and this could make the proposed methods ineffective.

In this chapter we propose an approach which is free of the above-mentioned disadvantages. We deal with the semantics of the symbols. We assume a deeper representation of real world events and facts. Concretely, we assume that a fact is represented not by a symbol, but by a pair (a, v) (called a *term*) where a is an attribute representing the feature of the fact and v is its value. Owing to this the dependencies of facts or events can be exposed by themselves and a metalanguage is not needed. Also, it is not necessary to use a large set of symbols, because each value of v in pair (a, v) can refer to one fact or event. Thus the representation power is greater than in the case of symbols. Term (a, v) is understood as an interpretation of some logic formula, and therefore solving inconsistency with taking into account the interpretations of logic formulae we call the *semantic level* of inconsistency resolution.

Similarly as on the syntactic level, on the semantic level we also consider two kinds of relationships between terms: conjunction and disjunction. By means of the conjunction structure it will be possible for an agent to connect several facts in one opinion for representing a complex event. By means of the disjunction structure an agent may represent his uncertainty, and furthermore, represent the rules in the precondition–postcondition form. For each structure a consensus problem is formulated and the definition is given. Algorithms for consensus choice are also presented. The original idea for defining inconsistency on the semantic level has been introduced in [108]. In this chapter this approach is modified, extended, and more deeply analyzed.

6.2. Conjunction Structure

6.2.1. Basic Notions

In this chapter we use the notions defined in Chapter 4, Section 4.2.1. These notions refer to representing a real world by a multiattribute and multivalue relational structure.

Let (A, V) be a real world. For the requirements of this chapter we introduce the following additional notions.

- An expression $(a = v)$ where $a \in A$, $v \subseteq V_a$ is called a *positive literal* based on the real world (A, V), or (A, V)-based for short. An expression $\neg(a = v)$ is called a *negative literal*. Positive literals serve agents to express their positive knowledge, that is, knowledge consisting of statements "*something should take place,*" whereas negative literals serve to express their negative knowledge, that is, knowledge consisting of statements "*something should not take place.*"
- Notice that the value v of literal $(a = v)$ is a set of elementary values. We accept the following interpretation of this literal. It represents a fact or event for which the value of attribute a (or parameter a) is a subset of v. For example, a meteorological agent may give her forecast

referring to temperature in the form of a literal (*temperature* = [15–20]). That is, in her opinion the temperature will be between 15 and 20 degrees centigrade. If $v = \varnothing$ then according to this interpretation we understand that in the agent's opinion the fact referring to this attribute has no value. In other words, attribute a does not concern this fact. Consider again the meteorological example; if the forecast refers to the time of rain, then an agent may believe that there will be no rain, and she should give a literal (*rain* = $\varnothing$). A positive literal in fact is a one-attribute tuple.

- In this sense, by means of a negative literal $\neg(a = v)$ an agent can express her opinion that the value of attribute a referring to the considered fact may not be a subset of v.

- Notice that literal $\neg(a = v)$ is not equivalent to literal $(a = V_a \backslash v)$. For example, a meteorological agent can believe that there will be no rain between 10 a.m. and 12 a.m., but this does not mean that in the opinion of the agent it will rain during some period the rest of the day.

- Instead of $(a = v)$ we write (a, v) and instead of $\neg(a = v)$ we write $\neg(a, v)$.

6.2.2. Conjunctions of Literals

In this approach an element of a conflict profile representing an agent opinion is a formula in the form of a conjunction of literals:

$$l_1 \wedge l_2 \wedge \cdots \wedge l_n$$

where $l_1, l_2, \ldots, l_n$ are (A, V)-based literals. By $Conj(A,V)$ we denote the set of all conjunctions of (A, V)-based literals. The set of attributes appearing in a conjunction is called its *type*.

Let's consider an example.

Example 6.1. Let A be a set of attributes *Type, Direction, Wind_Speed* which represent the parameters of wind in a meteorological system. The domains of these attributes are the following.

- $V_{Type} = \{$gusty, moderate$\}$.

- $V_{Direction} = \{$N, W, E, S, N–W, N–E, S–W, S–E$\}$.

- $V_{Wind\_Speed} = [0$ km/h, 250 km/h$]$ (this interval represents the set of integers not smaller than 0 and not greater than 250).

Examples of formulae representing opinions of agents A_1, A_2, and A_3 are the following:

A_1: *(Type*, {gusty}) $\land$ *(Direction*, {N}) $\land$ $\neg$*(Wind_Speed*, {90}).

A_2: *(Type*, {gusty}) $\land$ $\neg$*(Direction*, {N–W, N})

$\land$ *(Wind_Speed*, [100, 150]).

A_3: *(Type*, $\varnothing$) $\land$ *(Wind_Speed*, [20, 50]).

As assumed above, the empty value of attribute *Type* in the third conjunction means that in the opinion of the agent this attribute should not have any value.

As we can see, by means of a conjunction an agent may represent his positive knowledge (in positive literals; see Table 6.1) as well as negative knowledge (in negative literals; see Table 6.2).

Table 6.1. Positive knowledge

Agent	Type	Direction	Wind_Speed
A_1	{gusty}	{N}	
A_2	{gusty}		[100, 150]
A_3	$\varnothing$		[20, 50]

Table 6.2. Negative knowledge

Agent	Type	Direction	Wind_Speed
A_1			[90, 90]
A_2		{N-W, N}	
A_3			

♦

The set of attributes occurring in a literal is called its type. Note that in a conjunction the same attribute may appear more than one time. For example, in conjunction

(Type, {gusty}) $\land$ *(Direction*, {N}) $\land$ $\neg$*(Direction*, {W})

$\land$ $\neg$*(Wind_Speed*, {90})

attribute *Direction* appears twice. The type of this literal is set

{*Type, Direction, Wind_Speed*}.

We now define the semantics of conflict profile elements.

Definition 6.1.
As the semantics of conjunctions we understand the following function,

$$S_C: Conj(A,V) \rightarrow 2^{\bigcup_{T \subseteq A} 2^{E-TUPLE(T)} \cup \theta_E},$$

such that:

(a) $S_C((a,v)) = \{r \in \text{E-TUPLE}(\{a\}): r_a \in v\}$ *for* $v \subseteq V_a$ *and* $v \neq \varnothing$.

(b) $S_C((a,\varnothing)) = \{(a, \varepsilon)\}$.

(c) $S_C(\neg(a,v)) = \{r \in \text{E-TUPLE}(\{a\}): r_a \in V_a \setminus v\} \cup \{(a, \varepsilon)\}$
for $v \subseteq V_a$ *and* $v \neq \varnothing$.

(d) $S_C(\neg(a, \varnothing)) = \{r \in \text{E-TUPLE}(\{a\}): r_a \in V_a\}$.

(e) $S_C(l_1 \wedge l_2 \wedge \cdots \wedge l_k)$

$$= \big\{r \in \text{E-TUPLE}(B) \cup \theta_E:$$
$$(\forall a \in B)(\forall i \in \{1, 2, \ldots, k\})([a \text{ appears in } l_i] \Rightarrow$$
$$(a, r_a) \in S_C(l_i))\big\},$$

where B is the type of conjunction $l_1 \wedge l_2 \wedge \cdots \wedge l_k$.

Some commentary should be made for this definition:

- The semantics of a one-literal conjunction (a, v) where $v \subseteq V_a$ and v is nonempty, consists of those elementary tuples which are included in (a, v). This is consistent with the assumption that the value of parameter a of the fact represented by this literal is a subset of v. Thus an elementary tuple included in (a, v) should be a potential scenario of the fact.

- The semantics of conjunction $(a, \varnothing)$ consists of only one elementary tuple which is (a, ε). This is because such kind of opinion means that the agent believes that referring to an event attribute a should not have any value.

- For an attribute a the set of all potential scenarios is equal to

  $$\text{E-TUPLE}(\{a\}) \cup \{(a, \varepsilon)\}.$$

  The semantics of literal $\neg(a, v)$ should be complementary to the semantics of (a, v); that is, the sum of the semantics of $\neg(a, v)$ and the semantics of (a, v) should be equal to the set of all possible scenarios referring to attribute a, and they must be also disjoint. This property follows from the definition.

- At last, the semantics of a complex conjunction should be built on the basis of the semantics of particular literals. Note that the definition in (d) is consistent with that in (a)–(c) for the case when $k = 1$. Besides, if an attribute a appears in more than one literal in conjunction $l_1 \wedge l_2 \wedge \cdots \wedge l_k$ then the elementary tuple (a, r_a) must belong to the semantics of each of these literals.

Thus the semantics of conjunction x is a set of all elementary tuples which are included in the tuple x' representing x, and their values referring to an attribute are empty if and only if the value of x' is empty for this attribute. The idea of this definition is based on the aspect that if conjunction x represents the opinion of an agent for some issue then set $S_C(x)$ consists of all possible scenarios which are included in x and may take place according to the agent's opinion. Example 6.2 should illustrate the intuition.

Example 6.2. For the real world defined in Example 6.1 the semantics of agent's opinions is determined as follows.

For conjunction

$$x = \neg(Type, \{gusty\}) \wedge (Direction, \{N\text{--}W, N\})$$
$$\wedge (Wind\_Speed, [100\text{--}150]),$$

the semantics is presented by Table 6.3.

Table 6.3. The semantics of formula x

Type	Direction	Wind_Speed
moderate	N–W	100
moderate	N–W	101
. . .	. . .	. . .
moderate	N–W	150
moderate	N	100
moderate	N	101
. . .	. . .	. . .
moderate	N	150
ε	N	100
ε	N	101
. . .	. . .	. . .
ε	N	150

For conjunction:

$$x' = (\textit{Type}, \{\text{gusty}\}) \wedge (\textit{Direction}, \{\text{N–W, N, E}\})$$
$$\wedge (\textit{Direction}, \{\text{N–W, N, S}\}) \wedge (\textit{Wind\_Speed}, [200\text{–}202])$$

its semantics is presented by the following table.

Table 6.4. The semantics of formula x'

Type	Direction	Wind_Speed
gusty	N–W	200
gusty	N–W	201
gusty	N–W	202
gusty	N	200
gusty	N	201
gusty	N	202

Each of the elementary tuples from this table represents a scenario which in the opinion of the agent should take place.   ♦

From Definition 6.1 the following properties follow immediately.

Remark 6.1.
For any $a \in A$ the following dependencies are true:

(a) $S_C(\neg(a,\varnothing)) = S_C((a,V_a)) = \textit{E-TUPLE}(\{a\})$.

(b) $S_C((a,\varnothing)) = S_C(\neg(a,V_a)) = \{(a, \varepsilon)\}$.

(c) $S_C((a,v)) \neq S_C(\neg(a,V_a\backslash v))$ *for $v \neq \varnothing$.*

(d) $S_C((a, v)) \cap S_C(\neg(a, v)) = \varnothing$ *for any $v \subseteq V_a$.*

(e) $S_C((a, v)) \cup S_C(\neg(a, v)) = \textit{E-TUPLE}(\{a\}) \cup \{(a, \varepsilon)\}$
for any $v \subseteq V_a$.

Remark 6.2.
Function S_C has the following properties:

(a) *Commutativity, that is,*

$$S_C(x \wedge x') = S_C(x' \wedge x).$$

(b) *Associativity, that is,*

$$S_C((x \wedge x') \wedge x'') = S_C(x \wedge (x' \wedge x'')).$$

Now we present the definition of such notions as equivalence, complement, inconsistency, and conflict of conjunctions.

Definition 6.2.

  (a) *Two conjunctions x and x' ($x, x' \in Conj(A,V)$) are equivalent if and only if*

$$S_C(x) = S_C(x').$$

  (b) *Two literals x and x' are conflicting if and only if*

$$S_C(x) \cap S_C(x') = \varnothing.$$

  (c) *Two literals x and x' of the same type $\{a\}$ are complementary if and only if*

$$S_C(x) \cap S_C(x') = \varnothing$$

and

$$S_C(x) \cup S_C(x') = E\text{-}TUPLE(\{a\}) \cup \{(a, \varepsilon)\}.$$

  (d) *A conjunction x is inconsistent if and only if $S_C(x) = \varnothing$*

  (e) *Two conjunctions x and x' ($x, x' \in Conj(A,V)$) are conflicting if and only if conjunction $x \wedge x'$ is inconsistent.*

A conjunction which is not inconsistent, is called *consistent*. Thus two consistent conjunctions x and x' are conflicting if and only if there exist a literal l in x and a literal l' in x' such that l and l' are conflicting.

We prove the following.

Theorem 6.1.
The following dependencies are true.

  (a) *If two conjunctions are equivalent then they must be of the same type.*

  (b) *Any two literals (a, v) and (a, v') are conflicting if and only if*

$$v \cap v' = \varnothing;$$

any two literals $\neg(a, v)$ and $\neg(a, v')$ are conflicting if and only if

$$v = \varnothing \text{ and } v' = V_a \text{ or vice versa.}$$

  (c) *Any two literals (a, v) and (a, v') are complementary if and only if*

$$v = \varnothing \text{ and } v' = V_a \text{ or vice versa.}$$

(d) For any two literals $l = (a, v)$ and $l' = (a, v')$ there should be

$$S_C(l \wedge l') = S_C(l) \cap S_C(l'),$$

and if l and l' are nonconflicting then

$$S_C(l \wedge l') = S_C((a, v \cap v')).$$

(e) For any two nonconflicting literals $l = \neg(a, v)$ and $l' = \neg(a, v')$ there should be

$$S_C(l \wedge l') = S_C(l) \cap S_C(l') = S_C(\neg(a, v \cup v')).$$

(f) Two literals (a, v) and $\neg(a, v')$ are complementary if and only if

$$v = v'.$$

Proof.

(a) Two conjunctions are equivalent if they have the same semantics. Assume that they are of different types. That is, there exists an attribute a which appears in one conjunction but does not appear in the second. In this case the semantics of the conjunction containing a should include elementary tuple (a, ε) if a occurs in a negative literal or in literal $(a, \varnothing)$, or tuple (a, w) for some $w \in V_a$ if a occurs in a positive literal, whereas the second conjunction does not have this property.

(b) For any two positive literals (a, v) and (a, v') where $v \cap v' = \varnothing$ it is obvious that $S_C(x) \cap S_C(x') = \varnothing$; that is, they are conflicting. Assume that literals (a, v) and (a, v') are conflicting; that is, $S_C(x) \cap S_C(x') = \varnothing$. Then $v \cap v' = \varnothing$. For the proof for the case when literals $\neg(a, v)$ and $\neg(a, v')$ are conflicting, see the proof for (c).

(c) Any two positive literals (a, v) and (a, v') where $v \neq \varnothing$ and $v' \neq \varnothing$ cannot be conflicting because their semantics does not contain tuple $\{(a, \varepsilon)\}$. If one of them is empty then the other must equal V_a because only literal (a, V_a) has semantics equal to E-$TUPLE(\{a\})$.

(d) Let $l = (a, v)$ and $l' = (a, v')$; according to Definition 6.1 we have immediately:

$$S_C(l \wedge l') = \left\{ r \in E\text{-}TUPLE(\{a\}) \cup \theta_E : (a, r_a) \in S_C(l) \cap S_C(l') \right\}$$

$$= S_C(l) \cap S_C(l').$$

On the other hand, if $v \cap v' \neq \varnothing$ then we have:

$$S_C((a, v \cap v')) = \{r \in E\text{-}TUPLE(\{a\}) : r_a \in v \cap v'\} = S_C(l) \cap S_C(l').$$

If l and l' are nonconflicting then there should be $v \cap v' \neq \varnothing$. Thus according to Definition 6.1 we have

$$S_C(l) \cap S_C(l') = S_C((a, v \cap v')) = S_C(l \wedge l').$$

Notice that in the case when $v \cap v' = \varnothing$ the equality is not true because

$$S_C((a, v \cap v')) = \{(a, \varepsilon)\}$$

whereas $S_C(l) \cap S_C(l') = \varnothing$.

(e) Two literals $l = \neg(a, v)$ and $l' = \neg(a, v')$ are nonconflicting if

$$(V_a \backslash v) \cap (V_a \backslash v') \neq \varnothing \text{ or } V_a \backslash (v \cup v') \neq \varnothing.$$

Thus we have

$$S_C(l \wedge l') = S_C(l) \cap S_C(l') = S_C(\neg(a, (v \cup v'))).$$

Notice that if l and l' are conflicting, that is, $V_a \backslash (v \cup v') = \varnothing$, then the equation is not true because $V_a = (v \cup v')$ and then $S_C(l) \cap S_C(l') = \varnothing$ but

$$S_C(\neg(a, (v \cup v'))) = S_C(\neg(a, V_a)) = \{(a, \varepsilon)\}.$$

(f) Literals (a, v) and $\neg(a, v)$ are complementary. This statement follows from Remarks 6.1d and 6.1e. We show now that if two literals (a, v) and $\neg(a, v')$ are complementary then there should be $v = v'$. From Definition 6.2 it follows that

$$S_C((a, v)) \cap S_C(\neg(a, v')) = \varnothing, \text{ and}$$

$$S_C((a, v)) \cup S_C(\neg(a, v')) = E\text{-}TUPLE(\{a\}) \cup \{(a, \varepsilon)\}.$$

We can note that $v \cap (V_a \backslash v') = \varnothing$ because otherwise sets $S_C((a, v))$ and $S_C(\neg(a, v'))$ will not be disjoint. Also, there should be $v \cup V_a \backslash v' = V_a$ because if $v \cup V_a \backslash v' \neq V_a$ then

$$S_C((a, v)) \cup S_C(\neg(a, v')) \subset E\text{-}TUPLE(\{a\}) \cup \{(a, \varepsilon)\}.$$

Thus it follows that $v = v'$.   ♦

From Theorem 6.1 it implies that the equivalence relation between conjunctions refers only to conjunctions of the same type, whereas the conflict relation refers to literals with the same attribute. Inconsistency is a feature of single conjunctions which contain two conflicting literals. As stated above these two literals being conflicting must contain the same attribute.

Theorem 6.2.
If conjunctions $x_1, x_2, \ldots, x_k$ are of the same type then

$$S_C(x_1 \wedge x_2 \wedge \ldots \wedge x_k) = S_C(x_1) \cap S_C(x_2) \cap \ldots \cap S_C(x_k).$$

Proof.

First we prove that for any two conjunctions x and x' of the same type there should be

$$S_C(x \wedge x') = S_C(x) \cap S_C(x').$$

From Theorem 6.1 it follows that it is true for the case when x and x' are literals. In the case when x and x' are conjunctions of the same type but consisting of more than one literal then using the properties of associativity and commutativity in conjunction $x \wedge x'$ we can group the literals of the same type. More concretely, let

$$x = l_1 \wedge l_2 \wedge \ldots \wedge l_k$$

and let

$$x' = l_{1'} \wedge l_{2'} \wedge \ldots \wedge l_{l'}.$$

Notice that although conjunctions x and x' are of the same type, the numbers of literals in each of them need not be equal. The reason is that in x or x' there may be more than one literal with the same attribute. Let T be the type of these conjunctions. Let $r \in S_C(x \wedge x')$. According to Definition 6.1 for an attribute $a \in T$ tuple r should have such value r_a that elementary tuple (a, r_a) belongs to the semantics of each literal containing attribute a in both conjunctions. Thus it is obvious that $r \in S_C(x) \cap S_C(x')$. On the other hand, if r is such an elementary tuple that $r \in S_C(x) \cap S_C(x')$ then for each attribute $a \in T$ pair (a, r_a) belongs to the semantics of each literal containing attribute a in both conjunctions, so $r \in S_C(x \wedge x')$.

For the proof of the general case we may use the result presented above for two conjunctions and a simple induction method.   ♦

Theorem 6.2 shows a very important property of the semantics of conjunctions: the relationship between conjunctive structure and the product operation on sets. It also facilitates calculating semantics of complex conjunctions.

6.2.3. Distance Function between Attribute Values

In Section 4.2.2 (Chapter 4) we defined several distance functions between attribute values. For an attribute a we defined two kinds of distance functions: functions of type δ minimizing the transformation costs and functions of type ρ minimizing the element shares in the distance. Both of them are metrics. We have also defined proportional functions δ^P, ρ^P, and quasi-proportional functions δ^{QP} and ρ^{QP}, respectively. We mention that a propositional distance function assigns to a pair of two sets of attribute values a larger distance if the symmetrical difference between them is larger. A quasi-proportional distance function additionally requires the sum of these two sets to be constant.

The defined distance functions are used in the next sections for performing the integration process of knowledge in conjunctive structure.

6.2.4. Inconsistency Representation

In this section we deal with the representation of a conflict profile using conjunctions. As a conflict profile we understand a finite set with repetitions of (A,V)-based conjunctions. We assume that the conjunctions are consistent; that is, each of them does not contain conflicting literals. This assumption is needed because an agent or expert should give a sensible opinion; that is, he cannot state simultaneously in his opinion that the same scenario should take place as well as it should not take place.

For a conflict profile we can also assume that in each conjunction each attribute may occur at most in one positive literal and one negative literal. This assumption is possible owing to Theorem 6.1, which enables replacing two positive (or negative) literals with the same attribute by one positive (or negative) literal with this attribute and a proper value.

Definition 6.3.
Let $X = \{x_1, x_2, \ldots, x_n\}$ where $x_i \in Conj(A,V)$ and x_i is a consistent conjunction for $i = 1, 2, \ldots, n$, be a conflict profile. We say that X represents a conflict if there exist two conjunctions x and x' such that

$$S_C(x) \neq S_C(x').$$

Thus a conflict profile consists of at least two opinions of agents (or experts) that do not have the same semantics.

A conjunction may also be divided into two parts: the first consists of positive literals and the second consists of negative literals. Thus similarly as in Chapter 5 a conjunction x can be represented by a pair:

$$x = (x^+, x^-).$$

A conflict profile X may then be written as

$$X = \{x_i = (x_i^+, x_i^-) \in Conj(A,V) : i = 1, 2, \ldots, n\}.$$

Let T_X be the sum of all types of conjunction belonging to X. For each attribute $a \in T_X$ we determine

- $X^+(a)$ as the set with repetitions consisting of all positive literals containing attribute a which occur in the conjunctions from X
- $X^-(a)$ as the set with repetitions consisting of all negative literals containing attribute a which occur in the conjunctions from X

Notice that in each of sets $X^+(a)$ and $X^-(a)$ a conjunction from X may have at most one literal. These sets may be treated as positive and negative profiles restricted to attribute a. We call them *subprofiles*. Notice that one of sets $X^+(a)$ and $X^-(a)$ may be empty, however, both of them may not be empty; that is, $X^+(a) \cup X^-(a) \neq \varnothing$.

Example 6.3. Let A be a set of attributes a, b, and c. The domains of the attributes are the following:

- $V_a = \{1, 2, \ldots, 10\}$.
- $V_b = \{N, W, E, S\}$.
- $V_c = [6\ \text{a.m.–}6\ \text{p.m.}]$ (this interval represents the set of hours between 6 a.m. and 6 p.m.

Let profile X consist of the following conjunctions:

- $(a, \{1, 2\}) \wedge (b, \{N\}) \wedge \neg(c, \{6\ \text{a.m.–}8\ \text{a.m.}\})$.
- $\neg(a, \{1\}) \wedge \neg(b, \{S\}) \wedge (c, \{6\ \text{a.m.–}10\ \text{a.m.}\})$.
- $(a, \{1, 3, 8\}) \wedge \neg(a, \{1\}) \wedge \neg(c, \{8\ \text{a.m.–}9\ \text{a.m.}\})$.
- $(a, \varnothing) \wedge (b, \{N, S, E\}) \wedge \neg(c, \{6\ \text{a.m.–}6\ \text{p.m.}\})$.
- $(a, \{1, 5, 9\}) \wedge \neg(b, \{N\})$.

Notice that conjunctions belonging to the profile have different types. On the basis of the profile we determine the subprofiles as follows.

Subprofiles	a	b	c
X^+	$(a, \{1, 2\})$ $(a, \{1, 3, 8\})$ $(a, \varnothing)$ $(a, \{1, 5, 9\})$	$(b, \{N\})$ $(b, \{N, S, E\})$	$(c, \{6\ \text{a.m.–}10\ \text{a.m.}\})$
X^-	$\neg(a, \{1\})$ $\neg(a, \{1\})$	$\neg(b, \{S\})$ $\neg(b, \{N\})$	$\neg(c, \{6\ \text{a.m.–}8\ \text{a.m.}\})$ $\neg(c, \{8\ \text{a.m.–}9\ \text{a.m.}\})$ $\neg(c, \{6\ \text{a.m.–}6\ \text{p.m.}\})$

♦

6.2.5. Integration Problem

The integration problem is defined as follows.

Given a profile

$$X = \{x_i = (x_i^+, x_i^-) \in Conj(A,V) : i = 1, 2, \ldots, n\}$$

one should determine a conjunction x* which best represents the given conjunctions.

For this problem with the assumption that attributes occurring in profile X are independent of each other (attribute dependencies are analyzed later in this chapter),[1] we can accept the following scheme for solving this integration problem:

1. For each attribute a occurring in X determine positive and negative subprofiles $X^+(a)$ and $X^-(a)$.
2. Determine the consensus for $(X^+(a), X^-(a))$.
3. Perform the concatenation of consensuses for all attributes occurring in X creating conjunction x^*.

If the attributes are independent, the above-defined scheme is very intuitive. Because for each attribute we have the best representative for the subprofiles, then the concatenation of the representatives should be the best for all given conjunctions. However, in the case of attribute dependencies this scheme cannot be used. We propose a model for attribute dependencies and a method for consensus determining for those profiles in which attribute dependencies appear.

The first of the above-mentioned tasks is simple, and its realization has been shown above. The third task is also not complex. The second task is the most complex and important.

6.2.6. Consensus Determination for Subprofiles

As stated above, realization of the second task is essential for the integration process of conjunctions. Below we present the definition of a consensus function for subprofiles referring to an attribute a.

Definition 6.4.
By a consensus function for subprofiles of literals of type $\{a\}$ we understand a function C_a which for a pair

---

[1] Here we understand generally that two attributes are independent of each other if for each real world object to which they refer the values of one of them do not determine the values of the other.

$$X(a) = (X^+(a), X^-(a))$$

assigns a set $C_a(X(a))$ of conjunctions of type $\{a\}$ which satisfies one or more of the following postulates.

P1a. *If $X^+(a) = \varnothing$ then each element of set $C_a(X(a))$ should have only positive components.*

P1b. *If $X^-(a) = \varnothing$ then each element of set $C_a(X(a))$ should have only negative components.*

P1c. *If $X^+(a) \neq \varnothing$ and $X^-(a) \neq \varnothing$ then each element of set $C_a(X(a))$ should have both components.*

P2. *If an element of $C_a(X(a))$ has positive component (a, v) then:*

$$\bigcap_{(a,v') \in X^+(a)} v' \subseteq v$$

and

$$v \subseteq \bigcup_{(a,v') \in X^+(a)} v'.$$

P3. *If an element of $C_a(X(a))$ has negative component $\neg(a, v)$ then:*

$$\bigcap_{(a,v') \in X^-(a)} v' \subseteq v$$

and

$$v \subseteq \bigcup_{(a,v') \in X^-(a)} v'.$$

P4. *Any element of $C_a(X(a))$ should be consistent.*

P5a. *If literal (a, v) occurs in an element of $C_a(X(a))$ then it should minimize the sum of distances:*

$$\sum_{(a,w) \in X^+(a)} d_a(v, w) = \min_{w' \subseteq V_a} \sum_{(a,w) \in X^+(a)} d_a(w', w).$$

P5b. *If literal $\neg(a, v')$ occurs in an element of $C_a(X(a))$ then it should minimize the sum of distances:*

$$\sum_{(a,w) \in X^-(a)} d_a(v, w) = \min_{w' \subseteq V_a} \sum_{(a,w) \in X^-(a)} d_a(w', w).$$

An element of $C_a(X(a))$ is called a *consensus* of subprofile $X(a)$.

Postulates *P1a–P1c* express a very general requirement for the consensus. Concretely, the positive component will occur in the consensus only if the agents or experts generate their positive knowledge. The same is true for the negative component of the consensus. These requirements seem to be very natural inasmuch as the consensus should reflect the knowledge of conflict participants. Postulates *P2* and *P3* are very popular because they require the consensus to satisfy the Pareto criterion (the common part of agents' opinions should be in consensus) and not to exceed the knowledge of the agents.

Postulate *P4* is characteristic for conjunctions; that is, a consensus should not be inconsistent: its semantics should not be an empty set. Notice that inconsistency may refer to the case when a consensus contains both positive and negative components. If it contains only positive or only negative components then the inconsistency does not exist, because in these cases the semantics is always nonempty. Last, postulate *P5* is known as the criterion O_1 defined and analyzed in Chapter 3. Notice that distance function d_a has been defined in Section 4.2.2 as a function minimizing the transformation cost for two subsets of V_a, or a function calculating the shares of elements of set V_a in the distance of two its subsets.

We show now some properties of the consensus functions referring to the defined postulates.

Theorem 6.3.
If a consensus function C_a satisfies postulates P1 and P5 then it should also satisfy postulates P2 and P3; that is,

$$(C_a \vdash P1 \land C_a \vdash P5) \Rightarrow (C_a \vdash P2 \land C_a \vdash P3).$$

Proof.
Let a consensus function C_a satisfy postulates *P1* and *P5*. For proving that postulate *P2* is satisfied let profile *X* be such that $X^+(a) \neq \emptyset$ and let an element of $C_a(X(a))$ contain a positive literal (a, v). In this case we have

$$\sum_{(a,w)\in X^+(a)} d_a(v,w) = \min_{w'\subseteq V_a} \sum_{(a,w)\in X^+(a)} d_a(w',w).$$

Assume that

$$\bigcap_{(a,v')\in X^+(a)} v' \not\subset v.$$

Denote by

$$u = \bigcap_{(a,v')\in X^+(a)} v',$$

of course $u \neq \emptyset$. For a literal $(a, w) \in X^+(a)$ we have

$$u \subseteq w \text{ but } u \not\subset v.$$

In this case

$$d_a(v, w) > d_a(v \cup u, w)$$

for $d_a \in \{\rho_a, \delta_a\}$. This inequality should take place because:

- For function ρ_a: adding elements of set u to set v causes the shares of these elements to be equal to 0, whereas previously they were not equal to 0.
- For function δ_a: adding elements of set u to set v causes decreasing the cost for transformation of set w into set v because these elements now belong to both sets.

Thus the sum of distances should be smaller for literal $(a, v \cup u)$ than for literal (a, v). The first condition of postulate $P2$ should then be satisfied. For the second condition we assume that

$$v \not\subset \bigcup_{(a,v') \in X^+(a)} v'.$$

Denote then

$$u = v \setminus \bigcup_{(a,v') \in X^+(a)} v',$$

of course $u \neq \varnothing$. For a literal $(a, w) \in X^+(a)$ we have

$$u \subseteq v \text{ but } u \not\subset w.$$

In this case arguing similarly as above we have

$$d_a(v \setminus u, w) > d_a(v \cup u, w).$$

Thus the sum of distances may not be minimal for v. This proves that postulate $P2$ should be satisfied.

The proof for postulate $P3$ is identical.   ♦

Postulates $P4$ and $P5$ in general are not consistent; that is, satisfying one of them may cause nonsatisfying of the other. Below we give an example.

Example 6.4. Let's consider the subprofiles for attribute a defined in Example 6.3.

Subprofiles	a
$X^+(a)$	$(a, \{1, 2\})$ $(a, \{1, 3, 8\})$ $(a, \varnothing)$ $(a, \{1, 5, 9\})$
$X^-(a)$	$\neg(a, \{1\})$ $\neg(a, \{1\})$

As the distance function ρ_a we accept:

$$\rho_a = \frac{card(v \div w)}{card(V_a)}.$$

For this function it has been proved [31] that an element will occur in the consensus of a profile of sets if it occurs in at least half the sets. Thus for this case set v which minimizes the sum of distances for subprofile $X^+(a)$ should be $\{1\}$, and the same should be for subprofile $X^-(a)$. Because literals $(a, \{1\})$ and $\neg(a, \{1\})$ are conflicting, the consensus

$$(a, \{1\}) \wedge \neg(a, \{1\})$$

should be inconsistent. So postulate $P4$ is not satisfied. On the other hand, we can see that any consistent conjunction may not minimize the sum of distances; that is, satisfying postulate $P4$ yields nonsatisfying postulate $P5$.

♦

We present now an important property of consensus satisfying postulates $P2$ and $P3$.

Theorem 6.4.
If a consensus function C_a satisfies postulates P2 and P3 then the following relationships are true.

(a) If an element of $C_a(X(a))$ has a positive component (a, v) then

$$\bigcap\nolimits_{(a,v') \in X^+(a)} S_C((a,v')) \subseteq S_C((a, v))$$

and

$$S_C(a, v) \subseteq \bigcup\nolimits_{(a,v') \in X^+(a)} S_C((a,v')).$$

(b) If an element of $C_a(X(a))$ has a negative component $\neg(a, v)$ then

$$\bigcap\nolimits_{\neg(a,v') \in X^-(a)} S_C(\neg(a,v')) \subseteq S_C(\neg(a, v))$$

and

$$S_C(\neg(a, v)) \subseteq \bigcup\nolimits_{\neg(a,v') \in X^-(a)} S_C(\neg(a,v')).$$

Proof.
The proof follows directly from the content of postulates $P2$ and $P3$ and Definition 6.1.   ♦

Theorem 6.4 shows some strong justification for postulates $P2$ and $P3$, because it turns out that the common part of the semantics of positive (or negative) components of the profile should be included in the semantics of the consensus, and on the other hand, the semantics of the consensus should be included in the sum of semantics of the profile components. From Theorem 6.3 it is implied that the consensus function satisfying $P1$ and $P5$ should have this property.

Because of the sensibility of the consensus (it may not be inconsistent), and in light of the above consideration it is known that a heuristic algorithm for determining a consensus satisfying both postulates $P4$ and $P5$ should be worked out. Notice that only the determination of a consensus satisfying postulate $P5$ is in many cases (referring to the structures of elements of domain V_a) a NP-hard problem. Thus only for postulate $P5$ do we need a separate heuristic algorithm. We consider the cases of distance functions between sets of elementary values:

- For function ρ_a: if we use distance function η defined in Section 5.2.5 then Algorithm 5.1 should be useful. If we use distance function

$$d_a = \frac{card(v \div w)}{card(V_a)}$$

  then the simple and effective algorithm proposed in [31] is useful; in this case the problem is not NP-complete.

- For function δ_a: the algorithm needs to be more complex. The idea of this algorithm is the following. First we start from a set of one element, which may be selected from those appearing in the elements of the subprofile. Next we consider adding those elements to this set which improve the sum of distances. The algorithm is presented as follows.

Algorithm 6.1.

Input: Subprofile $X^+(a)$ and distance function δ_a.

Output: Set $x^* \subseteq V_a$, which minimizes the sum of distances to the values of the literals belonging to $X^+(a)$.

Procedure:

BEGIN

1. Set $Z := \bigcup_{(a,v) \in X^+(a)} v$;

2. Set $x^* := \bigcap_{(a,v) \in X^+(a)} v$; $x^{*\prime} := x^*$;

3. Set $S := \sum_{(a,v) \in X^+(a)} \delta_a(x^*, v)$;

4. Select from $Z \backslash x^{*\prime}$ an element z such that the sum

$$\sum_{(a,v) \in X^+(a)} \delta_a(x^* \cup \{z\}, v)$$

is minimal;

5. Set $x^{*\prime} := x^{*\prime} \cup \{z\}$;

6. If $S < \sum_{(a,v) \in X^+(a)} \delta_a(x^* \cup \{z\}, v)$ then

Begin

    6.1. Set $S := \sum_{(a,v) \in X^+(a)} \delta_a(x^* \cup \{z\}, v)$;

    6.2. Set $x^* := x^* \cup \{z\}$;

End;

7. If $Z \backslash x^{*\prime} \neq \varnothing$ then GOTO 4;

END.

The algorithm for subprofile $X^-(a)$ is similar.

We can see that the consensus x^* determined by Algorithm 6.1 satisfies postulates $P2$ and $P3$. This follows from steps 1 and 2, where set x^* contains the common part of the given sets and does not exceed set Z being the sum of these sets. Steps 4–7 realize the heuristic aspect for satisfying postulate $P5$. Postulate $P1$ is also satisfied because in the worst case x^* will be empty, but literal $(a, x^*) = (a, \varnothing)$ will be the consensus.

The computational complexity of Algorithm 6.1 is $O(m^2 \cdot n)$ where $n = card(Z)$ and $m = card(X^+(a))$.

Now we present an algorithm which determines a consensus satisfying (partly, of course) both postulates $P4$ and $P5$. This algorithm uses Algorithm 6.1 and modifies the consensuses for subprofiles $X^+(a)$ and $X^-(a)$ so that the sums of distances minimally change.

Algorithm 6.2.

Input: Subprofiles $X^+(a)$ and $X^-(a)$ and a distance function d_a.

Output: Conjunction y^* being a consensus satisfying postulates $P4$ and $P5$.

Procedure:

BEGIN

    1. Using Algorithm 6.1 determine consensus (a, w) for subprofile $X^+(a)$; Set $S := \sum_{(a,v) \in X^+(a)} d_a(w, v)$;

    2. Using Algorithm 6.1 determine consensus $\neg(a, w')$ for subprofile $X^-(a)$; Set $S' := \sum_{\neg(a,v) \in X^-(a)} d_a(w', v)$;

    3. If $w \neq w'$ then GOTO END;

4. Set $Z: = \bigcup_{(a,v) \in X^+(a)} v$; $Z': = \bigcup_{\neg(a,v) \in X^-(a)} v$;

5. If $w = w'$ then
    Begin
        5.1. Determine such $z \in Z$ that sum
$$s = \sum_{(a,v) \in X^+(a)} d_a(w \cup \{z\}, v) \text{ is minimal;}$$
        5.2. Determine such $z' \in Z'$ that sum
$$s' = \sum_{(a,v) \in X^-(a)} d_a(w' \cup \{z'\}, v) \text{ is minimal;}$$
        5.3 If $(s - S) < (s' - S')$ then set $w: = w \cup \{z\}$
             else set $w': = w' \cup \{z'\}$;
    End;
    6. Set $y^*:= (a, w) \wedge \neg(a, w')$
END.

Satisfying postulate *P5* follows from steps 1 and 2, where Algorithm 6.1 is used for determining the consensuses of subprofiles. However, these consensuses may create an inconsistent conjunction; that is, postulate *P4* is not satisfied. Thus for satisfying this postulate it is necessary to change one of the chosen consensuses. This is done by steps 5.1–5.3, where only one of the values w and w' is changed, which causes the minimal increase of the sum of distances. As we see, the determined consensus $y^* = (a, w) \wedge \neg(a, w')$ only partly satisfies both postulates *P4* and *P5*, because they are in general inconsistent with each other.

6.3. Disjunction Structure

6.3.1. Basic Notions

Similarly as on the syntactic level (Chapter 5), by a disjunction we call an expression:

$$l_1 \vee l_2 \vee \cdots \vee l_k,$$

where l_i is a (A, V)-based literal (positive or negative) for $i = 1, 2, \ldots, k$ and $k \in \aleph$.

This structure was proposed for the first time in [107, 108]. In this chapter we provide its deeper analysis.

Notice that owing to this structure an agent may express another type of its opinion than in the conjunction structure; viz. an agent can now give its opinion in the form of a disjunction referring to a number of scenario attributes.

Similarly as in Section 5.3 of Chapter 5 formula $(l_1 \vee l_2 \vee \cdots \vee l_m)$ can be treated in an equivalent way as a clause. We can then write

$$(l_1 \vee l_2 \vee \cdots \vee l_k) \equiv (b_1 \wedge b_2 \wedge \cdots \wedge b_{k''}) \rightarrow (h_1 \vee h_2 \vee \cdots \vee h_{k'}),$$

where $h_1, h_2, \ldots, h_{k'}$ are positive literals and $b_1, b_2, \ldots, b_{k''}$ are negative literals.

Formula $(b_1 \wedge b_2 \wedge \cdots \wedge b_{k''})$ is called the *body* of the clause, and formula $(h_1 \vee h_2 \vee \cdots \vee h_{k'})$ is called the *head* of the clause. It is a well-known form of clauses. It has been mentioned earlier that owing to this property the disjunction structure is very useful in practice for experts to express their opinions.

By *Clause(A,V)* we denote the set of all (A,V)-based clauses.

As a equivalent form for clause

$$(b_1 \wedge b_2 \wedge \cdots \wedge b_{k''}) \rightarrow (h_1 \vee h_2 \vee \cdots \vee h_{k'})$$

we use the following,

$$b_1, b_2, \ldots, b_{k''} \rightarrow h_1, h_2, \ldots, h_{k'}.$$

Or more general:

$$b \rightarrow h,$$

where b is the body and h is the head of the clause, and b, h are sets of positive (A,V)-based literals.

Similarly as for conjunctions, a clause

$$x = b \rightarrow h$$

can be then represented by a pair

$$(x^+, x^-),$$

where x^+ is the set of literals included in the head of x and x^- is the set of literals included in the body of x, that is $x^+ = h$ and $x^- = b$.

Example 6.5. Let A be a set of attributes *Age, Education, Int-Quotient* (representing intelligence quotient), *Perception, Receiving, Processing,* and *Understanding*, which describe a student's parameters necessary for his classification in an E-learning system [42]. The domains of the attributes are the following.

- V_{Age} = {young, middle, advanced}.

- $V_{Education}$ = {elementary, secondary, graduate, postgraduate}.

- $V_{In\text{-}Quotient}$ = {low, middle, high}.

- $V_{Perception}$ = {sensitive, intuitive}.

- $V_{Receiving}$ = {visual, verbal}.

- $V_{Processing}$ = {active, reflective}.

- $V_{Understanding}$ = {sequential, global}.

Examples of the formulae representing the rules generated by experts E_1, E_2, E_3, and E_3 about the learner preferences are the following.

$E_1 = \neg(Age, \{young\}) \vee \neg(Education, \{graduate, postgraduate\}) \vee$
$\quad \neg(Int\text{-}Quotient, \{high\}) \vee (Understanding, \{global\}).$

$E_2 = \neg(Age, \{advanced\}) \vee \neg(Education, \{elementary, secondary\}) \vee$
$\quad \neg(Int\text{-}Quotient, \{low\}) \vee (Perception, \{sensitive\}).$

$E_3 = \neg(Education, \{graduate, postgraduate\}) \vee \neg(Int\text{-}Quotient, \{high\})$
$\quad \vee \neg(Receiving, \{verbal\}) \vee (Processing, \{active\}).$

$E_4 = (Perception, \{sensitive\}) \vee (Processing, \{active\}).$ ◆

We now define the semantics of clauses. The semantics of literals (positive and negative) has been defined in Definition 6.1. Here we extend this definition by adding the semantics of disjunctions of literals. Therefore, we use the same symbol S_C for defining the semantics of clauses.

Definition 6.5.
As the semantics of clauses we understand the following function,

$$S_C\colon Clause(A,V) \to 2^{\bigcup_{T \subseteq A} 2^{E\text{-}TUPLE(T)} \cup \theta_E},$$

such that:

(a) $S_C((a,v)) = \{r \in E\text{-}TUPLE(\{a\}): r_a \in v\}$ *for* $v \subseteq V_a$ *and* $v \neq \varnothing$.

(b) $S_C((a,\varnothing)) = \{(a, \varepsilon)\}$.

(c) $S_C(\neg(a,v)) = \{r \in E\text{-}TUPLE(\{a\}): r_a \in V_a \setminus v\} \cup \{(a, \varepsilon)\}$
$\quad$ *for* $v \subseteq V_a$ *and* $v \neq \varnothing$.

(d) $S_C(\neg(a,\varnothing)) = \{r \in E\text{-}TUPLE(\{a\}): r_a \in V_a\}$.

(e) $S_C(l_1 \vee l_2 \vee \ldots \vee l_k)$

$$= \left\{ r \in \bigcup_{a \in B} E - TUPLE(\{a\}) \cup \{(a, \varepsilon)\}: \right.$$

$$(\forall a \in B)(\forall i \in \{1, 2, \ldots, k\})([a \; occurs \; in \; l_i] \Rightarrow (a, r_a) \in S_C(l_i)) \left. \right\},$$

where B is the type of clause $l_1 \vee l_2 \vee \cdots \vee l_k$..

We can see that in comparison with Definition 6.1, the semantics of single literals defined in Definition 6.5 is identical. The new element is the semantics of a clause for which an element of the semantics is not an elementary tuple of type B (where B is the type of the clause), but an elementary tuple of 1-attribute type. The reason for this difference follows from the disjunction structure of clauses. If such an elementary tuple refers to an elementary event in the real world then the clause should be true.

Below we present an example.

Example 6.6. Let's consider the first clause defined in Example 6.7. Its equivalent disjunction form is:

$\neg(Age, \{young\}) \vee \neg(Education, \{graduate, postgraduate\}) \vee$
$$\neg(Int\text{-}Quotient, \{high\}) \vee (Understanding, \{global\}).$$

The semantics of this clause is presented in the following table.

Age	Education	Int-Quotient	Understanding
middle			
advanced			
ε			
	elementary		
	secondary		
	ε		
		low	
		middle	
		ε	
			global

Each of the rows in the above table represents an elementary event, which, if taking place, will cause the truth of the clause.   ♦

Let's notice that because Definitions 6.1 and 6.5 only complete each other, all statements in Remarks 6.1 are also true for clauses. Remark 6.2 has now the following corresponding remark.

Remark 6.3.
Function S_C for clauses has the following properties.

a) *Commutativity, that is,*

$$S_C(x \vee x') = S_C(x' \vee x)$$

b) *Associativity, that is,*

$$S_C((x \vee x') \vee x'') = S_C(x \vee (x' \vee x''))$$

The definitions of such notions as equivalence, complement, inconsistency, and conflict of literals have been included in Definition 6.2. Definition 6.6 below completes the notion of equivalence and inconsistency of clauses.

Definition 6.9.

(a) *Two clauses x and x' ($x, x' \in Clause(A,V)$) are equivalent if and only if*

$$S_C(x) = S_C(x').$$

(b) *A clause x is inconsistent if and only if $S_C(x) = \varnothing$.*

(c) *Two clauses x and x' ($x, x' \in Clause(A,V)$) are conflicting if and only if clause $x \vee x'$ is inconsistent.*

A clause which is not inconsistent is called *consistent*. However, notice that there does not exist any clause from *Clause(A,V)*, which is inconsistent. The reason is that all (A,V)-based literals are consistent, even literal $(a, \varnothing)$ for which the semantics is equal $\{(a, \varepsilon)\}$. In this way we do not have conflicting clauses either. This phenomenon is similar to classical logic where only the constant logic *false* can always have logic value *false* and the constant logic *true* can always have logic value *true*. Thus conditions (b) and (c) of Definitions 6.6 have been given only for formal reasons.

Now we prove the following.

Theorem 6.5.
The following dependencies are true.

(a) *If two clauses are equivalent then they must be of the same type.*

(b) *For any two literals $l = (a, v)$ and $l' = (a, v')$ there should be*

$$S_C(l \vee l') = S_C(l) \cup S_C(l'),$$

and if $v, v' \neq \emptyset$ then

$$S_C(l \vee l') = S_C((a, v \cup v')).$$

(c) For any two negative literals $l = \neg(a, v)$ and $l' = \neg(a, v')$ where $v \cap v' \neq \emptyset$ there should be

$$S_C(l \vee l') = S_C(l) \cup S_C(l') = S_C(\neg(a, v \cap v')).$$

Proof.

(a) Two clauses are equivalent if they have the same semantics. Assume that they are of different types. That is, there exists an attribute a which appears in one clause but does not appear in the second. In this case the semantics of the clauses containing a should include an elementary tuple (a, ε) if a occurs in a negative literal or in literal $(a, \emptyset)$, or tuple (a, w) for some $w \in V_a$ if a occurs in a positive literal, whereas the second clause does not have this property.

(b) This property follows from Definition 6.5e on the basis of which we can write

$$S_C(l \vee l') = \{r \in E\text{-}TUPLE(\{a\}) \cup \{(a, \varepsilon)\}: (a, r_a) \in S_C(l) \text{ or } (a, r_a) \in S_C(l')\}$$
$$= S_C(l) \cup S_C(l').$$

Let literals l and l' be such that $v, v' \neq \emptyset$, it follows that there should be:

$$(a, \varepsilon) \notin S_C(l) \quad \text{and} \quad (a, \varepsilon) \notin S_C(l').$$

Owing to this we have

$$S_C(l \vee l') = S_C((a, v \cup v')).$$

(c) For any two negative literals $l = \neg(a, v)$ and $l' = \neg(a, v')$ such that $v \cap v' \neq \emptyset$ it is obvious that $v \neq \emptyset$ and $v' \neq \emptyset$. We have

$$S_C(l) = S_C((a, V_a \backslash v)) \cup \{(a, \varepsilon)\}$$

and

$$S_C(l) = S_C((a, V_a \backslash v')) \cup \{(a, \varepsilon)\}.$$

Thus

$$S_C(l \vee l') = S_C((a, V_a \backslash v)) \cup S_C((a, V_a \backslash v')) \cup \{(a, \varepsilon)\}$$
$$= S_C((a, (V_a \backslash v) \cup (V_a \backslash v'))) \cup \{(a, \varepsilon)\}$$

$$= S_C((a, V_a\backslash(v \cap v'))) \cup \{(a, \varepsilon)\}$$

$$= S_C(\neg(a, v \cap v')). \qquad \blacklozenge$$

From Theorem 6.5 it is implied that the relation of equivalence between clauses also refers only to those of the same type. Similarly as in Theorem 6.1, dually here the semantics of a clause $l \vee l'$ containing the same attribute can be calculated as the sum of the semantics of l and l'. Below we present a more general statement.

Theorem 6.6.

If clauses $x_1, x_2, \ldots, x_k$ are of the same type then

$$S_C(x_1 \vee x_2 \vee \cdots \vee x_k) = S_C(x_1) \cup S_C(x_2) \cup \cdots \cup S_C(x_k).$$

Proof.

First we prove that for any two clauses x and x' of the same type there should be

$$S_C(x \vee x') = S_C(x) \cup S_C(x').$$

From Theorem 6.4 it follows that it is true for the case when x and x' are literals. In the case when x and x' are clauses of the same type but consisting of more than one literal then using the properties of associativity and commutativity in clause $x \vee x'$ we can group the literals of the same type. More concretely, let

$$x = l_1 \vee l_2 \vee \cdots \vee l_k$$

and let

$$x' = l_1' \vee l_2' \vee \cdots \vee l_l'.$$

Notice that although clauses x and x' are of the same type, the numbers of literals in each of them need not be equal. The reason is that in x or x' there may be more than one literal with the same attribute. Let T be the type of these clauses and let $r \in S_C(x \vee x')$. According to Definition 6.5 if an attribute $a \in T$ occurs in r then value r_a should be such that elementary tuple (a, r_a) belongs to the semantics of one literal containing attribute a in one of clauses. Thus it is obvious that $r \in S_C(x) \cup S_C(x')$. On the other hand, if r is such an elementary tuple that $r \in S_C(x) \cup S_C(x')$ then there should be an attribute $a \in T$ such that pair (a, r_a) belongs to the semantics of one literal containing attribute a in one of clauses, so $r \in S_C(x \vee x')$.

For the proof of the general case we may use the result presented above for two clauses and a simple induction method. $\qquad \blacklozenge$

Theorem 6.6 shows that the semantics of clauses has a dual property to the semantics of conjunctions, which is represented by the relationship between disjunctive structure and the sum operation on sets. It surely facilitates calculating semantics of complex clauses.

6.3.2. Inconsistency Representation

In this section we deal with representation of a conflict profile using clauses. As a profile we understand a finite set with repetitions of (A,V)-based clauses.

For a profile we can also assume that in each clause each attribute may occur at most in one positive literal and one negative literal. This assumption is possible owing to Theorem 6.5 which enables replacing two positive (or negative) literals with the same attribute by one positive (or negative) literal with this attribute and proper value.

Definition 6.7.
Let $X = \{x_1, x_2, \ldots, x_n\}$, where $x_i \in Clause(A,V)$ for $i = 1, 2, \ldots, n$, be a profile. We say that X contains inconsistency if there exist two clauses x and x' such that

$$S_C(x) \neq S_C(x').$$

A clause may be divided into two parts: the first consists of positive literals, and the second consists of negative literals. Thus a clause x can be represented by a pair:

$$x = (x^+, x^-).$$

Then profile X may be written as

$$X = \{x_i = (x_i^+, x_i^-) \in Clause(A,V): i = 1, 2, \ldots, n\}.$$

Let T_X be the sum of all types of clauses belonging to X. For each attribute $a \in T_X$ we determine

- $X^+(a)$ as the set with repetitions consisting of all positive literals containing attribute a, which occur in the clauses from X
- $X^-(a)$ as the set with repetitions consisting of all negative literals containing attribute a, which occur in the clauses from X.

Notice that in each of the sets $X^+(a)$ and $X^-(a)$ a clause from X may have at most one literal. These sets may be treated as the positive and negative profiles restricted to attribute a. We call them *subprofiles*. Notice that one of the sets $X^+(a)$ and $X^-(a)$ may be empty, however, they may not both be empty; that is, $X^+(a) \cup X^-(a) \neq \emptyset$.

Example 6.7. For the clauses defined in Example 6.7 we create the subprofiles as follows.

Subprofiles	Perception	Processing	Understanding
X^+	{sensitive}	{active} {active}	{global}

and

Subprofiles	Age	Education	Int-Quotient	Receiving
X^-	{young} {advanced}	{graduate, postgraduate} {elementary, secondary} {graduate, postgraduate}	{high} {low} {high}	{global}

♦

6.3.3. Integration Problem and Consensus

Similarly as for conjunctions, the integration problem for clauses is defined as follows.

Given a profile

$$X = \{x_i = (x_i^+, x_i^-) \in Clause(A,V): i = 1, 2, \ldots, n\}$$

one should determine a clause x* which best represents the given clauses.

This problem can be solved in the same way as for conjunctions. We can use the same scheme as defined in Section 6.2.5, which consists of three tasks:

1. For each attribute a occurring in X determine positive and negative subprofiles $X^+(a)$ and $X^-(a)$.
2. Determine the consensus for $(X^+(a), X^-(a))$.
3. Perform the concatenation of consensuses for all attributes occurring in X creating clause x^*.

Assuming the independence of attributes from set A, we can define the consensus in the same way as in Definition 6.4 and next use Algorithms 6.1 and 6.2 for consensus choice. The properties included in Theorems 6.3 and 6.4 are also true for this case.

In the next section we deal with the case of consensus choice when some attributes are dependent on some others.

6.4. Dependencies of Attributes

The algorithms for consensus choice presented in previous sections are useful only when we can assume that the attributes appearing in conjunctions (or clauses) belonging to the profile are independent of each other. Owing to this assumption we can calculate consensus for each attribute and next make the concatenation of consensuses creating the final consensus.

However, in practice, a real world (A, V) may contain dependencies of attributes; that means values of an attribute may determine values of another attribute. Below we present the definition of attribute dependency.

Definition 6.8.
Let $a, b \in A$; we say that attribute b is dependent on attribute a if and only if there exists a function

$$f_b^a : V_a \to V_b .$$

For $v \subseteq V_a$ we denote

$$f_b^a (v) = \bigcup_{z \in v} \{f_b^a (z)\} .$$

The dependency of attribute b on attribute a means that in the real world, if for some object the value of a is known then the value of b is also known. In practice, owing to this property for determining the values of attribute b it is enough to know the value of attribute a.

The fact that attribute b is dependent on attribute a is represented by the following expression,

$$a \mapsto b.$$

Definition 6.9.
Let $a, b \in A$, $a \mapsto b$, and let x be a conjunction $x \in Conj(A,V)$; we say that dependence $a \mapsto b$ is satisfied in x if the following conditions are fulfilled.
   a)   If literals (a, v) and (b, v') (or $\neg(a, v)$ and $\neg(b, v')$) appear in x then

$$v' = f_b^a(v).$$

b) *If literals (a, v) and $\neg(b, v')$ appear in x then literals*

$$(b, f_b^a(v)) \text{ and } \neg(b, v')$$

may not be conflicting.

c) *If literals $\neg(a, v)$ and (b, v') appear in x then literals*

$$(b, v') \text{ and } \neg(b, f_b^a(v))$$

may not be conflicting.

Definition 6.9 requires in the first case that because attribute b is dependent on attribute a then values v and v' have to be consistent with this fact. In the second case notice that literal $(b, f_b^a(v))$ may be treated as the consequence of literal (a, v), thus literals $(b, f_b^a(v))$ and $\neg(b, v')$ may not be conflicting. The third case may be interpreted in the same way as the second case.

Consensus determining for the case of dependencies of attributes may not be performed in independent ways for each attribute, as assumed in Algorithms 6.1 and 6.2 because the consensus (a, v) for subprofile $X^+(a)$ and consensus (b, v') for subprofile $X^-(a)$ may not satisfy dependence $a \mapsto b$ as indicated in Definition 6.9.

Let's consider an example illustrating this case.

Example 6.8. Let

- $A = \{a, b\}$.

- $V_a = \{a_1, a_2, a_3, a_4, a_5\}$.

- $V_b = \{b_1, b_2\}$.

Let $a \mapsto b$ and function f_b^a be the following.

Function $f_b^a : V_a \to V_b$	
a_1	b_2
a_2	b_1
a_3	b_2
a_4	b_1
a_5	b_1

Let subprofiles be the following.

$X^+(a)$	$X^+(b)$
$(a, \{a_1,a_3\})$	$(b, \{b_2\})$
$(a, \{a_2,a_3\})$	$(b, \{b_1,b_2\})$
$(a, \{a_1,a_4\})$	$(b, \{b_1,b_2\})$
$(a, \{a_1,a_4,a_5\})$	$(b, \{b_1,b_2\})$
$(a, \{a_1\})$	$(b, \{b_2\})$

As the distance function between sets we use the function of type ρ:

$$\gamma(X_1,X_2) = \frac{1}{card(V_a)} card(X_1 \div X_2).$$

Then the consensus for $X^+(a)$ is $(a, \{a_1\})$ whereas the consensus for $X^+(b)$ is $(b, \{b_1, b_2\})$, of course.

$$\{b_1, b_2\} \neq f_b^a(\{a_1\}) = \{b_1\}. \qquad \blacklozenge$$

Thus we propose two ways for performing consensus choice. First, we assume that each conjunction belonging to a profile should contain both attributes a and b in positive (or negative) literals.

Consensus (a, v) for subprofile $X^+(a)$ and consensus (b, v') for subprofile $X^-(a)$ may be determined in one of the following ways.

1. Because of dependence $a \mapsto b$ the relationship between subprofile $X^+(a)$ and subprofile $X^+(b)$ is the following.

$$X^+(b) = \{(b, f_b^a(w)) : (a, w) \in X^+(a)\}.$$

Thus we can first calculate a consensus (a, v) for subprofile $X^+(a)$ using postulates defined in Definition 6.4, and next calculate the consensus (b, v') for subprofile $X^+(b)$ where

$$v' = f_b^a(v).$$

This approach may be justified in practice; because of dependence $a \mapsto b$ the values of attribute b do not need to be determined, if the values of attribute a are known. Thus consensus for subprofile $X^+(b)$ may also be determined on the basis of the consensus of subprofile $X^+(a)$. However, if consensus (a, v) satisfies postulate $P5$ then consensus (b, v') may not satisfy this postulate, as shown in Example 6.8.

2. The second approach is based on calculating such consensuses (a, v) and (b, v') that together they satisfy postulate $P5$; that is, the following sum of distances

$$\sum_{(a,w)\in X^+(a)} d_a(v,w) + \sum_{(b,w')\in X^+(b)} d_b(v',w')$$

is minimal. Thus attributes a and b are treated equivalently. However, the algorithm for this case is more complex than in the first case. We present it later. For consensus choice in this case it is interesting to investigate the relationship between literal (a, v^*) which minimizes the sum

$$\sum_{(a,w)\in X^+(a)} d_a(v^*,w)$$

and literal $(b, v^{*\prime})$ which minimizes the sum

$$\sum_{(b,w')\in X^+(b)} d_b(v^{*\prime},w').$$

We prove the following.

Theorem 6.7.
Let $a \mapsto b$; using distance function ρ^P or δ^P if literal (a, v^*) is a consensus for subprofile $X^+(a)$ then there exists literal $(b, v^{*\prime})$ being a consensus for subprofile $X^+(b)$ such that $f_b^a(v^*) \subseteq v^{*\prime}$.

Proof.
First we prove a lemma.
Let there be given sets of elementary values $X_1, \ldots, X_n \subseteq V_a$ for some $a \in A$ and let $\sigma \in \{\rho^P, \delta^P\}$; then the sum $\sum_{i=1}^{n} \sigma(X,X_i)$ is minimal if and only if for each $x \in X$ the following inequality is true,

$$occ(x) \geq \frac{n}{2},$$

where $occ(x)$ is the number of occurrences of element x in sets $X_1, X_2, \ldots, X_n$.

Proof of Lemma.
   (a) For $\sigma = \rho^P$ notice that from Theorem 4.1c it follows that

$$\rho^P(X,X_1) = v \cdot card(X \div X_1) ,$$

where $\qquad v = \dfrac{1}{card(V_a)(2card(V_a)-1)} .$

The share of an element $x \in X$ in the sum of distances $\sum_{i=1}^{n}\rho^P(X,X_i)$ is then equal to $v \cdot (n - occ(x))$, and the share of an element $y \notin X$ the sum of distances $\sum_{i=1}^{n} \rho^P(X,X_i)$ is equal to $v \cdot occ(y)$. Thus for the sum $\sum_{i=1}^{n} \rho^P(X,X_i)$ to be minimal, it is necessary to add to X such elements x, for which the inequality $occ(x) \geq n/2$ is true.

(b) For a distance function $\sigma \in \delta^P$ the proof is similar.

Now we can give the proof of the theorem. From the above lemma it follows that if set $v*$ is included in a consensus for subprofile $X^+(a)$ then for each element $x \in X^+(a)$ the number of its occurrences in the elements of subprofile $X^+(a)$ should not be smaller than half of the elements of $X^+(a)$. Thus element $f_b^a(x)$ should also appear in at least half of the elements of $X^+(b)$. Then it may be included in a consensus $(b, v*')$ of subprofile $X^+(b)$. Of course apart from the elements of $f_b^a(v*)$ consensus $(b, v*')$ may contain other elements. So we have

$$f_b^a(v*) \subseteq v*'. \qquad\qquad \blacklozenge$$

In Example 6.8 we can notice that the consensus for $X^+(a)$ is literal $(a, \{a_1\})$, whereas the consensus for $X^+(b)$ is $(b, \{b_1,b_2\})$, and

$$f_b^a(\{a_1\}) = \{b_1\} \subseteq \{b_1,b_2\}.$$

Theorem 6.7 implies that if distance functions ρ^P and δ^P are used then the dependency between attributes does not disturb the condition of optimality. That is, if an element $x \in V_a$ occurs in the consensus of subprofile $X^+(a)$ then $f_b^a(x)$ should appear in the consensus of subprofile $X^+(b)$. Using distance functions other than ρ^P and δ^P does not always result in the above property. Below we give an example.

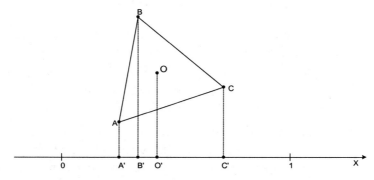

Figure 6.1. Subprofiles $X^+(a)$ and $X^+(b)$.

Example 6.9. Let the values in literals of subprofile $X^+(a)$ be represented by three points (A, B, and C) on the plane creating an equilateral triangle (see Figure 6.1). The location of this triangle is such that any of its sides is not parallel to axis X. The function f_b^a assigns for each point of the triangle a point on axis X being its projection on X. These points (A', B', and C') represent the values in literals of subprofile $X^+(b)$.

Let the distances between these points be measured by the Euclidean distance function. It is easy to note that the consensus of subprofile $X^+(a)$ is the center of gravity of triangle ABC, whereas the consensus of subprofile $X^+(b)$ is point B', but not point $f_b^a(O)$, that is, O'.　　　　◆

The above example shows that using distance functions other than ρ^P and δ^P can cause the inconsistency of consensuses for subprofiles $X^+(a)$ and $X^+(b)$ in the sense that if an element x belongs to the consensus of $X^+(a)$ then $f_b^a(x)$ does not have to belong to the consensus of $X^+(b)$.

Theorem 6.7 facilitates to a certain degree the consensus choice in the second approach mentioned above, because the component (a, v) of the retrieved consensus should be the consensus of subprofile $X^+(a)$ and the value v' of component (b, v') should contain set $f_b^a(v)$. Thus the space of the retrieval is not large.

From Theorem 6.7, Remark 6.4 follows directly.

Remark 6.4.

Let $a \mapsto b$ and $b \mapsto a$; using distance function ρ^P or δ^P if literal (a, v^*) is a consensus for subprofile $X^+(a)$ then there exists literal (b, $v^{*\prime}$) being a consensus for subprofile $X^+(b)$ such that

$$f_b^a(v^*) = v^{*\prime} \quad and \quad f_a^b(v^{*\prime}) = v^*.$$

In this case it is enough to determine a consensus for $X^+(a)$ or $X^+(b)$; the second consensus is determined by function f_b^a or function f_a^b.

Now we present an algorithm for determining a consensus for the second approach with the assumption of any distance function. The idea of this algorithm relies on the following steps:

- First we determine the consensuses (a, v^*) and $(b, v^{*\prime})$ satisfying postulate $P5$ for subprofiles $X^+(a)$ and $X^+(b)$ independently.
- Next, as the beginning value of v' we take the common part of $f_b^a(v^*)$ and $v^{*\prime}$.
- As the beginning value of v we take such value x that $f_b^a(x) = v'$.
- Next, values v and v' are successively modified by adding to v such elements $z \in V_a$ which improve the sum of distances

$$\sum_{(a,w)\in X^+(a)} d_a(v,w) + \sum_{(b,w')\in X^+(b)} d_b(v',w').$$

Of course, adding an element to v causes modification of v'.

The details of the algorithms are presented as follows.

Algorithm 6.3.
Input: Dependence $a \mapsto b$, subprofiles $X^+(a)$ and $X^+(b)$ and distance functions $d_a \in \{\rho_a, \delta_a\}$ and $d_b \in \{\rho_b, \delta_b\}$.
Output: Consensus (a, v) and (b, v') satisfying dependence $a \mapsto b$ and minimizing sum

$$\sum_{(a,w)\in X^+(a)} d_a(v,w) + \sum_{(b,w')\in X^+(b)} d_b(v',w').$$

Procedure:

BEGIN

1. Using Algorithm 6.1 determine consensus (a, v^*) for subprofile $X^+(a)$;
2. Using Algorithm 6.1 determine consensus $(b, v^{*\prime})$ for subprofile $X^+(b)$;
3. If $f_b^a(v^*) = v^{*\prime}$ then set $v := v^*$, $v' := v^{*\prime}$ and GOTO END;
4. Set $v' := f_b^a(v^*) \cap v^{*\prime}$;
5. Calculate $x \subseteq V_a$ such that $f_b^a(x) = v'$;
6. Set $v := x$;

7. Set $S := \sum_{(a,w) \in X^+(a)} d_a(v,w) + \sum_{(b,w) \in X^+(b)} d_b(v',w)$;

8. For each $z \in V_a \backslash v$ do
    Begin
        8.1. Set $x := v \cup \{z\}$ and $x' := f_b^a(x)$;
        8.2. Calculate
            $S_z := \sum_{(a,w) \in X^+(a)} d_a(v,w) + \sum_{(b,w) \in X^+(b)} d_b(x',w)$;
        8.3. If $S < S_z$ then
            Begin
               Set $v := x$; $v' := x'$; $S := S_z$;
            End;
    End;
END.

The computational complexity of Algorithm 6.3 is $O(m \cdot n^2)$ where $m = card(V_a)$ and $n = card(X^+(a)) = card(X^+(b))$.

The dependencies of attributes taking into account other structures of the values have been investigated in [161, 162].

6.5. Conclusions

In this chapter the problem of knowledge integration is considered on the semantic level. As stated, the semantic level differs from the syntactic level investigated in Chapter 5 in the power of inconsistency representation. On the semantic level the possibility for expressing the inconsistency is larger. However, this causes the larger complexity of algorithms for consensus choice.

The idea of these approaches was first presented in papers [107, 108]. However, the materials included in Chapters 5 and 6 differ from those presented in these papers. The differences are based on defining the semantics of literals, conjunctions, and clauses. In the mentioned papers the literal (a, V_a) represents the expert statement "*Everything is possible*," and the empty attribute value represents the ignorance of the expert. In this chapter we assume that the empty value represents the expert's statement that the attribute for which the empty value is assigned has no value. This difference causes other differences in defining not only the semantics, but also the distance between attribute values and, in consequence, the consensus of conflict profiles. In addition, in these chapters we present a deeper analysis of the approaches.

7. Consensus for Fuzzy Conflict Profiles

In Chapter 3 (Section 3.6) we used weights for achieving consensus susceptibility. These weights serve to express the credibility and competence of experts or agents who generate opinions on some common matter. In this chapter we present an approach in which weights are used for expressing the credibility of opinions. We call a set of such opinions a *fuzzy conflict profile*.

7.1. Introduction

The idea of fuzzy sets initialized by Zadeh [160] has been proved to be very useful for experts in expressing their opinions on any matter. In previous chapters a conflict profile has been defined as a set, among others, of expert opinions on some matter. Thus using fuzzy sets in representing and analyzing conflicts should be natural.

In Chapter 5 we used fuzzy values for conjunction structure. In this chapter we assume generally that an element belongs to a conflict profile with some degree. That is, an element x appears in a profile in a pair (x, v) where $v \in [0, 1]$. This pair represents an opinion of an expert on some matter and is interpreted as follows. In the opinion of the expert element x should be the proper solution (or alternative, scenario, etc.) in the degree of v. Because a conflict profile is a set of such opinions, it may contain several occurrences of the same pair as well as several pairs with the same element x may occur. An example of such kind of profiles is:

$$X = \{(a, 0.6), (a, 0.9), (a, 0), (b, 0.3), (b, 0.3), (b, 1), (c, 1)\},$$

in which element a appears three times with values 0.6, 0.9, and 0; element b also appears three times with values 0.3 and 1, and element c one time with value 1. We call conflict profiles of such kind *fuzzy conflict profiles*.

In Chapter 3 we dealt with solving the consensus problem for nonfuzzy conflict profiles. A nonfuzzy conflict profile can be treated as a special case of fuzzy profile where all values are equal to 1.

In this chapter a similar consensus problem is formulated and the consensus functions defined. The distance function is the basis of consensus functions. As shown, distance functions for a fuzzy universe are very interesting and cannot be defined strictly on the basis of distance functions for nonfuzzy universes. Next, specific postulates for fuzzy consensus functions are formulated and analyzed. Finally, some algorithms for consensus determining are worked out.

7.2. Basic Notions

Let U be a finite universe; by U_F we denote the *fuzzy universe* which is defined as

$$U_F = U \times [0, 1].$$

An element of set U_F is called a *fuzzy element* of the fuzzy universe. An element of set $\prod(U_F)^1$ is called a *fuzzy conflict profile.*

Now we deal with the distance function between fuzzy elements of the universe. We assume that a distance function d between the elements of universe U is known:

$$d : U \times U \rightarrow [0,1]$$

which is a half-metric. We need to define the distance function d_F between the fuzzy elements of universe U_F,

$$d_F : U_F \times U_F \rightarrow [0, 1].$$

It seems that it could be good if there were a possibility for defining function d_F on the basis of function d. However, we should investigate if it is possible. First, we formulate some intuitive conditions which should be satisfied by function d_F.

Definition 7.1.
Distance function d_F should satisfy the following conditions:

- *Function d_F should be a half-metric*

- $d_F((x, 1), (y, 1)) = d(x, y)$

- $d_F((x, v_1), (x, v_2)) = |v_1 - v_2|$

for any $x, y \in U$ and $v_1, v_2 \in [0, 1]$.

---

[1] We mention that $\prod(X)$ denotes the set of all finite subsets with repetitions of set X.

The first condition in Definition 7.1 is natural for distance functions. It should be mentioned that function d_F must not be a metric because conditions for metrics are too strong for distance functions. The second condition is also intuitive because a nonfuzzy element $x \in U$ can be treated as a special case of fuzzy element $(x, 1) \in U_F$. For the third condition notice that two fuzzy elements (x, v_1) and (x, v_2) refer to the same nonfuzzy element x and may represent, for example, two opinions of two experts. The first expert states that x should be proper in the degree of v_1 and the second expert states that x should be proper in the degree of v_2. Thus the difference between these two opinions seems to equal $|v_1 - v_2|$.

If it is possible to define function d_F on the basis of function d then we should have

$$d_F\big((x, v_1), (y, v_2)\big) = \begin{cases} |v_1 - v_2| & \text{for } x = y \\ g\big(d(x, y), v_1, v_2\big) & \text{for } x \neq y \end{cases},$$

where $(x, v_1), (y, v_2) \in U_F$.

Thus according to Definition 7.1 there should be

$$g\big(d(x, y), v_1, v_2\big) = g\big(d(x, y), v_2, v_1\big) > 0$$

for $x \neq y$ because d_F is a half-metric, and

$$g\big(d(x, y), 1, 1\big) = d(x, y).$$

Two functions which satisfy these equalities may be the following.

$$d_{F_1}\big((x, v_1), (y, v_2)\big) = \begin{cases} |v_1 - v_2| & \text{for } x = y \\ \big(d(x, y)\big)^{\frac{v_1 + v_2}{2}} & \text{for } x \neq y \end{cases},$$

and

$$d_{F_2}\big((x, v_1), (y, v_2)\big) = \sqrt{\big(d(x, y)\big)^2 + (v_1 - v_2)^2},$$

for all $(x, v_1), (y, v_2) \in U_F$.

Notice that if function d_F is defined by means of function g then for $x \neq y$ and $v_1 = v_2 = 0$ value $d_F((x, 0), (y, 0))$ should be determined. However, it is difficult to interpret this fact. Let's come back to the example functions d_{F_1} and d_{F_2} defined above; for $x \neq y$ we have

$$d_{F_1}\big((x, 0), (y, 0)\big) = 1$$

and

$$d_{F_2}\big((x, 0), (y, 0)\big) = d(x, y).$$

That is, if $x \neq y$ then the value of function d_F is always maximal for each pair $(x, 0)$, $(y, 0)$ in the first case, and equal to $d_F\big((x, 1), (y, 1)\big)$ in the second case. The question is how to interpret this fact, especially if we have such x and y that $d(x, y) = 1$; then $d_F\big((x, 1), (y, 1)\big) = 1$ and there also should be $d_{F_1}\big((x, 0), (y, 0)\big) = d_{F_2}\big((x, 0), (y, 0)\big) = 1$. It is hard to find a good interpretation for this case. So this is the justification for the assumption that function d_F should not depend only on parameters $d(x, y)$, v_1, and v_2.

Another justification for this assumption is that the structure of a fuzzy element is more complex than the structure of a nonfuzzy element, thus the relationship between distance functions d_F and d should be generalization, not dependency. As an example consider U as the universe of points on the plane $\Re \times \Re$ and U_F as the universe of points in the space $\Re \times \Re \times [0, 1]$. In this case functions d and d_F could be the cosine distance functions for two- and three-dimensional spaces, respectively. However, such a defined function d_F is not dependent on function d. This consideration suggests defining function d_F as independent of function d. It seems that the proposed function is a good distance function for this case.

Some additional comments should be made referring to function d_{F_1}. Apart from the fact that $d_{F_1}\big((x, 0), (y, 0)\big) = 1$, which is hard to be interpreted, this function seems to be good for practice. The reasons are:

- In the case when $x = y$ the values of the function are very intuitive.
- For the case $x \neq y$ if $d(x, y) = 1$ then $d_{F_1}\big((x, v_1), (y, v_2)\big) = 1$ for all values of v_1 and v_2.
- For the case $x \neq y$ when $d(x, y) < 1$ then the value of d_{F_1} changes as in Figure 7.1. We can see that $d_{F_1}\big((x, v_1), (y, v_2)\big)$ is a monotonous function referring to the sum $v_1 + v_2$. The maximal value is equal to 1 for $v_1 = v_2 = 0$ and the minimal value is equal to $d(x, y)$ for $v_1 = v_2 = 1$. The interpretation of this phenomenon is that if the sum $v_1 + v_2$ is small then the difference between $d_{F_1}\big((x, v_1), (y, v_2)\big)$ and $d(x, y)$ should be large because the degrees of belief of the experts (or agents) who give opinions x and y are small. This means the smaller the values v_1 and v_2 are, the larger the value of the distance is.

In what follows we assume that distance function d_F is known.

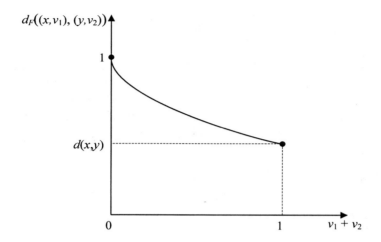

Figure 7.1. The dependency between value $v_1 + v_2$ and d_F.

7.3. Postulates for Consensus

In Chapter 3 by **Con**(U) we denoted the set of all consensus functions for (nonfuzzy) universe U. Consequently, by **Con**(U_F) we now denote the set of all consensus functions for fuzzy universe U_F, that is, functions of the following signature,

$$C: \prod(U_F) \to 2^{U_F}.$$

In a fuzzy profile we can make a clustering of its elements referring to their first components. That is, a profile $X \in \prod(U_F)$ can be divided into such sets (with repetitions) $X(x)$ where $x \in U$, defined as follows.
Let

$$S_X = \{x \in U: x \text{ occurs in } X\},$$

and

$$X(x) = \{(x, v): (x, v) \in X \text{ and } x \in S_X\}.$$

We also define a nonfuzzy profile as a set $\check{X}$ with repetitions corresponding to fuzzy profile X as follows.

$$\check{X} = \{x: (x, v) \in X \text{ for some } v \in [0, 1]\}.$$

A profile $X \in \prod(U_F)$ is

- *Fuzzily homogeneous*, if profile $\check{X}$ is homogeneous.
- *Fuzzily regular*, if profile $\check{X}$ is regular.[2]

Now we present the postulates for consensus functions for fuzzy profiles. Notice that all postulates defined for consensus functions for non-fuzzy profiles (Definition 3.2, Chapter 3) can be used for fuzzy profiles. In Definition 7.2 presented below the postulates included in positions 1–10 are adopted from Definition 3.2. Postulates included in positions 11–15 are new and typical for fuzzy profiles.

Definition 7.2.

A consensus choice function $C \in \textbf{Con}(U_F)$ satisfies the postulate of:

1. *Reliability (Re) iff*

$$C(X) \neq \varnothing.$$

2. *Simplification (Si) iff*

$$\left(\text{Profile } X \text{ is a multiple of profile } Y\right) \Rightarrow C(X) = C(Y).$$

3. *Unanimity (Un), iff*

$$C(\{n * x\}) = \{x\}$$

for each $n \in \aleph$ and $x \in U_F$.

4. *Quasi-unanimity (Qu) iff*

$$\left(x \notin C(X)\right) \Rightarrow \left(\exists n \in \aleph : x \in C(X \cup (n * x))\right)$$

for each $x \in U_F$.

5. *Consistency (Co) iff*

$$\left(x \in C(X)\right) \Rightarrow \left(x \in C(X \cup \{x\})\right)$$

for each $x \in U_F$.

6. *Condorcet consistency (Cc), iff*

$$\left(C(X_1) \cap C(X_2) \neq \varnothing\right) \Rightarrow \left(C(X_1 \cup X_2) = C(X_1) \cap C(X_2)\right)$$

for each $X_1, X_2 \in \Pi(U_F)$.

7. *General consistency (Gc) iff*

---

[2] The notions of homogeneous and regular profiles are given in Definition 2.1 (Chapter 2).

$$C(X_1) \cap C(X_2) \subseteq C(X_1 \,\dot{\cup}\, X_2) \subseteq C(X_1) \cup C(X_2)$$

for any $X_1, X_2 \in \Pi(U_F)$.

8. *Proportion (Pr) iff*

$$\big(X_1 \subseteq X_2 \wedge x \in C(X_1) \wedge y \in C(X_2)\big) \Rightarrow \big(d_F(x,X_1) \le d_F(y,X_2)\big)$$

for any $X_1, X_2 \in \Pi(U_F)$.

9. *1-Optimality (O_1) iff for any $X \in \Pi(U_F)$*

$$\big(x \in C(X)\big) \Rightarrow \big(d_F(x,X) = \min_{y \in U_F} d_F(y,X)\big),$$

where $d_F(z,X) = \sum_{y \in X} d_F(z,y)$ for $z \in U_F$.

10. *2-Optimality (O_2) iff for any $X \in \Pi(U_F)$*

$$\big(x \in C(X)\big) \Rightarrow \big(d_F^2(x,X) = \min_{y \in U_F} d_F^2(y,X)\big),$$

where $d_F^2(z,X) = \sum_{y \in X}\big(d_F(z,y)\big)^2$ for $z \in U_F$.

11. *Closure (Cl) iff*

$$S_{C(X)} \subseteq S_X.$$

12. *Two-level choice (TLC), iff*

$$\big(X \text{ is fuzzily regular}\big) \Rightarrow C(X) = C\big(\bigcup\nolimits_{x \in S_X} C(X(x))\big).$$

13. *Fairness (Fa) iff*

$$\big(X \text{ is fuzzily homogeneous}\big) \Rightarrow C(X) = \Big\{(x, v^*)\colon v^* = \frac{\sum_{(x,v) \in X} v}{card(X)}\Big\}.$$

14. *Fuzzy simplification (Fs) iff*

$$\big(\forall (x, v), (x', v') \in X\colon v = v' = v^*\big) \Rightarrow$$
$$C(X) = \{(x, v^*)\colon x \in C'(\breve{X})\}$$

for some $C' \in \mathbf{Con}(U)$.

15. *Fuzzy proposition (Fp) iff a consensus from $C(X)$ should be built on the basis of consensuses from $C(X(x))$ for $x \in S_X$ where the share of a consensus from $C(X(x))$ is equal to*

$$\frac{card(X(x))}{card(X)}.$$

Some comments should be made for the new postulates *Cl*, *TLC*, *Fa*, *Fs*, and *Fp*. Postulate *Cl* requires that in a consensus for a fuzzy profile X only elements from set S_X may appear. This means that the consensus must refer only to those objects for which experts or agents have generated their opinions. For the remaining postulates notice that the elements of a fuzzy profile can be classified into such groups that in each of them there are occurrences of only one element from universe U. Such a group is denoted by symbol $X(x)$ where $x \in S_X$.

The fact that profile X is fuzzily regular means that the cardinality of set $X(x)$ is identical for each $x \in S_X$. Postulate *TLC* enables calculating a consensus for a fuzzily regular profile in two steps. In the first step the consensus for subprofiles $X(x)$ is determined, and in the second step a consensus of the set of these consensuses is calculated. The basis of this approach is that each element $x \in S_X$ occurs in profile X the same number of times. This idea is shown in Figure 7.2.

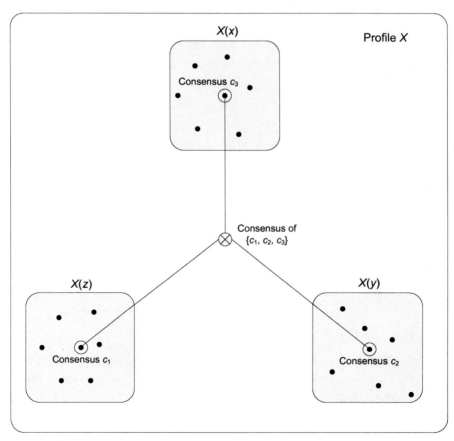

Figure 7.2. Two-level consensus choice.

The postulate of *Fairness*, in turn, enables calculating a consensus for a subprofile $X(x)$. It requires that the consensus of such a subprofile should consist of x and the value equal to the average of all values appearing in the subprofile. As proved in Theorem 7.2, this condition guarantees that postulate O_2 should be satisfied for the subprofile; that is, the sum of squared distances between the consensus and the subprofile elements is minimal.

The postulate of *Fuzzy simplification* treats the situation in which all elements have the same value, as follows. In such a profile one can omit all values and treat the profile as a nonfuzzy profile in consensus determination. Next, the same value is added to the consensus and the final consensus for the fuzzy profile is determined.

The postulate of *Fuzzy proposition* is a general requirement. According to this postulate a consensus for a fuzzy profile X should be chosen on the basis of consensuses for subprofiles $X(x)$ where $x \in S_X$. Each of these consensuses has a share equal to the proportion of the number of occurrences of x in the profile. Merging this postulate with postulate O_1 gives the following consensus function C_{F_1}, such that $x^* \in C_{F_1}(X)$ if and only if

$$\sum_{x_z \in Z} \frac{card(X(z))}{card(X)} d(x^*, x_z) = \min_{x \in U_F} \sum_{x_z \in Z} \frac{card(X(z))}{card(X)} d(x, x_z),$$

where x_z is a consensus of subprofile $X(z)$ for $z \in S_X$ and Z is the set of consensuses of all subprofiles such that each subprofile has exactly one consensus in Z. The consensuses from set Z may be chosen by using function C_1 defined in Section 3.3.3 (Chapter 3).

In the next section we show some properties of these postulates and some relationships between them and the postulates defined for nonfuzzy profiles.

7.4. Analysis of Postulates

Because a fuzzy universe U_F can be treated as a nonfuzzy universe U, all properties of postulates defined for nonfuzzy universes are true. Thus all theorems presented in Section 3.3.3 (Chapter 3) can be translated to the case of fuzzy universes. We now deal with the properties of new postulates *TLC*, *Fa*, *Fs*, and *Fp* which have been specially formulated for fuzzy universes, also their relationships with the previously defined postulates.

Similarly as in Chapter 3 we say that a postulate p

- is *satisfied* if there exist a universe U_F and a function in $\mathbf{Con}(U_F)$ which satisfies postulate p
- is *c-satisfied* if for any universe U_F there exists a function in $\mathbf{Con}(U_F)$ which satisfies postulate p
- is *u-true* if there exists a universe U_F for which p is satisfied by all functions from $\mathbf{Con}(U_F)$
- is *true* if it is *u*-true referring to all universes
- is *false* if it is not satisfied

We can build complex formulae on the basis of atomic formulae using logic quantifiers and such logical connectives as $\vee$, $\wedge$, $\neg$, $\Rightarrow$. For these formulae we accept the same semantics as defined for atomic formulae and the semantic rules of classical logic.

Theorem 7.1.
Formula $Cl \wedge TLC \wedge Fa \wedge Fs \wedge Fp$ is c-satisfied; that is, for each universe U_F there exists a consensus function $C \in \mathbf{Con}(U_F)$ which satisfies all these postulates.

Proof.
For this proof we present a procedure in which for a fuzzy universe a consensus function satisfying postulates *TLC*, *Fa*, *Fs*, and *Fp* is defined. Let then be given a fuzzy universe U_F and let $X \in \Pi(U_F)$ be a profile. We propose to determine a consensus for X as follows.

- Create set (without repetitions)

$$S_X = \{x \in U: x \text{ occurs in } X\}.$$

- Create subprofiles

$$X(x) = \{(x, v): (x, v) \in X \text{ and } x \in S_X\}.$$

- For each $x \in S_X$ calculate the consensus c_x of $X(x)$ as follows,

$$c_x = (x, v_x) \quad \text{where } v_x = \frac{\sum_{(x,v)\in X} v}{card(X)}.$$

- Create a new profile with weights

$$Y = \{c_x: x \in S_X\}$$

where for an element $x \in S_X$ its weight w_x is equal to

$$w_x = \frac{card(X(x))}{card(X)}.$$

- Determine the consensus for profile Y taking the weights into account. For this aim we may use function $C_i^w(Y)$ for $i = 2$ defined in Section 3.6.2 (Chapter 3).

It is obvious that the above procedure guarantees satisfaction of postulate Cl. As we can see from the third step of this procedure it follows that the chosen consensus should satisfy postulate Fa. We may note also that if all fuzzy values of all profile elements are identical then the final consensus should have the same value; that is, postulate Fs is satisfied. Notice that in the case of a fuzzily regular profile the weights of all elements calculated in the fourth step are equal to each other. Owing to the fourth and fifth steps postulate Fp is satisfied and the whole procedure guarantees the two-level consensus choice, that means satisfying for postulate TLC. In this way the procedure determines a consensus function which satisfies all above-mentioned postulates.   ◆

Theorem 7.1 shows that postulates TLC, Fa, Fs, and Fp are not contradictory. Theorem 7.2 below presents some interesting properties of postulate Fa.

Theorem 7.2.
The following formulae are true.

(a) $O_2 \wedge Cl \Rightarrow Fa.$

(b) $Fa \Rightarrow Re \wedge Si \wedge Un \wedge Co \wedge Cc.$

Proof.
(a) Let X be a fuzzily homogeneous profile; that is,

$$X = \{(a, v_i): i = 1, \ldots, n\}$$

for some $a \in U$ and $n \in \aleph$. Let C be a consensus function satisfying postulates O_2 and Cl. Let $x \in C(X)$, because of satisfying postulate Cl we have $x = (a, v)$ for some $v \in [0, 1]$, and

$$\sum_{i=1}^{n}(d_F(x,(a,v_i)))^2 = \min_{y \in U_F} \sum_{i=1}^{n}(d_F(y,(a,v_i)))^2.$$

That is, the sum $\sum_{i=1}^{n}(v - v_i)^2$ is minimal. To develop this sum we have

$$\sum_{i=1}^{n}(v-v_i)^2 = n \cdot v^2 - 2v \cdot \sum_{i=1}^{n}v_i + \sum_{i=1}^{n}(v_i)^2 ,$$

which is minimal if and only if

$$v = \frac{1}{n}\sum_{i=1}^{n}v_i .$$

Thus postulate Fa should be satisfied.

(b) Let X be a fuzzily homogeneous profile; that is,

$$X = \{(a, v_i): i = 1, \ldots , n\}.$$

Let consensus function C satisfy postulate Fa; that is,

$$C(X) = \{(x, v^*): v^* = \frac{1}{n}\sum_{i=1}^{n}v_i \}.$$

Thus satisfaction of postulate Re is obvious. For the postulate of *Simplification* notice that if profile Y is a multiple of profile X then Y is fuzzily homogeneous if and only if X is fuzzily homogeneous. Also each element $(a, v_i) \in X$ appears the same number of times (say k, i.e., $Y = k * X$) in profile Y. Thus the average of values v in profile Y is equal to the average value of v in profile X. That is, postulate Si is satisfied. The satisfaction of postulates Un and Co is obvious. For postulate Cc notice that according to postulate Fa we have $card(C(X)) = 1$. Let X_1 and X_2 be fuzzily homogeneous profiles and let $C(X_1) \cap C(X_2) \neq \varnothing$, thus it should be $C(X_1) = C(X_2)$, so $C(X_1) \cap C(X_2) = C(X_1) = C(X_2)$. We show that $C(X_1 \cup X_2) = C(X_1)$. For this statement it is enough to prove that the following equality is true,

$$\frac{1}{n}\sum_{i=1}^{n}v_i + \frac{1}{m}\sum_{i=1}^{m}v'_i = \frac{1}{n+m}\left(\sum_{i=1}^{n}v_i + \sum_{i=1}^{m}v'_i\right)$$

with the assumption that $\frac{1}{n}\sum_{i=1}^{n}v_i = \frac{1}{m}\sum_{i=1}^{m}v'_i$. The proof of this equality is simple.   ♦

Theorem 7.3.
The following formulae are not true.

(a) $O_1 \Rightarrow Fs$

(b) $TLC \wedge O_1$

(c) $TLC \wedge O_2$

(d) $Fa \wedge O_1$

(e) $Fp \wedge O_1$

(f) $Fp \wedge O_2$.

Proof.

(a) We show that not all consensus functions from $\boldsymbol{Con}(U_F)$ which satisfy postulate O_1 also satisfy postulate Fs. Notice that for applying postulate O_1 we need to define distance function d_F which may cause that postulate Fs will not be satisfied. We give an example of such a function:

$$d_F\big((x, v_1), (y, v_2)\big) = \begin{cases} |v_1 - v_2| & \text{for } x = y \\ 1 & \text{for } x \neq y \text{ and } v_1 = v_2 = 1 , \\ \max\left\{\dfrac{v_1 + v_2}{2}, 0.1\right\} & \text{otherwise} \end{cases}$$

where $(x, v_1), (y, v_2) \in U_F$. This function of course satisfies all conditions formulated in Definition 7.1. Let profile X be

$$X = \{(a, 0.6), (b, 0.6), (c, 0.6)\}.$$

We have: if consensus function C has to satisfy postulate O_1 then

$$C(X) = \{(x, 0): x \in U \setminus S_X\};$$

that is, postulate Fs may not be satisfied.

(b) and (c) Let distance function d_F be

$$d_F\big((x, v_1), (y, v_2)\big) = \begin{cases} |v_1 - v_2| & \text{for } x = y \\ 1 & \text{otherwise} \end{cases},$$

and let profile X be

$$X = \{(a, 0), (a, 1), (a, 0.5), (b, 0.5), (b, 0.5), (b, 0.5)\}.$$

Let a consensus function C satisfy postulate O_1; then we have

$$C(X) = \{(b, 0.5)\},$$

$$C(X(a)) = \{(a, 0.5)\},$$

$$C(X(b)) = \{(b, 0.5)\},$$

$$C\left(\bigcup\nolimits_{x \in S_X} C(X(x)) \right) = \{(a, 0.5), (b, 0.5)\}.$$

So function C does not satisfy postulate *TLC*.

(d) Let the distance function be defined as in (b) and (c) and let profile X be defined as follows,

$$X = \{(a, 0), (a, 1), (a, 0.2)\}.$$

We have: if a consensus function C satisfies postulate O_1 then

$$C(X) = \{(a, 0.2)\},$$

Thus it cannot satisfy postulate *Fa*.

The results in (e) and (f) are implied directly from (b) and (c), respectively.

♦

From this theorem it follows that in general postulates *TLC*, *Fa*, *Fs*, and *Fp* are not consistent with postulates O_1 and O_2; that is, those consensus functions which satisfy one of these postulates do not satisfy postulate O_1 or postulate O_2.

7.5. Algorithms for Consensus Choice

In this section we present some algorithms for consensus determining for fuzzy profiles. Referring to postulates O_1 and O_2, the algorithms should be dependent on the structures of the elements of universe U. In Chapters 4 through 6 one can find several algorithms for such structures as multi-attribute and multivalue relation, conjunction, disjunction, and clause. Here we present general algorithms (without assumption about the structures of the universe elements) which focus on the fuzzy values. In fact a fuzzy value is an element of the fuzzy universe and may be treated as an additional dimension of the element structure. For example, if the structure is multiattribute then the fuzzy value may be treated as the value of an additional attribute.

In working out the algorithms we take into account the special postulates for fuzzy profiles. These postulates are *Cl*, *TLC*, *Fa*, *Fs*, and *Fp*.

Algorithm 7.1.

Input: Fuzzy profile $X \in \prod(U_F)$ and distance function d_F.

Result: A consensus x^* for profile X satisfying postulates *Cl*, *TLC*, *Fa*, *Fs*, and *Fp*.

Procedure:

BEGIN

    1. Create set (without repetitions)

$$S_X = \{x \in U: x \text{ occurs in } X\};$$

    2. For each $x \in S_X$ create subprofile

$$X(x) = \{(x, v): (x, v) \in X\};$$

    3. For each $x \in S_X$ calculate the consensus c_x of $X(x)$

$$c_x = (x, v_x) \quad \text{where } v_x = \frac{\sum_{(x,v) \in X} v}{card(X)};$$

    4. Create a new profile with weights

$$Y = \{c_x: x \in S_X\},$$

    where for an element $x \in S_X$ its weight w_x is equal to

$$w_x = \frac{card(X(x))}{card(X)};$$

    5. Determine the consensus for profile Y taking the weights into account. For this aim use a function $C_i^w(Y)$ defined in Section 3.6.2 (Chapter 3), for $i = 1, 2$. That is, determine an element $x^* \in U_F$ such that

$$\sum_{y \in Y} w_y \big(d_F(x^*, y)\big)^i = \min_{z \in U_F} \sum_{y \in Y} w_y \big(d_F(z, y)\big)^i;$$

END.

The proof that the consensus determined by Algorithm 7.1 satisfies all postulates *Cl*, *TLC*, *Fa*, *Fs*, and *Fp* is included in the proof of Theorem 7.1. The complexity of Algorithm 7.1 is to a large degree dependent on the complexity of step 5 which, in turn, depends on distance function d_F and the structure of the elements of universe U_F.

Now we investigate the relationship between a consensus determined for a fuzzy profile X by using distance function d_F and postulate O_1 and a consensus determined for its corresponding nonfuzzy profile $\breve{X}$ by using distance function d and the same postulate.

We mention that nonfuzzy profile $\breve{X}$ corresponding to fuzzy profile X is defined as follows,

$$\breve{X} = \{x : (x, v) \in X\}.$$

We assume that distance function d_F is defined on the basis of distance function d between nonfuzzy elements in the following way.

$$d_F\big((x, v_1), (y, v_2)\big) = \begin{cases} \big|v_1 - v_2\big| & \text{for } x = y \\ (d(x,y))^{\frac{v_1 + v_2}{2}} & \text{for } x \neq y \end{cases}$$

for $(x, v_1), (y, v_2) \in U_F$.

As mentioned in Section 7.2 this function seems to be useful in practice because of some its advantages.

The function C_1 defined in the proof of Theorem 3.2 (Section 3.3.3) has the following form:

$$C_1(\breve{X}) = \{x \in U : d(x,X) = \min_{y \in U} d(y,X)\}.$$

A similar function may be defined for fuzzy profiles:

$$C_{1F}(X) = \{x \in U_F : d_F(x,X) = \min_{y \in U_F} d_F(y,X)\},$$

where $d_F(z,X) = \sum_{y \in X} d_F(z, y)$ for $z \in U_F$.

The problems are the following:

1. If $(x, v) \in C_{1F}(X)$ *then could there be* $x \in C_1(\breve{X})$?

2. If $x \in C_1(\breve{X})$ *then does there exist* v *such that* $(x, v) \in C_{1F}(X)$?

If the answers for the above questions are positive they should be very useful in practice because this means that a consensus for a fuzzy profile may be determined on the basis of a consensus for its corresponding non-fuzzy profile.

Unfortunately, the answers to these questions are negative. Below we give an example for proving this statement referring to the first question.

Let $U = \{x, y, z, u\}$ and the fuzzy profile X be defined as follows,

$$X = \{(x, 0), (y, 0)\}.$$

The distance function d assigns the following values,

$$d(x, y) = 1; \quad d(z, x) = 0.49; \quad d(z, y) = 0.01; \quad d(u, x) = d(u, y) = 0.22;$$

Taking into account the fact that $a^b \geq a^{b'}$ for $a, b, b' \in [0, 1]$ and $b \leq b'$, we have the following,

$$C_{1F}(X) = \{(z, 1)\},$$

because

$$d_F((z, 1), (x, 0)) = 0.49^{0.5} = 0.7,$$

$$d_F((z, 1), (y, 0)) = 0.01^{0.5} = 0.1,$$

and

$$d_F((x, 0), (y, 0)) = 1,$$

$$d_F((u, 1), (x, 0)) = d_F((u, 1), (y, 0)) \approx 0.469.$$

However,

$$d(z, x) + d(z, y) = 0.5 > d(u, x) + d(u, y) = 0.44.$$

Thus z may not be a consensus for profile $\{x, y\}$; that is, $z \notin C_1(\breve{X})$.

For the second question using the same example notice that u is a consensus for profile $\breve{X} = \{x, y\}$. However, (u, v) may not be a consensus for profile X for any v because

$$d_F((u, v), (x, 0)) \geq d_F((u, 1), (x, 0)) \approx 0.469,$$

$$d_F((u, v), (y, 0)) \geq d_F((u, 1), (y, 0)) \approx 0.469,$$

and

$$d_F((z, 1), (x, 0)) = 0.7,$$

$$d_F((z, 1), (y, 0)) = 0.1.$$

So the answer is also negative in this case.

Our main aim is to determine a consensus for a fuzzy profile satisfying postulate O_1. This task may be very complex because the cardinality of universe U_F is greater than the cardinality of universe U and in fact is an equal *continuum*. Thus it seems that for determining a value of function C_{1F} one should search whole set U_F. However, owing to the theorem presented below, in many cases only universe U should be searched.

Theorem 7.4.
Let $X \in \prod(U_F)$; for each $(x, v) \in C_{1F}(X)$ if $x \notin S_X$ then there should be

$$(x, 1) \in C_{1F}(X).$$

Proof.
For each $(y, w) \in X$, because $x \neq y$ we have $d(x, y) > 0$ and

$$d_F((x, v), (y, w)) = \left(d(x,y)\right)^{\frac{v+w}{2}}$$

$$\geq \left(d(x,y)\right)^{\frac{1+w}{2}} = d_F((x,1),(y,w)).$$

The inequality becomes an equality if and only if $v = 1$ or $d(x, y) = 1$.
Thus if (x, v) is a consensus of profile X then element $(x, 1)$ should also be
a consensus for X. ◆

This theorem, although simple, is very useful in consensus determining.
Owing to it we may search a consensus for a given profile not in universe
U_F but in U if we know that it does not belong to the nonfuzzy profile corresponding to the fuzzy profile.

However, there may be such a consensus $(x, v) \in C_{1F}(X)$ that $x \in S_X$.
How can we find it in an effective way? Assume that we have to deal with
such a situation. Because $x \in S_X$ we know that $X(x)$ is not empty. Let's
consider the following problem:

*For given $x \in S_X$ determine such (x, v_x) which minimizes the sum of dis-
tances to all elements of X; that is,*

$$\sum_{y \in X} d_F((x,v),y) = \min_{v' \in [0,1]} \sum_{y \in X} d_F((x,v'),y).$$

We know that

$$\sum_{y \in X} d_F((x,v'),y) = \sum_{(x,w) \in X(x)} |w - v'| + \sum_{(z,w) \in X \setminus X(x)} \left(d(x,z)\right)^{\frac{w+v'}{2}}.$$

If the values of v' in the two components of the above sum were independent then for minimizing the first component the value of v' could be calculated by the following algorithm.

Algorithm 7.2.

Input: A subprofile $X(x)$.

Result: A consensus (x, v_x) for $X(x)$ satisfying postulate O_1.

Procedure:

BEGIN

    1. Create set with repetitions $Y = \{w: (x, w) \in X(x)\}$;

    2. Create a sequence from Y by sorting its the elements in an increas-
       ing order;

    3. Set v_1 as the $\left\lfloor \dfrac{l+1}{2} \right\rfloor$ th element of the sequence, where $l = card(Y)$,

       and set v_2 as the $\left\lfloor \dfrac{l+2}{2} \right\rfloor$ th element of the sequence;

4. Set v' as any value from interval $[v_1, v_2]$;
5. Set $v_x := v'$;
END.

For minimizing the second component the value of v' could be equal to 1 (according to Theorem 7.4). From these statements it follows that the common value for v' minimizing sum $\sum_{y \in X} d_F((x,v'),y)$ should be included in interval $[v_1, 1]$. Notice that the two components can be treated as functions of parameter v', and in this interval the first component is a nondecreasing function, and the second component is a nonincreasing function. In addition, both functions are continuous. Therefore, although determining a precise value of v' minimizing the sum of the two components is hard, it is rather simple to determine an approximate value of v', for example, by discretisation of the interval, and checking the discrete values of v' referring to the value of the sum. The above problem can then be solved in an effective way.

Now we present an algorithm for determining a consensus for a fuzzy profile X satisfying postulate O_1 using the results presented above. The idea of this algorithm is the following. First, for each $x \in S_X$ determine a fuzzy element (x, v_x) which minimizes the sum of distances to all elements of X; that is,

$$\sum_{y \in X} d_F((x,v),y) = \min_{v' \in [0,1]} \sum_{y \in X} d_F((x,v'),y).$$

Next, determine an element $x' \notin S_X$ such that the sum of distances from $(x', 1)$ to elements of X is minimal. According to Theorem 7.4 such an element $(x', 1)$ could be a candidate for a consensus of profile X. Finally compare element $(x', 1)$ with elements (x, v_x) where $x \in S_X$ concerning their sums of distances to elements of X determining the consensus.

This algorithm is presented as follows.

Algorithm 7.3.

Input: Fuzzy profile $X \in \prod(U_F)$ and distance function d_F.

Result: A consensus x^* for profile X satisfying postulates O_1.

Procedure:

BEGIN
    1. Create set (without repetitions)

$$S_X = \{x \in U: x \text{ occurs in } X\};$$

    2. For each $x \in S_X$ do
        Begin

2.1. Create subprofile

$X(x) = \{(x, v): (x, v) \in X\}$;

2.2. Using Algorithm 7.2 determine consensus (x, v_x) for subprofile $X(x)$;

2.3. Determine element (x, v'_x) which minimizes sum

$$\sum_{y \in X} d_F((x, v'_x), y) = \min_{v \in [0,1]} \sum_{y \in X} d_F((x, v), y)\,;$$

End;

3. Determine such (z, w) from set $\{(x, v'_x): x \in S_X\}$ which minimizes sum $\sum_{y \in X} d_F((z, w), y)$;

4. Set $x^* := (z, w)$ and $T := \sum_{y \in X} d_F((z, w), y)$;

5. For each $x \in U \backslash S_X$ do

  Begin

    5.1. Calculate sum $T(x) = \sum_{y \in X} d_F((x, 1), y)$;

    5.2. If $T(x) < T$ then set $x^* := (x, 1)$ and $T := T(x)$;

  End;

END.

The computational complexity of Algorithm 7.3 is hard to be determined because the microstructure of universe U is unknown. The most complex may be the operation included in step 5, where it is needed to search set $U \backslash S_X$ which may be large. However, as we have stated earlier, it is always much less complex than searching the whole (or even a part) of the fuzzy universe U_F.

7.6. Conclusions

In this chapter a model for fuzzy consensus is presented. This model can be treated as a special case of the general model of consensus presented in Chapter 3. Therefore, some specific postulates for fuzzy profiles have been defined and analyzed. Although the microstructure of the fuzzy universe is not assumed, several concrete algorithms for consensus determining have been proposed and analyzed.

8. Processing Inconsistency of Expert Knowledge

In this chapter an analytical approach to quality analysis of expert knowledge is presented. We show different types of conflict profiles consisting of expert solutions of some problem and investigate the relationship between the consensus of a profile to the proper solution of this problem. Although the proper solution is not known, we show that in certain situations the consensus is more similar to it than the solutions proposed by the experts.

8.1. Introduction

An expert, in a general understanding, is someone who is widely recognized as a reliable source of knowledge, technique, or skill, and has the capability to make autonomous decisions which can be considered as sustained. Thus an expert is characterized by two attributes: possessing knowledge and capability for autonomous decision making. Most often for an expert these two attributes refer only to a narrow field of science and technique. Therefore, very often, a complex problem needs to be solved by several experts simultaneously.

Using expert knowledge is very popular and practically necessary in many fields of life. By an expert we understand not only a human expert in a field of science and technology, but also some intelligent program, for example, an expert system or an intelligent agent. One can say that in almost every task we need expert knowledge and we use it for making proper (at least we hope so) decisions, from fixing a car to the purchase of a house. It very often happens that before making an important decision we often ask opinions of not one, but several experts. If the opinions of all these experts are identical or very similar, we are happy and have no trouble with making the final decision, but if these opinions are to a large degree different from each other then our decision-making process will be difficult. However, this observation is not always true, and this is the subject of this chapter.

More generally, if solving a task is entrusted to several experts then one can expect that some of the solutions generated by the experts may differ from each other. Thus the set of expert solutions creates a conflict profile. As stated in Chapter 3, consensus methods turn out to be useful in reconciling inconsistency of agent and expert opinions. The inconsistency in this context is seen as "something wrong" and needs to be solved.

However, very often inconsistency has its positive aspects and is very useful because it helps to present different aspects of a matter. In this chapter we present a mathematical model which shows that for many practical cases the inconsistency is necessary.

Let's start with an example. In the television game show, *Who Wants to Be a Millionaire?*, a player with a difficult question may have three lifebuoys: removing two of four variants in the answer; a telephone call to his friend; and a question to the public. In the second and third case the decision of the player to a larger degree is dependent on the answer of a specialist (his friend) or of a larger number of people (the public). According to the statistics given by Shermer in the book, *The Science of Good and Evil* [142], it is known that using the help of specialists only 65% of them have given good answers, whereas using the help of the public as many as 91% have given good answers. From this observation the author of the above-mentioned book put forward a hypothesis that in solving a number of problems a group of people is more intelligent than a single person. This hypothesis is confirmed by another author, James Surowiecki, in his book, *The Wisdom of Crowds* [150]. In this work Surowiecki has described several experiments which prove that the reconciled decision of a group of people is in general more proper than single decisions.

As one of these experiments Surowiecki presented the following. A number of people have been asked to guess how many beans are in a jar. The average of results given by the experiment participants is 871 grains, and in fact the number of beans in the jar is 850; the error is only 2.5%. Surowiecki's book also contains other interesting experiments proving that inconsistency of experts may give a more proper solution for a problem than only one solution.

What then is the basis of this phenomenon?

In this chapter we try, to a certain degree, to answer this question. We build a mathematical model with this aim. We formulate the following problem. To discover the proper solution of a problem a number of agents or experts are asked to give their solutions. The set of these solutions (as a set with repetitions) is called a conflict profile (see Chapter 2). For the

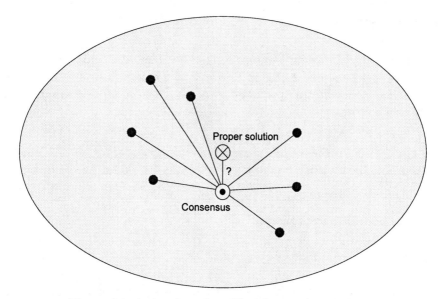

Figure 8.1. A situation of conflict of expert knowledge.

conflict profile a consensus may be determined. Assuming that the elements of the profile are placed in a certain distance space, we should answer the following question. What is the relationship between the distance from the consensus to the proper solution and the distances from the proposed solutions to the proper solution?

Figure 8.1 illustrates this problem, where the black points represent the elements of the conflict profile.

In Figure 8.1 we have a conflict situation in which elements of the conflict profile represent the solutions given by experts. On their basis we can determine the consensus. A very interesting question is: what are the conditions for which the distance between the consensus and the proper solution is smaller than the average of distances from the proper solution to the profile elements? Knowing the answer to this question one can for a concrete task generate the set of experts or agents so that the consensus of their solutions will not be far from the proper solution which is needed to be found. The other advantage of this fact is also the possibility for explaining why the wisdom of crowds is larger than the wisdom of a sole person.

In this chapter we do not deal with the uncertainty of experts. This is the subject of many publications, among others [97].

8.2. Basic Notions

In this chapter we use the notions defined in Chapters 2 and 3. We assume that the distance space (U, d) defined in Chapter 2 is a nonnegative m-dimension Euclidean space for $m \in \aleph$. That is, an element x of the space is a vector

$$x = (x_1, x_2, \ldots, x_m)$$

for $x_i \in \Re^+$ ($\Re^+$ is the set of nonnegative real numbers) for $i = 1, 2, \ldots, m$. In addition, the distance function is Euclidean; that is, for two elements

$$x = (x_1, x_2, \ldots, x_m) \quad \text{and} \quad x' = (x'_1, x'_2, \ldots, x'_m)$$

we have their distance equal to

$$d(x, x') = \sqrt{\sum_{i=1}^{m} (x_i - x'_i)^2} \ .$$

Here is some commentary referring to the representation power of m-dimension Euclidean spaces. As is well known, a vector in such a space has m dimensions and represents a potential problem solution given by an expert. A dimension may represent an attribute and its value. The value of the vector component under this dimension describes in what degree the attribute may have the given value. Below we give an example illustrating this idea.

Example 8.1. Let (U, A) be a real world, where

$$A = \{a, b, c, d\},$$
$$V_a = \{0, 1\},$$
$$V_b = \{+, -\},$$
$$V_c = \{\alpha, \beta\},$$
$$V_a = \{\mu, \eta\}.$$

A group of experts is asked to describe an object belonging to U referring to the above-given attributes. Their fuzzy-based opinions are presented as follows.

Expert	$(a, 1)$	$(b, +)$	(c, β)	(d, μ)
E_1	0.5	1	0.7	0.3
E_2	1	0.1	0.5	0.8
E_3	0.8	0.5	0.9	0.5
E_4	0.3	0.1	0.7	0.7
E_5	0.7	0	0.6	0.2

Thus an opinion of an expert is a vector in four-dimensional Euclidean space. Each dimension in this space represents an attribute and each component of a vector represents the degree in which, in the opinion of an expert, the given object may have a concrete value referring to an attribute. Notice that an attribute may have more than one dimension if an expert opinion refers to its different values. ♦

8.3. Consensus Determination Problems

For further investigation we need to mention the problem of consensus determination. As stated in Chapter 3, for consensus choice two postulates (criteria) are most popular:

- Criterion O_1 which requires the sum of distances from a consensus to the profile elements to be minimal
- Criterion O_2 which requires the sum of squares of distances from a consensus to the profile elements to be minimal.

For the first criterion the consensus choice is a complex problem for Euclidean space. The problem of finding a point in the space which is nearest to a set of points is a classical problem of optimization theory. An effective algorithm does not exist for this problem and it is necessary to use heuristic strategies. However, as we have shown in Chapter 3, if the points belonging to the profile are placed on an axis (in an m-dimensional space there are m axes), then we have an effective method for determining a consensus. This method may be generalized for the case when profile elements are placed on a line.

For the second criterion there exists an effective method for consensus determination. We prove the following.

Theorem 8.1.
For given profile

$$X = \{ x^{(i)} = (x_1^{(i)}, x_2^{(i)}, \ldots, x_m^{(i)}): i = 1, 2, \ldots, n\},$$

a vector

$$x = (x_1, x_2, \ldots, x_m)$$

is a consensus satisfying criterion O_2 if and only if

$$x_j = \frac{1}{n}\sum_{i=1}^{n} x_j^{(i)}$$

for j = 1, 2, . . . , m.

Proof.

Criterion O_2 requires the sum

$$\sum_{i=1}^{n}(d(x,x^{(i)}))^2$$

to be minimal. Furthermore we have

$$\sum_{i=1}^{n}(d(x,x^{(i)}))^2 = \sum_{i=1}^{n}(\sum_{j=1}^{m}(x_j - x_j^{(i)})^2) = \sum_{i=1}^{n}\sum_{j=1}^{m}[(x_j)^2 - 2\cdot x_j \cdot x_j^{(i)} + (x_j^{(i)})^2]$$

$$= \sum_{j=1}^{m}\sum_{i=1}^{n}[(x_j)^2 - 2\cdot x_j \cdot x_j^{(i)} + (x_j^{(i)})^2]$$

$$= \sum_{j=1}^{m}[n\cdot(x_j)^2 - 2\cdot x_j \cdot \sum_{i=1}^{n} x_j^{(i)} + \sum_{i=1}^{n}(x_j^{(i)})^2] = \sum_{j=1}^{m}F(x_j),$$

where

$$F(x_j) = n\cdot(x_j)^2 - 2\cdot x_j \cdot \sum_{i=1}^{n} x_j^{(i)} + \sum_{i=1}^{n}(x_j^{(i)})^2 .$$

Notice that sum $\sum_{i=1}^{n}(d(x,x^{(i)}))^2$ is minimal if for each $j = 1, 2, \ldots, m$ value $F(x_j)$ is minimal. This value, in turn, is minimal for such value x_j for which the differential coefficient is e qual to 0; that is,

$$\frac{\partial F(x_j)}{\partial x_j} = 0 ;$$

it follows

$$x_j = \frac{1}{n}\sum_{i=1}^{n} x_j^{(i)} .$$ ♦

From Theorem 8.1 it follows that the consensus satisfying criterion O_2 should be the centre of gravity of profile X.

As stated above, there is no effective algorithm determining the consensus satisfying criterion O_1 for profile X. However, we prove an interesting property of this consensus.

Theorem 8.2.
For given profile

$$X = \{ x^{(i)} = (x_1^{(i)}, x_2^{(i)}, \ldots, x_m^{(i)}): i = 1, 2, \ldots, n \},$$

let vector

$$x = (x_1, x_2, \ldots, x_m)$$

be its consensus satisfying criterion O_1. Then in the space there does not exist any vector y for which

$$d(y, x) > d(y, x^{(i)})$$

for all $i = 1, 2, \ldots, n$.

Proof.
We mention that criterion O_1 requires the sum

$$\sum_{i=1}^{n} d(x, x^{(i)})$$

to be minimal. We carry out the proof by contradiction. Let's assume that there exists a vector p for which

$$d(p, x) > d(p, x^{(i)})$$

for all $i = 1, 2, \ldots, n$. Thus for an $i = 1, 2, \ldots, n$ consider the triangle $\Delta_{px^{(i)}x}$ (see Figure 8.2). Because $d(p, x) > d(p, x^{(i)})$ we have the following inequality of angles,

$$\alpha_i > \beta_i.$$

Thus we may determine a point p_i being on line px and between these points ($p_i \neq p$) so that $\alpha_i > \alpha'_i = \sphericalangle p x^{(i)} p_i$ and $\alpha'_i > \beta'_i = \sphericalangle x^{(i)} p_i p$ (see Figure 8.2). In the new triangle $\Delta_{px^{(i)}p_i}$ the following inequality is true,

$$d(p, p_i) > d(p, x^{(i)}).$$

Let $p_k \in \{p_1, p_2, \ldots, p_n\}$ be such that

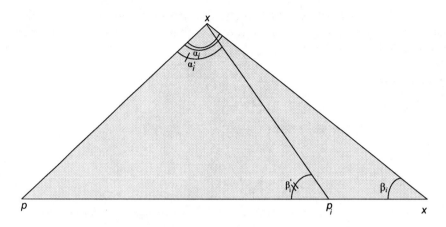

Figure 8.2. Triangle $\Delta_{px^{(i)}x}$.

$$d(p_k, x^{(i)}) = \max_{j \in \{1,2,...,n\}} d(p_j, x^{(i)}).$$

Notice that in triangle $\Delta_{px^{(i)}p_k}$ there should be $\beta'_k < 90°$ because $\alpha'_i > \beta'_i$. Thus $\vartriangleleft x^{(i)}p_k x > 90°$; it follows that $d(p_k, x^{(i)}) < d(x, x^{(i)})$ and, as the consequence:

$$\sum_{i=1}^{n} d(p_k, x^{(i)}) < \sum_{i=1}^{n} d(x, x^{(i)}).$$

This result causes the contradiction because x is the consensus satisfying criterion O_1. ◆

Theorem 8.2 is also true for the consensus satisfying criterion O_2. The proof is identical.

From Theorem 8.2 it follows that the distance from a consensus of profile X satisfying criterion O_1 (or O_2) to any point of the space should not be greater than the maximal distance from this point to the elements of the profile.

More generally, we can state that if x is a consensus of profile X satisfying criterion O_1 (or O_2), then x should be intrinsic referring to X in the sense that there may not exist a plane T such that consensus x is placed on one side and the elements of profile X on the other side of plane T. Figure 8.3 illustrates this situation, where profile X consists of four points $x^{(1)}, x^{(2)}, x^{(3)},$ and $x^{(4)}$. It is assumed that plane T shares profile X and consensus x.

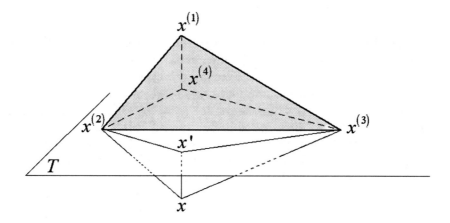

Figure 8.3. Consensus x and profile X should be intrinsic.

This situation may not take place because we may make the projection x' of x on plane T and for each profile element $x^{(i)}$ we have:

$$d(x,\ x^{(i)}) > d(x',\ x^{(i)})$$

because angle $\sphericalangle xx'\,x^{(i)} > 90°$. Thus x may not be a consensus satisfying either criterion O_1 or criterion O_2.

Notice that the property included in Theorem 8.2 is not true for each distance space. Let's consider an example.

Example 8.2. Let the distance space (U, d) be defined as

$$U = 2^{\{a,\ b,\ c\}},$$

$$d(y,z) = card(y \div z) \text{ for } y, z \subseteq \{a, b, c\}.$$

Let profile $X = \{\{a, b\}, \{a, c\}\}$. Then a consensus satisfying criterion O_1 is

$$x = \{a, b, c\}.$$

Letting $y = \{a\}$ we have:

$$2 = d(y,x) > d(x,\{a,b\}) = d(x,\{a,c\}) = 1.$$

Thus the property from Theorem 8.2 is not true.   ◆

8.4. The Quality Analysis

In this section we deal with the quality analysis of expert knowledge. In the Introduction we stated that it is often good that the opinions generated by experts for some matter are different from each other. Here we try to prove this statement. We assume that some problem requires to be solved and has a proper solution which has to be "guessed" by a group of experts. It is then the first case mentioned in Section 3.2.2 (Chapter 3). First we notice that an expert generates a solution of this problem but her decision is made in a situation of uncertainty and incompleteness. Thus it is not known if her solution is exactly the same as the proper solution. The example with the jar of beans is an illustration of this case. An expert (i.e., experiment participant) does know exactly how many beans there are in the jar. Her decision is made only on the basis of her experiences and visual evaluation. In this experiment the average of the results given by the participants has been taken as the final solution of experts. From Theorem 8.1 we know that it is the consensus satisfying criterion O_2.

Let's consider the following aspects:

- If there is only one expert who is entrusted to solve the given problem, then his solution may be good (close to the proper solution) or wrong (far from the proper solution). According to the statistic made for the television game show *Who Wants to Be a Millionaire?*, 65% of telephone calls to friends were on target. The reason for a not so high pertinence degree of one expert is based on the fact that the problem to be solved is multidimensional (interdisciplinary) whereas an expert is a good specialist only in one or two dimensions (fields). Thus entrusting the problem to only one expert may be risky in the sense that the solution given by this expert can be very dissimilar to the proper solution.
- If not one, but several experts are trusted to solve the problem and their solutions are identical, we have a homogeneous profile with the maximal consistency and of course the consensus will be the same. However, if the problem is not simple, this fact may mean that the experts are very similar referring to their profiles (i.e., they are specialists in the same field). In this case the consensus of their solutions can be wrong. Let's return to the experiment with the jar of 850 beans. The problem of guessing this number is not simple. So if all results given by the participants were identical, it would seem that this is not a good solution.

- For many problems which are complex (multidimensional) and contain many uncertain parameters we would wish to entrust to experts of different specializations for solution and we would be happier if the solutions given by them were not consistent. Why? Owing to this the solutions given by the experts will reflect more aspects of the problem and in consequence, their reconciled solution could be similar to the proper solution. As Surowiecki has suggested in the book, *The Wisdom of Crowds*, the condition for achieving a good result of experiments is the autonomy of the participants and the differentiation of their profiles. In this section we use Euclidean space to prove this hypothesis.

First we prove that if we use a group of experts to solve a problem then the consensus of their solutions should not be worse than the worst solution.

Theorem 8.3.
For given profile

$$X = \{ x^{(i)} = (x_1^{(i)}, x_2^{(i)}, \ldots, x_m^{(i)}): i = 1, 2, \ldots, n\},$$

containing the solutions given by experts, let vector

$$x = (x_1, x_2, \ldots, x_m)$$

be its consensus satisfying criterion O_1 or O_2. Let x^* be the proper solution; then

$$d(x, x^*) \leq \max_{i \in \{1,2,\ldots,n\}} d(x^*, x^{(i)})$$

and if $x \notin X$ then there should be

$$d(x, x^*) < \max_{i \in \{1,2,\ldots,n\}} d(x^*, x^{(i)}).$$

Proof.
We prove the theorem for criterion O_1; for criterion O_2 the proof is similar.

From Theorem 8.2 we know that there does not exist any vector y for which

$$d(y, x) > d(y, x^{(i)})$$

for all $i = 1, 2, \ldots, n$. It follows that for vector x^* there should be

$$d(x^*, x) = d(x, x^*) \leq d(x^*, x^{(j)})$$

for some $j = 1, 2, \ldots, n$. So

$$d(x^*, x) \leq \max_{i \in \{1,2,\ldots,n\}} d(x^*, x^{(i)}).$$

Let's now assume that $x \notin X$. In this case we prove that

$$d(x^*, x) < \max_{i \in \{1,2,\ldots,n\}} d(x^*, x^{(i)}).$$

Assume that it is not true; that is,

$$d(x^*, x) = \max_{i \in \{1,2,\ldots,n\}} d(x^*, x^{(i)}).$$

Because $x \notin X$ then for each $i = 1, 2, \ldots, n$ the plane determined by three points x^*, x, and $x^{(i)}$ has the following property. We may introduce a circle with the centre x^* and radius equal to $d(x^*, x)$, which contains point $x^{(i)}$. Because $x \neq x^{(i)}$ we may introduce a line l upright to line x^*x so that points x and $x^{(i)}$ are on both sides of l (see Figure 8.4). Let line l cut line x^*x in point y_i.

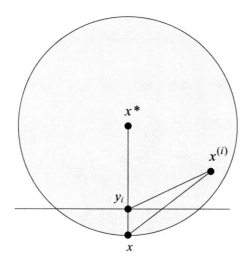

Figure 8.4. The plane determined by three points x^*, x, and $x^{(i)}$.

We have the following inequality of angles:

$$\sphericalangle xy_i x^{(i)} > 90°$$

because x and $x^{(i)}$ are on both sides of l and l is upright to x^*x. It should follow that in triangle $\Delta_{xx^{(i)}y_i}$ the following inequality is true,

$$d(y_i, x^{(i)}) < d(x, x^{(i)}).$$

Let's now determine point y among points $y_1, y_2, \ldots, y_n$ such that the distance $d(x^*, y)$ is maximal. We have

$$d(y, x^{(i)}) < d(x, x^{(i)})$$

for all $i = 1, 2, \ldots, n$. This is a contradiction because in this case x may not be a consensus for profile X satisfying neither criterion O_1 nor O_2. Thus there should be

$$d(x^*, x) < \max_{i \in \{1,2,\ldots,n\}} d(x^*, x^{(i)}). \qquad \blacklozenge$$

Notice that the inequality

$$d(x^*, x) < \max_{i \in \{1,2,\ldots,n\}} d(x^*, x^{(i)})$$

is true only for the case when $x \notin X$; that is, profile X should be non-homogeneous. That is, it should contain at least two elements different from each other. In other words, in profile X there is inconsistency.

For a consensus satisfying criterion O_2 we have a stronger result. It turns out that if profile X is nonhomogeneous then the distance between consensus and the proper solutions should always be smaller than the maximal distance between the proper solution and the elements of the profile.

Theorem 8.4.
For given nonhomogeneous profile

$$X = \{ x^{(i)} = (x_1^{(i)}, x_2^{(i)}, \ldots, x_m^{(i)}): i = 1, 2, \ldots, n\},$$

containing the solutions given by experts, let vector

$$x = (x_1, x_2, \ldots, x_m)$$

be its consensus satisfying criterion O_2. Let x^* be the proper solution; then

$$d(x, x^*) < \max_{i \in \{1,2,\dots,n\}} d(x^*, x^{(i)}).$$

Proof.

If $x \notin X$ then on the basis of Theorem 8.3 we have immediately

$$d(x, x^*) < \max_{i \in \{1,2,\dots,n\}} d(x^*, x^{(i)}).$$

Assume now $x \in X$; that is, consensus x is one of the profile elements. Without losing generality we can assume that $x = x^{(1)}$. In this case notice that for each dimension j ($j = 1, 2, \dots, m$), on the basis of Theorem 8.1 we have:

$$x_j = \frac{1}{n} \sum_{i=1}^{n} x_j^{(i)},$$

or

$$x_j^{(1)} = \frac{1}{n} \sum_{i=1}^{n} x_j^{(i)}.$$

After reduction and noting that $n > 1$ because profile X is nonhomogeneous we have

$$x_j^{(1)} = \frac{1}{n-1} \sum_{i=2}^{n} x_j^{(i)}.$$

This equation for all dimensions $j = 1, 2, \dots, m$ means that x is still a consensus satisfying criterion O_2 for profile X after removing element $x^{(1)}$ from it. In this way we can remove from the profile all elements identical to the consensus x and x will still be a consensus for a new profile. Finally, owing to the nonhomogeneity of profile X we will have a situation that there is profile $X' \subseteq X$ such that x is a consensus satisfying criterion O_2 for X' and $x \notin X'$. Using Theorem 8.3 we have

$$d(x, x^*) < \max_{x' \in X'} d(x^*, x'),$$

and because

$$\max_{x' \in X'} d(x^*, x') \le \max_{i \in \{1,2,\dots,n\}} d(x^*, x^{(i)}),$$

thus

$$d(x, x^*) < \max_{i \in \{1,2,\ldots,n\}} d(x^*, x^{(i)}).$$ ◆

Theorems 8.3 and 8.4 give us some very important properties of a profile containing inconsistency. In practice it means that if solving some problem is entrusted to several experts, and the consensus of their given solutions is different from those solutions, then it is not only not worse than the worst solution (in the sense of distance to the proper solution), but also better than this solution. The property included in Theorem 8.4 is stronger than in Theorem 8.3. It means that if profile X is nonhomogeneous then the consensus satisfying criterion O_2 is better than the worst solution.

These properties explain why the inconsistency of expert solutions is useful, because only in this case can one learn that the consensus should be better than the worst result generated by the experts.

Now we deal with a situation in which it is assumed that the distance from the proper solution to the elements of a nonhomogeneous profile are identical. We prove that in this case the consensus is better than the solutions generated by the experts.

Theorem 8.5.
For given profile

$$X = \{ x^{(i)} = (x_1^{(i)}, x_2^{(i)}, \ldots, x_m^{(i)}): i = 1, 2, \ldots, n\},$$

containing the solutions given by experts, let vector

$$x = (x_1, x_2, \ldots, x_m)$$

be its consensus satisfying criterion O_1 or O_2. Let x^* be the proper solution and let

$$d(x^*, x^{(1)}) = d(x^*, x^{(2)}) = \cdots = d(x^*, x^{(n)}).$$

If $x \notin X$ then there should be

$$d(x, x^*) < d(x^*, x^{(1)}).$$

Proof.
The proof of this theorem follows directly from the proof of Theorem 8.3 with the notice that

$$d(x^*, x^{(1)}) = \max_{i \in \{1,2,\dots,n\}} d(x^*, x^{(i)}). \qquad \blacklozenge$$

In the case of a consensus satisfying criterion O_2 and on the basis of Theorem 8.4 we have the following stronger property.

Theorem 8.6.
For a given nonhomogeneous profile

$$X = \{ x^{(i)} = (x_1^{(i)}, x_2^{(i)}, \dots, x_m^{(i)}) : i = 1, 2, \dots, n\},$$

containing the solutions given by experts, let vector

$$x = (x_1, x_2, \dots, x_m)$$

be its consensus satisfying criterion O_2. Let x^* be the proper solution and let

$$d(x^*, x^{(1)}) = d(x^*, x^{(2)}) = \cdots = d(x^*, x^{(n)}).$$

Then there should be

$$d(x, x^*) < d(x^*, x^{(1)}).$$

From Theorems 8.5 and 8.6 it follows that it is true that if the expert solutions reflect the proper solution to the same degree then their consensus satisfying criterion O_1 should be better than the expert solutions if this consensus does not belong to the profile. In the case of nonhomogeneous profiles it is always true that a consensus satisfying criterion O_2 should be better than all expert solutions.

The practical sense of the above results is that if we invite several experts to solve some problem and we assume the same degree of confidence in these experts, then the consensus of the profile containing all expert solutions should be better than each of them separately. By the degree of confidence in an expert we mean the distance between the proper solution and the solution given by this expert. As an example let's take the situation when a president of a country has to make an important decision which is related to the interests of many people. Before making his decision the president asks his experts for their opinions on this matter. If the president conditions his decision on the opinions of the experts, and his confidence degrees toward them are the same, then the consensus of expert opinions in general should be nearer to the president's decision than each of these individual opinions.

These results are very suitable for the case when the solution of the problem is dependent on the opinions of experts. As analyzed in Section

3.2.2, it is the solutions of experts that decide about the final solution of the problem. If the proper solution is assumed to exist then the best criterion for consensus choice is postulate O_1. If the proper solution is assumed to be dependent on the expert solutions then the best criterion for consensus choice is postulate O_2.

8.5. Conclusions

Future work should concern the relationships between consistency measures for conflict profiles and the quality of the consensus. We can consider other notions of consensus quality than that defined in Section 3.4. The quality of consensus is here understood as the difference between a consensus solution generated by experts and the proper solution of the problem. As defined in Chapter 2, the consistency value for a conflict profile informs us about the coherence degree of the profile elements. It has been stated that sometimes it is better to deal with a more consistent profile than with a less consistent profile, because in the first profile the opinions of conflict participants are more similar to each other, and therefore it is easier to solve the conflict. We can suggest another aspect of inconsistency degree. We show that the credibility of the consensus can be better when the value of profile consistency degree is low; that is, the expert solutions are in large degree different from each other.

9. Ontology Integration

Ontology can be treated as the background of an information system. If integration of some systems has to be performed, their ontologies must also be integrated. In this process it is often necessary to resolve conflicts (or inconsistency) between ontologies. In this chapter we present a classification of ontology conflicts and consensus-based methods for their resolution.

9.1. Introduction

Ontology has been known to be a very useful tool in defining the "spirit" or a "background" of an information system. In database systems this background is the conceptual scheme which consists of such elements as a set of attributes with their domains, a set of dependencies between the attributes, and a set of relationships between data objects. The data or knowledge which appear in the database have to comply with this scheme. Most often ontology is defined by the following elements [43, 51]:

- C – Set of concepts (classes)
- I – Set of instances of concepts
- R – Set of binary relations defined on C
- Z – Set of axioms which are formulae of first-order logic and can be interpreted as integrity constraints or relationships between instances and concepts, and which cannot be expressed by the relations in set R, nor as relationships between relations included in R

Recently, there has been an increased interest in ontologies and in various problems related to inconsistency processing, such as ontology mismatch, ontology conflict, ontology merging, or ontology integration [28, 45, 136]. Ontology mismatch or ontology conflict could be treated as synonymies defining a specific relation between two or more ontologies. Ontology merge (or ontology integration) refers to some activities performed on ontologies. Ontology integration (we use this term in this chapter) is an important task which needs to be realized in many practical cases, especially when several systems with knowledge bases have to be merged for some purpose, or when they want to share or exchange their knowledge in order to have a uniform point of view. Because ontology in these systems is a distinguished element of their knowledge bases, the knowledge integration process very often begins with ontology integration.

According to Pinto and others [137], ontology integration is a process which may be done on one of the following three levels.

- Building a new ontology reusing other available ontologies: One wants to build a new ontology using some other ontologies which have been built. It is the simplest case of ontology integration.
- Merging different ontologies about the same domain into a single one that "unifies" all of them: One wants to build an ontology merging ideas, concepts, distinctions, axioms, and the like, that is, knowledge, from other existing ontologies about exactly the same domain.
- Introducing ontologies into applications: In this case, several ontologies are introduced into an application; they underlie and are shared among several software applications. It is also possible to use several ontologies to specify or implement a knowledge-based system on the basis of distributed resources.

Noy and Musen [130], on the other hand, formulate two general approaches for ontology integration process:

- Merging several ontologies for creating one consistent ontology
- Adjustment of several ontologies by determining the references between them for the possibility of using all of these ontologies

In the first case one has to deal with several ontologies which are inconsistent or in conflict. The notion of inconsistency (or conflict) of ontologies is not so simple, and is defined and analyzed further in this chapter. Here we roughly understand that two ontologies are in conflict (or are inconsistent) if they reflect the same real world for different systems, and contain different states of knowledge referring to the same real world element. It is necessary to determine one ontology on the basis of given ontologies. The ontology for Esperanto language is an example of this case.

In the second approach for two ontologies one needs to find a mechanism which fixes the relationships between elements of one ontology and elements of another and owing to this it is possible to use both ontologies toward some aim without creating one unified ontology. As an example consider two agents, one of whom occupies car sales and the other occupies marketing strategy. Assume that the first agent would like to use the ontology of the second agent. Toward this aim the agent should "translate" the concepts of his ontology to those of the second ontology.

The first approach is one of the subjects of this chapter. We characterize the conflicts between ontologies and make a classification of these conflicts. Next, we propose consensus-based methods for conflict resolution.

Figure 9.1 presents a situation where for the same real world there are four ontologies defined for four systems. These ontologies may differ from each other. However, this definition of inconsistency between ontologies is not always accurate because the difference of ontologies may appear on different levels and in different parameters. Also, the areas of the real world occupied by these systems may be different, or only partly overlap.

The idea of the integration method presented in this chapter was initiated in [111]. Some application of this method for integrating ontologies of information retrieval agents is presented in [121]. In [143] the authors present a method for integrating ontologies of biomedical databases.

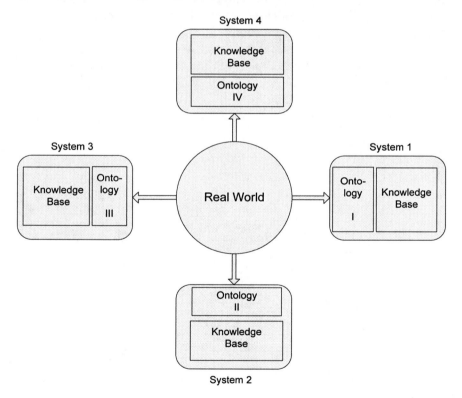

Figure 9.1. A possible inconsistency situation of ontologies.

9.2. Problem of Ontology Integration

In general, one of the ontology integration problems can be formulated as follows.

For given ontologies $O_1, \ldots, O_n$ one should determine one ontology which best represents them.

The realization of this task of ontology integration is useful when there is a need to fuse n systems in which ontologies $O_1, \ldots, O_n$ are used. The final system needs the ontology which arises as the result of integration of these ontologies. The process of ontology integration is illustrated in Figure 9.2.

Notice that not always in ontology integration processes is it necessary to solve conflicts of ontologies. A conflict of some ontologies may arise only when they refer to the same real world. As stated in the Introduction, the subject of our work is focused on the aspect that the same real world object is differently reflected in ontologies. Thus during the integration process there will be the problem of choosing the proper description of the object.

In this chapter we consider three levels of ontology conflicts: *instance level*, *concept level*, and *relation level*. For each level the conflict is defined and analyzed using consensus methods.

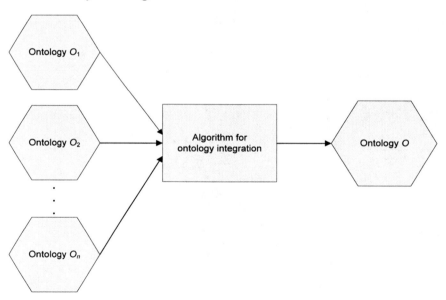

Figure 9.2. Scheme for ontology integration.

9.3. Inconsistency between Ontologies

9.3.1. Basic Notions

As mentioned in Section 9.1, by an ontology we understand a quadruple:

$$(C, I, R, Z).$$

We assume a real world (A, V) where A is a finite set of attributes and V is the domain of A; that is, V is a set of attribute values, and

$$V = \bigcup_{a \in A} V_a \,,$$

where V_a is the domain of attribute a.

We consider the domain ontologies referring to the real world (A, V); such ontologies are called (A, V)-based. In this chapter we define the following notions.

Definition 9.1.
A concept of an (A, V)-based ontology is defined as a triple:

$$Concept = (c, A^c, V^c) \,,$$

where c is the unique name of the concept, $A^c \subseteq A$ is a set of attributes describing the concept, and $V^c \subseteq V$ is the attributes' domain: $V^c = \bigcup_{a \in A^c} V_a$.

Pair (A^c, V^c) is called the *structure* of concept c. It is obvious that all concepts belonging to the same ontology are different from each other. However, notice that within an ontology there may be two or more concepts with the same structure. Such a situation may take place, for example, for concepts "*person*" and "*body*". For expressing the relationship between them the relations from set R will be very useful.

Set C in the ontology definition is a set of ontology names.

Definition 9.2.
An instance of a concept c is described by the attributes from set A^c with values from set V^c and is defined as a pair:

$$instance = (i, v) \,,$$

where i is the unique identifier of the instance in world (A, V) and v is the value of the instance, a tuple of type A^c, and can be presented as a function:

$$v: A^c \rightarrow V^c$$

such that $v(a) \in V_a$ for all $a \in A^c$.

Value v is also called a description of the instance within a concept. A concept may be interpreted as a set of all instances described by its structure. We can then write $i \in c$ for presenting the fact that i is an instance of concept c.

All instances of the same concept within an ontology should be different from each other. The same instance may belong to different concepts and may have different descriptions. However, the following *Instance Integration Condition* (IIC) should be satisfied.

Let instance i belong simultaneously to concept c as (i, v) and to concept c′ as (i, v'). If $A^c \cap A^{c'} \neq \varnothing$ then there should be

$$v(a) = v'(a)$$

for each $a \in A^c \cap A^{c'}$.

The instance integration rule means that if the same instance is described differently in different concepts then in referring to the same attribute they should have the same value.

Similarly, we define the *Concept Integration Condition* (CIC) as follows.

Let concept c occur twice in the same ontology or in two (A, V)-based ontologies, such as (c, A^c, V^c) and $(c, A^{c'}, V^{c'})$. Then there should be $A^c = A^{c'}$ and $V_a^c = V_a^{c'}$ for each $a \in A^c$.

This condition requires that a concept should occur with the same structure.

By *Ins(O,c)* we denote the set of all instances belonging to concept c in ontology O. We define the set *Ins(O)* of all instances in ontology O:

$$Ins(O) = \bigcup_{c \in C} Ins(O,c).$$

In an ontology within a pair of concepts there may be defined one or more relations.

Let O and O' be (A, V)-based ontologies. A concept (c, A^c, V^c) belonging to O is identical with a concept $(c', A^{c'}, V^{c'})$ belonging to O' if and only if $c = c'$, $A^c = A^{c'}$ and $V^c = V^{c'}$. Thus two identical concepts should have the same name as well as the same structure; that is, they are in fact the same concept. As mentioned above, a concept is identified by its name, so saying "a concept" we have in mind its name. This means that the same concept may have different structures in different ontologies.

The same instance may be described in different ways in different ontologies. Two instances (i, v) and (i', v') may have then identical identifiers (i.e., $i = i'$), but their values may be different (i.e., $v \neq v'$). We should notice that an identifier of an instance serves to indicate this instance in the real world; its value may be dependent on an ontology to which it belongs. So in saying "an instance" we have in mind a real world object.

In this way instances can be identified on the physical level, that is, referring to their being in the real world, whereas concepts are identified only on the logical level, that is referring to their names and their structures.

Inconsistency between ontologies is considered on the following levels:

- *Inconsistency on the instance level*: The same instance belonging to different ontologies does not satisfy the instance integration condition.
- *Inconsistency on the concept level*: The concept integration condition is not satisfied for some concept. In other words, there are several concepts with the same name having different structures in different ontologies.
- *Inconsistency on the relation level*: Between the same two concepts there are inconsistent relations in different ontologies.

The kinds of inconsistency mentioned above are very general and inaccurate. In the following sections we provide their concrete definitions.

We assume that within an ontology there is no inconsistency; that is, all integration conditions should be satisfied.

9.3.2. Inconsistency on the Instance Level

On this level we assume that two ontologies differ from each other only in values of instances. That means they may have the same concepts and relations between them.

Definition 9.3.
Let O_1 and O_2 be (A,V)-based ontologies including concepts (c, A^c, V^c) and $(c', A^{c'}, V^{c'})$, respectively. Let $(i, v) \in Ins(O_1,c)$ and $(i, v') \in Ins(O_2,c')$. We say that an instance inconsistency takes place if

$$v(a) \neq v'(a)$$

for some $a \in A^c \cap A^{c'}$.

From Definition 9.3 it follows that referring to instance i the instance integration condition is not satisfied. Let's consider an example.

Example 9.1. As an example let's consider ontologies of two information systems of a university and a company. Consider concept *Student* belonging to the ontology for the university system, which has the following structure,

$$(\{St\_id, Name, Age, Address, Specialization, Results\}, V^{Student})$$

and concept *Employee* belonging to the ontology for the company system, which has the following structure,

$$(\{Emp\_id, Name, Address, Position, Salary\}, V^{Employee}).$$

Assume that there is an instance *i* which belongs to both concepts (i.e., somebody is a student of the university and an employee of the company, simultaneously). The value of this instance referring to concept *Student* is

St_id	Name	Age	Address	Specialization
1000	Nowak	20	Wroclaw	Information Systems

and the value of this instance referring to concept *Employee* is

Emp_id	Name	Address	Position	Salary
1000	Nowak	Warsaw	Designer	15.000

Thus there is inconsistency on the instance level because the instance in the university ontology referring to attribute *Address* has value "Wroclaw" and in the company ontology referring to the same attribute has value "Warsaw". ◆

9.3.3. Inconsistency on the Concept Level

On this level we assume that two ontologies differ from each other in the structure of the same concept. That means they contain the same concept but the structure is different in each ontology. This situation is very frequent inasmuch as each ontology serves to represent knowledge of a specific object and therefore concepts are defined from the point of view of the needs resulting from the subject.

Definition 9.4.
Let O_1 and O_2 be (A, V)-based ontologies. Let the same concept c belong to O_1 as (c, A^{c_1}, V^{c_1}) and belong to O_2 as (c, A^{c_2}, V^{c_2}). We say that the inconsistency takes place on the concept level if $A^{c_1} \neq A^{c_2}$ or $V^{c_1} \neq V^{c_2}$.

Definition 9.4 specifies such situations in which two ontologies define the same concept in different ways.

Example 9.2. Concept *Person* in one ontology may be defined by attributes:

$$\{Name, Age, Address, Sex, Job\}$$

whereas in the other ontology it is defined by attributes:

$$\{Id, Name, Address, Date\_of\_birth, TIN,^1 Occupation\}.$$

Another example refers to the situation in which the sets of attributes are identical, but their domains vary. Let's take attribute *Age*: for concept *Person* one ontology assigns domain $V_{Age} = [1, 17]$ and the other ontology assigns domain $V_{Age} = [18 - 65]$. In this case the inconsistency appears. ♦

As we can see, attributes play a very important role referring to the inconsistency on the concept level. An attribute belonging to set A is identified only by its name and this may cause a very "easy" inconsistency on this level because the inconsistency may arise as a result of the syntactic difference between attributes. For example, attributes *AGE* and *age* could be interpreted as different. Therefore, we propose to deal with the relationships between attributes using their semantics and domains. As the semantics of an attribute we understand its role in describing real world objects. Such a definition of attribute semantics is too generic and requires a deeper specification. For representation of the semantics of attributes we use the following triple

$$(i, a, x)$$

presenting the fact that instance i referring to attribute a has value x.

We define the following relations between attributes:

- *Equivalence*: Two attributes a and b are equivalent if for any instance i we have: (i, a, x) if and only if (i, b, x). That means that these attributes have different names, but reflect the same feature of instances. For example, attributes *Occupation* and *Job* are equivalent. We denote this relation by symbol "↔", for example:

$$Occupation \leftrightarrow Job.$$

---

[1] Tax Identification Number.

- *Generalization*: An attribute a is more general than another attribute b if the information included in fact (i, a, x), that is, attribute a referring to instance i has value x, may be implied from the information included in fact (i, b, y) for some x and y. For example, attribute *Age* is more general than *Day_of_birth* because if the day of birth of somebody is known, then his or her age should also be known. This relation is denoted by symbol "$\rightarrow$"; for the above-mentioned example we have

$$Day\_of\_birth \rightarrow Age.$$

- *Contradiction*: An attribute a is contradictory with an attribute b if their domains are the same two-element set, for example $\{0, 1\}$, for the same instance i if $(i, a, 0)$ then there must be $(i, b, 1)$, and if $(i, a, 1)$ then there must be $(i, b, 0)$. For example, attribute *Is_free* referring to books in a library is contradictory to attribute *Is_lent* where their domain is set $\{Yes, No\}$. That is, if a book is lent then it may not be free for lending, and if it is free for lending then it may not be lent. This relation is denoted by symbol "$\downarrow$"; for the example we have:

$$Is\_free \downarrow Is\_lent.$$

From the definitions of these relations we can easily prove the following properties.

Theorem 9.1.

For any $a, a', b, b, c' \in A$ the following dependencies are true.

(a) $a \leftrightarrow b$ iff $a \rightarrow b$ and $b \rightarrow a$.

(b) If $a \leftrightarrow b$ and $b \leftrightarrow c$ then $a \leftrightarrow c$.

(c) If $a \leftrightarrow b$ and $a \rightarrow c$ then $b \rightarrow c$.

(d) If $a \leftrightarrow b$ and $c \rightarrow a$ then $c \rightarrow b$.

(e) If $a \rightarrow b$ and $b \rightarrow c$ then $a \rightarrow c$.

(f) If $a \leftrightarrow b$ and $a \downarrow a'$ and $b \downarrow b'$ then $a' \leftrightarrow b'$.

(g) If $a \rightarrow b$ and $a \downarrow a'$ and $b \downarrow b'$ then $b' \rightarrow a'$.

(h) If $a \downarrow b$ and $b \downarrow c$ then $a \leftrightarrow c$.

(i) $a \downarrow b$ iff $b \downarrow a$.

These dependencies show the relationships between attributes, which will be useful for ontology integration.

9.3.4. Inconsistency on the Relation Level

Relations between concepts describe the relationships between them. For example, between two concepts being terms in ontology WordNet there may be defined such relations as *Synonym* relation or *Antonym* relation. Relations between concepts are included in set **R** of the ontology definition, whereas the relationships between them may be included in set **Z** (see Section 9.1).

As the inconsistency on the relation level we understand the situation where referring to the same two concepts in one ontology there is defined a relation which is not present in another ontology. Consider an example.

Example 9.3. Consider two ontologies defined for a university information system and a company information system. Let two concepts *Employee* and *Course* belong to both ontologies. In the first ontology there is defined the relation *Teaching* (i.e., an employee teaches a course), and in the second ontology instead of the relation *Teaching* there is also defined the relation *Completing* (i.e., an employee has completed a course). Thus we have inconsistency on the relation level.   ♦

Of course a concept may be in some relation with itself. As an example consider concept *Person*: in one ontology it is in relation *Marriage* with itself, and in another ontology there may be relation *Consanguinity*. Notice that within the same ontology two concepts may be in more than one relation.

Denote by $R_O(c,c')$ the set of relations between concepts c and c' within ontology O.

As mentioned above, set **Z** contains among others some constraints referring to relations between concepts. We are interested in such kind of constraints which do not allow contradictory relations to coexist. For example, within an ontology if between concepts *Friend* and *Colleague* in WordNet if there is relation *Synonym* then there may not be relation *Antonym*.

Formally, we use classical logic symbols for presenting the constraint that relation r may not coexist with relation r' referring to the same concepts, as follows,

$$r \Rightarrow \neg r',$$

and for the constraint that between two concepts there must be exactly one of relations r or r' is written that

$$r \Leftrightarrow \neg r'.$$

Below we give the definition of the ontology inconsistency on the relation level.

Definition 9.5.
Let O and O' be (A, V)-based ontologies containing concepts c and c'. Let $r \in R_O(c,c')$ and let $r' \in R_{O'}(c,c')$. We say that ontology inconsistency takes place on the relation level if the coexisting of relations r and r' between concepts c and c' may cause nonsatisfaction of the constraints defined for ontology O or O'.

If the set of constraints is empty then the inconsistency on the relation level may be considered as referring to a given relation independently. However, if between relations some specified constraints are fixed then it is necessary to take these constraints into account in inconsistency solving.

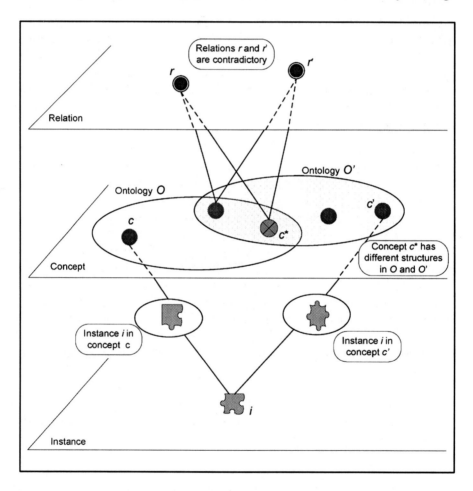

Figure 9.3. Three levels of ontology inconsistency.

9.3.5. Some Remarks

The levels of ontology inconsistencies are illustrated in Figure 9.3. In this figure we can see that two concepts are in contradictory relations, the same concept has different structures in different ontologies, and the same instance is described differently in different concepts.

9.4. Inconsistency Resolution and Ontology Integration

The general problem of ontology integration has been formulated in Section 9.2; it requires determining an ontology for a given set of ontologies. This problem is solved according to the levels of ontology inconsistency. For each level we formulate the integration problem and propose an algorithm for its solving.

9.4.1. For the Instance Level

We mention that the inconsistency on the instance level is based on the fact that the same instance is described differently within different concepts of different ontologies (Definition 9.3). We have assumed that within an ontology the instance integration condition must be satisfied.

For solving inconsistency of ontologies on the instance level consensus methods seem to be very useful. As mentioned in previous chapters, consensus methods in general deal with determining for a set of different versions of data (so called a *conflict profile*) such a version which best represents the given versions. Different criteria, structures of data, and algorithms have been worked out. Here as the conflict profile we have to deal with a set of versions of the same instance. A version of an instance (i, x) can be represented by the value x. The task is to determine a version (a value) which best represents the given versions.

For this kind of consistency the consensus problem can be defined as follows.

Given a set of values $X = \{v_1, \ldots, v_n\}$ where v_i is a tuple of type $A_i \subseteq A$, that is:

$$v_i: A_i \to V_i$$

for $i = 1, \ldots, n$ and $V_i = \bigcup_{a \in A_i} V_a$ one should find a tuple v of some type, which best represents the given values.

This problem is a typical problem for knowledge integration described in Chapter 4. For this problem a formal conflict model, which enables describing multivalued and multiattribute conflicts has been defined and analyzed. The structures of tuples representing the contents of conflicts are defined as distance functions between these tuples. Two kinds of distance functions (ρ and δ) have been defined. The consensus and the postulates for its choice have been defined and analyzed. For the defined structures and particular postulates several algorithms for consensus determination have been worked out.

It has turned out that in this case the best criterion for determining value v is

$$\sum_{i=1}^{n} d(v, v_i) = \min_{v' \in TYPE(A)} \sum_{i=1}^{n} d(v', v_i),$$

where $A = \bigcup_{i=1}^{n} A_i$ and d is a distance function between tuples.

Algorithms for determining consensus for the above problem can be found in Chapter 4. Value v which is determined by one of these algorithms can be assumed to be the value of instance i in the final ontology.

9.4.2. For the Concept Level

As stated in Section 9.3.3, in ontology integration some concept may have different structures in different ontologies. Let the subject of the ontology inconsistency on this level be a concept c. We assume that in ontology O_i concept c has structure (A^i, V^i) for $i = 1, \ldots, n$.

The problem is the following.

For the given set of pairs

$$X = \{(A^i, V^i): (A^i, V^i) \text{ is the structure of concept } c \text{ in ontology } O_i$$
$$\text{for } i = 1, \ldots, n\}$$

it is necessary to determine a pair (A^*, V^*) which best represents the given pairs.

The word "best" means one or more postulates for satisfying by pair (A^*, V^*). In general, we would like to determine such set A^* of final attributes that all attributes appearing in sets A^i $(i = 1, \ldots, n)$ are taken into account in this set. However, we cannot simply make the sum of A^i.

For this problem we formulate the following postulates for determination of pair (A^*, V^*).

P1. *For $a, b \in A = \bigcup\limits_{i=1}^{n} A^i$ and $a \leftrightarrow b$ then all occurrences of a in all sets*

  A^i may be replaced by attribute b or vice versa.

P2. *If in any set A^i attributes a and b appear simultaneously and $a \rightarrow b$ then attribute b may be removed.*

P3. *For $a, b \in A = \bigcup\limits_{i=1}^{n} A^i$ and $a \downarrow b$, all occurrences of a in all sets A^i*

  may be replaced by attribute b or vice versa.

P4. *Occurrence of an attribute in set A^* should be dependent only on the appearances of this attribute in sets A^i.*

P5. *An attribute a appears in set A^* if it appears in at least half of sets A^i.*

P6. *Set A^* is equal to A after applying postulates P1–P3.*

P7. *For each attribute $a \in A^*$ its domain is V_a (from the real world (A, V)).*

Postulate P1 uses the equivalence of attributes: one of them may replace another and vice versa. Postulate P2 uses the generality relation between attributes. Postulate P3 also replaces one attribute by its contradictory attribute (in some sense they are equivalent). After applying the first three postulates each of the attributes may be treated independently in performing the integration (postulate P4). Postulate P5 guarantees A^* to be the best representation of sets A^i in the sense of consensus. Postulate P6, on the other hand, makes the sum of all attributes after removing those equivalent, general, and contradictory. This postulate guarantees the lack of loss of attributes and in many cases is suitable for the integration sense. Postulate P7 helps to define the domains of chosen attributes. It is clear that postulates P5 and P6 cannot be satisfied simultaneously. Therefore, set A^* may be determined on the basis of postulates P1–P5 and P7, or on the basis of postulates P1–P4, P6, and P7.

We propose the following algorithms for ontology integration on the concept level. Algorithm 9.1 is built on the basis of postulates P1–P5 and P7 and Algorithm 9.2 is built on the basis of postulates P1–P4, P6, and P7.

Algorithm 9.1.

Input: Concept structures (A^i, V^i) where A^i is a set of attributes and V^i is their domain for $i = 1, \ldots, n$.

Output: Pair (A^*, V^*) which is the integration of the given pairs.

Procedure:

BEGIN

    1. Set $A^* = \bigcup\limits_{i=1}^{n} A^i$;

    2. For each pair a, b of attributes from A^* do

        Begin

            If $a \leftrightarrow b$ then set $A^* := A^* \setminus \{a\}$ if a does not occur in relationships with other attributes from A^*;

            If $a \rightarrow b$ then set $A^* := A^* \setminus \{b\}$ if b does not occur in relationships with other attributes from A^*;

            If $a \downarrow b$ then set $A^* := A^* \setminus \{b\}$ if b does not occur in relationships with other attributes from A^*;

        End;

    3. For each attribute a from set A^* do

        If the number of occurrences of a in pairs (A^i, V^i) is smaller than $n/2$ then set $A^* := A^* \setminus \{a\}$;

    4. For each attribute a from A^* add to A^* attribute b if there is relationship $a \leftrightarrow b$ or $a \downarrow b$;

    5. For each attribute a from set A^* determine its domain V_a as the sum of its domains in pairs (A^i, V^i);

END.

Algorithm 9.2.

Input: Concept structures (A^i, V^i) where A^i is a set of attributes and V^i is their domain for $i = 1, \ldots, n$.

Output: Pair (A^*, V^*) which is the integration of the given pairs.

Procedure:

BEGIN

    1. Set $A^* = \bigcup\limits_{i=1}^{n} A^i$;

    2. For each pair a, b of attributes from A^* do

If $a \rightarrow b$ then set $A^* = A^* \setminus \{b\}$ if b does not occur in relationships with other attributes from A^*;

3. For each attribute a from set A^* determine its domain V_a as the sum of its domains in pairs (A^i, V^i);

END.

These algorithms seem to be computationally very simple. However, checking the conditions in steps 2 and 4 of Algorithm 9.1 may be complex if the set of relationships between attributes is numerous. Step 2 of Algorithm 9.1 is needed because step 3 can cause inconsistencies referring to the attribute relationships. These removed attributes (except those from generation relationships) are completed back in step 4. Algorithm 9.1 should be used in such cases where the new ontology to be created should contain the most often used knowledge from the given ontologies. In this case the most representative ontology must satisfy postulate P5; owing to it the newly created ontology will be most similar to that given referring to the set of concepts. Algorithm 9.2, on the other hand, should be used in such cases where one wants to get into the new ontology all elements of knowledge included in the given ontologies. In this case the newly created ontology is in some sense a sum of the given ontologies.

The computational complexity of each of Algorithms 9.1 and 9.2 is $O(m^2 n)$ where $m = card(A^i)$. Because m is not very large, these algorithms are effective.

Below we present an example.

Example 9.4. Let the real world (A, V) be defined as follows.

$$A = \{a, b, c, d, e, f\}$$

$$V_a = [1, 200].$$

$$V_b = \{0, 1\}.$$

$$V_c = \{Yes, No\}.$$

$$V_d = \{Mon, Tue, Wed, Thurs, Fri, Sat, Sun\}.$$

$$V_e = \{+, -, \pm\}.$$

$$V_f = \{Yes, No\}.$$

The set of relationships among these attributes is:

$$\{b \leftrightarrow c, c \downarrow f, e \rightarrow a\} \ .$$

Let the structures of some concept in five ontologies be presented as follows.

Ontology	Attributes
O_1	$\{a, b, c\}$
O_2	$\{a, d, e, f\}$
O_3	$\{a, e\}$
O_4	$\{f\}$
O_5	$\{e, f\}$

Set A^* determined by step 1 of both algorithms 9.1 and 9.2 is equal to

$$A^* = \{a, b, c, d, e, f\}.$$

According to Algorithm 9.1, by applying step 2 we can remove attributes b, c, and a. Thus after Step 2 we have:

$$A^* = \{d, e, f\}.$$

Step 3 causes the removal of attribute d, step 4 does not cause any change, and step 5 adds the domains of the remaining attributes. Finally we have:

$$A^* = \{e, f\}.$$

According to Algorithm 9.2, step 2 causes the removal of attribute a and step 3 adds the domains of the remaining attributes. Finally we have:

$$A^* = \{b, c, e, f\}. \qquad \qquad \blacklozenge$$

9.4.3. For the Relation Level

We consider the situation in which between concepts c and c' different ontologies assign different relations. Let c and c' be two concepts. We have the following integration problem.

For a given profile

$$X = \{ R_{O_i}(c,c'): i = 1, \ldots, n\}$$

it is necessary to determine set $R(c,c')$ of final relations between c and c', which best represents the given sets.

If between relations on concepts c and c' there is a lack of relationships, then the solution for this problem seems to be simple. One can determine $R(c,c')$ as the sum of sets $R_{O_i}(c,c')$, or select to $R(c,c')$ only those relations from $R_{O_i}(c,c')$ which appear most frequently. However, the solution will not be so simple if we take into account the relationships between these relations. For example, if relation r is between c and c', and relation r' is between c' and c'', then there must be relation r'' between c and c''. Such kind of relationships may make the choice of set $R(c,c')$ hard. Here we consider the contradiction relationship between relations on concepts. As defined in Section 9.3.4, relations included in set $R(c,c')$ must satisfy the condition for noncontradiction: that is, two contradictory relations cannot occur between the same two concepts.

Let Y be a set consisting of pairs of relations contradictory to each other. We assume that both relations belonging to a pair in Y appear in sets $R_{O_i}(c,c')$. Let's see an example.

Example 9.5. Let the sets of relations between concepts c and c' given by ontologies $O_1, \ldots, O_5$ and restrictions included in set T be as follows.

Set X	Relations between c and c'	Set Y
$R_{O_1}(c,c')$	$\{r_1, r_2, r_3\}$	
$R_{O_2}(c,c')$	$\{r_1, r_2, r_4\}$	$\{(r_1, r_6),$
$R_{O_3}(c,c')$	$\{r_3, r_5, r_6\}$	$(r_3, r_4),$
$R_{O_4}(c,c')$	$\{r_1, r_5\}$	$(r_2, r_5)\}$
$R_{O_5}(c,c')$	$\{r_2, r_3, r_6\}$	

It follows, for example, that between concepts c and c' in ontology O_1 there are three relations r_1, r_2, and r_3, and among others relations r_1 and r_6 may not occur together.   ♦

Similarly as in solving inconsistency on the concept level, here we propose two algorithms. The first integrates all relations between concepts c and c' given by the ontologies, and next removes those causing contradiction. The second algorithm includes in the final set of relations only those relations which appear most often in the ontologies, and of course do not cause contradiction. These algorithms are presented as follows.

Algorithm 9.3.

Input: Sets $R_{O_i}(c,c')$ including relations between concepts c and c' given by the ontologies O_i for $i = 1, \ldots, n$ and set Y including restrictions.

Output: Set $R(c,c')$ consisting of final relations, which is the integration of the given sets.

Procedure:

BEGIN

1. Set $R(c,c') = \bigcup\limits_{i=1}^{n} R_{O_i}(c,c')$;

2. For each relation $r \in R(c,c')$ calculate the number $\gamma(r)$ of its occurrences in sets $R_{O_i}(c,c')$ for $i = 1, \ldots, n$;

3. For each relation r occurring in Y calculate

$$\lambda(r) = \sum\nolimits_{(r,r') \in Y} \gamma(r');$$

4. Determine such r in Y that $\lambda(r)$ is maximal and set

$$R(c,c') = R(c,c') \setminus \{r\};$$

5. Remove from Y all pairs in which r occurs;

6. If $Y \neq \varnothing$ then GOTO 4;

END.

Step 1 of the above algorithm integrates all relations occurring in given ontologies. Step 2 calculates the numbers of occurrences of each relation in sets $R_{O_i}(c,c')$. Owing to numbers $\lambda(r)$ calculated in step 3 one can get to know if relation r remains in the final set $R(c,c')$ then it is needed to remove $\lambda(r)$ occurrences of other relations. Number $\lambda(r)$ in some sense can be treated as the cost of maintenance of relation r in set $R(c,c')$. Therefore, we propose to remove those relations for which the maintenance costs are maximal (steps 4 and 5). Step 6 checks if all contradictory relations have been eliminated. Algorithm 9.3 guarantees then the maximal number of relations in set $R(c,c')$, and if it is necessary to remove a relation, it chooses the relation causing the minimal loss.

The computational complexity of Algorithm 9.3 is $O(m^2 n)$ where $m = card(C)$. This is the worst case. However, the cardinality of set $R(c,c')$ is not very large. Therefore, Algorithm 9.3 is an effective one.

For the situation given in Example 9.5 we have these numbers calculated as follows.

	r_1	r_2	r_3	r_4	r_5	r_6
γ	3	3	3	1	2	2
λ	2	2	1	3	3	1

From this result it follows that the first relation to be removed is r_6 and after this it is necessary to remove r_4 and r_5. Thus finally set $R(c,c')$ should consist of relations r_1, r_2, and r_3.

The idea of Algorithm 9.4 is based on collecting to set $R(c,c')$ only those relations which appear often in sets $R_{O_i}(c,c')$. We use the same rule for contradiction elimination as given in Algorithm 9.3. This algorithm is presented as follows.

Algorithm 9.4.

Input: Sets $R_{O_i}(c,c')$ including relations between concepts c and c' given by the ontologies O_i for $i = 1, \ldots, n$ and set Y including restrictions.

Output: Set $R(c,c')$ consisting of final relations, which is the integration of the given sets.

Procedure:

BEGIN

1. Set $R(c,c') = \varnothing$ and $Z = \bigcup_{i=1}^{n} R_{O_i}(c,c')$;

2. For each relation $r \in Z$ calculate the number $\gamma(r)$ of its occurrences in sets $R_{O_i}(c,c')$ for $i = 1, \ldots, n$;

3. For each relation $r \in Z$ if $\gamma(r) \geq n/2$ then set

$$R(c,c') = R(c,c') \cup \{r\};$$

4. Modify set Y so that each pair belonging to Y consists of relations from $R(c,c')$;

5. For each relation r occurring in Y calculate

$$\lambda(r) = \sum_{(r,r') \in Y} \gamma(r');$$

6. Determine such r in Y that $\lambda(r)$ is maximal and set

$$R(c,c') = R(c,c') \setminus \{r\};$$

7. Remove from Y all pairs in which r occurs;

8. If $Y \neq \varnothing$ then GOTO 5;

END.

The difference between Algorithms 9.3 and 9.4 is that in Algorithm 9.4 for the beginning value of set $R(c,c')$ we collect only those relations which appear at least in half the number of all ontologies. This condition is well-known in consensus theory for the best representation of set $R(c,c')$ referring to given sets $R_{O_i}(c,c')$. The process for eliminating the contradiction is similar in both algorithms.

For the situation in Example 9.5 using Algorithm 9.4 we should obtain set $R(c,c')$ equal also to $\{r_1, r_2, r_3\}$.

9.5. Conclusions

In this chapter a classification of ontology inconsistencies has been proposed. According to this classification, inconsistency of ontologies may refer to one of three levels: instance level, concept level, and relation level. For each level we propose a method for inconsistency solving.

The advantages of the proposed algorithms are based on the fact that they are not complex and can work for different structures of ontologies. They do not require well-valuating the parameters in ontologies, as subject logics do [60].

In this chapter we do not consider the inconsistency of ontologies on the axiom level. However, this problem can be solved using the results presented in Chapter 5 referring to inconsistency resolution on the syntactic level. On this level it is possible to reconcile the inconsistency of a set of logic formulae.

10. Application of Inconsistency Resolution Methods in Intelligent Learning Systems

This chapter deals with some applications of the methods for inconsistency resolution presented in previous chapters. Its subject is related to recommendation processes in intelligent learning systems. Using methods for rough classification, a model for representation of learner profiles, learning scenarios, and the choice of a proper scenario for a new learner is proposed. The recommendation mechanisms are based on consensus methods and clustering algorithms. Owing to them there is a possibility to adapt the learning path to learner profiles.

10.1. Introduction

Nowadays one of the most important aims of information systems is to serve the user in an effective way and to offer the highest quality services. The interaction between a user and a system should not be one way, as took place in the past, but should be two way, in the sense that the system should have some knowledge about the user for better serving him. The past systems treated all users in rather the same way, because for the same query the reaction of the system was also the same. Modern systems behave in another way. They "know" a lot about the user and can adapt their services to her needs. In addition, these systems try to guess what the user needs; in other words, they can perform recommendation processes.

Recommendation is a very important feature of such kind of systems as information retrieval systems, tutoring systems, or E-learning systems. A recommender system, as defined in [138], is a system which can suggest to the user potential elements he may be interested in on the basis of knowledge about the user. Intelligent learning systems seem to be required to have this feature.

Adaptive hypermedia systems are very popular in delivering personalized information and in the area of E-learning [24]. Below we present a brief overview of the following adaptive systems of this kind: INSPIRE, CS388, AEC-ES, and EDUCE.

In the INSPIRE system [131] the learning styles classification based on Kolb's theory of experimental learning [73] is applied for developing adaptive presentation techniques. Learners having different learning styles receive educational materials presented in different ways. Thus to a certain degree the adaptation process is realized.

System CS388 [25] uses the learning style model defined by Felder and Silvermann [41, 42] in which such parameters as learner modes of thinking, remembering, and problem solving are distinguished. Different types of media are also used for knowledge presentation and make them appropriate for different learning styles.

AEC-ES [154] is an adaptive educational system that is based on field dependent/field independent (FD/FI) cognitive styles. In this system instructional strategies are recommended according to their cognitive styles by means of different adaptive navigation support tools and adaptive presentation techniques.

In system EDUCE [66] a cognitive learner's characteristics model is applied to adaptation aims. It uses students' classification in two dimensions: Gardner's multiple intelligences concept and Bloom's learning goals concept. In EDUCE a learner can choose material according to his needs and preferences. These decisions are recorded in order to modify the learner profile which in turn helps to recommend proper educational materials to learners. EDUCE offers two types of adaptation concerning presentation of text: multimedia and modality adaptation. It also offers navigation support concerning direct guidance and link annotation.

The subject of this chapter is the recommendation process in intelligent learning systems. This kind of system provides the possibility of learning at any time and anywhere. In most traditional learning systems only one learning strategy is accessible. This strategy is prepared by specialists (i.e., teachers or tutors) for the so-called typical learner, the main user of the system. The main disadvantage of such a system is keeping the same strategy for different learners. Therefore, the learning process is not always effective, and not convenient for the learner. To overcome this disadvantage a recommendation mechanism should be proposed.

For working out a recommendation mechanism for an intelligent learning system we first define the knowledge structure of the system. Knowledge is divided into several concepts, each of them expressed by so-called *presentations*. A concept may be presented to the learner by different sequences of presentations. Next we define a path usage called a *scenario*. A scenario sets the order of concepts to be presented and the presentation sequences within the concepts. The system gathers two kinds of data about a learner: user data and usage data. User data consist of such information about the learner as age, gender, education level, learning styles, and so on. Usage data, on the other hand, include one or more scenarios with which the learner has passed the course with success.

The idea for recommendation is based on determining the opening scenario for a new learner. Toward this aim first a new learner is classified into a class; next the opening scenario for this learner is calculated on the basis of the passed scenarios of other members of this class. Although members of a class are assumed to be similar, there may be inconsistency in the set of their passed scenarios in the sense that these scenarios may not be identical. Therefore, the consensus method should be useful for determining the opening scenario for a new learner.

For a learner classification process the attributes from user data are used. These attributes are most often indicated by experts. However, we assume that the set of these attributes should not be permanent for the whole life of the system. We note that the main criterion for the similarity of learners should be the similarity of their passed scenarios. Owing to this similarity we can determine the set of user data attributes responsible for the classification process in the following way. First we use these scenarios as the basis for performing a clustering process for the set of learners. Next we propose a rough classification-based method which enables determining the smallest set of attributes generating a partition of the set of learners maximally similar to the partition given by the clustering process. This set of attributes will be the actual criterion for classification for new learners. Such a process should be repeated ever and again for updating this criterion for the system to adapt to new characteristics of learners.

As mentioned above, the aspect of inconsistency appears in the fact that learners who are assumed to be similar (i.e., belonging to the same class of the classification) may have different passed scenarios of learning. The reason for this fact may be included in the following elements: First, the attributes creating the classification criterion are badly chosen. Second, the criterion is proper but only for a certain universe of learners; for other universes it may be improper. This argument justifies the necessity of treating classification criteria in a nonpermanent way, and our proposed method toward this aim should be useful.

This chapter is organized as follows. In Section 10.2 the structure of knowledge of an intelligent learning system is presented. Section 10.3 includes the structure of a learner profile and the procedure for learner classification. In Section 10.4 the recommendation mechanism is presented, which enables determining the opening scenario for a new learner. Next, the method for learner clustering using the passed scenarios is presented in

Section 10.5, and finally in Section 10.6 a rough classification-based method for determining new criteria for learner classification is included.

10.2. Structure of Knowledge

10.2.1. Basic Notions

First we mention the notion of *linear order* (or weak *linear order*) on some set X.

A binary relation $R \subseteq X \times X$ is called a linear order on X if the following conditions are satisfied:

(a) $\forall x \in X: (x,x) \in R$.

(b) $\forall x,y,z \in X: (x,y) \in R \wedge (y,z) \in R \Rightarrow (x,z) \in R$.

(c) $\forall x,y \in X: (x,y) \in R \wedge (y,x) \in R \Rightarrow x = y$.

(d) $\forall x,y \in X: (x,y) \in R \vee (y,x) \in R$.

A linear order R on X is called a *strong linear order* if it satisfies conditions (b), (d), and
$$\forall x,y \in X: (x,y) \in R \Rightarrow (y,x) \notin R.$$
Relation R is called a *partial linear order* (*partial linear relation*) on X if only conditions (a) through (c) are satisfied. Thus it is a linear order on some subset of X.

The knowledge base of an intelligent learning system should contain the following elements:

- A set of concepts: They represent the notions of the field of learning. A concept can be treated as an integrated element of knowledge.
- A set of linear relations between concepts: Each of such relations defines the order in which the notions should be presented to the learner.
- A set of presentations of concepts: A presentation refers to a notion and contains one piece of this notion. In the system a presentation may be understood as a multimedia screen, a page of text, and the like. Each concept has its set of presentations.[1]

---

[1] Some justification for representing a concept by presentations is given in [74].

- A set of partial linear relations: Each of them is defined on the set of presentations of a particular concept. Each of these relations refers to the set of presentations of one concept and shows an order in which the presentations should be presented to the learner. A concept may have different relations between its presentations, which means that there are different ways to show the same material to the learner.

Below we present an example.

Example 10.1. Figure 10.1 illustrates the knowledge structure on the level of concepts and the level of presentations. Between the three concepts there are two linear relations

$$\alpha_1 = \{(c_1, c_2), (c_2, c_3)\}$$

and

$$\alpha_2 = \{(c_1, c_3), (c_3, c_2)\}.$$

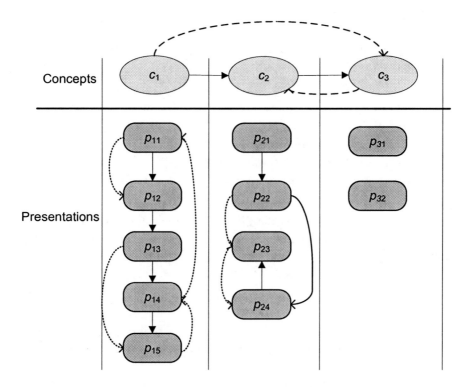

Figure 10.1. Structure of knowledge.

Instead of a set of pairs a linear order can be written as a sequence. For example,

$$\alpha_1 = <c_1, c_2, c_3>.$$

Between the presentations of concept c_1 there are two linear orders: the first is:

$$<p_{11}, p_{12}, p_{13}, p_{14}, p_{15}>,$$

and the second is:

$$<p_{13}, p_{15}, p_{14}, p_{11}, p_{12}>.$$

Between the presentations of concept c_2 there are two partial linear orders and between the presentations of concept c_3 there are also two partial linear orders. (Notice that a linear order is a special case of partial linear orders and in a linear relation an element is in relation with itself.) ♦

Ontology seems to be the best tool for defining the structure of knowledge of learning systems.

Definition 10.1.
The ontology of knowledge of an E-learning system is defined by the following quadruple,

$$(C, P, R_C, R_P),$$

where

- *C is a finite set of concepts.*
- *P is a set of presentations of concepts.*
- *R_C is a set of linear relations on set C.*
- *R_P is a set of partial linear relations on subsets of set P.*

Example 10.2. For the lesson on subject "Relational algebra" from the field of databases the system should show learners the basic notions such as "attribute", "attribute domain", "tuple", "relation", and the definition of such operations on relations as "project", "selection", and so on. The elements of a knowledge base are defined as follows.

- C = {*Attribute, Attribute_domain, Tuple, Relation, Project, Selection, Join, Sum, Product, Difference*}.
- Two linear relations between concepts are presented in Figure 10.2. A relation represents an order in which the notions should be presented to the learner.
- Presentations of concept "Join" and their relations are shown in Figure 10.3. We can see that this concept can be learned using one of two ways for ordering the presentations. In the first way two

presentations are used, "Example 1" and "Example 2," whereas in the second way these presentations are omitted. We can then assume that the second way is for more advanced learners.

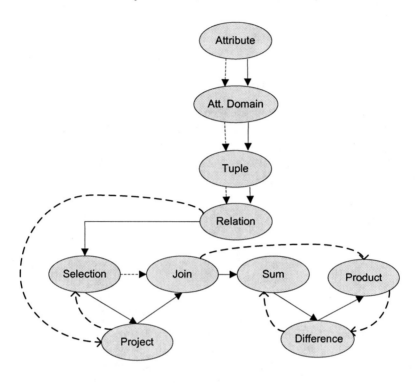

Figure 10.2. Relations among concepts.

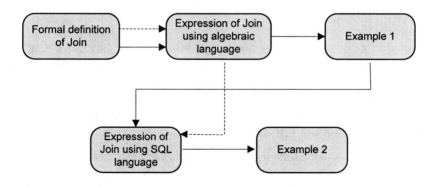

Figure 10.3. Presentations of concept "Join".

Because set C is finite, we can denote $n = card(C)$.

Let $c \in C$; by $P(c)$ we denote the set of presentations of concept c and by $R_P(c)$ we denote the set of partial linear orders on set $P(c)$. Thus we have

$$P = \bigcup_{c \in C} P(c)$$

and

$$R_P = \bigcup_{c \in C} R_P(c).$$

Now we define the notion of *scenario* which is understood as a sequence of sequences of presentations containing all concepts and each concept is presented in total in such a sense that a whole partial linear relation on its set of presentations is included in the sequence. Each scenario is based on an order of concepts.

Definition 10.2.

Let $\alpha \in R_C$, be a scenario based on order α (or an α-based scenario); we call a sequence

$$s = <r_1, r_2, \dots, r_n>,$$

where

- *For each i $(1 \le i \le n)$ $r_i \in R_P(c_i)$ for some $c_i \in C_i.$*
- *For each i $(1 \le i < n)$ $c_i \ne c_{i+1}$ and $(c_i, c_{i+1}) \in \alpha$.*

Thus a scenario should firstly be based on some linear order from R_C, and secondly it is a sequence of partial linear orders on sets of presentations of the concepts. The relation α determines the order in which the presentations of particular concepts will be presented to the learner, and within a concept c_i relation r_i will type the order for showing the presentations.

A scenario can be treated as a learning path for a learner to learn the knowledge in the system. Owing to different relations on the set of concepts and different partial linear relations between presentations within concepts there may be defined various scenarios for different learners.

So a scenario has two kinds of orders: the first (called the *external order*) refers to one order of concepts and the second (called the *internal order*) refers to orders of presentations within concepts.

Example 10.3. As an example of a scenario consider the knowledge structure described in Example 10.1. As known, there are two linear orders on concepts. Let α be relation α_1. For each concept one of the partial linear orders may be included in a scenario. Some α_1-based scenarios are defined as follows.

$$s_1 = \left\langle <p_{13}, p_{15}, p_{14}, p_{11}, p_{12}>, <p_{31}>, <p_{21}, p_{22}, p_{23}, p_{24}> \right\rangle .$$

$$s_2 = \left\langle <p_{11}, p_{12}, p_{13}, p_{14}, p_{15}>, <p_{21}, p_{22}, p_{23}, p_{24}>, <p_{32}> \right\rangle .$$

$$s_3 = \left\langle <p_{13}, p_{15}, p_{14}, p_{11}, p_{12}>, <p_{22}, p_{23}, p_{24}>, <p_{31}> \right\rangle .$$

As we can see, each scenario consists of a sequence of sequences. The external sequence refers to α and each internal sequence refers to a partial linear order within a concept. For example, in scenario s_1 the external sequence refers to order $<c_1, c_3, c_2>$, whereas in scenario s_2 the external sequence refers to order $<c_1, c_2, c_3>$. In scenario s_2 for concept c_1 the internal order is $<p_{11}, p_{12}, p_{13}, p_{14}, p_{15}>$, for concept c_2 it is $<p_{21}, p_{22}, p_{23}, p_{24}>$, and for concept c_3 it is $<p_{32}>$.

A scenario may be represented by a table where each column represents a concept, and the order of rows represents the order of presentations within a concept. The orders of columns and rows refer exactly to the order of concepts in the relation α and the order of presentations within concepts, respectively. Thus scenario s_3 may be represented by Table 10.1.

♦

By S_C we denote the set of all potential scenarios for set C of concepts. Notice that the cardinality of set S_C is dependent on the number of knowledge pieces occurring in C and the numbers of partial linear relations on sets of presentations of the concepts. Generally, this number may be very large, but always finite.

Table 10.1. Scenario s_3

c_1	c_2	c_3
p_{13}	p_{22}	p_{31}
p_{15}	p_{23}	
p_{14}	p_{24}	
p_{11}		
p_{12}		

10.2.2. Distance Functions between Scenarios

Now we deal with defining the distance functions for scenarios. Before this we need to define the distance function between two partial linear relations on a set. The distance functions for linear orders on a set have been

defined by several authors [68, 159]. There are two most popular functions. The first counts the number of pairs (x, y) for $x, y \in X$ such that they
appear only in one relation. This function takes into account the difference
between the positions of an element in both relations. For example, the distance between relations

$$<x_1, x_2, x_3, x_4, x_5>,$$

and

$$<x_3, x_5, x_4, x_1, x_2>$$

should be equal to 14.

In the second function for each element from X its position indexes in
each relation are determined and its share in the distance is calculated as
the absolute difference of these indexes. For example, element x_1 occurs in
the first relation (presented above) on the first position and in the second
relation on the fourth position, so its share in the distance is 3. In this way
we can calculate the distance between these two relations, which is equal
to 12.

Our task for defining a distance function differs from that solved in the
literature in that the relations are partial; that is, there may exist an element
from set X which appears in one relation but does not appear in the second.

Let β_1 and β_2 be partial linear relations on a finite and nonempty set X.
We define a distance function of type ρ (see Section 4.2.2.2 in Chapter 4).
We mention that a function of type ρ reflects the shares of elements from
set X in the distance between two relations.

The share $S_x(\beta_1, \beta_2)$ of an element $x \in X$ in the distance between relations
β_1 and β_2 is defined as follows.

a) If x does not occur in either β_1 or β_2 then

$$S_x(\beta_1, \beta_2) = 0.$$

b) If x occurs in β_1 on position k and in β_2 on position k' then

$$S_x(\beta_1, \beta_2) = \frac{|k - k'|}{card(X)}.$$

c) If x occurs in β_1 on position k and does not occur in β_2 (or x occurs
in β_2 on position k and does not occur in β_1) then

$$S_x(\beta_1, \beta_2) = \frac{card(X) - (k - 1)}{card(X)}.$$

Although the conditions (a) and (b) are rather intuitive, some comments
should be added for condition (c). Notice that if an element x appears only

in one relation (e.g., in β_1) then the intuition is that the smaller its position in β_1 the greater is its share in the distance. The reason is that a smaller position index means a higher position in the order.

The distance function σ for partial linear relations is defined as follows.

Definition 10.3.
By the distance between two partial linear relations on set X we understand the following value,

$$\sigma(\beta_1,\beta_2) = \frac{\sum_{x \in X} S_x(\beta_1,\beta_2)}{card(X)}.$$

Example 10.4. Let $X = \{x_1, x_2, x_3, x_4, x_5\}$ and let

$$\beta_1 = \langle x_1, x_2, x_3, x_4, x_5 \rangle,$$
$$\beta_2 = \langle x_3, x_5, x_1 \rangle.$$

We have:

$$S_{x_1}(\beta_1,\beta_2) = \frac{1}{5}|1-3| = \frac{2}{5},$$

$$S_{x_2}(\beta_1,\beta_2) = \frac{5-(2-1)}{5} = \frac{4}{5},$$

$$S_{x_3}(\beta_1,\beta_2) = \frac{1}{5}|1-3| = \frac{2}{5},$$

$$S_{x_4}(\beta_1,\beta_2) = \frac{5-(4-1)}{5} = \frac{2}{5},$$

$$S_{x_4}(\beta_1,\beta_2) = \frac{5-(5-1)}{5} = \frac{1}{5}.$$

Thus

$$\sigma(\beta_1,\beta_2) = \frac{\frac{2}{5}+\frac{4}{5}+\frac{2}{5}+\frac{2}{5}+\frac{1}{5}}{5} = \frac{11}{25}. \qquad \blacklozenge$$

Notice that in the case when β_1 and β_2 are linear orders on X then function σ corresponds to the second distance function described above. We have the following theorem.

Theorem 10.1.
The following properties are true.
(a) For each $x \in X$ function S_x is a metric.

(b) For each $x \in X$ and any two partial linear relations on X there should be $S_x(\beta_1,\beta_2) \leq 1$, and $S_x(\beta_1,\beta_2) = 1$ iff x occurs on the first position of one relation and does not occur in the second.

(c) Function σ is a metric.

(d) For any two partial linear relations β_1 and β_2 on X there should be $\sigma(\beta_1,\beta_2) \leq 1$, and $\sigma(\beta_1,\beta_2) = 1$ iff $card(X) = 1$, $\beta_1 = <y>$ for $y \in X$ and $\beta_2 = \varnothing$, or $card(X) = 2$, $\beta_1 = <y>$, $\beta_2 = <z>$ for $y, z \in X$.

Proof.

(a) Notice that function S_x is nonnegative and symmetric. For transitivity consider three partial linear relations β_1, β_2, and β_3. Let's consider the following cases:

- Element x occurs in all of them on positions k, k', and k'', respectively. Then we have

$$S_x(\beta_1,\beta_2) + S_x(\beta_2,\beta_3) = \frac{|k-k'|+|k'-k''|}{card(X)} \geq \frac{|k-k''|}{card(X)} = S_x(\beta_1,\beta_3).$$

- Element x appears in β_1 and β_2 on positions k and k' but does not appear in β_3. We can assume that $k \geq k'$ and have

$$S_x(\beta_1,\beta_2) + S_x(\beta_2,\beta_3)$$
$$= \frac{(k-k')+card(X)-(k'-1)}{card(X)} \geq \frac{card(X)-(k-1)}{card(X)} = S_x(\beta_1,\beta_3).$$

- Element x appears in β_1 and β_3 on positions k and k'' but does not appear in β_2. Because $card(X) + 1 > k$ and $card(X) + 1 > k''$ we have

$$S_x(\beta_1,\beta_2) + S_x(\beta_2,\beta_3) = \frac{2card(X)-(k-1)-(k''-1)}{card(X)} \geq \frac{|k-k''|}{card(X)}$$
$$= S_x(\beta_1,\beta_3).$$

- Element x appears only in β_1 on position k. We have

$$S_x(\beta_1,\beta_2) + S_x(\beta_2,\beta_3) = \frac{card(X)-(k-1)}{card(X)} = S_x(\beta_1,\beta_3) .$$

- Element x appears only in β_3 in position k''. We have

$$S_x(\beta_1,\beta_2) + S_x(\beta_2,\beta_3) = \frac{card(X)-(k''-1)}{card(X)} = S_x(\beta_1,\beta_3).$$

- Element x does not appear in any of these relations. Of course, we have the following equation:

$$S_x(\beta_1,\beta_2) + S_x(\beta_2,\beta_3) = S_x(\beta_1,\beta_3) = 0.$$

(b) Inequality $S_x(\beta_1,\beta_2) \leq 1$ follows from the fact that the position index of x in any relation may not be larger than $card(X)$. The equality occurs if and only if x occurs in the first position of one relation and does not appear in the second.

(c) This property follows from the fact that function S_x is a metric for any $x \in X$.

(d) The fact that $\sigma(\beta_1,\beta_2) \leq 1$ should be implied from Definition 10.3. We can quickly check that if $X = \{y\}$, $\beta_1 = <y>$, and $\beta_2 = \varnothing$ (or $\beta_1 = \varnothing$ and $\beta_2 = <y>$), also if $X = \{y, z\}$, $\beta_1 = <y>$, and $\beta_2 = <z>$, then there should be $\sigma(\beta_1,\beta_2) = 1$. On the other hand, let $\sigma(\beta_1,\beta_2) = 1$; then for each $x \in X$ there should be $S_x(\beta_1,\beta_2) = 1$. From (c) it is known that x should occur in the first position of one relation and not appear in the second. The number of elements with this property may be maximally equal to 2. If 2, each of them should occur only in one relation, and the cardinality of X should also be equal to 2. If 1, the only element should occur in one relation, and the cardinality of X should be equal to 1.   ◆

Now we deal with the distance function for scenarios. Let two scenarios

$$s_1 = <r_1^{(1)}, r_2^{(1)}, \ldots, r_n^{(1)}>$$

and

$$s_2 = <r_1^{(2)}, r_2^{(2)}, \ldots, r_n^{(2)}>$$

be given where n is the number of concepts.

For comparing two scenarios s_1 and s_2 we should take into account the following aspects:

- The difference between the linear orders on the set of concepts in these scenarios for this component in the distance a weight w_1 will be destined.
- The difference between partial linear relations on the set of presentations within each concept, weight w_2 will be destined for this component.

For each concept $c \in C$ denote by $g(c)$ and $h(c)$ the positions referring to c in scenarios s_1 and s_2, respectively.

Definition 10.4.

By distance function between scenarios we understand a function

$$d : S_C \times S_C \to [0,1],$$

where for an α_1-based scenario s_1 and an α_2-based scenario s_2 the distance between them is defined as follows,

$$d(s_1, s_2) = w_1 \cdot \sigma(\alpha_1, \alpha_2) + w_2 \cdot \sum_{c \in C} \sigma(r^{(1)}_{g(c)}, r^{(2)}_{h(c)})$$

and

$$0 < w_1, w_2 < 1; \qquad w_1 + w_2 = 1.$$

The first component of the distance function refers to the distance between external orders in scenarios, and the second component refers to the distance between internal orders of the scenarios.

Example 10.5. Consider two scenarios defined in Example 10.3:

$$s_1 = \left\langle <p_{13}, p_{15}, p_{14}, p_{11}, p_{12}>, <p_{31}>, <p_{21}, p_{22}, p_{23}, p_{24}> \right\rangle.$$

$$s_2 = \left\langle <p_{11}, p_{12}, p_{13}, p_{14}, p_{15}>, <p_{21}, p_{22}, p_{23}, p_{24}>, <p_{32}> \right\rangle.$$

Their representations are as follows.

s_1

c_1	c_2	c_3
p_{13}	p_{31}	p_{21}
p_{15}		p_{22}
p_{14}		p_{23}
p_{11}		p_{24}
p_{12}		

s_2

c_2	c_3	c_2
p_{13}	p_{21}	p_{32}
p_{15}	p_{22}	
p_{14}	p_{23}	
p_{11}	p_{24}	
p_{12}		

The distance between external orders $<c_1, c_2, c_3>$ and $<c_1, c_3, c_2>$ is equal to 2/9. The distance between internal orders for

concept c_1 is 0,
concept c_2 is 0,
concept c_3 is 1.

Thus the second component of the scenarios' distance is 1. Assuming $w_1 = w_2 = 0.5$ we have

$$d(s_1, s_2) = 0.5 \cdot \frac{2}{9} + 0.5 \cdot 1 = \frac{11}{18}. \qquad \blacklozenge$$

Values w_1 and w_2 may be treated as weights for the components of external and internal order differences in the distance. They may be regulated for adapting to a practical situation.

Because function σ is a metric (see Theorem 10.1), then it is easy to prove that function d is also a metric.

10.3. Learner Profile and Classification

An intelligent learning system should have the properties of adaptation and recommendation. They are very useful features for learners. In adaptive and recommender systems the user model is a very important element. The task of the user model is to deliver information about the user and simplification for her to understand the interaction process [57]. It is the basis for description and prediction of the user potential behaviors during her work with the interactive system [96]. Most often there are two elements of a user model: the user data and usage data [71]. User data contain mainly the demographic data, such as: record data (name, address, e-mail, etc.), geographic data (zip code, city, state, country), user's characteristics (gender, education, occupation), and some other qualifying data (IQ, skills and capabilities, interests and preferences, etc.). The usage data, on the other hand, consist of information about the user related to the user's interactions with the system. For example, often-given queries or often-used use paths belong to usage data. The usage data may concern users' interests, preferences, or temporal viewing behavior, as well as ratings concerning the relevance of these elements [71].

The term "user model" is general for all types of systems where there is two-way interaction between the user and the system. For learning systems the most important user is a learner (or a student). Therefore, instead of "user model" we use the "learner profile" term [74–76]. As stated above, a learner profile should include user data and usage data. We propose to concretize these kinds of data as follows.

10.3.1. User Data

This kind of data should contain such parameters of a user which characterize him as a learner [77]. The attributes and their domains are given in Table 10.2.

The attributes of personal data are clear and do not need comments. To classify purpose attributes *Age*, *Gender*, *Education level*, and *Intelligence Quotient* seem to be very useful. The attributes for the individual learning style are adopted from the model of Felder and Silverman [42]. Apart from this model we can find many other models of learning styles in the literature. It is worthwhile mentioning Dunns's model [38], Kolb's model [73], and Herrmann's model [56]. All these models enable describing the individual learning styles of learners. However, their practical use seems to be strongly limited because of the complexity of their structures. Felder and

Silverman's model appears to be simpler and its attributes seem to be sufficient to cover the information about learners for the adaptation and recommendation goal. Its application and usefulness in practice has been described in [163]. Some experiments of applications of Felder's model to the learning styles modeling in the hypermedia environment are presented in [25]. The advantages of this model have also been widely analyzed in [76, 77].

Table 10.2. Attributes of user data

Attribute Name	Attribute Domain
Personal Data	
Learner identifier (login)	STR
Password	STR
Surname	STR
Age	Integer
Gender	{*male, female*}
Education level	{*elementary, secondary, graduate, postgraduate*}
Intelligence Quotient (I.Q.)	{*low, middle, high*}
Individual Learning Style	
Perception	$\{0.0, 0.1, 0.2, \ldots, 1.0\}$
Receiving	$\{0.0, 0.1, 0.2, \ldots, 1.0\}$
Processing	$\{0.0, 0.1, 0.2, \ldots, 1.0\}$
Understanding	$\{0.0, 0.1, 0.2, \ldots, 1.0\}$

According to Felder's model the style of a learner should be concerned with four dimensions: *perception, receiving, processing,* and *understanding* [41, 42]. Each of these dimensions is measured in two values:

- *Perception* may be sensitive or intuitive.
- *Receiving information* may be visual or verbal.
- *Processing information* may be active or reflective.
- *Understanding* may be sequential or global.

Owing to this we can use a fuzzy domain for each of these attributes. The domain is a set of discrete values from 0 to 1 (see Table 10.2). We can assume that a value of an attribute represents the degree of the learner referring to the first value mentioned above, and the difference between 1 and this number represents the second value. For example, if for a learner the value for attribute *Perception* is equal to 0.4 then one should understand that the ability of the learner is sensitive in the degree of 0.4 and is intuitive in the degree of 0.6.

10.3.2. Usage Data

The usage data of a learner should contain such data as

- Opening scenarios proposed by the system: Learners are classified into classes on the basis of their user data. When a new learner logs onto the system, it may propose one or more scenarios to him. This scenario is chosen on the basis of the scenarios passed by other learners belonging to the same class. The way to choose a beginning scenario for a new learner is presented in the next section.
- Realized learning scenarios: The beginning scenario suggested by the system may turn out to be unsuitable for the learner, and it is necessary to change it. Thus the final scenario on the basis of which the learner passes the course may be different from the first one. This kind of scenario will serve to reclassify the process for the set of learners.

10.3.3. Learner Classification Process

The classification process for learners is done on the basis of attributes defined in user data. The aim of the classification is to enable the process of adaptation and recommendation. We would like to have in one class the learners who have passed similar learning scenarios. Owing to this a new learner after classifying may be recommended with a good scenario so that he will be probably able to pass it.

It turns out that not all attributes are proper for the classification process. For example, attributes *Learner Identifier* and *Password* are obviously useless for classification. The choice of the attributes for the classification process should be done by experts.

Below we present a description of the classification process.

Let A be the set of attributes from user data. For an attribute domain the discretisation process may be done. For example, for attribute Age its domain (Integer) may be divided into three intervals: up to 18 (*young*), between 18 and 50 (*middle*), and above 50 (*elder*). For each attribute a denote its domain (after possible discretisation) by V_a.

Let L denote the set of all learners who have used the system. Let $B \subseteq A$ be the set of attributes for classification. Let C_B be the classification of the set of learners on the basis of attributes from B. A class of the classification is defined by the following elementary tuple of type B,

$$r : B \to \bigcup_{a \in B} V_a \, ,$$

where

$$r(a) \in V_a$$

for each $a \in B$. The set of all elementary tuples of type B has been denoted $E\text{-}TUPLE(B)$ (see Section 4.2.1, Chapter 4).

Thus the number of classes is equal to the number of all tuples of type B; that is,

$$card(\textstyle\prod_{a \in B} V_a).$$

By $C_B(r)$ we denote the class of classification C_B defined by tuple r. A learner $l \in L$ is classified into class $C_B(r)$ if and only if for each attribute $a \in B$ its value referring to this learner is equal to $r(a)$. We have the following properties,

$$\bigcup_{r \in E\text{-}TUPLE(B)} C_B(r) = L,$$

and

$$C_B(r) \cap C_B(r') = \varnothing \quad \text{for any } r, r' \in E\text{-}TUPLE(B) \text{ and } r \neq r'.$$

In this way the set

$$C_B = \{ C_B(r) \colon r \in E\text{-}TUPLE(B) \}$$

can be treated as a partition of L. However, some of its classes may be empty and should be removed from C_B.

Because the values of the attributes describing a learner's individual learning style may not be precisely known when the learner begins her interaction with the system, we may assume that these values may be modified during her learning process.

In the next section we present a method for learner recommendation.

10.4. Recommendation Process

At the beginning of the interaction with the system, a learner gives his parameters (user data) to the system and next he is classified into a class. Using the usage data of the learners belonging to the class the system determines the beginning scenario for this new learner. We propose to use consensus methods toward this aim. The algorithm for this choice is presented later. First we show the general procedure for recommendation.

10.4.1. Recommendation Procedure

As presented in Figure 10.4, the recommendation procedure consists of eight steps:

- In step 1 a new learner gives his temporal user data to the system. The temporality refers mainly to the values of attributes concerning learning style.
- In step 2 the new learner is classified into a class on the basis of his user data.
- In step 3 the system determines the opening scenario for the learner on the basis of the passed scenarios of the learners belonging to the class with using consensus method.
- In steps 4 through 6 the learning process takes place. According to the given scenario within a concept the system presents to the learner a sequence of presentations. At their end the learner's knowledge is verified (e.g., by some test). If the verification process fails the system can change to an alternative sequence of presentations, and modify the scenario. Some elements of the learning style of the learner may also be modified because some of its elements may be really different than assumed at the beginning. For example, for attribute *Receiving* it may turn out that for the learner the verbal form is better, not the visual form as he has declared.
- After the learner has been shown all concepts, if the system evaluates the process as positive then it should perform step 7 which relies on completing usage data that are the opening scenario and the passed scenario. Otherwise step 8 should be performed, in which the learner should be reclassified and directed to step 3. Note that reclassification is sensible because the user data of the learner could be changed, and a new opening scenario could bring learning success.

In the next section we deal with the algorithm for determination of the opening scenario.

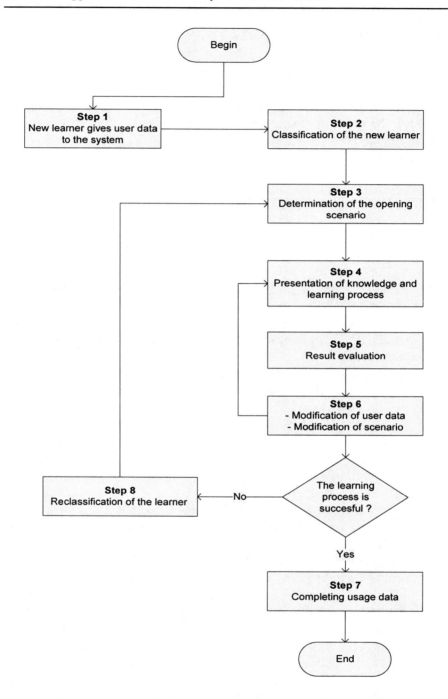

Figure 10.4. Recommendation procedure.

10.4.2. Algorithm for Determination of Opening Scenario

We now present an algorithm for determination of the opening scenario for a new learner. We assume that after the classification process the new learner will belong to a class which consists of learners similar to her. These learners have passed the course with success, and it is the basis for us to assume that the scenario for the new learner should be determined on the basis of the scenarios of her colleagues. Along with this assumption we would like the scenario for the new learner:

- To be maximally similar to the scenarios passed by her colleagues
- To have maximally steady similarities to the scenarios passed by her colleagues

As analyzed in Chapter 3, a scenario which satisfies the first condition is a consensus fulfilling criterion O_1 (requiring minimization of the sum of distances between the consensus and profile elements, in this case passed scenarios), and a scenario which satisfies the second condition is a consensus fulfilling criterion O_2 (requiring minimization of the sum of squared distances between the consensus and profile elements). It has been proved that in general such a consensus satisfying both conditions simultaneously does not exist. Therefore, we work out separately an algorithm for each condition.

First we deal with consensus fulfilling criterion O_1. Toward this aim we use the distance function d defined for scenarios in Section 10.2.2. The consensus problem is defined as follows.

For a given set with repetitions of scenarios

$$X = \{s_i \in S_C : s_i \text{ is } \alpha_i\text{-based for } i = 1, 2, \ldots, n\},$$

one should determine an α^*-based scenario $s^* \in S_C$ such that sum

$$\sum_{i=1}^{n} d(s^*, s_i)$$

is minimal.

According to Definition 10.3 we have:

$$d(s^*, s_i) = w_1 \cdot \sigma(\alpha^*, \alpha_i) + w_2 \cdot \sum_{c \in C} \sigma(r^*_{g(c)}, r^{(i)}_{h_i(c)}),$$

where $g(c)$ and $h_i(c)$ denote the position indexes referring to concept c in scenarios s^* and s_i, respectively. Thus we further have

$$\sum_{i=1}^{n} d(s^*, s_i) = w_1 \cdot \sum_{i=1}^{n} \sigma(\alpha^*, \alpha_i) + w_2 \cdot \sum_{i=1}^{n} \sum_{c \in C} \sigma(r^*_{g(c)}, r^{(i)}_{h_i(c)})$$

$$= w_1 \cdot \sum_{i=1}^{n} \sigma(\alpha^*, \alpha_i) + w_2 \cdot \sum_{c \in C} \sum_{i=1}^{n} \sigma(r^*_{g(c)}, r^{(i)}_{h_i(c)}).$$

From the above equality it follows that the sum $\sum_{i=1}^{n} d(s^*, s_i)$ is minimal if one determines such concept order α^*; thus sum $\sum_{i=1}^{n} \sigma(\alpha^*, \alpha_i)$ is minimal, and for each concept c such partial linear relation $r^*_{g(c)}$ which minimizes the sum $\sum_{i=1}^{n} \sigma(r^*_{g(c)}, r^{(i)}_{h_i(c)})$. Therefore, we need an algorithm for the following two optimization problems:

Problem 1.
For a given set of linear orders on set C of concepts

$$Y = \{\alpha_i : i = 1, 2, \ldots, n\}$$

one should determine a linear order α^* on C such that sum

$$\sum_{i=1}^{n} \sigma(\alpha^*, \alpha_i)$$

is minimal.

and

Problem 2.
For a given set of partial linear orders on some finite set Z

$$Y = \{\gamma_i : i = 1, 2, \ldots, k\}$$

one should determine a partial linear order γ^* on Z such that sum

$$\sum_{i=1}^{k} \sigma(\gamma^*, \gamma_i)$$

is minimal.

For Problem 1 there is a known branch and bound algorithm worked out by Barthelemy, Guenoche, and Hudry [12] on the basis of standard distance functions between linear orders. We propose here another algorithm using the distance function σ defined in Section 10.2.2. The idea of this algorithm is based on the following steps:

- For each concept determine a set of indexes of the positions on which this concept occurs in orders α_i for $i = 1, 2, \ldots, n$.
- In relation α^* the order of concepts will be consistent with the increasing order of the sums of their indexes.

The algorithm is presented as follows.

Algorithm 10.1.

Input: Set of linear orders on set C

$$Y = \{\alpha_i: i = 1, 2, \ldots, n\}.$$

Output: Linear order α^* on C minimizing sum $\sum_{i=1}^{n} \sigma(\alpha^*, \alpha_i)$.

Procedure:

   BEGIN

      1. For each $c \in C$ determine a set with repetitions:

         $I_c = \{j$: there exists an order from Y such that concept c occurs on its jth position$\}$;

      2. For each $c \in C$ calculate $J_c = \sum_{j \in I_c} j$;

      3. Set in order the concepts in relation α^* according to the increasing order of values J_c;

   END.

We give an example:

Example 10.5. Let $C = \{c_1, c_2, c_3, c_4\}$, and let set Y consist of the following orders,

$$\alpha_1 = \langle c_1, c_2, c_3, c_4 \rangle$$
$$\alpha_2 = \langle c_2, c_1, c_4, c_3 \rangle$$
$$\alpha_3 = \langle c_4, c_3, c_1, c_2 \rangle$$
$$\alpha_4 = \langle c_1, c_4, c_2, c_3 \rangle$$
$$\alpha_5 = \langle c_4, c_3, c_1, c_2 \rangle.$$

We have:

$$I_{c_1} = \{1, 2, 3, 1, 3\}$$
$$I_{c_2} = \{2, 1, 4, 3, 4\}$$
$$I_{c_3} = \{3, 4, 2, 4, 2\}$$
$$I_{c_4} = \{4, 3, 1, 2, 1\}$$

and

$$J_{c_1} = 10, \quad J_{c_2} = 13, \quad J_{c_3} = 15, \quad J_{c_4} = 11.$$

Thus $\alpha^* = \langle c_1, c_4, c_2, c_3 \rangle.$ ◆

The computational complexity of this algorithm is $O(n \cdot m)$ where $m = card(C)$.

For Problem 2 the algorithm may be more complex, because the relations may be partial. First let's notice that if relation γ^* may have a weak linear order then we have the following method.

The idea of this method is based on the observation that the position of each element from set Z may be determined in an independent way. For an element $x \in Z$ we may determine the set of indexes of its positions in relations γ_i ($i = 1, 2, \ldots, k$). If z does not occur in some relation then we may assume its index equal to $card(Z) + 1$. This follows from the definition of the share of x in the distance of two partial linear orders where x occurs only in one relation on position k; then its share is equal to

$$\frac{card(X)-(k-1)}{card(X)} = \frac{(card(X)+1)-k}{card(X)}.$$

This value is the same as if in the second relation x occurred in position $card(Z) + 1$ which, of course, does not exist.

For example, let $Z = \{x_1, x_2, x_3, x_4\}$, and let set Y consist of the following orders,

$$\gamma_1 = <x_1, x_2, x_4>$$
$$\gamma_2 = <x_1, x_2, x_4, x_3>$$
$$\gamma_3 = <x_4, x_2, x_3>$$
$$\gamma_4 = <x_1, x_4, x_3>$$
$$\gamma_5 = <x_3, x_1, x_2>.$$

Thus $card(Z) + 1 = 5$ and we have:

$$I_{x_1} = \{1, 1, 5, 1, 2\} = \{1, 1, 1, 2, 5\}$$

$$I_{x_2} = \{2, 2, 2, 5, 3\} = \{2, 2, 2, 3, 5\}$$

$$I_{x_3} = \{5, 4, 3, 3, 1\} = \{1, 3, 3, 4, 5\}$$

$$I_{x_4} = \{3, 3, 1, 2, 5\} = \{1, 2, 3, 3, 5\}.$$

Based on Algorithm 5.5 (see Section 5.4.3 in Chapter 5) we can imply that if the position index of x_1 in relation γ^* is 1 then its share in the sum of distances between γ^* and the given partial linear relations will be minimal (this means the best position for x_1 in γ^*). Similarly for x_2 the index should be 2, for $x_3 - 3$, and for $x_4 - 3$. Thus if γ^* could be a weak linear order then it should have the form:

$$<x_1, x_2, \{x_3, x_4\}>.$$

However, it is required that γ^* should be a (nonweak) linear order. This problem seems to be NP-complete (its proof is not presented here), thus a heuristic algorithm is needed to be worked out.

Fortunately, despite the NP-completeness we can notice that in fact within a concept we must choose one of its presentation orders which minimizes the sum of distances to given presentation orders. This means $\gamma^* \in R_P(c)$ where $R_P(c)$ is the set of partial linear orders on the set of presentations of concept c. Because set $R_P(c)$ should not be large, we can allow making a full search for finding the optimal element from $R_P(c)$ that minimizes the sum of distances.

The algorithm is presented as follows.

Algorithm 10.2.

Input: Set of partial linear orders on set $P(c)$ for $c \in C$.

$$Y = \{\gamma_i : \gamma_i \in R_P(c) \text{ for } i = 1, 2, \ldots, k\}.$$

Output: Partial linear order $\gamma^* \in R_P(c)$ minimizing sum

$$\sum_{i=1}^{k} \sigma(\gamma^*, \gamma_i).$$

Procedure:

BEGIN

1. Set $\gamma \in R_P(c)$ as any relation belonging to $R_P(c)$;

2. Set $\gamma^* := \gamma$; Calculate $\Omega := \sum_{i=1}^{k} \sigma(\gamma^*, \gamma_i)$;

3. For each $\gamma \in R_P(c)$ do if $\sum_{i=1}^{k} \sigma(\gamma, \gamma_i) < \Omega$ then

  Begin

  Set $\Omega := \sum_{i=1}^{k} \sigma(\gamma, \gamma_i)$;

  $\gamma^* := \gamma$

  End;

END.

Example 10.6. Let's consider the sequel of Example 10.5. For each concept the set of its presentations and partial linear orders is presented as in Figure 10.5 (symbol r_{ij} represents a presentation's partial order for concept c_i). Assume that in a class the passed scenarios are the following (where scenario s_i is α_i-based, for $i = 1, 2, 3, 4$, respectively).

$$s_1 = \left\langle <p_{11}, p_{13}, p_{14}, p_{12}>, <p_{22}, p_{23}, p_{24}>, <p_{33}, p_{35}, p_{34}>, \right.$$
$$\left. <p_{43}, p_{45}, p_{44}, p_{41}, p_{42}> \right\rangle.$$

$$s_2 = \left\langle <p_{21}, p_{23}, p_{24}, p_{22}>, <p_{11}, p_{13}, p_{14}, p_{12}>, <p_{43}, p_{45}, p_{44}, p_{41}, p_{42}>, \right.$$
$$\left. <p_{31}, p_{33}> \right\rangle.$$

$$s_3 = \left\langle <p_{42}, p_{43}, p_{44}>, <p_{31}, p_{33}>, <p_{11}, p_{13}, p_{14}, p_{12}>, \right.$$
$$\left. <p_{21}, p_{23}, p_{24}, p_{22}> \right\rangle.$$

$$s_4 = \left\langle <p_{12}, p_{13}, p_{14}>, <p_{42}, p_{43}, p_{44}>, <p_{22}, p_{23}, p_{24}>, <p_{31}, p_{33}> \right\rangle.$$

$$s_5 = \left\langle <p_{42}, p_{43}, p_{44}>, <p_{31}, p_{33}>, <p_{13}, p_{15}, p_{14}, p_{11}, p_{12}>, \right.$$
$$\left. <p_{21}, p_{23}, p_{24}, p_{22}> \right\rangle.$$

As known from Example 10.5, in the consensus the order α^* for concepts should be:

$$\alpha^* = <c_1, c_4, c_2, c_3>.$$

For each concept the partial linear order is given in Table 10.3. This order is also the opening scenario for the new learner.   ◆

c_1

r_{11}	r_{12}	r_{13}	r_{14}
p_{13}	p_{11}	p_{12}	p_{12}
p_{15}	p_{13}	p_{13}	p_{13}
p_{14}	p_{14}	p_{14}	p_{15}
p_{11}	p_{12}		p_{11}
p_{12}			

c_2

r_{21}	r_{22}	r_{23}
p_{23}	p_{22}	p_{21}
p_{22}	p_{23}	p_{23}
p_{24}	p_{24}	p_{24}
p_{21}		p_{22}

c_3

r_{31}	r_{32}	r_{33}
p_{33}	p_{33}	p_{31}
p_{35}	p_{35}	p_{33}
p_{34}	p_{34}	
	p_{31}	
	p_{32}	

c_4

r_{41}	r_{42}
p_{43}	p_{42}
p_{45}	p_{43}
p_{44}	p_{44}
p_{41}	
p_{42}	

Figure 10.5. Partial orders of presentations of concepts.

Table 10.3. Opening scenario for the new learner

c_1	c_4	c_3	c_2
p_{11}	p_{22}	p_{31}	p_{21}
p_{13}	p_{23}	p_{33}	p_{23}
p_{14}	p_{24}		p_{24}
p_{12}			p_{22}

10.5. Learner Clustering Process

As described above, in the classification of learners their user data play a key role. Experts indicate these attributes from the user data which are the basis of the classification process. In this section we propose a novel approach for determining these attributes. It is based on the usage data, more concretely, on determining the attributes for classification on the basis of the passed scenarios of learners. We assume that it is the passed scenarios which decide about the similarity of learners. However, the tool for classification should be based on user data. Thus we propose to use passed scenarios for determining the attributes from user data which will be used for the classification process. The idea of this approach is similar to the one for user interfaces presented in our recent article [126] concerning the method for creating effective user interfaces. For learner clustering this idea is shown in Figure 10.6. Here we can see some circle of the system life. Although the idea is presented in a clear way in the figure, below we add some comments.

- Step 1: The beginning of the system; there is a lack or simply a small number of learners. The experts are asked to suggest attributes from user data for learner classification.
- Step 2: Set A of attributes has been generated by the experts. Each new learner is classified on the basis of values of these attributes (see Section 10.3.4). Set A can be understood as the criterion for learner classification. This process gives a partition P of the set of all learners.
- Step 3: Owing to learning processes the usage data of learners are gathered. Very important are the passed scenarios of learners.
- Step 4: We may expect that the passed scenarios will not be similar even for learners of the same class. If so, the situation means that it is necessary to have a new criterion for classification. Using the

passed scenarios we may perform clustering for the set of learners generating a new partition Q of the learners' set.

- If partition P differs meaningfully from partition Q then using the rough classification method (see Section 10.7) we can determine the new criterion for learner classification (steps 5 and 6). Next this new criterion is used for new learners (step 2).
- If partition P differs a little from partition Q then there is no need for a new criterion for learner classification. The system will wait for new learners who may cause the large distance between partitions P and Q (step 3).

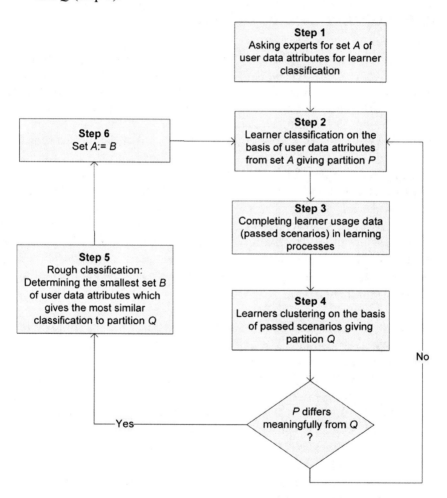

Figure 10.6. A cycle of the system life.

Generally, clustering a finite set is a process for creating a partition of this set which satisfies some criterion. A number of algorithms for clustering have been worked out in the literature. One of the most popular criteria is based on minimizing the sum of squared distances from elements of a cluster to the cluster centre. A very popular clustering strategy has been named "k-mean" [62] which relies on partitioning the set of elements into k nonoverlapping clusters that are identified by their centres. This problem is known to be NP-complete [94], although it is still attractive because of its simplicity and flexibility.

Here we present in short the algorithm worked out by Kanungo et al. [62]. This algorithm is one of the most popular algorithms based on the k-mean strategy. The main steps of this algorithm are organized as follows.

- Step 1: Select randomly k elements as the starting centres (called *centroides*) of the clusters. Each centroid represents a cluster.
- Step 2: Assign each element of the set to this cluster for which the distance between this element and the centroid is smallest.
- Step 3: Redetermine the centroid of each cluster, for example, by choosing the new centroid as the center of gravity of the cluster.
- Step 4: Repeat steps 2 and 3 until some convergence conditions have not been met (e.g., the centroids do not change).

The advantages of this algorithm lie in its simplicity and the finite time for its performance. It always reaches the end when using the above-mentioned convergence condition. The largest disadvantage of this k-means algorithm is its large computational complexity. Namely, the time cost of this algorithm is $O(k \cdot m \cdot N)$, where m is the dimension of an element and N is the number of elements of the set which is rather a large number.

For the set of learners in the learning system each learner is represented by his passed scenario. Thus in fact we need to perform the clustering process for a set of scenarios. Calculation of distances between scenarios is not complex. However, the determination of the gravity centre for a cluster (needed in step 3) may be a complex task. However, it turns out that this task is very simple for Euclidean vectors. Therefore, here we propose to determine the new centroid as the consensus of the cluster. For this task the algorithms presented in Section 10.4.2 may be used.

As the result of the clustering process we obtain a partition of the set of learners, which may differ meaningfully from the partition created in the classification process. As stated above, two learners belonging to the same cluster (i.e., having similar passed scenarios) should be considered to be more similar than those in the same class of the classification. Therefore, we propose to use the results of clustering to redefine the criterion of the classification process. Toward this aim we use the rough classification method. The conception of this method has been included in papers [125, 126]; here we present this approach in more detail.

The term "rough classification" is borrowed from the rough classification of Pawlak [134]. However, the conception presented here is different from that of Pawlak and is an original and novel one.

The details are presented in the next section.

10.6. Rough Learner Classification Method

10.6.1. Pawlak's Concept

The concept of rough classification has been defined by Pawlak [134]. The idea of this conception can be briefly described as follows.

An information system according to Pawlak is presented by the following quadruple [132],

$$S = (U, A, V, \rho),$$

where

U is a set of objects,
A is a set of attributes which describe the objects,
V is the set of attribute values,
$\rho: U \times A \rightarrow V$ is the information function, such that $\rho(x,a) \in V_a$ for each $x \in U$ and $a \in A$.

An information system can be represented by a table in which columns represent the attributes and rows represent the objects. A real world object is characterized by a row (tuple) in this table. Owing to this description objects can be classified into classes and the criterion for classification is a subset B of the set A in such way that objects belonging to the same class should be characterized by an identical tuple of type B.

Pawlak worked out a method which enables us to determine the minimal set of attributes (called a *reduct*) that generates the same classification as the whole set of attributes. From a practical point of view, this method is very useful because owing to it the same classification may be created on the basis of a smaller number of attributes.

In short, Pawlak's concept of rough classification is the following. For given classification C of set U a rough classification is the approximation of C. Assume that classification C is generated by set B of attributes; then the approximation of C is based on determining a proper subset B' of B

such that the classification defined by B' differs "a little" from C. The small difference between these classifications is illustrated by the difference of their accuracy measure which should not be larger than a threshold ε; that is,

$$\mu_B(X) - \mu_{B \setminus B'}(X) \le \varepsilon,$$

for each $X \subseteq U$, where

$$\mu_R(X) = \frac{card(\underline{A}X)}{card(\overline{A}X)}$$

for $\underline{A}X$ and $\overline{A}X$ being the lower approximation and upper approximation of set X, respectively, in information system S reduced to set R of attributes. For more information the reader can refer to Pawlak's work [134].

Thus the aim of Pawlak's concept for rough classification is based on determining a subset set B' of set B which generates a partition similar to this one generated by set B.

10.6.2. Our Concept

In this work we consider another approach and other problems of rough classification. The aim of this approach is to solve the following problem. *For a given classification of set U one should determine such minimal set B of attributes from A that the distance between the classification generated by attributes from B and the given classification is minimal.* The application of this method for intelligent learning systems is based on determining the minimal set of user data attributes which generate a similar classification to that generated by a learner clustering process. After these attributes of set B have been determined, they should enable the classification of new learners more properly and as a consequence, assign good scenarios to them.

This problem differs from the one formulated by Pawlak. Also, in solving it we use distance functions between classifications to generate the attributes. This approach was originally presented in [126, 148]; here we present it with some extension, improvement, and a deeper analysis.

10.6.3. Basic Notions

We define the following basic notions.

- *Partition of a set*:
By a partition of set U we call a finite set of nonempty and disjoint with each other classes which are subsets of U, such that their union is equal to

U. By $\pi(U)$ we denote the set of all partitions of set U. Let $P, Q \in \pi(U)$, the product of P and Q (written as $P \cap Q$) be defined as

$$P \cap Q = \{p \cap q : p \in P, q \in Q \land p \cap q \neq \varnothing\}.$$

Thus product $P \cap Q$ is also a partition of U.

• *Distances between partitions*:
We define two distance functions (μ and ω) between partitions.

Function μ:
The idea of this function is based on measuring the distance between partitions P and Q of set U as the minimal number of elementary transformations needed to transform partition P into partition Q. This number may be normalized by value $card(U)$ (with the assumption that U is a finite set) [34].
There are two elementary transformations which are defined as follows.

- *Removal of an element*: transforms a partition P of set U into a partition Q of set $U\backslash\{x\}$ by removing element x from P. We denote this operation by symbol $\hat{x}$:

$$P \xrightarrow{\hat{x}} Q.$$

- *Addition of an element*: transforms a partition P of set $U \cup \{x\}$ into a partition Q of set U by including an element x in one of the existing classes from P or by creating a new class with only one element x. We denote this operation by symbol $\check{x}$:

$$P \xrightarrow{\check{x}} Q.$$

The following example illustrates these operations.

Example 10.7. Let

$$U = \{x_1, \ldots, x_7\},$$
$$P = \{\{x_1\}, \{x_2, x_3, x_4, x_7\}, \{x_5, x_6\}\},$$
$$Q = \{\{x_1, x_2\}, \{x_3, x_4\}, \{x_7\}, \{x_5, x_6\}\}.$$

The necessary elementary transformations are presented as follows.

$$P = \{\{x_1\}, \{x_2, x_3, x_4, x_7\}, \{x_5, x_6\}\}$$
$$\xrightarrow{\check{x}_7} \{\{x_1\}, \{x_2, x_3, x_4\}, \{x_5, x_6\}\}$$
$$\xrightarrow{\hat{x}_7} \{\{x_1\}, \{x_2, x_3, x_4\}, \{x_5, x_6\}, \{x_7\}\}$$
$$\xrightarrow{\check{x}_2} \{\{x_1\}, \{x_3, x_4\}, \{x_5, x_6\}, \{x_7\}\}$$
$$\xrightarrow{\hat{x}_2} \{\{x_1, x_2\}, \{x_3, x_4\}, \{x_5, x_6\}, \{x_7\}\} = Q.$$

Thus $\mu(P,Q) = 4/7$. It has been proved that function μ is a metric [34]. In this work the author also presented an algorithm for determining values of function μ, for which the complexity is $O(card(U)^2)$.   ◆

Function ω:

For $P, Q \in \pi(U)$ let $M(P) = [p_{ij}]_{n \times n}$ be such a matrix that

$$p_{ij} = \begin{cases} 1 & \text{if} \quad x_i, x_j \text{ are in different classes of } P \\ 0 & \text{if} \quad x_i, x_j \text{ are in the same class of } P \end{cases}$$

and matrix $M(Q) = [q_{ij}]_{n \times n}$ be defined in a similar way, where $n = card(U)$. Notice that these matrixes are symmetric.

The distance between partitions P and Q is defined as

$$\omega(P,Q) = \frac{1}{2 \cdot card(U)} \sum_{i,j=1}^{n} \left| p_{ij} - q_{ij} \right|.$$

The distance function defined in this way should also be a metric. It is easy to show that the algorithm for determining distance of this kind requires $O(n^2)$ time. The distance between partitions defined in Example 10.7 is equal to 12/14.

- *Inclusion of partitions*:

Let $P, Q \in \pi(U)$. We say that partition P is included in partition Q (written $P \subseteq Q$) if each class of P is a subset of some class in Q. It is obvious that $P \cap Q \subseteq P$ and $P \cap Q \subseteq Q$.

- *Set of attributes as a criterion for partition (classification)*:

As stated earlier, if U denotes the set of learners and A is the set of attributes from user data then a learner may be represented by a tuple of type A. For $a \in A$ we define the following binary relation P_a on set U: For $x_1, x_2 \in U$ pair $<x_1, x_2>$ belongs to P_a if and only if learners x_1 and x_2 are assigned with the same value referring to attribute a. It is easy to prove that P_a is an equivalence relation, and therefore it is a partition of set U.

More general, a set B of attributes determines an equivalent relation P_B of set U as follows. A pair of two elements from U belongs to P_B if and only if referring to each attribute $b \in B$ these elements are assigned with the same value. Thus P_B is also a partition of U and it is not hard to show that

$$P_B = \bigcap_{b \in B} P_b.$$

It is also obvious that

$$P_B \subseteq P_{B'}$$

for each $B' \subseteq B$.

10.6.4. Rough Learner Classification

As we have assumed above, after registering with the learning system, a new learner is classified into an appropriate class of learners according to his or her user data. This class is the basis for determination of an opening scenario for this learner.

Let's mention:

- U = the set of learners of the system; notice that U is a dynamic set.
- A = the set of all attributes included in user data.

Assume that actually a set $B \subseteq A$ is the criterion for learner classification which is the partition P_B of set U. Assume also that the clustering process on the basis of passed scenarios gives partition Q of set U.

Because partition Q is dependent only on the learners' passed scenarios, and the aim for the system is to recommend for a new learner such a scenario with which the learner may pass the course, the partitions P_B and Q should be maximally similar. Therefore, if P_B differs from Q (or their distance is greater than a given threshold) then we say that the system is weakly adaptive. The smaller the difference is between P_B and Q the more adaptive the system. A system is then fully adaptive if $P_B = Q$.

Thus to make a system more adaptive, the set B of attributes, which is the classification criterion, should be determined on the basis of Q. Notice that set B determines exactly one partition P_B, but different sets of attributes may determine the same partition. Therefore, there is an additional problem to select a minimal set B (i.e., a set with a minimal number of elements) for which P_B and Q are equal. However, for a given partition Q such a set B may not exist; it is then reasonable to require that the distance between P_B and Q be minimal. In Figure 10.7 we can see an illustration of this situation. The squares represent set U of users, and partitions are shown by lines splitting these squares. There are three attributes a, b, and c, where only the partition generated by set $\{a, c\}$ is minimally different from partition Q.

Let $d \in \{\mu, \omega\}$ be a distance function between partitions. We formulate the following problems of rough classification.

Problem RC-1:

For a given partition Q of set U one should determine a minimal set $B \subseteq A$ such that $P_B \subseteq Q$ and $d(P_B, Q)$ is minimal.

In this problem set B represents such a classification which is included in Q and their distance is minimal. Owing to relation $P_B \subseteq Q$ two learners who have different passed scenarios, should not belong to the same class in classification P_B. However, if the second condition is not required then set U will needlessly be too narrowly fragmented.

Notice, however, that the solutions of this problem do not always exist, because no B exists for each Q such that $P_B \subseteq Q$. According to the property of inclusion relation between partitions, $P_A \subseteq P_B$ for each $B \subseteq A$, we have the following remark.

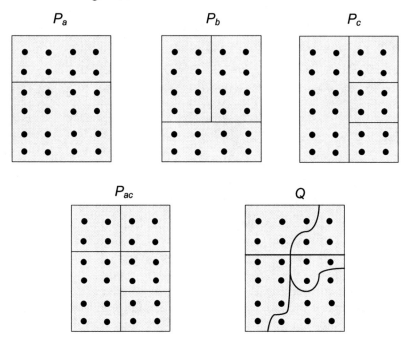

Figure 10.7. The distance between P_{ac} and Q is minimal.

Remark 10.1.
The necessary and sufficient condition for Problem RC-1 to have a solution is
$$P_A \subseteq Q.$$

So if $P_A \not\subseteq Q$ then there will not be any solution. In this case the solutions of Problem RC-2 or RC-3 should be found.

Problem RC-2:
For a given partition Q of set U one should determine a minimal set $B \subseteq A$ such that $Q \subseteq P_B$ and $d(P_B,Q)$ is minimal.

In this problem set B represents such classification which includes Q and minimally differs from this partition; that is, partition P_B is less narrow than partition Q. Therefore, two learners with different passed scenarios may be classified in the same class in P_B. However, owing to the second condition the number of learners of this kind will be minimal. Thus we deal with some kind of rough classification. The only advantage of the solution to this problem is that the number of attributes needed for classification P_B is often smaller than in the solutions of Problem RC-1. Similarly as with RC-1 this problem also may have no solutions. Because $P_B \subseteq P_b$ for each $b \in B$ we have the following.

Remark 10.2.
The necessary and sufficient condition for Problem RC-2 to have a solution is

$$Q \subseteq P_a$$

for some $a \in A$.

Problem RC-3:

For a given partition Q of set U one should determine a minimal set $B \subseteq A$ such that $d(P_B, Q)$ is minimal.

This problem is the most general and should always have solution(s), which may be useful if solutions of Problems RC-1 and RC-2 do not exist. In this case we say that set B represents a rough classification referring to Q. In the majority of practical cases this problem needs to be solved. Problem RC-3 here has been modified referring to its primal form defined in [126] by adding the second condition. This condition is needed because it guarantees the minimal cardinality of set B being very useful in practice.

Before solving these problems we present an example.

Example 10.8. Let $U = \{l_1, \ldots, l_7\}$ and $A = \{a, b, c, d, e, f\}$. The profiles of the learners with their user data are given in Table 10.4.

Table 10.4. Example user data of learners

Learners	a	b	c	d	e	f
l_1	a_1	b_2	c_3	d_1	e_2	f_3
l_2	a_2	b_1	c_2	d_2	e_1	f_1
l_3	a_2	b_2	c_3	d_2	e_2	f_2
l_4	a_1	b_3	c_2	d_2	e_2	f_3
l_5	a_2	b_1	c_2	d_2	e_1	f_2
l_6	a_2	b_2	c_1	d_1	e_2	f_1
l_7	a_2	b_1	c_2	d_2	e_1	f_2

From this table we have the following partitions:

$$P_a = \{ \{l_1, l_4\}, \{l_2, l_3, l_5, l_6, l_7\} \},$$
$$P_b = \{ \{l_1, l_3, l_5\}, \{l_2, l_5, l_7\}, \{l_4\} \},$$
$$P_c = \{ \{l_1, l_3\}, \{l_2, l_4, l_5, l_7\}, \{l_6\} \},$$
$$P_d = \{ \{l_1, l_6\}, \{l_2, l_3, l_4, l_5, l_7\} \},$$
$$P_e = \{ \{l_1, l_3, l_4, l_6\}, \{l_2, l_5, l_7\} \},$$
$$P_f = \{ \{l_1, l_4\}, \{l_2, l_6\}, \{l_3, l_5, l_7\} \}.$$

Thus

$$P_A = \{ \{l_1\}, \{l_2\}, \{l_3\}, \{l_4\}, \{l_5, l_7\}, \{l_6\} \}.$$

Let the partition determined by the learners clustering process be the following,

$$Q = \{ \{l_1, l_4\}, \{l_2, l_3, l_6\}, \{l_5, l_7\} \}.$$

We have $P_A \subseteq Q$, thus the problem RC-1 should have a solution. This solution is $B = \{e, f\}$ which generates partition

$$P_B = \{ \{l_1, l_4\}, \{l_2\}, \{l_3\}, \{l_6\}, \{l_5, l_7\} \}.$$

For problem RC-2 notice that $Q \subseteq P_a$, so it should have a solution in which $B = \{a\}$; we have

$$P_B = \{ \{l_1, l_4\}, \{l_2, l_3, l_5, l_6, l_7\} \}.$$

In this case we say that B does not represent the classification as accurately as Q, but maximally near to Q. If now

$$Q = \{ \{l_1, l_7\}, \{l_2, l_3\}, \{l_5, l_6\}, \{l_4\} \},$$

then we can see that $P_A \not\subseteq Q$, thus RC-1 has no solution. Similarly RC-2 has no solution because $Q \not\subseteq P_a$ for each $a \in A$. It is then necessary to solve problem RC-3.   ♦

Now we present the solutions for the above-defined problems.

For Problem RC-1:

From Remark 10.1 it follows that if $P_A \not\subseteq Q$ then the solution for this problem does not exist. In the case of relationship $P_A \subseteq Q$ the solution should exist and set B may be equal to set A, but for the condition that $d(P_B, Q)$ should be minimal some attributes from A should be considered for removal. The basis of these operations relies on the following theorem.

Theorem 10.2.
For any $P, Q, R \in \pi(U)$ and $d \in \{\mu, \omega\}$ if $R \subseteq P$ and $P \subseteq Q$ then
(a) $d(P,Q) \leq d(R,Q)$.
(b) $d(R,P) \leq d(R,Q)$.

Proof.

(a) The idea for this proof is based on the fact that partition P is narrower than partition Q and partition R is narrower than partition P. Thus, the distance between P and Q should not be larger than the distance between R and Q. Formally referring to distance functions we have two cases:

- For distance μ: We notice that in determining distance μ between partitions a pair of two operations, the removal of an element from a class and addition of the element to another class (this class may be newly created), is equivalent to a transformation operation which is based on moving this element from the first class to the second. Indeed, the distance $\mu(P,Q)$ is equal to half the minimal number of removal and addition operations on elements of U for transforming P to Q. From the fact that $P \subseteq Q$ it is implied that for each $q \in Q$ we have

$$q = \bigcup_{p \in P'} p$$

for some $P' \subseteq P$. For determining the distance $\mu(P,Q)$ it is necessary and sufficient to transform P to Q by moving some elements in P from some classes to other existing classes, because a class of Q is the sum of some classes of P. Thus for achieving class q the minimal amount of element moving is equal to $card(q\backslash p')$ where p' is the class in P' with the maximal number of elements. The general formula for distance between P and Q is:

$$\mu(P,Q) = \frac{1}{card(U)} \sum_{q \in Q} card(q \backslash p'),$$

where

$$card(p') = \max \{card(p): p \in P \text{ and } p \subseteq q\}.$$

If now we would like to measure the distance between R and Q we should notice that for each $q \in Q$ the value $card(q\backslash p')$ in distance $\mu(P,Q)$ is not larger than its corresponding component in distance $\mu(R,Q)$ because

$$\max\{card(p): p \in P \wedge p \subseteq q\}$$
$$\geq \max\{card(r): r \in R \wedge p \in P \wedge r \subseteq p \subseteq q\}.$$

From the above it follows that

$$\mu(P,Q) \leq \mu(R,Q).$$

- For distance ω: For this distance function from its definition we can see that because $P \subseteq Q$ the distance $\omega(P,Q)$ may be divided into classes belonging to partition Q. For each class $q \in Q$ its part in the distance is equal to the product of the cardinalities of those classes in partition P which are proper subsets of q. If such classes do not exist then it follows that there exists exactly one class in P which is identical to q. In this case the part of q in the distance is equal to 0. We have then the following equality

$$\omega(P,Q) = \frac{1}{2 \cdot card(U)} \sum_{q \in Q} (\prod_{\substack{p \in P \\ p \subset q}} card(p)).$$

Indeed, the fact $P \subset Q$ means that set q is "broken" into one or several sets $p \in P$. In the first case the part of q in distance $\omega(P,Q)$ is 0; in the second it is equal to the product of cardinalities of sets p. Notice that the sum of cardinalities of these sets is equal to the number of elements of q. In the case $R \subseteq P$ sets p are further broken, and as the consequence, in distance $\omega(R,Q)$ the part of set q is the product of cardinalities of smaller sets r where $r \in R$. Notice that for any natural number n the following dependency is always true,

$$n \leq k \cdot m ,$$

where $n = k + m$.

From this dependency it follows immediately that $\omega(P,Q) \leq \omega(R,Q)$.

(b) For distance function μ: Assume that $R \subseteq P \subseteq Q$; then let us see that for any two elements $x, y \in U$ there are the following cases:

- x and y occur in the same class of partition R. Thus because $R \subseteq P \subseteq Q$ they must occur together in partitions P and Q. Owing to this their share in distances $\mu(R,P)$ and $\mu(R,Q)$ is equal to 0.
- x and y occur in different classes in partition R, but in the same class in partition P. Hence they must also occur in the same class in partition Q. Thus their share in distances $\mu(R,P)$ and $\mu(R,Q)$ is equal to $2/card(U)$ (one removal and one adding operation).
- x and y occur in different classes in partitions R and P. If they occur in different classes in partition Q then their share referring to themselves in distances $\mu(R,P)$ and $d(R,Q)$ equals 0. If they occur in the same class in partition Q then their share referring to themselves in distances $\mu(R,P)$ equals 0, and in distance $\mu(R,Q)$ is equal to $2/card(U)$.

In all of the above cases the share of elements x and y referring to themselves in distance $\mu(Q,P_a)$ is always nongreater than in distance $\mu(Q,P_b)$. Thus there should be

$$\mu(Q,P_a) \le \mu(Q,P_b).$$

For distance function ω the proof is similar.   ◆

According to Theorem 10.2 it follows that if $P \subseteq Q$ then

$$d(P \cap S,Q) \le d(P,Q)$$

for any $S \in \pi(U)$. Next we can imply that if for some attribute a we have

$$P_{A\setminus\{a\}} \subseteq Q$$

then after eliminating a from A the distance should be improved; that is,

$$d(P_{A\setminus\{a\}},Q) \le d(P_A,Q)$$

because $P_A = P_{A\setminus\{a\}} \cap P_a$.

The algorithm for problem RC-1 can be presented as follows.

Algorithm 10.3.

Input: Partition Q of set U.

Output: Minimal set $B \subseteq A$ such that $P_B \subseteq Q$ and $d(P_B,Q)$ is minimal.

Procedure:

BEGIN

    1. Calculate P_A;

    2. If $P_A \not\subseteq Q$ then print "The solution does not exist"
       and GOTO END.

    3. Set $B := A$;

    4. For each $a \in B$
       if $P_{B\setminus\{a\}} \subseteq Q$ then set $B := B\setminus\{a\}$;

END.

The idea of this algorithm is rather simple and we can easily prove that so-determined set B fulfills the condition that $d(P_B,Q)$ is minimal for $d \in \{\mu, \omega\}$ and the cardinality of B is also minimal. The computational complexity of this algorithm is $O(m \cdot n^2)$ for m being the number of attributes in A and n being the number of learners, that is, the cardinality of set U.

For Problem RC-2:

To solve this problem first we prove the following theorem.

Theorem 10.3.

For any attributes $a, b \in A$ and partition $P \in \pi(U)$ if $P \subseteq P_a$ and $P \subseteq P_b$ then

$$d(P_{ab},P) \le d(P_a,P) \quad and \quad d(P_{ab},P) \le d(P_b,P),$$

where $d \in \{\mu, \omega\}$.

Proof.

From the assumption that $P \subseteq P_a$ and $P \subseteq P_b$ it is implied that $P \subseteq P_a \cap P_b = P_{ab}$. This follows from the definition of partition product. Of course we have $P \subseteq P_{ab} \subseteq P_a$ and $P \subseteq P_{ab} \subseteq P_b$. Hence from Theorem 10.2a it is implied that $d(P,P_{ab}) \leq d(P,P_a)$ and $d(P,P_{ab}) \leq d(P,P_b)$ for $d \in \{\mu, \omega\}$. ♦

Theorem 10.2 shows some proportion of the distance between partitions to their hierarchy determined by the inclusion relation. Theorem 10.3, on the other hand, shows that if a partition is included in two other partitions then its distance to the product of these partitions is smaller than the distances to each of them.

Now notice that $Q \subseteq P_B$ if and only if $Q \subseteq P_b$ for each $b \in B$. So if $P_A \subseteq Q$ (the necessary condition for Problem RC-2 to have a solution) then on the basis of Theorem 10.3 the value $d(P_B,Q)$ where $Q \subseteq P_B$ should be minimal if B contains all such attributes $a \in A$ that $Q \subseteq P_a$. Set B may next be minimized by eliminating dependent attributes from itself (attribute a is dependent on attribute b if $P_b \subseteq P_a$). That is, if a is dependent on attribute b then a should be eliminated. The algorithm for Problem RC-2 should consist of the following steps.

Algorithm 10.4.

Input: Partition Q of set U; $d \in \{\mu, \omega\}$.

Output: Minimal set $B \subseteq A$ such that $Q \subseteq P_B$ and $d(P_B,Q)$ is minimal.

Procedure:

    BEGIN

        1. Calculate P_A;

        2. If $Q \not\subset P_A$ then print "The solution does not exist"
           and GOTO END.

        3. Set $B:=\varnothing$;

        4. For each $a \in A$
           if $Q \subseteq P_a$ then $B:= B \cup \{a\}$;

        5. For each $a, b \in A$ and $a \neq b$
           if $P_b \subseteq P_a$ then $B:= B \backslash \{a\}$;

    END.

It is not hard to prove that set B determined in this way should be minimal and fulfill the condition that $d(P_B,Q)$ is minimal for $d \in \{\mu, \omega\}$. This proof follows immediately from Theorem 10.3. The computation complexity of this algorithm is also $O(m \cdot n^2)$.

For Problem RC-3:

It has been proven that this problem is NP-complete for both distance functions μ and ω [94]. Below we present two heuristic algorithms for this problem.

The idea of the first algorithm is based on building set B from the whole set A by eliminating from set A these attributes which "spoil" the distance between partition P_A and partition Q. It is based on the following intuitive steps:

- First we determine such set $B \subseteq A$ that $d(P_B,Q)$ is minimal. To realize this aim in the first iteration from A we set $B = A$ and eliminate from B those attributes which "spoil" the distance; that is, if $d(P_{B\setminus\{b\}},Q) < d(P_B,Q)$ for some b then this attribute should be moved. Next this iteration should be repeated for new set B until any attribute will not be removed.

- Next, if among attributes from B there exist attributes a, b such that $P_a \subseteq P_b$ then eliminate b (according to Theorem 10.3); this should minimize set B.

Following we present the algorithm.

Algorithm 10.5.
Input: Partition Q of set U, $d \in \{\mu, \omega\}$.
Output: Minimal set $B \subseteq A$ such that $d(P_B,Q)$ is minimal.
Procedure:

    BEGIN
      1. Set $B := A$;
      2. For each $b \in B$
            if $d(P_{B\setminus\{b\}},Q) < d(P_B,Q)$ then set $B := B\setminus\{b\}$;
      3. Repeat step 2 until any attribute will not be removed;
      4. For each $a, b \in B$ and $a \neq b$
            if $P_a \subseteq P_b$ then $B := B\setminus\{b\}$;
    END.

The description of this algorithm is short. However, its computational complexity is not so small. It is known that for calculating a distance between two partitions the cost is $O(n^2)$ where $n = card(U)$. For step 2 the cost is $O(m \cdot n^2)$ where $m = card(A)$. For step 3 $O(m^2 \cdot n^2)$ is needed; the same is also needed for step 4. So the summary complexity for Algorithm 10.5 is $O(m^2 \cdot n^2)$.

The idea of the second algorithm is dual to the idea of Algorithm 10.5 in the sense that the building of set B will begin from the best element of set A referring to distance to partition Q and next adding to it those attributes from A that cause improvement of the distance. Owing to this it will not be necessary to remove dependent attributes. The following steps should be included:

- Select such an attribute a from A that the distance between partitions P_a and Q is minimal.
- Let $B = \{a\}$.
- Add to B such an attribute from $A \backslash B$ that the new partition P_B is nearer to Q.
- Repeat the third step until the new partition P_B is nearer to Q than the previous one.

This algorithm is presented as follows.

Algorithm 10.6.
Input: Partition Q of set U, $d \in \{\mu, \omega\}$.
Output: Minimal set $B \subseteq A$ such that $d(P_B, Q)$ is minimal.
Procedure:
  BEGIN
    1. Choose $a \in A$ such that $d(P_a, Q) = \min\limits_{b \in A} d(P_b, Q)$;
    2. Set $B = \{a\}$;
    3. Set $C := A \backslash B$
    4. For each $c \in C$ do
        if $d(P_{B \cup \{c\}}, Q) < d(P_B, Q)$ then $B := B \cup \{c\}$;
    5. If $C \neq A \backslash B$ then GOTO 3;
  END.

Similarly as for Algorithm 10.5, the computational complexity of this algorithm is also $O(m^2 \cdot n^2)$. Note that this complexity is dependent among others on the square of the number of learners which is often large and may cause the process to be time consuming. However, the need for redefinition of the classification criterion arises only along with the appearance of a large number of new learners. Thus it is not needed to be performed too often and may be performed in an offline mode. In this case the complexity should not disturb the functioning of the system.

10.7. Conclusions

In this chapter an approach for using inconsistency resolution methods to perform recommendation processes in intelligent learning systems is presented. The inconsistency is considered here in two aspects. In the first aspect inconsistency refers to difference of the passed scenarios of similar learners (belonging to the same class of the classification). In this case to determine an opening scenario for a new learner it is necessary to calculate the consensus of the passed scenarios of the members of the class. The second aspect of inconsistency refers to the fact that learners assumed to be similar (belonging to the same class of the classification) may have very miscellaneous passed scenarios. This may cause a lack of efficiency of the procedure proposed in the first aspect. Here we propose to use a rough classification based method to redefine the criterion for classification.

The ideas of knowledge structures, learning recommendation processes, and using consensus methods in determining opening scenarios for new learners were first introduced in [76, 77]. In this chapter these conceptions are modified, extended, and described in a more precise way.

It should be emphasized that the difference between our approach and Pawlak's approach to rough classification is that we do not use the upper and lower approximations of partitions defined by Pawlak, but we use the distance functions between partitions to determine the nearest partition to the given. Distance functions have not been considered in Pawlak's approach. The problems RC-1, RC-2, and RC-3 defined in this chapter are novel and their solutions should help in determining the most effective (and also the most economic) set of attributes which are needed for an effective classification process.

11. Processing Inconsistency in Information Retrieval

This chapter includes a detailed conception of a metasearch engine using multiagent technologies. A consensus-based approach for integrating answers given by different agents for a given query is presented. Moreover, this multiagent system uses the features of agent technology for making the system be a recommender system. The aim of the project is to create a consensus-based multiagent system to aid users in information retrieval from the Internet.

11.1. Introduction

Information retrieval is one of the tasks which are most often realized by Internet users. Nowadays, a large number of methods, technologies, and search engines have been proposed for aiding them in this task. However, a user utilizes only a single search engine. He or she trusts it in the sense that for a query the obtained answer is relevant and complete. However, an interesting question arises. Although there are so many existing search engines, why use only one?

For this question we suggest using not only one search engine for a query. The reason for this suggestion consists of the following elements:

- *Low relevance of answers generated by a search engine*: caused by a noneffective work of filters. As a consequence, many unrelated pages (e.g., advertisements, but also pages loosely associated with the subject of the query) may be displayed. For example, for query "mp3" it seems that the most relevant answer is URL[1] http:// www.mp3.com. However, different search engines give this URL on different positions: Google, 15th position, AltaVista, 6th position, Yahoo, 1st position, Ask Jeeves, 4th position, Homerweb, 1st position, WebCrawler,

---

[1] URL is the abbreviation of *Uniform Resource Locator*, the global address of documents and other resources on the World Wide Web.

6th position, Teoma, 1st position, Amfibi, 3rd position, and Findelio, 1st position.[2]

- *Displaying repeating URLs*: which are identical or very similar to each other. This is a burden for the user because he loses a lot of time scrolling many screens to find the information of interest.
- It is quite possible that different search engines provide "best" answers to different queries.

The idea for creating multisearch engines is not novel. Several systems have arisen called metasearch engines. In general, a metasearch engine is a server which passes on queries to many search engines and/or directories and then summarizes all the results. Examples of metasearch engines are: Metacrawler, Ask Jeeves, Dogpile, Infind, Metacrawler, Metafind, and Metasearch. The mechanisms of metasearch engines are most often based on using several independent search engines to a query achieving several ranked lists of documents, and next, a linear combination of the ranks in the lists is performed giving the final list presented to the user.

Some improvements have been done in this scope: a metasearch engine named SOFIA (SOft Fusion of Information Access) applies a soft and flexible integration of the ranked lists of documents retrieved by distinct search engines available over the Internet [21]. In this metasearch engine the authors built an operator that allows the realization of fusions between the intersection and the union of the lists. In addition, it allows the user to specify her retrieval preference for better adaptation. A feedback to the user is also ensured in the metasearch engine described in [49]. The adaptation causes users with different preferences, but with the same keyword query, to obtain different component search engines, and have results ordered differently [92].

The foundation for metasearch engines is saying, "More heads are better than one."

However, one may ask the following question. Is the use of several search engines better than the use of only one? For the answer let's consider the following aspects referring to search engines.

- Each search engine has its own database, with its own techniques of document indexing and retrieval.
- Processing of a search engine for a query is a process independent of other search engines.

---

[2] This is the result of the experiment performed June 15, 2006.

- Each search engine uses an intelligent algorithm for ranking documents in an answer.
- Because of the enormous number of documents and the limited possibility of the database of a search engine we may assume that the answer for a query is not fully relevant and not complete.

We can treat the task of information retrieval of a user as a problem which should be solved, and may be formulated as follows. For a given information need one should find a set of relevant documents which are ordered by their relevance degrees to the query. From the above points of view referring to search engines we can treat each of them as an expert, and using it for this retrieval task is equivalent to entrusting the problem to the expert. As shown in Chapter 8, it is worth entrusting the solution of a problem to not one, but several, experts and to accept the consensus of their solutions as the final solution. In Chapter 8 we have proven that if the solution of some problem is entrusted to several experts, and the consensus of their given solutions is different from those solutions, then it is not only not worse than the worst solution (in the sense of distance to the proper solution), but also better than this solution. Moreover, if the set of expert solutions is a nonhomogeneous profile then the consensus satisfying criterion O_2 should be always better than the worst solution.

The above consideration suggests using several search engines for a retrieval task, and as the final answer accepting the consensus of answers given by the search engines.

As stated above, using metasearch engines is not a new idea. However, the application of consensus methods for the integration process of answers given by component search engines could be novel.

In this chapter we propose a consensus-based approach for integrating answers gathered by a metasearch engine. Along with this aim we present the conception of a multiagent system which realizes the tasks of the metasearch engine. Moreover, this multiagent system uses the features of agent technology for making the system be a recommender system.

The aim of the project is to create a consensus-based multiagent system, the task of which is based on aiding users in information retrieval from the Internet. This approach enables us to solve the following two problems often occurring in information retrieval processes.

The proposed system exploits the answers generated by multiple search engines. Utilizing the consensus algorithm, their optimal combination is determined and displayed to the user. Answer sets (and also search engines) are evaluated on the basis of their differences from the consensus answer. This information is fed back to searching agents, stored, and utilized in subsequent queries to select the search engine to be used in the next retrieval tasks.

11.2. Agent Technology for Information Retrieval

The use of agent technology in information retrieval has been more and more popular because of the possibilities of agents to adapt to user needs, its mobility, and the ability of processing with uncertainty.

The main task of an information agent is to build user profile structures and to use algorithms that adapt to changes of user information needs. An agent of this kind usually gathers information about user needs from implicit and explicit feedback. Implicit feedback is based on the agent observing the behavior of the user referring to documents usually without user's involvement. Explicit feedback consists in explicit evaluation of the user of a document. For example, if a user selects a document, it can be interpreted implicitly that in some degree she is interested in the content of this document [149].

An information agent called Letizia which assists a user in Web browsing was built by Lieberman [78]. The tasks of Letizia are based on monitoring the user's behavior, developing a user profile, and searching for potentially interesting pages for recommendations. An important aspect of Letizia's evaluation of the relevance of a document is that the relevance degree is determined not on the basis of the document content, but on the basis of the links to and from this document.

The advantage of the use of the information from the feedback is that it makes the information agent more user-friendly. However, the ambiguity in the interpretation of user reactions may bring about imprecise results in adaptation and recommendation processes. For examples, an unread document could be treated by a search engine as irrelevant to the user query, or the factor *"time of reading"* has sense if it is assumed only that the user never takes a break while reading an article. Therefore, accurate interpretation of user needs through feedback information is a very difficult task and requires sophisticated tools for observing user behaviors [29, 30].

Chen and Sycara [26] have developed an agent named WebMate which helps users effectively browse and search the Web. WebMate keeps track of user interests in different domains through multiple weighted vectors. The domains are treated as a subject of the information agents' learning process which takes place automatically when users give their positive feedback. A new domain is created for user feedback if the number of domains is still below some upper limit. If the number of domains is equal to its maximum limit then the document should be used to modify the vector with the greatest similarity.

Apart from agent autonomy, multiagent technology adds to these features communication profit, which has been particularly useful for exchanging knowledge between agents [44]. At the same time, there are very few such systems in existence. Menczer [91] has designed and implemented *Myspiders*, a multiagent system for information discovery on the Internet and has shown that augmenting search engines with adaptive intelligent searching agents can lead to significant competitive advantages.

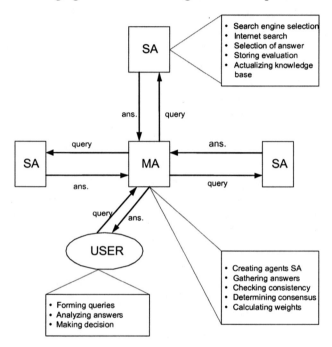

Figure 11.1. Architecture of system AGWI.

The team under the leadership of the author of this book has built two metasearch engines based on the IBM Aglets platform. The first (named AGWI) [113, 116], includes two kinds of agents: searching agents and managing agents. The tasks of a searching agent (SA) consist of (see Figure 11.1):

- Selecting in its knowledge base the best search engine for a given query.
- Generating an answer using the chosen search engine.
- Actualizing its knowledge base on the basis of the final result determined as the consensus of results generated by all searching agents.

As the result of the actualization the used search engine obtains a weight referring to a given query.

The tasks of a managing agent (MA) consist of:

- Creating searching agents
- Determining consensus of answers generated by searching agents and checking consistency degree of the set of these answers
- Calculating the distances between the consensus and answers generated by searching agents and sending the results to these agents for actualizing their knowledge bases.

After each retrieval process and evaluation given by a MA, a SA writes the query to its knowledge base with the accuracy degree (i.e., the distance between its answer and the consensus). For the next query a SA does not draw the search engine but determines it in the following way. The agent compares the query to queries stored in the base and chooses such query which is the nearest and has accuracy degree greater than 50%. The chosen search engine will be that which has been used for this query. SAs have three algorithms for comparing queries and they can draw one of them. Owing to this their query bases are not similar to each other.

After all SAs have finished their retrieval processes a MA determines the consistency degree of answers generated by SAs taking into account their weights. At the beginning the weights are equal to one for all SAs. If the set of answers is not consistent enough (the consistency degree is too low) then the MA shows the user all answers. The user can choose the answer of a SA which in his opinion is the best or requires renewing the retrieval process. If the set of answers is consistent (the consistency level is high) then the MA determines the consensus and calculates the weights for SAs.

If a URL is repeated in many answers then it means that the relevance degree of this URL is large. If a URL occurs many times in an answer then a SA must eliminate the duplications first. The way to eliminate duplicated URLs in the answer of an agent is based on comparison of this URL to other URLs; if they are 80% similar then the system decides that they are identical. Owing to this, the answers of SAs are "clearer" before the consensus choice.

If a URL occurs in few answers or occurs on lower positions of the answers then in the consensus it should not occur at all, or if so, only at a lower position. The consensus determining algorithm allows omitting irrelevant URLs or at least placing them in the last positions of the final ranking. Concretely, assume that a URL (e.g., an advertising page) occurs at the first position of the answer generated by one agent, but it does not occur in the rankings of other agents. Then, in dependence on the number of SAs taking part in the retrieval, this URL may not appear in the final ranking, and even if so, it should be at a very low position. The larger the number of SAs is, the lower the position for this URL. So one can expect that the final ranking should be more relevant than each generated by a SA.

The second multiagent system is called MASE [127, 151, 152]. The mechanisms for retrieval in this metasearch engine are also based on consensus methods. However, the communication between agents and the interface are improved to a large degree. The agents in this system can learn about the preferences of users and also gather experience in determining the best component engines for queries.

11.3. A Conception for a Metasearch Engine

In this section we present a conception for designing a metasearch engine using multiagent technology and consensus methods. As opposed to AGWI and MASE we propose to build only one kind of agent, viz. a searching agent (SA). Owing to this we can save on agent communication costs. However, we plan other activity scopes for these agents. Their structure is presented as follows.

11.3.1. Knowledge Base of Searching Agents

The knowledge base of a SA consists of the following main components:

- Knowledge about queries and the best search engines for these queries (KQ)
- User profiles including user preferences (UP)

The component KQ of the knowledge base of SA should contain the following elements.

1. Base *Query_base* of queries which have been serviced by the agent in the past
2. Function *Sim* for measuring the similarity of queries
3. Procedure *Clu* for clustering the set of queries
4. Set *SE* of search engine identifiers
5. Procedure *Consensus* for calculating consensus of a set of answers delivered by search engines

6. Procedure *Con* for calculating the consistency level of the set of answers
7. Procedure *BeSE* which determines the best search engine for a query
8. Procedure *Weight* for calculating the weight of a search engine referring to a query

Below we present detailed descriptions of the above-mentioned elements.

1. The base *Query_base* of queries

The base *Query_base* of queries consists of queries clustered in classes. First we assume that a query has the following structure

$$t_1 \wedge t_2 \wedge \cdots \wedge t_k \wedge (\neg t_0)$$

or

$$t_1 \wedge t_2 \wedge \cdots \wedge t_k ,$$

where $t_0, t_1, t_2, \ldots, t_k$ are phrases (as a phrase we understand one or a sequence of several worlds of a natural language). Phrases $t_1, t_2, \ldots,$ and t_k are called *positive*, and phrase t_0 is called *negative*. This query structure is used in the majority of search engines. Notice that although in the query defined above there is a lack of a disjunction operator, in fact this operator may be included in phrases. For example, for the phrase *"knowledge integration"* a search engine will interpret it as \

$$\text{"}knowledge\text{"} \vee \text{"}integration\text{"}.$$

2. Function *Sim* for measuring the similarity of queries

Queries are clustered on the basis of similarity function between queries. The similarity function is calculated as follows.

- A query
$$t_1 \wedge t_2 \wedge \cdots \wedge t_k \wedge (\neg t_0)$$
may be transformed into the form:
$$t \wedge (\neg t_0),$$
where t is the phrase being the concatenation of phrases $t_1, t_2, \ldots,$ and t_k. For example, if

$$t_1 = \text{"}knowledge\ integration\text{"}$$

and

$$t_2 = \text{"}knowledge\ inconsistency\text{"}$$

then the concatenation will be the phrase

$$t = \text{"}knowledge\ integration\ knowledge\ inconsistency\text{"}.$$

If in a query there is no negative phrase then we may accept its form as $t \wedge (\neg t_0)$ where t_0 is an empty phrase. The same goes for positive phrases. By $len(t)$ we denote the length of phrase t. It is the number of characters occurring in t including the spaces between the words of the phrase. For example $len(\text{"knowledge integration"}) = 21$. Of course an empty phrase has length equal to 0.

- By $t \cap t'$ we denote the sequence of characters of maximal length length, which is included in both phrases t and t'. The similarity $\tau(t, t')$ of two phrases t and t' is calculated by the following formula,

$$\tau(t, t') = \begin{cases} 1 & \text{if } len(t) = len(t') = 0 \\[2mm] \dfrac{len(t \cap t')}{\max \{len(t), len(t')\}} & \text{otherwise.} \end{cases}$$

For example, for

$$t = \text{"knowledge integration"}$$

and

$$t' = \text{"knowledge inconsistency"}$$

we have

$$t \cap t' = \text{"knowledge in" and } \tau(t, t') = 12/23.$$

It is easy to show that if $t = t'$ then $\tau(t, t') = 1$, and if one of these phrases is empty then $\tau(t, t') = 0$.

- For two queries

$$q = t \wedge (\neg t_0)$$

and

$$q' = t' \wedge (\neg t'_0)$$

their similarity is defined as follows,

$$sim(q, q') = \frac{\tau(t,t') + \tau(t_0,t'_0)}{2}.$$

It obvious that $sim(q, q') = 1$ if and only if $q = q'$, $0 \le q, q' \le 1$, and function sim is a metric.

3. Procedure *Clu* for clustering the set of queries

Now having defined the similarity function between queries we may perform clustering of the set of queries.

Here similarly as in Chapter 10 for learners we propose to use the algorithm worked out by Kanungo et al. [62]. This algorithm is one of the most popular algorithms based on the *k*-mean strategy. The main steps of this algorithm for a set of queries are organized as follows.

- Step 1: Select randomly *k* queries as the starting centers (called *centroides*) of the clusters. Each centroid represents a cluster.
- Step 2: Assign each query of the set to the cluster for which the similarity between this query and the centroid is smallest.
- Step 3: Redetermine the centroid of each cluster, for example, by choosing the new centroid as the center of gravity of the cluster.
- Step 4: Repeat steps 2 and 3 until some convergence conditions have not been met (e.g., the centroids do not change).

As a result, the set of queries is divided into classes of a partition. For each class of queries there is a central query represented by centroid. The clustering process should be done time and again because of new queries, which may cause the clustering and the centroids to be inaccurate.

Denote then by Q the clustering of the query set,

$$Q = \{Q_1, Q_2, \ldots, Q_n\},$$

where $Q_1, Q_2, \ldots, Q_n$ are classes of similar queries with centroids $q_1, q_2, \ldots, q_n$, respectively.

A new query is classified to a class on the basis of the criterion that the distance between this query and the centroid of the class is minimal.

4. Set *SE* of search engines' identifiers

This is a simple set including such information about existing search engines as their identifiers and links enabling to run them. By E we denote the set of search engines which can potentially be used by the searching agent.

5. Procedure *Consensus* for calculating the consensus of a set of answers delivered by search engines.

As is known, when a new query comes, the agent runs not one but several search engines (the choice of these search engines is presented later in this section), and gathers the answers from them. For the set of answers the agent calculates their consensus. We assume that each answer is a ranking of URLs of documents.

Before the consensus choice the following actions should be taken into account.

- In an answer the number of URLs may be very large. For example, using Google the number of documents for a query often exceeds

100.000. For the effectiveness of the consensus choice procedure this number should be decreased. This action may have such practical justification that a user rarely reads more than 100 documents given by a search engine. In fact, most often the user only reads documents on the first screen (i.e., about 30 documents).

- In an answer one URL may repeat many times, as well as many URLs similar to each other may appear. It is then necessary to remove the similar URLs. For performing this we can treat a URL as a phrase and use function τ defined above to measure the similarity of URLs. A threshold can be proposed to accept two URLs to be similar, and one of them should be removed. Notice, however, that this procedure requires an overview of all pairs of URLs to get to know which of them should be removed. Therefore, the cost of this procedure may be large. For improving this we propose to sort the URLs first and this should help in decreasing the cost.

Now let's define a profile of N rankings of URLs as follows,

$$X = \{U_1, U_2, \ldots, U_N\},$$

where U_i is a ranking of different URLs. We do not assume the same number of URLs in each ranking as well as a URL must appear in all rankings. The distance function for this kind of ranking has been proposed in Chapter 10 (see Section 10.2.2). For rankings of URLs the distance function has the form:

$$\sigma(U_i, U_j) = \frac{\sum_{u \in Url} S_u(U_i, U_j)}{card(Url)},$$

where $S_u(U_i, U_j)$ is the share of a URL u in the distance and Url is the set of all URLs occurring in rankings belonging to X.

We assume that each ranking U_i is assigned with a weight w_i ($0 \leq w_i \leq 1$) of the search engine which has generated the ranking. These weights are calculated for the search engines generating these rankings. How to calculate the weights is presented in Paragraph 7 in this section.

We propose the procedure *Consensus* for choosing the consensus of given rankings, which is similar to Algorithm 10.1 presented in Chapter 10. The idea of this procedure is based on calculating for each URL a number equal to the sum of the indexes of positions on which this URL appears on the given rankings. The idea is very intuitive.

Algorithm 11.1.

Input: Set of N rankings of URLs

$$X = \{U_1, U_2, \ldots, U_N\}$$

with weights $w_1, w_2, \ldots, w_N$, respectively.

Output: A URL's ranking U^* minimizing sum $\sum_{i=1}^{N} w_i \cdot \sigma (U^*, U_i)$.

Procedure:

BEGIN

1. Determine *Url* as the set (without repetitions) of all URLs occurring in rankings belonging to X;

2. For each $u \in Url$ determine set with repetitions:

   $I_u = \{j \cdot w_i$: URL u occurs on the jth position

   of ranking U_i for $i = 1, 2, \ldots, N\}$;

3. For each $u \in Url$ calculate $J_u = \sum_{x \in I_u} x$;

4. Set in order the URLs in ranking U^* according to the increasing order of values J_u;

END.

This algorithm is simple and effective. If a URL is in a high-ranking position but in others it is in low positions then in the consensus this URL should not occupy a high position.

Notice also that Algorithm 11.1 may also be used for consensus determination for all profiles of rankings of elements (not necessarily of URLs). We later use this algorithm for other aims, such as consensus determination for lists of search engines.

6. Procedure *Con* for calculating the consistency level of the set of answers

For measuring the consistency level of answers delivered by component search engines we propose use of the function c_4 defined in Section 2.4.4 of Chapter 2. For calculation of the values of this function the following values are needed:

- The sum of distances between a ranking R and the rankings from set X:

$$\sigma_1(R,X) = \sum_{R' \in X} w' \cdot \sigma(R,R'),$$

where w' is the way of the search engine generating ranking R' (see Paragraph 7).

- The set of all sums of distances:

$$D(X) = \{\sigma_1(R,X): R \text{ is a ranking of some URLs from set } Url\}.$$

- The minimal sum of distances from a ranking to the elements of profile X:

$$\sigma_{min}(X) = \min (D(X)).$$

These parameters are now applied for defining the following consistency functions:

$$c_4(X) = 1 - \frac{1}{N}\sigma_{min}(X).$$

As we can see, value $\sigma_{min}(X)$ is in fact the sum of distances from the consensus to the rankings from X. This consensus is calculated by Algorithm 11.1, so it is very convenient to calculate the consistency level.

The consistency value informs us about the coherence of the answers delivered by the component search engines. The large value of consistency means that the rankings generated by the component search engines are similar to each other. In this case the consensus is more credible. So the aim of calculating the consistency of search engines' answers is to evaluate the pertinency of the consensus which is presented to the user as the final answer for his query. Here a threshold for consistency level may be used for making the decision as to whether the consensus should be given to the user. If the consistency is lower than the threshold then the consensus should not be assumed to be a good answer for the user query, and the agent should organize a new searching process choosing new search engines for this purpose.

The procedure described above is in some sense contradictory to the considerations presented in Chapter 8, where we have stated that for expert knowledge analysis the low value of consistency is better than the high value because this means the experts are from different fields and have different points of view. Owing to this the consensus is more precise (more similar to the proper solution of the problem they solve). However, in the case of search engines, although they are treated as experts (as we have considered in the Introduction) they are rather not experts in the full meaning. An answer given by a search engine is dependent only on the documents it has in the database and the way of indexing these documents, not on knowledge processing. Their autonomy is restricted to the search process and making a ranking of the retrieved documents. For these reasons we may assume that a document is really relevant to a user (i.e., in her opinion the document is useful to her) if a large number of search engines rank it in high positions. Owing to this assumption a document occurring in a high position only in one component ranking should not be presented to the user in a high position in the consensus.

7. Procedure *BeSE* which determines the best search engine for a query

Each query is assigned a search engine as the best engine determined by procedure *BeSE*. For a query *q* the component search engine which gives the nearest answer to the consensus is called the best search engine for this query.

Formally, let for query q there be used N component search engines $e_1, e_2, \ldots, e_N$, which generate the URL rankings $U_1, U_2, \ldots, U_N$, respectively. Let U^* be the consensus of profile $X = \{U_1, U_2, \ldots, U_N\}$, and let e_k be such a search engine that

$$\sigma(U_k, U^*) = \min \{\sigma(U_1, U^*), \sigma(U_2, U^*), \ldots, \sigma(U_N, U^*)\};$$

then e_k is the best search engine for query q.

8. Procedure *Weight* for calculating the weight of a search engine in a class of queries

We notice that there are n classes $Q_1, Q_2, \ldots, Q_n$ of queries. We denote $e_i(q)$ as the best search engine for query q in class Q_i for $i = 1, 2, \ldots, n$.

Thus in each class of queries each query is assigned with its best search engine. Denote by $E(Q_i)$ the set of best search engines for queries in class Q_i for $i = 1, 2, \ldots, n$. Of course set $E(Q_i)$ has repetitions, so the numbers of occurrences of different search engines may be different. For a search engine $e \in E(Q_i)$ let $occ(e)$ be the number of occurrences of e in set $E(Q_i)$. Then the weight $w(e,i)$ of search engine e in class Q_i is equal to

$$w(e,i) = \frac{occ(e)}{card(E(Q_i))}.$$

Of course we have $0 \le w(e,i) \le 1$ and

$$\sum_{e \in E(Q_i)} w(e,i) = 1.$$

Notice that when a new query appears in class Q_i the weights of search engines in set $E(Q_i)$ should be modified. Besides, the same search engine may have different weights in different classes.

Now we present the scheme of activities of the searching agent.

11.3.2. Retrieval Process of a Searching Agent

The scheme of the retrieval activities of a searching agent consists of the following steps:

1. User sends a query to the agent.
2. The new query is classified into a class.
3. The agent determines a list of search engines for the new query. The search engines are determined on the basis of their weights. The larger

the weight the higher chance a search engine has to be chosen. To restrict the list some threshold may be introduced.
4. The agent runs the chosen search engines with the new query; next it
gathers the answers from them and calculates their consensus and the
consistency.
5. If the consistency is low then the agent adds to the list new search
engines and reperforms step 4. If the consistency is high then the consensus is presented to the user as the result of the search.
6. The distances between the consensus and the answers given by component search engines are calculated, and on their basis the best
search engine for the query is chosen.
7. The agent actualizes the weights of the best search engines of queries
belonging to the class to which the new query has been classified.
8. The agent is now ready for serving a next new query.

The above steps present a cycle of the searching agent's life. To this cycle it is necessary to add a procedure of reclassification of the set of queries. Along with the inflow of new queries the actual classification may be
inaccurate, because the new queries may not be close to the centroids and
in consequence the centroids lose their role as the centres of the classes.

The cycle of a searching agent is presented in the case use diagram
(Figure 11.2) and activity diagram (Figure 11.3).

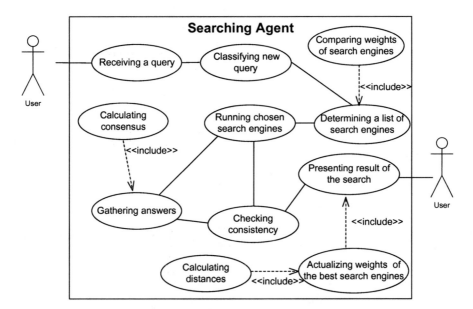

Figure 11.2. Case use diagram for a searching agent.

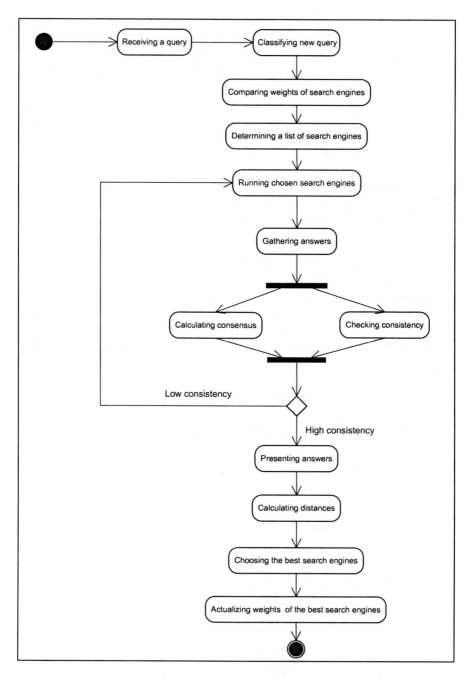

Figure 11.3. The activity diagram for a searching agent.

11.3.3. Cooperation between Searching Agents

Cooperation between searching agents is needed in the following situations.

- A searching agent cannot classify a new query to any class because the distances from the query to the centroids are too large.
- In the case of low consistency of the set of answers the agent cannot generate a new list of search engines because there are no search engines in reserve.
- For a new query there is not one but several best search engines. This may happen because a few search engines may obtain the same value of weight.
- Because of a very small number of users the knowledge base of a searching agent is too small for making any decision.

In these cases a searching agent can contact other searching agents and send them the query and a request for sending him the information needed for query processing. The cooperation steps are described as follows.

1. A searching agent a sends a query to other searching agents with a request to send him a list of search engines.
2. An agent who has obtained such a request processes the query performing steps 2 and 3 of the procedure defined in Section 11.3.2 for generating a list of the best search engines in her opinion, for the requested query.
3. Lists of search engines are sent to agent a.
4. Agent a makes the consensus choice of these lists using Algorithm 11.1 for rankings of search engines.
5. Agent a uses the consensus list for searching.

The details of this process are presented in Figure 11.4.

11.4. Recommendation Process

As is well known, in information retrieval systems recommendation can be effective if the user profile is used. A user profile includes information about the user, but its very important element is user feedback (this notion has been introduced in Section 11.2). Using a user profile for such purposes as recommendation, adaptation, or filtering documents for an information system is popular in the field of information retrieval.

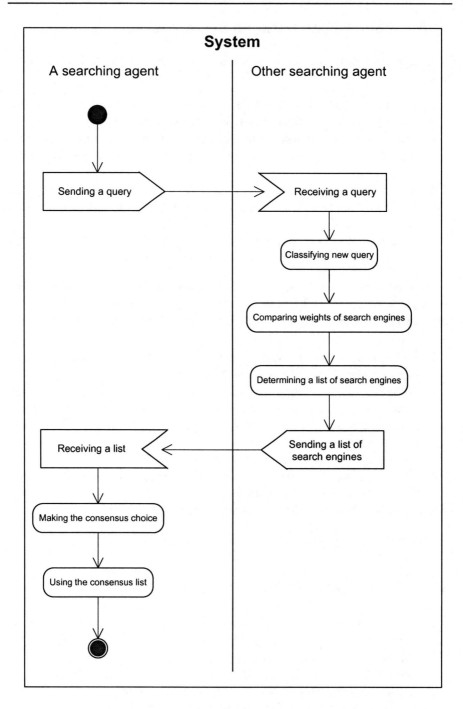

Figure 11.4. The cooperation diagram for searching agents.

McElligot and Sorensen [87] have developed a neural network approach employing a two-layer connectionist model to filter news documents in the Internet. Apart from the keywords, the system uses the context in which they occur to present a user profile. This system operates in two modes. The first mode is based on the learning phase, where sample documents are presented on input. The second mode is based on the comparison phase, where the retrieved documents are filtered before presenting them to the user. Owing to this mode the system can gather and learn about additional interesting documents.

In the model of Pazzani and others [135] the system asks the user to rank pages on a specific topic. Based on the content and ratings of these pages, the system learns a user profile that predicts if pages are of interest to the user. These authors have investigated a number of topics and in learning the system each user profile is considered referring to each topic. Pages are recommended from preselected Web sites. Similar to Pazzani et al.'s model, Balabanovic's system (called Fab) [10] requires the user to rank pages and it builds a user profile based on the rankings and content of pages. However, Fab considers recommendations based on profiles of all the other users of the system (although it does not identify users of similar interests). Fab possesses a collection agent that performs an offline best-first search of the Web for interesting pages.

In this work we have assumed that the multiagent metasearch engine uses the results of component search engines. Therefore for the recommendation aim we do not focus on the content of documents, but on the relationship between them and queries. We consider the recommendation process in two cases:

- Searching agents do not store data about users.
- Searching agents store user data.

These cases are analyzed in the next section.

11.4.1. Recommendation without User Data

In the first case similarly as in the majority of search engines the agents do not store the information about users; that is, they are anonymous. In this case we propose the following procedure for recommendation.

- A new query after being classified into a class, will be compared with other queries in the class for determining a list of queries which are maximally similar to it.

- The above-determined queries are recommended to the user for helping him to express his needs more precisely. In addition, it often happens that a user makes mistakes when writing the phrases. Owing to the recommendation of this type the agent can help the user remove the mistakes.
- If the user chooses one of the recommended queries then the agent can use the best engine determined for this query. If she does not choose any of the recommended queries then the procedure is the same as for a new query.

11.4.2. Recommendation with User Profiles

In the second case the searching agent has a possibility to gather information about users, among others owing to the logging-in procedure. A searching agent may be then treated as a personal agent of a user and it may build the user profile with the following structure.

- A set of queries which have been questioned by the user.
- Each such query is assigned with the best engine(s) (these data are from the knowledge base of the agent). A very important element of the user profile referring to a query is a set of documents (URLs) which the user has chosen (i.e., relevant documents) as the result of user feedback.

The structure of the user profile is represented by Table 11.1 with some example data.

Table 11.1. Structure of user profile

Query	Best engine	Relevant documents
q_1	e_1	u_1, u_4, u_{20}, u_{21}
q_2	e_1	$u_2, u_7, u_{22}, u_{30}, u_{32}$
q_3	e_2	u_8, u_9

The general procedure for recommendation is proposed as follows.

1. After identifying the user, the agent is ready to serve the user's new query.

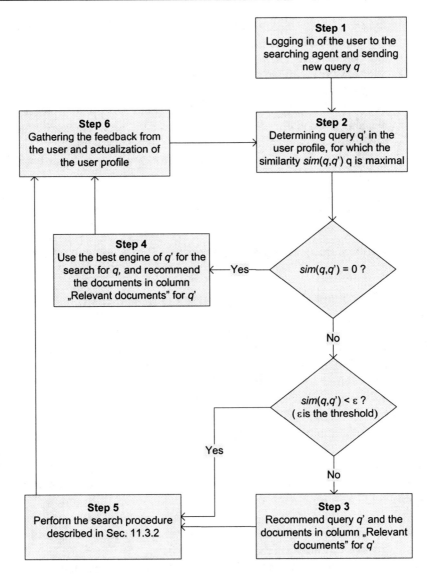

Figure 11.5. The recommendation scheme.

2. The new query is compared with other queries in her profile. The query which is most similar to the new query is chosen. To avoid the choice "by brute force" some threshold should be used. If the similarity between the new query and the chosen query is smaller than the threshold then the agent should treat the new query as "totally" new and should go to step 5.

3. If the new query is identical to one of the queries in the profile then the agent uses the best engine for this query for searching. Simultaneously the documents in column "Relevant documents" are recommended. Next the agent goes to step 6.

4. If the similarity between the new query and the chosen query is greater than or equal to the threshold then the agent recommends the chosen query and the documents related to this query. Simultaneously, step 5 is performed for generating the answer for this new query.

5. The procedure in Section 11.3.2 is run for generating the answer for this query.

6. The user may give some feedback. The agent remembers the query, its centroid, best search engine, and the list of chosen documents in the profile of the user.

The details of this procedure are presented by the scheme in Figure 11.5.

11.4.3. Recommendation by Query Modification

Note that the information included in the user profile may be used for query modification. Up to now we have suggested only that the user be recommended other queries similar to his new query, and the user makes the decision whether to modify the query. In this section we propose a procedure for an automatic query modification process. The aim of this procedure is to better reflect the need of the user in the query, without his acceptance. Automatic query modification process is a popular subject in the information retrieval field. Most often this process is organized for retrieval in vector models which is a very popular model for document organization because of its precision and possibilities for mathematical operations. The literature for this subject is very rich; see among others [9, 10]. In [30] the authors presented a vector model of user profiles and personalization for Web-based information retrieval system, and proposed a model for automatic query modification.

In this book we have assumed that we do not deal with the structures of document bases as well as the mechanisms for retrieval. We use only search engines and rely on their document bases. Therefore, for working out the query modification process we use only the information included in the user profile defined in the previous section.

However, without analyzing the relevant documents which have been indicated by the user in her feedback it is impossible to build credible needs of the user. Therefore, we propose to access these documents in the column "Relevant documents" of Table 11.1 in order to get to know if the needs of the user have changed, and if not, if they are correctly and completely expressed in the query. For this aim we may use an indexing algorithm to analyze these documents and build for a document one vector representing its content.

Formally, assume that we are analyzing a new query $q*$ of a concrete user who is included in our base and has a user profile. Let's denote by

- Q: The set of his queries stored in the profile
- $e(q)$: The best engine for query q
- $R(q)$: The set of relevant documents, which have been indicated by the user

For each document from $R(q)$ let's assume the existence of a set of terms $T = \{t_1, t_2, \ldots, t_n\}$[3] and let's build a vector

$$v_q = <v_{q1}, v_{q2}, \ldots, v_{qn}>,$$

where v_{qi} is the weight of term t_i for $0 \le v_{qi} \le 1$ and $i = 1, 2, \ldots, n$.

Our aim is to determine a new query which should better reflect the needs of the user than query $q*$. The idea of our method is based on the following general steps:

1. First choose those queries from set Q which are similar to query $q*$.
2. Create from the chosen queries the set of relevant documents and their vectors.
3. On the basis of the vectors calculate one vector best representing them.
4. On the basis of the calculated vector determine a query $q*'$ which replaces query $q*$.

Some commentary follows. The first step is intuitive and follows from the assumption that the stored queries in the user profile are more credible (in the sense of user needs representation) than the new query $q*$. It is further assumed that if there are queries similar to the new query, then the relevant documents referring to these queries should contain the real needs of the user. Therefore, the second and third steps should be performed for yielding a vector which will be the basis for determining query $q*'$. For the third step the vector to be calculated should be a consensus of the given vectors. As the criterion for consensus choice we may accept criterion O_2 (minimizing the sum of squared distances between the consensus and the

---

[3] The source of terms may be WordNet (http://wordnet.princeton.edu/).

given vectors). As has been proved in Chapters 3 and 8, this criterion guarantees the "fairness" of the consensus and small computational complexity for vector spaces. For the last step, a term which has high weight in the consensus vector should occur in the query $q^{*\prime}$ as a positive term, whereas a term with low weight should occur as a negative one.

The algorithm for query modification is presented as follows.

Algorithm 11.2.

Input: Profile of a user and a new query q^*, thresholds ε_1, ε_2, ε_3.

Output: A query $q^{*\prime}$ which could replace query q^*.

Procedure:

BEGIN

    1. Calculate $Q^* = \{q \in Q: sim(q,q^*) > \varepsilon_1\}$;

    2. If $Q^* = \varnothing$ then GOTO 9;

    3. Create $R(Q^*) = \bigcup_{q \in Q^*} R(q)$;

    4. Create $V(Q^*)$ as the set of vectors representing documents from set $R(Q^*)$;

    5. Calculate the consensus
$$v^* = <v_1, v_2, \ldots, v_n>$$
of set $V(Q^*)$ satisfying criterion O_2 using the results of Theorem 8.1;

    6. Determine sets:
$$T_1 = \{t_i \in T: v_i > \varepsilon_2 \text{ and } i = 1, 2, \ldots, n\}$$
    and
$$T_2 = \{t_i \in T: v_i < \varepsilon_3 \text{ and } i = 1, 2, \ldots, n\};$$

    7. Create a phrase $q^{*\prime}$ consisting of terms from sets T_1 and T_2 where terms from set T_1 are positive, and terms from set T_2 are negative;

    8. GOTO END;

    9. $q^{*\prime} := q^*$;

END.

The scheme for recommendation with query modification is presented in Figure 11.6.

An example is given below.

Example 11.1. Let the user profile be presented by Table 11.2, where

Table 11.2. Example of a user profile

Query	Best search engine	Relevant documents
q_1	e_1	u_1, u_4, u_{20}, u_{21}
q_2	e_1	$u_2, u_7, u_{22}, u_{30}, u_{32}$
q_3	e_2	u_{22}, u_{30}, u_8, u_9
q_4	e_3	u_8, u_{11}
q_5	e_3	u_6, u_{11}

- q_1 represents query *"knowledge base"*
- q_2 represents query *"database schemas integration"*
- q_3 represents query *"data integration"*
- q_4 represents query *"ontology integration"*
- q_5 represents query *"ontology"*

Let the thresholds be:
$$\varepsilon_1 = 0.5, \quad \varepsilon_2 = 0{,}5, \quad \text{and} \quad \varepsilon_3 = 0.2.$$
Let the new query of the user be
$$q^* = \text{"knowledge integration"}.$$
We have:
$$sim(q_1,q^*) = 10/21,$$
$$sim(q_2,q^*) = 12/28,$$
$$sim(q_3,q^*) = 12/21,$$
$$sim(q_4,q^*) = 12/21,$$
$$sim(q_5,q^*) = 0.$$
Because
$$sim(q_3,q^*) = sim(q_4,q^*) = 12/21 > \varepsilon_1 = \varepsilon_2$$
then
$$Q^* = \{q_3, q_4\} = \{\text{"data integration"}, \text{"ontology integration"}\}$$
and
$$R(Q^*) = \{u_{22}, u_{30}, u_8, u_8, u_9, u_{11}\}.$$
Notice that $R(Q^*)$ is a set with repetitions. This fact is essential for consensus choice. Let the vectors for documents for set $R(Q^*)$ be presented as follows.

Document	Terms				
	data model	*data integration*	*ontology integration*	*knowledge integration*	*data-base*
u_{22}	0.2	0.6	0.2	0.8	0.2
u_{30}	0.1	0.8	0.2	0.6	0.3
u_8	0.1	0.8	0.9	0.7	0.1
u_8	0.1	0.8	0.9	0.7	0.1
u_9	0.1	0.8	0.2	0.6	0.3
u_{11}	0.1	0.5	0.9	0.8	0
Consensus v^*	0.12	0.72	0.55	0.7	0.17

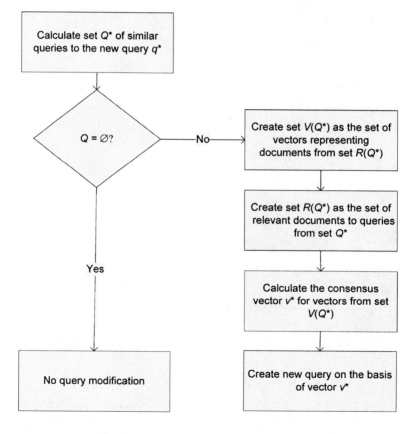

Figure 11.6. Query modification scheme.

From the consensus we have

$T_1 = \{data\ integration,\ ontology\ integration,$
$$knowledge\ integration\}$$
and
$T_2 = \{data\ model,\ database\}.$

Thus the modified query should have logical form:

$q^{*\prime} = data\ integration \wedge ontology\ integration$
$$\wedge\ knowledge\ integration \wedge \neg data\ model \wedge \neg database.$$

We can see that the modified query is more concrete than query q^*. ♦

11.5. Conclusions

The advantages of using agents in metasearch engines follow from their autonomy and their communication and cooperation abilities. Although utilization of several search engines for the same query is not novel, the method for reconciling the results presented here is. Its advantage is that it does not need information about the user (preferences, profiles, etc.). It works on the basis of an assumption that search engines may be treated as experts who are entrusted to solve the same problem of information retrieval. Then as stated in Chapter 8, the reconciled solution should be more credible than those proposed by individual experts.

The conception of a multiagent metasearch engine presented here differs fundamentally from the conceptions worked out earlier [113, 116]. In this chapter only one kind of agent (searching agents) is proposed. The knowledge base of searching agents is much richer. In addition, procedures for recommendation, adaptation, and query modification have been proposed. The procedures for determining the list of engines for a new query, as well as for reconciling the inconsistent answers generated by component search engines presented in this work are novel.

12. Conclusions

The main subject of this book is related to the distribution aspect of knowledge inconsistency resolution. In this book the author presents several methods for inconsistent knowledge processing which are based on using consensus computing mechanisms. Consensus computing is known in the decision-making field, but it is less known as a tool for reconciling inconsistency of knowledge. The book presents the extended, more complete, and unified versions of the latest research results of the author on this subject. These results have been included in over 50 scientific papers published in prestigious international journals (indexed by ISI), or in postproceedings published by, among others, Springer-Verlag, Kluwer Academic, and other international journals and conference proceedings [1, 30–32, 55, 63–65, 75–77, 83–85, 98–127, 146–148, 161, 162].

This book also includes several novel methods for processing inconsistent knowledge on syntactic and semantic levels, as well as for resolving inconsistency of ontologies. One can find here the definitions of knowledge inconsistency, consistency degree for conflict profiles, susceptibility to consensus, their properties, and inconsistency resolution for the abovementioned levels.

In this book several applications of the proposed methods from the fields of expert knowledge analysis, multiagent systems, information retrieval, recommender systems, and intelligent tutoring systems are also presented.

As mentioned in the Preface, the main contributions of this book include the following elements.

- A model for conflict and inconsistency of knowledge which contains such elements as conflict representation and consistency measures for conflict profiles.
- A model for consensus which contains postulates for consensus choice functions, their classes, an approach to set susceptibility to consensus, and methods for its achieving.
- A method for resolving knowledge inconsistency on the syntactic level, which is worked out for such knowledge structures as disjunctive, conjunctive, and fuzzy-based. In each of these structures the

manner of representing positive knowledge and negative knowledge is proposed.

- A method for resolving knowledge inconsistency on the semantic level which is worked out for such knowledge structures as disjunctive, conjunctive, and fuzzy-based.
- A method for knowledge integration with relational structures.
- A method for inconsistency resolution for ontologies based on consensus tools. A new classification of ontology conflicts is also proposed.
- A consensus-based method for reconciling inconsistency of expert knowledge. Assuming concrete structures of expert knowledge we have proved that inconsistency is often profitable and with some restrictions the consensus of expert opinions is better than any of these opinions separately.
- A method for determination of a learning scenario in intelligent tutoring systems using consensus methods and rough classification algorithms.
- A detailed conception of a metasearch engine for information retrieval on the Internet using multiagent technology. Inconsistency resolution methods are used in reconciling knowledge and answers given by different agents for the same query. Recommendation procedures are also proposed.

These results do not cover all problems of the subject related to inconsistent knowledge management. The following problems are very interesting and should be solved in the future.

- Inconsistency resolution on the syntactic and semantic levels for other (more complex) structures of logic formulae. This problem is useful also for resolving inconsistency of ontologies on the level of axioms.
- Inconsistency resolution on the mentioned levels taking into account the temporal aspect of knowledge.
- A more general model for expert knowledge processing and investigation of the relationships between expert solutions and the proper solution of a problem.
- Investigation of the influence of behavior of a profile element on consensus.
- Investigation of relationships of the so-called distributed consensuses (i.e., consensuses of particular classes of profiles) and the global consensus (i.e., the consensus of all elements of the profile).

References

1. Aftarczuk K, Kozierkiewicz A, Nguyen NT (2006) Using representation choice methods for a medical diagnosis problem. In: *Proc. of KES 2006, Lecture Notes in Artificial Intelligence* 4253, New York: Springer, pp. 805–812.
2. Aizerman MA (1985) New problems in the general choice theory. *Social Choice Welfare* 2: 235–382.
3. Amgoud L, Cayrol C (2002) Inferring from inconsistency in preference-based argumentation frameworks. *Journal of Automated Reasoning* 29: 125–169.
4. Arieli O (2003) Reasoning with different levels of uncertainty. *Journal of Applied Non-Classical Logics* 13: 317–343.
5. Arieli O, Avron A (1999) A model-theoretic approach for recovering consistent data from inconsistent knowledge bases. *Journal of Automatic Reasoning* 2: 253–309.
6. Arrow KJ (1963) *Social Choice and Individual Values*. New York: Wiley.
7. Avron A, Lev I (2005) Non-deterministic multiple-valued structures. *Journal of Logic and Computation* 15: 241–261.
8. Badache N, Hurfin M, Madeco R (1999) Solving the consensus problem in a mobile environment. In: *Proc. of IEEE International Performance, Computing and Communications Conference*. Piscataway NJ: IEEE, pp. 29–35.
9. Baeza YR, Ribeiro NB (1999) *Modern Information Retrieval*. New York: ACM Press.
10. Balabanovic M (1997) An adaptive web page recommendation service. In: *Proc. of 1st International Conference on Autonomous Agents*. New York: ACM Press, pp. 378–385.
11. Balzer R (1991) Tolerating inconsistency. In: *Proc. of the 13th International Conference on Software Engineering*. Washington, DC: IEEE Press, pp. 158–165.
12. Barthelemy JP, Guenoche A, Hudry O (1989) Median linear orders: Heuristics and a branch and bound algorithm. *European Journal of Operational Research* 42: 313–325.
13. Barthelemy JP, Janowitz MF (1991) A formal theory of consensus. *SIAM Journal of Discrete Mathematics* 4: 305–322.

14. Barthelemy JP, Leclerc B (1995) The median procedure for partitions. *DIMACS Series in Discrete Mathematics and Theoretical Computer Science* 19: 3–33.

15. Bazzi RA, Neiger G, Peterson GL (1997) On the use of registers in achieving wait-free consensus. *Distributed Computing* 10: 117–127.

16. Benferhat S, Dubois D, Prade H (1997) Some syntactic approaches to the handling of inconsistent knowledge bases: A comparative study. Part 1: The flat case. *Studia Logica* 58: 17–45.

17. Benferhat S, Garcia L (2002) Handling locally stratified inconsistent knowledge bases. *Studia Logica* 70: 77–104.

18. Birnbaum E, Lozinskii EL (2003) Consistent subsets of inconsistent systems: structure and behaviour. *Journal of Exp. Theory Artificial Intelligence*: 15, 25–46.

19. Bock HH, Day WHE, McMorris FR (1998) Consensus rules for committee elections. *Mathematical Social Sciences* 37: 219–232.

20. Bogart KP (1973) Preference structure I: Distance between transitive preference relations. *Journal of Math Sociology* 3: 455–470.

21. Bordogna G, Pasi G (2004) A model for a SOft Fusion of Information Accesses on the web. *Fuzzy Sets and Systems* 48: 105–118.

22. Bremer M (2005) *An Introduction to Paraconsistent Logics*. New York: Peter Lang.

23. Brown FN (1991) *Boolean Reasoning*. Hingham, MA: Kluwer Academic.

24. Brusilovsky P (1996) Methods and techniques of adaptive hypermedia. *User Modelling and User-Adapted Interaction* 6: 87–129.

25. Carver CA, Howard RA, Lavelle E (1996) Enhancing student learning by incorporating learning styles into adaptive hypermedia. In: *Proc. of Conf. on Educational Multimedia and Hypermedia*, Boston 1996, pp. 118–123.

26. Chen L, Sycara K (1998) Webmate – Personal agent for browsing and searching. In: *Proc. of the 2nd International Conference on Autonomous Agents*, St Paul. ACM Press, New York, pp. 132–139.

27. Coulouris G, Dollimore J, Kindberg T (2001) *Distributed Systems, Concepts and Design*. Reading, MA: Addison-Wesley.

28. Crow L, Shadbolt N (2001) Extracting focused knowledge from the semantic web. *International Journal of Human-Computer Studies* 54: 155–184.

29. Daniłowicz C, Nguyen HC (2002) Using user profiles in intelligent information retrieval. In: *Proc. of ISMIS'2002*, Lecture Notes in Computer Science 2366, New York: Springer, pp. 223–222.

30. Daniłowicz C, Nguyen HC, Nguyen NT (2003) Model of user profiles and personalization for web-based information retrieval systems. In: Abramowicz W (Ed.) *Knowledge Based Information Retrieval and Filtering from Internet*. Hingham, MA: Kluwer Academic, pp. 121–136.

31. Daniłowicz C, Nguyen NT (1988) Consensus-based partition in the space of ordered partitions. *Pattern Recognition* 21: 269–273.

32. Daniłowicz C, Nguyen NT (2003) Consensus methods for solving inconsistency of replicated data in distributed systems. *Distributed and Parallel Databases – An International Journal* 14: 53–69.

33. Date CJ (2004) *An Introduction to Database Systems*. Reading, MA: Addison-Wesley.

34. Day WHE (1981) The complexity of computing metric distances between partitions. *Mathematical Social Science* 1: 269–287.

35. Day WHE (1988) Consensus methods as tools for data analysis. In: Bock HH (Ed.), *Classification and Related Methods of Data Analysis, Proc. of IFC'87*. North-Holland, pp. 317–324.

36. De Kleer J (1986) An assumption-based TMS. *Artificial Intelligence* 28: 127–162.

37. Doyle J (1979) A truth maintenance system. *Artificial Intelligence* 12: 231–272.

38. Dunn R, Dunn K (1999) *The Complete Guide to the Learning Strategies in Service System*. Boston: Allyn & Bacon.

39. Ephrati E, Rosenschein JS (1998) Deriving consensus in multi-agent systems. *Artificial Intelligence* 87: 21–74.

40. Fehrer D (1993) A unifying framework for reason maintenance. In: Clark M et al (Eds.) *Symbolic and Qualitative Approaches to Reasoning and Uncertainty*, Lecture Notes in Computer Science 747, New York: Springer, pp. 113–120.

41. Felder R (1993) Reaching the second tier learning and teaching styles in college science education. *Journal of College Science Teaching* 23: 286–290.

42. Felder RM, Silverman LK (1988) Learning and teaching styles in engineering education. *Engineering Education* 78: 674–681.

43. Fensel D (2001) *Ontologies: Silver Bullet for Knowledge Management and Electronic Commerce*. New York: Springer-Verlag.

44. Ferber J (1999) *Multi-Agent Systems*. New York: Addison-Wesley.

45. Fernadez-Breis JT, Martinez-Bejar R (2002) A cooperative framework for integrating ontologies. *International Journal of Human-Computer Studies* 56: 665–720.

46. Fishburn PC (1977) Condorcet social choice functions. *SIAM Journal of Applied Mathematics* 33: 469–489.

47. Gardenfors P (1988) *Knowledge in Flux*. Cambridge, MA: MIT Press.

48. Gardner SP (2005) Ontologies and semantic data integration. *Drug Discovery Today* 14: 1001–1007.

49. Glover E, Lawrence S (1999) Architecture of a meta search engine that supports user information needs. In: *Proc. of the 8th International Conference on Information and Knowledge Management*. ACM Press, New York, pp. 210–216.

50. Grant J, Subrahmanian VS (1995) Reasoning in inconsistent knowledge bases. *IEEE Transactions on Knowledge and Data Engineering* 7: 177–189.

51. Gruber TR (1993) *A Translation Approach to Portable Ontology Specifications*. Knowledge System Laboratory. Academic Press Stanford University.

52. Guo P, Zeng DZ, Shishido H (2002) Group decision with inconsistent knowledge. *IEEE Transactions on Systems, Man and Cybernetics*, Part A, 32: 670–679.

53. Hameed A, Sleeman D., Preece A (2002) Detecting mismatches among experts' ontologies acquired through knowledge elicitation. *Knowledge-Based Systems* 15: 265–273.

54. Helpern JY, Moses Y (2001) Knowledge and common knowledge in distributed environment. *Journal of the Association for Computing Machinery* 37: 549–587.

55. Hernes M, Nguyen NT (2004) Deriving consensus for incomplete ordered partitions. In: Nguyen NT (Ed.) *Intelligent Technologies for Inconsistent Knowledge Processing*. Advanced Knowledge International, Adelaide, Australia, pp. 39–56.

56. Herrmann N (1988) *The Creative Brain*. Lake Lure, NC: Brain Books.

57. Holt J (2001) *UML (Unified Modelling Language) for Systems Engineers*. Institution of Electrical Engineers.

58. Hunter A (1998) Paraconsistent logics. In: Gabbay D, Smets P (Eds) *Handbook of Defeasible Reasoning and Uncertain Information*. Kluwer Academic Publishers, pp. 13–43.

59. Hunter A (2003) Evaluating the significance of inconsistencies. In: *Proc. of the International Joint Conference on AI (IJCAI'03)* San Mateo, CA: Morgan Kaufmann, pp. 468–473.

60. Jøsang A, Grandison T (2003) Conditional inference in subjective logic. In: Wang X. (Ed.) *Proc. of the 6th International Conference on Information Fusion*, 2003, pp. 279–311.

61. Juszczyszyn K, Nguyen NT, Kołaczek G et al. (2006) Agent-based approach for distributed intrusion detection system design. In: *Proc. of ICCS 2006*, Lecture Notes in Computer Science 3993, New York: Springer, pp. 208–215.

62. Kanungo T et al. (2002) An efficient k-means clustering algorithm: Analysis and implementation. *IEEE Transactions on Pattern Analysis and Machine Intelligence* 24: 881–892.

63. Katarzyniak RP, Nguyen NT (2000) Reconciling inconsistent profiles of agents' knowledge states in distributed multi-agent systems using consensus methods. *System Science* 26: 93–119.

64. Katarzyniak RP, Nguyen NT (2002) Modification of weights of conflict profile's elements and dependencies of attributes in consensus model. In: *Proc. of RSCTC 2002*, Lecture Notes in Artificial Intelligence 2475, New York: Springer, pp. 131–138.

65. Katarzyniak RP, Nguyen NT (2002) Solving conflicts of agent knowledge states in multi-agent systems. In: *Proc. of SOFSEM 2002*, Lecture Notes in Artificial Intelligence 2540, New York: Springer, pp. 231–239.

66. Kelly B, Tangney B (2002) Incorporating learning characteristics into an intelligent tutor. In: *Proc. of ITS 2002*, Lecture Notes in Computer Science 2363, New York: Springer, pp. 729–738.

67. Kiewra M, Nguyen NT (2005) Non–textual document ranking using crawler information and web usage mining. In: *Proc. of KES 2005*, Lecture Notes in Artificial Intelligence 3682, New York: Springer, pp. 520–526.

68. Kemeny JG (1959) Mathematics without numbers. *Daedalus* 88: 577–591.

69. Kifer M, Lozinskii EL (1992) A logic for reasoning with inconsistency. *Journal of Automatic Reasoning* 9: 179–215.

70. Knight K (2002) Measuring inconsistency. *Journal of Philosophical Logic* 31: 77–98.

71. Kobsa A, Koenemann J, Pohl W (2001) Personalized hypermedia presentation techniques for improving online customer relationships. *Knowledge Engineering Review* 16: 111–155.

72. Kołaczek G, Pieczynska A, Juszczyszyn K, Grzech A, Katarzyniak RP, Nguyen NT (2005) A mobile agent approach to intrusion detection in network systems. In: *Proc. of KES 2005*, Lecture Notes in Artificial Intelligence 3682, New York: Springer, pp. 514–519.

73. Kolb DA (1984) *Experimental Learning: Experience as a Source of Learning and Development*. Englewood Cliffs, NJ: Prentice-Hall.

74. Kukla E (2002) Outline of tutoring strategy construction method for multimedia intelligent tutoring systems. In: *Proc of Multimedia and Web-based Systems Conference – MISSI'2002, Wroclaw*, pp. 297–308 (in Polish).

75. Kukla E, Nguyen NT, Sobecki J et al. (2003) A model conception for learner profile construction and determination of optimal scenario in intelligent learning systems In: *Proc. of KES'2003 Oxford UK*, Lecture Notes in Artificial Intelligence 2774, New York: Springer, pp. 1216–1222.

76. Kukla E, Nguyen NT, Sobecki J et al. (2004) Determination of learning scenarios in intelligent web-based learning environment. In: *Proc. of IEA-AIE 2004*, Lecture Notes in Artificial Intelligence 3029, New York: Springer, pp. 759–768.

77. Kukla E, Nguyen NT, Sobecki J et al. (2004) A model conception for learner profile construction and determination of optimal scenario in intelligent learning systems. *International Journal of Interactive Technology and Smart Education* 1: 171–184.

78. Lieberman H (1995) Letizia: An agent that assists web browsing. In: *Proc. of International Joint Conference on Artificial Intelligence*. San Mateo, CA: Morgan Kaufmann, pp. 924–929.

79. Lipski W (1979) On semantic issues connected with incomplete information databases. *ACM Transactions on Database Systems* 4: 262–269.

80. Lipski W, Marek W (1986) *Combinatorial Analysis*. Warsaw: WTN (in Polish).

81. Loyer Y, Spyratos N, Stamate D (2000) *Hypothesis Support for Information Integration in Four-Valued Logics*. Lecture Notes in Computer Science, vol. 1872, New York: Springer, pp. 536–548.

82. Loyer Y, Spyratos N, Stamate D (2000) Integration of information in four-valued logics under non-uniform assumption. In: *Proc. of 30th IEEE International Symposium on Multiple-Valued Logic*, pp. 180–193.

83. Małowiecki M, Nguyen NT (2004) Consistency measures and consensus susceptibility for conflict profiles. In: *Proc. of 15th International Conference on System Science*. Wroclaw Univ. Tech Press, pp. 173–180.

84. Małowiecki M, Nguyen NT (2004) Consistency functions for reconciling knowledge inconsistency. In: Nguyen NT (Ed.) *Intelligent Technologies for Inconsistent Knowledge Processing*. Advanced Knowledge International, Adelaide, Australia, pp. 73–92.

85. Małowiecki M, Nguyen NT, Zgrzywa M (2004) Using consistency measures and attribute dependencies for solving conflicts in adaptive systems. In: *Proc. of ICCS 2004*, Lecture Notes in Computer Science 3038, New York: Springer, pp. 537–545.

86. Marcelloni F, Aksit M (2001) Leaving inconsistency using fuzzy logic. *Information and Software Technology* 43: 725–741.

87. McElligot M, Sorensen H (1994) An evolutionary connectionist approach to personal information filtering. In: *Proceeding of the Fourth Irish Neural Network Conference*, Dublin, Ireland, pp. 141–146.

88. McMorris FR, Mulder HM, Powers RC (2000) The median function on median graphs and semilattices. *Discrete Applied Mathematics* 101: 221–230.

89. McMorris FR, Powers RC (1995) The median procedure in a formal theory of consensus. *SIAM Journal of Discrete Mathematics* 14: 507–516.

90. McMorris FR, Powers RC (1997) The median function on weak hierarchies. *DIMACS Series in Discrete Mathematics and Theoretical Computer Science* 37: 265–269.

91. Menczer F (2003) Complementing search engines with online web mining agents. *Decision Support Systems* 35: 195–212.

92. Montaner M, Lopez B, De La Rosa JL (2003) A taxonomy for recommender agents on the Internet. *Artificial Intelligence Review* 19: 285–330.

93. Murray K, Porter B (1990) Developing a tool for knowledge integration: Initial results. *International Journal of Man-Machine Studies* 33: 373–383.

94. Musial K, Nguyen NT (1989) On the nearest product of partitions. *Bulletin of Polish Academy of Sciences* 36: 333–338.

95. Naqvi S, Rossi F (1990) Reasoning in inconsistent databases. In: *Logic Programming, Proc. of the North American Conference*. Cambridge, MA: MIT Press, pp. 255–272.

96. Newman WM, Lamming MG (1996) *Interactive System Design*. Harlow, UK: Addison-Wesley.

97. Ng KC, Abramson B (1990) Uncertainty management in expert systems. *IEEE Expert: Intelligent Systems and Their Applications* 5: 29–48.

98. Nguyen NT (2000) Using consensus methods for determining the representation of expert information in distributed systems. In: Cerri S (Ed.) *Proc. of AIMSA'2000*, Lecture Notes on Artificial Intelligence 1904, New York: Springer, pp. 11–20.

99. Nguyen NT (2000) Using consensus methods for solving conflicts of data in distributed systems. In: Bartosek M (Ed.) *Proc. of 27th SOFSEM*, Lecture Notes in Computer Science 1963, New York: Springer, pp. 409–417.

100. Nguyen NT (2001) Representation choice methods as the tool for solving uncertainty in distributed temporal database systems with indeterminate valid time. In: *Proc. of IEA-AIE 2001*, Lecture Notes in Artificial Intelligence 2070, New York: Springer, pp. 445–454.

101. Nguyen NT (2001) Using consensus for solving conflict situations in fault-tolerant distributed systems. In: *Proc. of First IEEE/ACM Symposium on Cluster Computing and the Grid 2001*. IEEE Computer Press, pp. 379–385.

102. Nguyen NT (2001) Consensus-based timestamps in distributed temporal databases. *The Computer Journal* 44: 398–409.

103. Nguyen NT (2001) Using distance functions to solve representation choice problems. *Fundamenta Informaticae* 48: 2001.

104. Nguyen NT (2002) *Methods for Consensus Choice and their Applications in Conflict Resolving in Distributed Systems*. Wroclaw University of Technology Press (in Polish).

105. Nguyen NT (2002) Consensus system for solving conflicts in distributed systems. *Journal of Information Sciences* 147: 91–122.

106. Nguyen NT (2003) Criteria for consensus susceptibility in conflicts resolving. In: Inuiguchi M, Tsumoto S, Hirano S (Eds.) *Rough Set Theory and Granular Computing. Series Studies in Fuzziness and Soft Computing* vol. 125. New York: Springer-Verlag, pp. 323–333.

107. Nguyen NT (2004) Consensus methodology for inconsistent knowledge processing. In: Nguyen NT (Ed.) *Intelligent Technologies for Inconsistent Knowledge Processing*. Advanced Knowledge International, Adelaide, Australia, pp. 3–20.

108. Nguyen NT (2005) Processing inconsistency of knowledge on semantic level. *Journal of Universal Computer Science* 11: 285–302.

109. Nguyen NT (2005) Modal time and processing its inconsistency in temporal data collections. In: Katarzyniak RP (Ed.) *Ontologies and Soft Methods in Knowledge Management*. Advanced Knowledge International, Adelaide, Australia, pp. 101–119.

110. Nguyen NT (2006) Methods for achieving susceptibility to consensus for conflict profiles. *Journal of Intelligent & Fuzzy Systems* 17: 219–229.

111. Nguyen NT (2006) Conflicts of ontologies – classification and consensus-based methods for resolving. In: Gabrys B, Howllet RJ, Jain LC (Eds.) *Proc.*

of KES 2006, Lecture Notes in Artificial Intelligence 4252, New York: Springer, pp. 267–274.

112. Nguyen NT (2006) Using consensus methodology in processing inconsistency of knowledge. In: Last M et al (Eds.) *Advances in Web Intelligence and Data Mining.* New York: Springer-Verlag, pp. 161–170.

113. Nguyen NT, Blazowski A, Malowiecki M (2005) A multi-agent system aiding information retrieval in Internet using consensus methods. In: *Proc. of SOFSEM 2005*, Lecture Notes in Computer Science 3381, New York: Springer, pp. 399–403.

114. Nguyen NT, Daniłowicz C (2003) Deriving consensus for conflict data in web-based systems. In: *Proc. of IEA-AIE 2003*, Lecture Notes in Artificial Intelligence 2718, New York: Springer, pp. 254–263.

115. Nguyen NT, Daniłowicz C (2004) Methods for reducing the number of representatives in representation choice tasks. In: *Proc. of IEA-AIE 2004*, Lecture Notes in Artificial Intelligence 3029, New York: Springer, pp. 154–163.

116. Nguyen NT, Gandza M, Paprzycki M (2006) A consensus-based multi-agent approach for information retrieval in Internet. In: *Proc. of ICCS 2006*, Lecture Notes in Computer Science 3993, New York: Springer, pp. 224–231.

117. Nguyen NT, Katarzyniak RP (Eds.) (2006) Multi-agent Systems, Ontologies and Conflict Resolution. Special Issue in *Journal of Intelligent & Fuzzy Systems* 17(3).

118. Nguyen NT, Małowiecki M (2004) Consistency function for conflict profiles. LNCS *Transactions on Rough Sets* 1: 169–186.

119. Nguyen NT, Małowiecki M (2004) Deriving consensus for conflict situations with respect to its susceptibility. In: *Proc. of KES 2004*, Wellington New Zealand, Lecture Notes in Artificial Intelligence 3214, New York: Springer, pp. 1179–1186.

120. Nguyen NT, Małowiecki M (2005) Using consensus susceptibility and consistency measures for inconsistent knowledge management. In: *Proc. of PAKDD'05*, Lecture Notes in Artificial Intelligence 3518, New York: Springer, pp. 545–554.

121. Nguyen NT, Rusin M (2006) A consensus-based approach for ontology integration. In: Butz C, Nguyen NT, Takama Y et al. (Eds.) *Proc. of WI/IAT'06 Workshops.* Piscataway, NJ: IEEE Computer Society, pp. 514–517.

122. Nguyen NT, Sobecki J (2001) Designing intelligent user interfaces using consensus-based methods for user profile determination. In: J. Zendulka (Ed.), *Proc. of Int. Conference on Information System Modelling.* Acta MOSIS, pp. 139–146.

123. Nguyen NT, Sobecki J (2003) Consensus versus conflicts – methodology and applications. In: *Proc. of RSFDGrC 2003*, Lecture Notes in Artificial Intelligence 2639, New York: Springer, pp. 565–572.

124. Nguyen NT, Sobecki J (2003) Using consensus methods to construct adaptive interfaces in multimodal web-based systems. *Journal of Universal Access in the Information Society* 2: 342–358.

125. Nguyen NT, Sobecki J (2005) Rough classification used for learning scenario determination in intelligent learning systems. In: Kłopotek M et al. (Eds.) *Intelligent Information Processing and Web Mining. Series Advances in Soft Computing.* New York: Physica-Verlag, pp. 107–116.

126. Nguyen NT, Sobecki J (2006) Determination of user interfaces in adaptive systems using a rough classification based method. *Journal of New Generation Computing* 24: 377–402.

127. Nguyen NT, Śliwko L (2006) Applications of multi-agent systems for information retrieval in Internet. In: Grzech A (Ed.) *Proc. of IWSE 2006.* Wroclaw University of Technology Press, pp. 155–164 (in Polish).

128. Nieger G (1995) Simplifying the design of knowledge-based algorithms using knowledge consistency. *Information & Computation* 119: 283–293.

129. Nilsson U, Maluszynski J (2000) *Logic, Programming and Prolog.* John Wiley & Sons.

130. Noy NF, Musen MA (1999) SMART: Automated support for ontology merging and alignment. In *Proc. of the 12th Workshop on Knowledge Acquisition, Modelling and Management (KAW'99)*, Banff, Canada, October 1999, pp. 1–20.

131. Papanikolaou AK et al. (2001) INSPIRE: An intelligent system for personalized instruction in a remote environment. In: Reich S et al. (Eds.) *Proc. of Int. Workshops OHS-7*, SC-3, AH-3, Lecture Notes in Computer Science 2266, New York: Springer, pp. 215–225.

132. Pawlak Z (1991) *Rough Sets - Theoretical Aspects of Reasoning about Data.* Hingham, MA: Kluwer Academic.

133. Pawlak Z (1998) An inquiry into anatomy of conflicts. *Journal of Information Sciences* 108: 65–78.

134. Pawlak Z (1999) Rough classification. *International Journal of Human-Computer Studies* 51: 369–383.

135. Pazzani M, Billsus D (1997) Learning and revising user profile: The identification of interesting web sites. *Machine Learning* 27: 313–331.

136. Pinto HS, Martins JP (2001) A methodology for ontology integration. In: *Proc. of the First International Conference on Knowledge Capture.* New York: ACM Press, pp. 131–138.

137. Pinto HS, Perez AG, Martins JP (1999) Some issues on ontology integration. In: Benjamins VR (Ed.) *Proc. of IJCAI99's Workshop on Ontologies and Problem Solving Methods*, vol. 18. CEUR Publications, pp. 7.1–7.11.

138. Rashid AM et al. (2002) Getting to know you: Learning new user preferences in recommender systems. In: *Proc. of International Conference on Intelligent User Interfaces 2002*, San Francisco, CA, pp. 127–134.

139. Reimer U (1998) Knowledge integration for building organizational memories. In *Proc. of the 11th Banff Knowledge Acquisition for Knowledge Based Systems Workshop*, vol. 12, pp. KM-61 – KM-620.

140. Roos N (1992) A logic for reasoning with inconsistent knowledge. *Artificial Intelligence* 57: 69–103.

141. Salton G (1989) *Automatic Text Processing The Transformation, Analysis, and Retrieval of Information by Computer.* Reading, MA: Addison-Wesley.

142. Shermer M (2004) *The Science of Good and Evil.* New York: Henry Holt.

143. Simon J et al. (2006) Formal ontology for natural language processing and the integration of biomedical databases. *International Journal of Medical Informatics* 75: 224–231.

144. Skowron A, Deja R (2002) On some conflict models and conflict resolution. *Romanian Journal of Information Science and Technology* 5: 69–82.

145. Skowron A, Rauszer C (1992) The discernibility matrices and functions in information systems. In: Słowiński E (Ed.) *Intelligent Decision Support, Handbook of Applications and Advances of the Rough Sets Theory.* Dordrecht: Kluwer Academic, pp. 331–362.

146. Sobecki J, Nguyen NT (2002) Using consensus methods to user classification in interactive systems. In: Grzegorzewski P et al. (Eds.) *Soft Methods in Probability, Statistics and Data.* New York: Physica-Verlag, pp. 346–354.

147. Sobecki J, Nguyen NT (2003) Consensus-based adaptive interface construction for multiplatform web applications. In: *Proc. of IDEAL'2003*, Lecture Notes in Computer Science 2690, New York: Springer, pp. 465–472.

148. Sobecki J, Nguyen NT, Małowiecki M (2004) Adaptive user interfaces modeling by means of rough classification methods and consistency measures. In: *Proc. of 1st International Workshop on Advanced Technologies for E-Learning and E-Science, 2004.* Piscataway, NJ, IEEE Computer Society Press, pp. 16–22.

149. Stadnyk I, Kass R (1992) Modeling users' interests in information filters. *Communications of the ACM* 35: 49–50.

150. Surowiecki J (2004) *The Wisdom of Crowds.* New York: Random House.

151. Śliwko L (2005) Applications of multi-agent systems in information retrieval in Internet. M.Sc. Thesis (Advisor: Ngoc Thanh Nguyen). Wroclaw University of Technology.

152. Śliwko L, Nguyen NT (2007) Using multi-agent systems and consensus methods for information retrieval in Internet. *International Journal of Intelligent Information and Database Systems* to appear in Vol. 1, issue 2.

153. Tessier C, Chaudron L, Müller HJ (2001) *Conflicting Agents: Conflict Management in Multiagent Systems.* Hingham, MA: Kluwer Academic.

154. Triantafillou E, Pomportsis A, Georiadou E (2002) AES-CS: Adaptive educational system based on cognitive styles. In: *Proc. of AH2002 Workshop, Second International Conference on Adaptive Hypermedia and Adaptive Web-Based Systems.* University of Malaga, Spain.

155. Wang JTL, Zhang K (2000) Identifying consensus of trees through alignment. *Journal of Information Sciences* 126: 165–189.

156. Yan KO, Wang SC, Chin YH (1999) Consensus under unreliable transmission. *Information Processing Letters* 69: 243–248.

157. Young HP (1974) An axiomatization of Borda's rule. *Journal of Economic Theory* 9: 43–52.

158. Young HP (1995) Optimal voting rules. *Journal of Economic Perspectives* 9: 51–64.

159. Young HP, Levenglick A (1978) A consistent extension of Condorcet's election principle. *SIAM Journal of Applied Mathematics* 35: 285–300.

160. Zadeh L (1965) Fuzzy sets. *Information and Control* 8: 338–353.

161. Zgrzywa M, Nguyen NT (2004), Determining consensus with simple dependencies of attributes. In: Nguyen NT (Ed.) *Intelligent Technologies for Inconsistent Knowledge Processing*. Adelaide, Australia: Advanced Knowledge International, pp. 57–72.

162. Zgrzywa M, Nguyen NT (2005) Estimating and calculating consensus with simple dependencies of attributes. In: Kurzyński M et al (Eds.) Computer recognition systems. New York: Physica-Verlag, pp. 320–329.

163. Zywno MS, Waalen JK (2002) The effect of individual learning styles on student outcomes in technology-enabled education. *Global Journal of Engineering. Education* 6: 35–43.

Index

Printed in the United States
102129LV00001B/37/A

9 781846 288883